THE WORKS OF LOVE

for Declan Deane

John F. Deane

The Works of Love
Incarnation, Ecology and Poetry

the columba press

First published in 2010 by
ᴄhe ᴄoʟᴜᴍʙᴀ ᴘʀᴇss
55A Spruce Avenue, Stillorgan Industrial Park,
Blackrock, Co Dublin

Cover by Bill Bolger
Cover Painting: Earth Lyre, 1990-1991, copyright Tony O'Malley,
used by kind permission of Jane O'Malley
Origination by The Columba Press
Printed in Ireland by ColourBooks Ltd, Dublin

ISBN 978 1 85607 709 5

Acknowledgements
The author and publisher gratefully acknowledge the permission of the
following to quote from work within their copyright: Anvil Press Ltd
for 'Of the Works of Love' by Ivan. V. Lalić from his collection of the
same title; Wendell Berry for quotations from his material; Carcanet for
quotations from *New Collected Poems* by Elizabeth Jennings; Thomas
Kinsella for his 'The Last Round: An Allegory'; The Word Works,
Washington, for 'Tipping Point' by Fred Marchant; Michael Longley
for 'All of these People' from his *Collected Poems*; Bruce Weigl for 'Song
of Napalm'; Kevin Bowen for 'Incoming'. The poems of Patrick
Kavanagh are reprinted from *Collected Poems*, edited by Antoinette
Quinn (Allen Lane, 2004), by kind permission of the Trustees of the
Estate of the late Katherine B. Kavanagh, through the Jonathan
Williams Literary Agency.

Contents

Preface

I see this book as a form of Testament, not definitive, as the final word will be found in my own poems. This is where my life has come to, at the moment, and whatever wisdom has been gained, if any, I offer to share with those who are taken by poetry, by Christ, by ecology, by love. The books I quote from are given a tag in each case that refers to the select bibliography at the end of the book. The scripture quotations contained herein are from the New Revised Standard Version Bible, copyright © 1989 by the Division of Christian Education of the National Council of the Churches of Christ in the USA used by permission. All rights reserved.

God's utterance of himself in himself is God the Word, outside himself is this world. This world then is word, expression, news of God. Therefore its end, its purpose, its purport, its meaning, is God and its life or work to name and praise him.

— *Gerard Manley Hopkins*

Life's Death, Love's Life

Who lives in love, loves least to live,
And long delays doth rue,
If Him he love by Whom he lives,
To Whom all love is due.

Who for our love did choose to live,
And was content to die;
Who loved our love more than His life,
And love with life did buy.

Let us in life, yea with our life,
Requite His living love;
For best we live when least we live,
If love our life remove.

Where love is hot, life hateful is,
Their grounds do not agree;
Love where it loves, life where it lives,
Desireth most to be.

And sith love is not where it lives,
Nor liveth where it loves,
Love hateth life that holds it back,
And death it best approves.

For seldom is He won in life
Whom love doth most desire;
If won by love, yet not enjoyed,
Till mortal life expire.

Life out of earth hath no abode,
In earth love hath no place;
Love settled hath her joy in heaven,
In earth life all her grace.

Mourn, therefore, no true lover's death,
Life only him annoys;
And when he taketh leave of life,
Then love begins his joys.

— *Robert Southwell*

The manifestation of the transcendent Creator God in the particular and temporal reaches its climax in Jesus of Nazereth. God's
engagement with the world from its creation through the beginnings of human failure, the call of Israel and the coming, as
Christians believe, of the promised Messiah and Redeemer in
Jesus Christ, involved divine fidelity to the covenant of Creation
and to the promise of God's 'doing a new thing', or as St Paul
called it, 'a new creation'. The labour pains of the New Creation
were the birth, the life and ministry, and the suffering and death
of his incarnate Son, Jesus Christ. The risen Christ was the witness and expression of that newness which Jesus had preached
and inaugurated in his lifetime as the kingdom or reign of God
and which John in his gospel had frequently described as eternal life. In the new divine project, the old was maintained,

healed or redeemed and transformed. The divine creative power had issued in the radical healing of the older broken and divided world. The tower of Babel, symbolising human pride and issuing in the breakdown of human communication, was overthrown by the gift of tongues at Pentecost. People with languages disparate all understood, each in their own language, the Spirit-inspired preaching of the disciples. One of the most potentially divisive ills of humanity had been in principle healed. The New Israel or the New Community established in the New Adam was the foretaste and symbol of the New Heavens and the New Earth for which the whole cosmos had been groaning (Rom 8).The redemption in Christ, in whom as Word of God, all things had been created, was also creation-wide.

The poet and the poem exercise their own limited saving and healing powers, first of all in regard to language and communication, but also in regard to people and community, and indeed the cosmos. A good poem renews the language in restoring its truthfulness, its honesty of expression, avoiding false and hon-eyed words of the courtier and the exploitation of the advertiser or lobbyist. It restores it further in re-exposing its beauty in combinations, vibrant and fresh, at times reviving words too long ignored or inventing new and true words. All of this work enriches the attentive and sensitive reader in self, in relation-ships with others and in perception of and delight in the world. The redress of poetry, to borrow Heaney's phrase, can affect reader, community and cosmos as reader and community are awakened anew to the beauty and fragility of that cosmos. So poets and poetry play a serious, if subordinate, and for those with eyes to see, a revealing and redemptive role in the divine economy of creation-redemption.

— *Enda McDonagh*

Sonnet

Poets love nature and themselves are love,
The scorn of fools and mock of idle pride
The vile in nature worthless deeds approve
They court the vile and spurn all good beside
Poets love nature like the calm of heaven
Her gifts like heaven's love spared far and wide
In all her works there are no signs of leaven
Sorrow abashes from her simple pride
Her flowers like pleasures have their season's birth
And bloom through regions here below
They are her very scriptures upon earth
And teach us simple mirth where e'er we go
Even in prison they can solace me
For where they bloom God is, and I am free.
                                    — *John Clare*

House at the Crossroads

I was born in the house at the crossroads. Bunnacurry, Achill Island, County Mayo. Turn left when you go out the front gate and you are heading 'back the island', towards Keel, Dooagh and Keem Bay. Turn right and you are heading 'out the island' towards Cashel and Achill Sound and the mainland. Straight across, the road heads 'down the island' towards Bunnacurry church, Dooniver and The Bull's Mouth, The Valley, Dugort and ultimately round to Keel.

The front door had a brass knocker with frosted, ice-coloured glass on either side. My memory suggests the frosting had a tinge of gold to it, autumnal, and warm when the sun shone through and fell in an oblong shape on the flagged hallway floor. When I heard Beethoven's 5th symphony for the first time, that call like a knock against the heart, the opening that goes ta – ta – ta – tum! mother reached anxiously for the door. Out there, beyond, in the universe of soul and thought, there is a blueprint of this family of which I was, and am, a part, but too much distance across the blank expanse of space, too many cloudy passageways of time and too much interference from manmade and un-created things, have blurred that blueprint. Old house, all dead, dispersed, and those present have no sense of the true occupants of this house, those of us who prowl about, like ghosts, where life first offered its difficult embrace.

I have come again, in mind and imagination, to listen to the old chants, to knock on that front door like one who has taken every road away and has returned, burdened; only the beloved dead will be there to answer, to throw open the familiar door. If you let reason fall, like a blue antique tureen, the scent of mystery will pervade the house; for now a storm plays about the walls, the wind, in a high soprano voice, intones Vivaldi: *nulla in mundo pax sincera* … the rain against the windows is Tallis's *miserere nostri* and down the chimneys an alto saxophone moans *Kyrie*. When I return thus, humbled in soul, feeling astray in the wide world in which I move, I am embraced again in protective

blankets, I am at home with the small light on the Pilot wireless,
while the bolted door is yet a bulwark between me and the world.

Entering from that hallway, turning right into the living-
room, I still find a picture of the Sacred Heart on the wall, a red
light perpetually burning before it. On the heavy, home-built
side-board, a statue of the Child Jesus of Prague, its small head
on that broad and triangular-shaped body glued back on several
times, a thick scar of glue holding it in place. All through the
house were pictures and crucifixes, and we knelt every night,
leaning our elbows on hard wooden chairs, to say the rosary, an
event more essential to each passing day than eating. Roman
Catholicism was wholly pervasive, a completely accepted and
unquestioned form of Christianity into which I was born and in
which I was wrapped, sometimes like a strait-jacket, sometimes
like an overcoat against the chill.

The Study

Over the deal table a flower-patterned oil-cloth;
the boy
has his Bible history open before him; its pictures

of deserts, and of stylised heroes of God's militias;
he is chewing on a pencil-end
as if hunger for knowledge frustrates him and he spits

small splinters out onto the stone-flagged floor;
outside
hydrangeas are in bloom, their sky-blue flowers

big as willow-pattern plates; on the kitchen wall
a picture of Jesus, stylised,
fingers long as tapers, ringlets honey-brown, and eyes

lifted querulously towards the ceiling;
a red, eternal light
flickers weakly below the picture;

but the saddened eyes have lowered, and peer
down on the restless
stooped-over boy, in anger or in mute and trenchant
pleading;

and only a summer bee
distraught against the window, makes any sound.

Grandfather, John Connors, always old in my eyes, was kind
and gentle towards us, his grandchildren. Mother told how hard
he had been, how his own children had to call him 'sir' and obey
his slightest wish. He had built the house, designed, worked
and furnished it with his own hands. Genuine medieval man-of-
all-trades, his workshop remained out in the sheds behind the
house, all his tools ranged perfectly around the walls, stocked in
the pouches of several rifle cartridge-belts. Everything ordered,
arranged, in place and immaculately regulated. Like the tick-
tock of the mantel clock, like the movements of his faith, like the
definition of his God.

Now his grave lies amongst rank disorder. A high stone cross
above where he lies holds the history of the world carved in
pastel-coloured lichens. The graveyard path hides in weeds and
grasses; St Joseph lilies flaunt white and unkempt surplices. It is
creation's original chaos of delight – where the old man lies, at
peace, like God before he shook himself out of lethargy and
spoke: In the beginning …

Behind him was his time in the Royal Irish Constabulary. A
small barracks in The Valley still stands, but there are only the
bare walls, it is roofless, holding itself to attention. It is almost
buried now in grasses, in rushes and wild flowers, the indisci-
pline of it all seriously contrasting with the strict discipline of
the RIC in grandfather's time. And it is that discipline I think of,
that strict adherence to rules and regulations he would have had
to adopt and it was adopted willingly. This I know because,
born in Waterford and named John O'Connor, he found that
name too Irish and changed it to Connors, feeling himself more
English then and more fitting for the Constabulary. After
Independence, when the RIC found themselves the target of
rebels and uncomfortable with the new Irishness, John Connors
took himself off to England where he lived, sulking, no doubt,
for several years.

Grandfather, every dusk, solemnly wound his big fob watch,
then the standing-clock, and finally the loud-ticking mantel
clock. Small beads of moisture gathered on the yellowing ends

of his moustache. His footsteps came sounding out of the nineteenth century; tick, and tock, and tick, and tock. I rummaged in
his carpenter's shed, hiding sometimes in the wooden-bodied
fragrant grain-bin, pulling a roof of darkness down over my
misbehaving.

Later I knelt by grandfather in the pew, proud to be on the
men's side; he kept nudging me to kneel up straight, stop fidgeting. I was looking up at Jesus' face to see if his eyes moved, if he
fidgeted out of his stiffness. And then, one afternoon, as I
walked desultorily home from school, chewing on the fresh
crust of a loaf handed out at the end of classes, father's car drew
up alongside me on the road. Excited, I was hopping up down,
up down, that pendulum irritation, tock, tick, tock, tick, on the
running-board till he told me – bad news, bad news, your
grandfather has died.

It was 1953 and I was ten years old. Grandfather John
Connors was gone out of my life but had left behind a strong
sense of discipline-and-put-up-with-it in my mother, an attitude she carried over from everyday living into the locks and
bolts of her Catholic faith. Now grandfather lies alone in his
earth bed, part of the ordering of time that is drawing coverlets
of mosses and grasses over him; above his name, faded too, a
face of Jesus wretched in a wreathe of thorns. And day by day
the slow dandelion clocks blow gently on the winds that cross
the world.

He left my mother to her freedom, to her own adulthood
unharrassed by such a possessive and disciplinarian father.
Mother, Mary Josephine Deane, nee Connors, primary school
teacher, Roman Catholic and long-suffering wife of Donald
Patrick Deane, civil servant and sometime heavy drinker. Later
I would understand how she turned her faith into a form of consolation for the difficulties of life, and erected that faith as a
fortress around her against which nothing would prevail.
Grandfather, though she would not be aware of it, watching always over her shoulder. Discipline. Faith. Regularity. Tick, tock,
tock, tick. And it was there I would find myself butting my head
against her walls as the world changed and as I changed and
grew. But that was later, much, much later, when I had to come
to terms with my own life and my own faith.

The Ship

She was sitting in the striped deck-chair, the dog
dog-dreaming at her feet; the summer garden,
a noon-time listless as a tide before the turn.
I was floating stick-ships on the drain, imagining

gardens greater than this, and more fabulous;
if I let them go they would float past almost
endless obstacles, into the chaos
of the sea; when mother

shivered, and sat up, startled suddenly
and said: somebody
has stepped across my grave. Now,
I remembered it, where I was sheening the black

marble headstone and at once –
wind in the puzzle-trees and rain spittling –
our world of clay was a fabulous boat
floating out on an ocean of darkness.

In every room of that Old Yellow House, a crucifix hung on a
wall. The man Jesus was manifest in so many contorted positions on the cross that his image, that eikon of huge suffering,
was deeply implanted in my mind. Grandfather, in his patient
coming-to-terms with the destruction of his policeman's way of
life, mother, in her coming-to-terms with the fact of two alcoholic
though beloved brothers, and one sister dead from tuberculosis
at far too young an age, suffering, putting-up-with-it because a
better world existed there beyond the darkness – and always
Christ Crucified, the Cross, the Rood, a deeply probing and
mortifying presence. Christ everywhere. Christ beside me,
Christ before me ...

Christ be with Me, Christ before ...

'Christianity in a thousand ways has shaped the history of Ireland', (De Paor, 3). This is fact, and it must not be forgotten when the Irish look at themselves in the contemporary world, or look at the state of Christianity today. Liam De Paor was speaking in terms of his study of Ireland around the beginning of the fifth century. He concludes that our St Patrick may indeed not have been the first to bring Christianity to Ireland. Before 432 there were Christians in the country as the chronicle of Prosper of Aquitaine, who lived in the fifth century, tells us; in 431 Pope Celestine sent one Palladius to be 'the first bishop of the Irish believers in Christ'. This suggests there were believers already in the country and that they needed guidance. Patrick, when he came, clearly had far greater success in spreading Christianity and it may well be that the facts and legends of both Paladius and Patrick have conflated into the one we now know as our Special Patron Saint. There are writings by St Patrick, this is clear, and they are written in Latin as it was used in the fifth century. However, the 'Lorica', (the Latin word for *cuirass* or breastplate), has an uncertain authorship, though there are indications that it may well have been greatly influenced by Patrick's teachings, if not actually written by Patrick himself. Fact and legend merge into one glimmering pearl of great price to which we Irish hold, with enthusiasm and with genuine love.

By the fifth century the Irish language was established everywhere: 'The unity of speech was reflected in a unity (not perhaps complete uniformity) of culture throughout the country' (De Paor 24). The culture was a rural one, with cattle and sheep vital to survival. Irish chieftains were used to leading plundering expeditions into the Roman world, mainly into Britain and from these they brought slaves and goods back into the country. Many of these slaves would already have been touched by Christianity and they formed their own groups throughout Ireland. All of this brought a 'new wealth' into the country, and with it a loyalty to one's chieftain who doled out generous portions of the plunder to those who rode the seas alongside them. These chiefs, or local 'kings', had a semi-sacral status; they were protectors and were inaugurated in a pagan ceremony of mating with a local goddess. 'The inauguration of the king of Tara was a symbolic mating (*feis*) with the goddess' (De Paor 28). Connected to the king's court were the *filid*, the poets, who were believed to have supernatural powers, and the *druí*, druids, who were believed to have access to wisdom and arcane knowledge. There was a pantheon of local gods and goddesses, the latter mainly spirits of place and, of course, of motherhood and fertility. Spells and incantations were common. 'Christian teaching had to find a way through a labyrinth of fear, superstitious observance and worship (ultimately of the elements of nature) – which included some form of sun worship' (De Paor 29), and *St Patrick's Breastplate* echoes the natural fear that wizards and incantations imposed.

March 17th; it began, of course, with a special Mass and we dressed accordingly, ensuring that we wore something green about us. We children wore a green badge with a golden harp on it, or a grey high tower, a spring-green ribbon dangling. At Mass we sang, or hum-hawed our way through *Hail Glorious Saint Patrick dear saint of our isle* ... or pretended we had some idea what we were murmuring as we glossed and glozed our way through *Dóchas linn Naomh Pádraig Aspal mór na hÉireann* ... The feast day often occurred during Lent and for that special day we were allowed break our fasting and eat sweets and chocolates to our hearts' content. Afternoon, when we had eaten our green cabbage, our green jelly, our roast lamb with rosemary and mint, we took the car and joined many of the island folk back in Keel, listening to the bands, perhaps cocking an ear to the commentary on the radio of the games going ahead up in Dublin, making ourselves slowly sick on an overdose of sweets.

St Patrick's Day on Achill Island was celebrated with special glee and enthusiasm, however chilly the winds were coming in off the Atlantic, however wet the weather at this vicious turning of the seasons. The harsh winds seemed always to come slicing in from the ocean on that particular day, racing across the sandy banks like Norse Invaders wielding swords, or whipping salt spray and stinging grains of sand against face and body as we stood huddled, watching the pipers' bands as they paraded and played their rousing tunes. They came marching down from the church in Pollagh, and you could hear the lift and urgent cries of their sharp high notes suffering against the low and throaty insistence of the chanters, all against the steady and unrelenting wham wham wham of the big drums. And the men came, proudly clothed in their tartan kilts and blazing jackets, their golden sporrans, their ghillie brogues, such polished mighty brooches and caps with jaunty feathers, seagull feather, peacock feather, black feather of the chough ... But were these not our neighbours, the fishermen, the small farmers, the sons of small farmers, the boys in the higher classes in the schools? All changed, utterly, and rousingly.

The tunes they played were patriotic tunes, *Faith of Our Fathers, A Nation Once Again,* and for those cold hours we stood proud and tall as Irish men and women, who had survived centuries of oppression and had held on to that old faith, that holy faith, to which we would be true to death, and all of that in spite of dungeon, fire and sword. Deep into my soul sank the great knot of Irish sentiment with a powerfully dominant Roman Catholic faith, never to be shaken, never to be questioned, and our hearts beat high with joy, oh yes we will be true to that faith till death.

And what of those hymns we sang, lustily and greedily, in chapel on Patrick's morning?

Dóchas linn Naomh Pádraig
Aspal mór na hÉireann
'Ainm oirirc gléigeal
Solas mór an tsaoil é
'S é do chloígh na draoithe
Croíthe dúra gan aon mhaith
D'ísligh dream an díomais
Tré neart Dé ar dtréanfhlaith

Sléibhte gleannta maighe
's bailte mór' na hÉireann
Ghlan sé iad go deo dúinn
Míle glóir dár Naomh dhil

Iarraimid ort, a Phádraig
Guí orainne Gaela
Dia linn lá 'gus oíche
's Pádraig Aspal Éireann

> Your aid to us St Patrick,
> Great Apostle of Ireland
> Name all brightly shining
> Powerful light across our life
> It was he destroyed the Druids
> Hard of heart they were and worthless
> Flung out that dreadful crowd
> Through God's power, our Hero.
>
> Mountains, glens and valleys
> And the mighty towns of Ireland
> He purified for us for ever
> A thousand glories to our darling saint
> We beg you now, dear Patrick
> Pray for us the Irish
> God be with us day and night
> And Patrick Apostle of Ireland.

This was our special saint, and we were a specially favoured people because of him. We believed in those times that when the end days of the universe were coming upon us, Ireland would be granted the grace of sinking gently beneath the waves of the Atlantic Ocean and the Irish Sea, and we would avoid the fire and brimstone that a thundering God would pour down on the earth in his judgemental rage and fury. We believed, too, that the safest place on earth, when and if those days came in our time, would be back on the high slopes of our own mountain, Slieve More, 'Big Mountain', some three thousand feet above sea-level. We were innocent. We were willing. We believed.

Hail, glorious St Patrick, dear saint of our isle,
On us thy poor children bestow a sweet smile;
And now thou art high in the mansions above,
On Erin's green valleys look down in thy love.

On Erin's green valleys, on Erin's green valleys,
On Erin's green valleys look down in thy love.

Hail, glorious St Patrick, thy words were once strong
Against Satan's wiles and a heretic throng;
Not less is thy might where in Heaven thou art;
Oh, come to our aid, in our battle take part!

In a war against sin, in the fight for the faith,
Dear Saint, may thy children resist to the death;
May their strength be in meekness, in penance, and prayer,
Their banner the Cross, which they glory to bear.

Thy people, now exiles on many a shore,
Shall love and revere thee till time be no more;
And the fire thou hast kindled shall ever burn bright,
Its warmth undiminished, undying its light.

Ever bless and defend the sweet land of our birth,
Where the shamrock still blooms as when thou wert on earth,
And our hearts shall yet burn, wherever we roam,
For God and St Patrick, and our native home.

How lustily we sang, 'On Erin's green valleys ...' for in those days they were green indeed, unpolluted, pristine, and lovely. This was our faith, this was our patriotism. We would fight the good fight against sin, guided infallibly by our special saint and by our mother church. Because, as the hymn insists, we are at war with sin, we are in a battle to save our souls, and we are in an ongoing fight to save our faith. Our banner was 'the Cross' and under it we would prevail. And we stood strong and emotionally stirred by it all.

Many years later I came across the other hymn, *Christ be beside me, Christ be before me, Christ be behind me, King of my Heart ...* I love the tune still, and I relish the sentiment. So I sought out the original and found a poem that must be one of the very first in these western islands to so encapsulate the sense of the all-pervasive and guardian presence of the Christ in our lives. Duns Scotus Eriugena (810-877) who left Ireland to take up important work abroad, laboured towards a reconciliation of faith and reason; his relationship to Celtic piety helped him with the idea that

'God alone has true being; he is the essence of everything that partakes of this. Every one of his creatures, therefore, is a theophany, a sign of God's presence' (Armstrong 199). This rings beautifully true throughout the poem.

The Trinity, it appears, was vitally important to St Patrick's teaching, and the presence of Christ being close to the people. He knew the scriptures and brought the story of the incarnation of the Second Person of the Trinity to a people already disposed to think of some higher Presence on our earth. The faith flourished under his ministry and the Celtic awareness of sacred things allowed great commitment to the new faith throughout Ireland, our 'Land of Saints and Scholars'. Rome and its authority seemed then very far away and the church in Ireland took upon itself the spreading of the faith amongst its nearest neighbours, in Wales and Scotland.

Patrick had spent six years in captivity where he acquired a knowledge of the Celtic tongue; his master, Milchu, was a high priest of the druids, and Patrick grew strong in his own faith, and in his wish to rid Ireland of what he saw as evil in the Celtic Druidic beliefs. Ultimately it was Pope Celestine I who entrusted Patrick to return to Ireland to gather the Irish into the Christian fold. The rest is history – and legend.

Amhairghin, 'birth of song', is the name given to our first poet, Amergin. He it was who first claimed in verse that his is this glorious island, to his soul Ireland belongs. Here is a poet who does not merely claim dominion over all of creation, but kinship with creation in all its aspects. Here is a poet for whom living is being part of the cosmos, and the cosmos is part of his living.

The Song of Amergin

I am a seven-antlered stag,
I am a flood of waters on the plain,
I am a wind on the deep wide ocean,
I am a gleaming tear shed by the sun,
I am a hawk on the high cliff ledge,
I am the fairest among the flowers,
I am the roaring of high tide and low,
I am the fire burning on every hill,

I am the fierce and charging boar,
I am the salmon of wisdom in the black pool,
I am the spear in the battle-fray,
I am a wave upon the ocean,
I am a hill aflame with poetry,
Who else is tree and the lightning on the tree,
Who else is the unhewn darkness of the dolmen,
Who else is aware of the sun's track, the seasons of the moon,
Who else directs the mountains, the rivers, the folk,
I am the queen of every hive,
I am the shield upon every breast,
I am the grave of every selfish hope,
I invoke the land of Ireland.

Echoes of this poem sound through the prayer attributed to
St Patrick. Centuries later, after Amergin, after Patrick, William
Butler Yeats wrote, in 1929:

I Am of Ireland

'I am of Ireland,
And the Holy Land of Ireland,
And time runs on,' cried she.
'Come out of charity,
Come dance with me in Ireland.'

One man, one man alone
In that outlandish gear,
One solitary man
Of all that rambled there
Had turned his stately head.
'That is a long way off,
And time runs on,' he said,
'And the night grows rough.'

'I am of Ireland,
And the Holy Land of Ireland,
And time runs on,' cried she.
'Come out of charity
And dance with me in Ireland.'

'The fiddlers are all thumbs,
Or the fiddle-string accursed,
The drums and the kettledrums
And the trumpets all are burst,
And the trombone,' cried he,
'The trumpet and trombone,'
And cocked a malicious eye,
'But time runs on, runs on.'

'I am of Ireland,
And the Holy Land of Ireland,
And time runs on,' cried she.
'Come out of charity
And dance with me in Ireland.'

St Patrick's Breastplate is contained in the ancient Book of Armagh, from the early ninth century, along with Patrick's authentic *Confession*. St Patrick is said to have written this prayer to strengthen himself with God's protection as he prepared to confront and convert Laoghaire, high king of Ireland. In Ephesians, chapter six, St Paul wrote:

> Finally, be strong in the Lord and in the strength of his power. Put on the whole armour of God so that you may be able to stand against the wiles of the devil. For our struggle is not against enemies of flesh and blood, but against the rulers, against the authorities, against the cosmic powers of this present darkness and against the spiritual forces of evil in the heavenly places. Therefore take up the whole armour of God, so that you may be able to withstand on that evil day, and having done everything, to stand firm. Stand therefore, and fasten the belt of truth around your waist, and put on the breastplate of righteousness. As shoes for your feet put on whatever will make you ready to proclaim the gospel of peace. With all of these, take the shield of faith, with which you will be able to quench all the flaming arrows of the evil one. Take the helmet of salvation and the sword of the Spirit, which is the word of God.

St Patrick is said to have offered this prayer when he and some of his followers were being pursued by the king's men;

they were all turned into deer and escaped, hence another title, *The Deer's Cry*. In the poem the soul girds itself with the armour of Christ's presence to face into the day, a prayer suitable for beginnings, suitable for the start of any journey, suitable for the ongoing pursuit of that journey of life. It breathes awareness of how Christ cared for the soul on its journey, and how the battle the soul has to fight is rich with a sense of the great wonder and beauty of that world, a freshness and blessed presence that remains centred on Christ and fused to the beauty of all creation. It remains in the Irish consciousness as a morning prayer, as a prayer of protection, and we breathe it out with great pleasure.

The Deer's Cry

I gather strength today
through invocation of the Trinity;
the Source and Sustenance of our being,
the Name and Nature of the Source
and the Breath that gives it being.

I gather strength today
through power of Christ's birth and baptism,
through power of His crucifixion and His burial,
through power of His resurrection and His ascension,
through power of His coming on the Final Day.

I gather to myself today
strength in the love of Cherubim,
strength in the obedience of angels
and in the service of archangels,
strength in the hope of resurrection,
in the prayers of patriarchs
and the foretelling of the prophets,
strength in apostles' preaching
and in confessors' faith,
strength in the innocence of virgins
and the actions of prudent men.

I gather strength today
through the great power of heaven,
light of the sun
and radiance of the moon,

strength in the lightning flash
and splendour of the fire,
in the swiftness of the winds
and in the depths of ocean,
stability of the earth
and steadfastness of rock.

I gather to myself today
the strength of God to guide me,
the power of God to uphold me,
wisdom of God to lead me,
the eye of God to watch for me,
ear of God to hear for me,
the word of God to speak for me,
hand of God to guard me,
God's way to stretch before me
and the shield of God to shelter;
the godly hosts to save me
out of the snares the devils set
and out of temptations of viciousness,
out of the clutches of those who wish me harm,
however far they be, however close,
singly, or in multitudes.

I call to myself today
God's strength against all evil,
against all cruel force and merciless
that may attack my body and my soul,
against incantation of false prophecy,
against the black laws of the heathen,
against the false laws of heresies,
against the lies and shams of idols,
against the spells of women, smiths and druids,
against those webs of knowledge that entrap
     the souls of men.

Oh Christ I pray protect me
against poisons, burnings, drownings,
and against all wounding powers
that I may reap abundant harvests of rewards.

Christ be with me, Christ before,
Christ behind and Christ within me,
Christ beneath and Christ above,
Christ on my right hand, Christ on my left,
Christ in my sleeping, and in my rising,
Christ in the courtyard, Christ at the wheel,
Christ in the heart of everyone who thinks of me,
Christ in the mouth of all who speak of me,
Christ in the eye of all who see me,
Christ in the ear of all who hear me.

I gather strength today
through invocation of the Trinity;
the Source and Sustenance of our being,
the Name and Nature of the Source
and the Breath that gives it being.

Our ideas of early Celtic Ireland bring us epic stories of kings and warriors, strange gods and learned Druids. There are hill-forts for defence against marauders, invaders, neighbours, some of which appear to have been magnificent places. There were complex religious tenets and their standing stones with incised patterns, attest to that. Their 'bards' were thought to have skills of prophecy and counselling as well as other powers; many and varied were the gods and goddesses. Their dead were important to them and were buried with great care and ceremony, the souls being transported to an Otherworld that appeared very similar to their status on earth. There were rules and customs of personal honour, loyalty and hospitality, festivals of fire, festivals to mark the change of seasons, of darkness and light, of birth and rebirth. Overall, the Celtic imagination is elusive, it twists and turns through a sensuous spiritual energy, an asymmetrical symbolic language; it is always anti-classical, anti-representational, anti-rational; all is flux and becoming. Patrick seems to capture this and steady it, placing it in the care of Christ and the Trinity. Here are the Trinity brought close, here are the phalanxes of the angels and here is creation, called upon to be a saving part in the living of the human being. In this view of living, to be is to become, and Celtic spirituality is the furthest from the static, it is a surging stream that brought its life and vitality out into a turgid Europe.

The Deer's Cry begins with an invocation of the sources of all being; in the move to Christianity, this was, of course, the Trinity. It goes on to call upon the events of the incarnation, and invokes the aid of all those who have achieved holiness in the new faith. The poem then moves to a call on the powers and forces of creation itself, a call for aid, for partnership, for presence and consolation; sun, moon, lightning, fire, wind, ocean, earth and rock:

> I gather strength today
> through the great power of heaven,
> light of the sun
> and radiance of the moon,
> strength in the lightning flash
> and splendour of the fire,
> in the swiftness of the winds
> and in the depths of ocean,
> stability of the earth
> and steadfastness of rock.

This echoes the poetry of Amergin, and the corresponding poetry of the Welsh original, Taliesin. Calling on all the strength and watchfulness of God, the poem moves on to a very special awareness of Christ's presence throughout creation, glorying and finding hope in the incarnation, in the fact that God became incarnate through his Son into the very veins and bones of his own creation and therefore will offer grace and help to humankind.

No wonder then that I found settling within me a religion and pride closely associated with the physical world in which I was born and raised, and with the Christ who knew everything I did and thought, and who guarded and watched over my every path. Except that in those days it was a thundering God the Father who was mostly taught to us, and a God the Father jealous of his authority and apt and keen to punish every inclination away from that authority. Achill Island is one of the glories of God's creation and its beauty and wildering grandeur entered through every pore of my being. It is an attempt to clarify, to expedite, to Christ-ian-ate my whole being in this world that urges me to look often at The Deer's Cry, and to explore its graces and promises through the centuries.

The awe of small things wonderful

Then there was father. Don. Donald Patrick Deane, former Kerryman, former Christian Brother, then Mayoman and Civil Servant. After the dust and dullness of his working day, there was nothing he liked more than to head out fishing. When I was still quite young he brought me with him down to the sea that runs between Achill and Inishbiggle. He parked the car on the grass near the pier and we headed along the rough-stone shore towards his favourite spot, where the sea rounded a corner and the wildering current came closest in to the shore. There was a sand-bank in the low cliff behind him and he would leave me there to play, and move the few yards down to the sea. There he stood, up to his thighs in slip-water, the great dark waders tied waist-high. I slid down the small Basse-Alps of the sand, I built my own imagined towns and cities among the stones, I looked into the still sea-pools that were left around the base of the rocks.

He was spinning. Eager, concentrated, his hands were exact with rod and water-coloured gut. I was safe, there behind him, out of the rush of the current. Periwinkles breathed their small bubbles in the pools and barnacles clung to the rough rock surfaces. I hammered on their backs with stones and watched the water-blood seep from the shattered shells. Sometimes father called out in excitement, when the shoals of mackerel broke into the shallows near him, famished, frenzied through the living mercury of sprat. Then he could almost reach down with his hand and fling one onto the rocks behind him. I would stand, picturing them, out there, the shoals, streaming through the cold, inhuman forests of the underworld, aghast, and wraith-like. But I was content, save when the dusk came closer and the midges appeared from undergrowth or shrubbery in the fields behind the sand-dunes. Then they nipped, invisibly, at every particle of exposed skin, or they found their way into my hair and I could not swish them away.

When we made our way homeward over the rocks, mackerel were strung by their gills on twine, fish-scales, fish-blood, ghosted his jacket, his waders, and I moved beside him, quietened, clinging once again to his big, red hands, for hold.

He was a gentle presence in my young life, strong, quiet, often wholly absorbed in his own worries or his books. But he was firm, without the exacting angers that mother displayed. He acted with a steady, quiet certainty that was acceptable but sometimes daunting. For him, too, as I came to know, the Christ was a central presence and focus in his life and he prayed, at Mass, upright in the pew with his eyes open, gazing towards the altar. Often, at night, as we snuggled down into our beds, he told us Pushkin, Tolstoy, Gogol, reading from the Russian in the few books he had been able to acquire in that language. He had taught himself how to read in German, French and Russian and had a rich, select collection of texts in those languages from which he chose the exciting tales to tell us before we went to sleep. So, out on the boglands around our home, we rarely played Cowboys and Indians, we were Tatars and Cossacks, I was Taras Bulba leading moustachioed hordes over drain and *árdán*, my short pants wide as the Black Sea, Bunnacurry the Ukraine and Stony River the Dnieper. Such readings and imaginings no doubt opened my mind to a world greatly wider than the one in which I moved as a child, and opened, too, the love of words and language and left a permeability in my imagination and thinking that no doubt made me susceptible, in later years, to the love of, and writing of, poetry.

Frenzy

A small row-boat on Keel Lake,
the water sluppering gently as he rowed,
the easy sh-sh-sshhhh of the reeds

as we drifted in, and all about us
tufts of bog-cotton like white moths,
the breathing heathers, that green-easy lift

into the slopes of Slievemore. All else
the silence of islands, and the awe
of small things wonderful: son,

father, on the one keel, the ripples
lazy and the surfaces of things unbroken.
Then the prideful swish of his line

fly-fishing, the curved rod graceful,
till suddenly may-fly were everywhere,
small water-coloured shapes like tissue,

sweet as the host to trout and – by Jove!
he whispered, old man astounded again
at the frenzy that is in all living.

Long summer evenings as the sun set, he would drive back
to Keel for fishing. When sea stroked shore as if peace had been
declared, he walked from the pier briskly, along the edge of a
field towards his favoured headland. I walked with him; excited,
child, carrying my own fishing rod. On our left the ocean, on
our right fields sloping up towards the village. I knew an exhilaration that I felt from his presence, from our adventure, from his
strength and comradeship; I knew exhilaration from the lark's
song and the half-heard background of the seagulls' calls. The
ground we walked on, along the top of the lower cliffs, was a
soft and mossy track, broken here and there with streamlets of
brownish water running down from the fields and peat banks; it
stood back from the sea-shore boulders where the great Atlantic
swell rose, broke, fell back and rose again. I relished the up and
down of the turfy slopes and small hillocks. My older brother
Declan strode along, too, and we each had a fishing-rod in our
hands, there was a song silent in my soul, and my father's stride
was powerful and assuring. Here and there great gleaming black
slugs were spreading themselves before our feet but we stepped
carefully around them; they had a life, too, and a purpose
though I was damned if I could sense it.

We passed the end of a deep cove where things were festering down in the cold dark. The sea cut in deep under the land
here and the waves sloshed and slapped against the walls
below. If you threw a stone down into the water it hit with an
echoing splash that was hugely exciting. But we stayed carefully
clear of the edge; there were stories, there were falls, there was
death.

We fished, at last, from the furthest point of rock, after clambering down over great boulders, again taking enormous care, following. We stood a good distance apart as we were spinning out as far as we could into the ocean, towards the edge of a current that came round the headland and moved swiftly past, out there beyond us. There were times when the mackerel shoals moved by out there, millions of them, the surface of the ocean sparkling with their feeding frenzy. Sometimes, behind them you could see a seal, diving, surfacing, relishing the feast as the mackerel relished their feast of sprat. Then was our pleasure wild as we drew in the mackerel, often three or four at a time, their sleek and many-coloured shape and arrowy excellence swiftly tarnished.

Came the moment I found truly difficult, the taking out of the hooks and the killing of these lovely and slimlined fish. The hooks were often caught in difficult places because the mackerel move so fast: in the gills, in the eye, deep in the back of the mouth. I held the mackerel in my left hand and tried to take the hook out. I could feel the trembling of that lithe body, I could see the eye already dulling, I could feel the warmth of my hand already burning against the scaly skin and I knew the cold sense of a salt ocean in the feel of that sublime mackerel shape. When the hook was out, I had to kill the fish, holding it still in my left hand and violently dragging the head back so that the neck broke. I hope it was painless and fast. I hoped so then, I have always hoped so, but I have always had doubts.

Then my father caught a pollock, heavy as stone, flabby as seaweed. He was angry at the fish as the mackerel were still running and none of us liked the flesh of the pollock. He drew it in with difficulty, the slender rod bending dangerously. He heaved the seemingly lifeless body up over the rocks; it was big, brown, and heavy. Its baleful eye seemed to watch towards me where I stood, my rod idle for the moment. I saw father looking down at the fish where it lay on the rock at his feet, the hook still stuck in its mouth. It was panting, slowly, its mouth opening and shutting, its body giving an occasional weak jerk where it lay. I could see the small but sharply pointed teeth. Father did not want to put his finger into that mouth; perhaps he felt, already, the sharpness of those teeth; perhaps he felt he would not

have the strength to draw back that head and snap the neck. I
saw him lift the pollock in both hands high over his head and
dash it down against the rock. It slithered back down to his feet,
leaving traces of moist dirt among the scales, leaving small
blood-stains. It jerked again, and once more he lifted it and
flung it down furiously against the rock. It was that awful slap
that hurt me, and that dreadful stain on the face of the boulder.
A sound that entered my spirit and my flesh and makes me jud-
der still when I remember it.

Far Country

He told us Pushkin, Tolstoy, Gogol;
we were Tatar and Cossack, I was Taras Bulba

leading moustachioed hordes over drain and árdán,
my short pants wide as the Black Sea,

Bunnacurry the Ukraine
and Stony River the Dnieper.

*

I watched him
pacing the stone flags of the kitchen floor,
hands in his pockets, eyes cast down;

but he was ranging across the steppes of his imagination,
bright meadow, ballroom, serf,
the immensity of his white land, his far country.

*

For years he worked at a deal table
cumbered with files and documents
while a harassed people, rough-handed, old,
came to him with forms;

sometimes he held a match to a stub of wax
and watched its one big drop of blood
fall heavily. His eyes were glazed with dust,
his long legs, under the table, curled.

*

Together we stepped down onto the tarmac,
he was silent, pleading,

home at last, reach, toe-tip, hold
like Daedalus after his hazardous flight;

old now, and slow, he was entering through the sliding
glass doors of his dream,

suffering the long
low customs hall, passport control,

questioned for currency, for proof
he was who he thought he was and no other.

*

By day we were Intourists, on an Intourist bus,
viewing mechanical glories of the Revolution.
We queued for hours to see the saint,
shambling, like convicts, between rows of guards;

stepped down, out of the sun, into a crypt,
where Lenin lies, uncorrupted, under glass,
plans for the reconstruction of the world
frozen in his head; a dead man's bedroom

but you cannot touch the folded hands
or put your lips to the alabaster brow.
Father was silent, pleading; at night I heard him
turn in his bed, utter small, hurt, animal cries.

*

At last, at dawn, in the airport terminal,
I saw him sitting, radiant

under the chandeliers of Russian words,
speaking with an old official at a desk

who dropped wax blood onto yellow forms;
they spoke of weather, traffic, snow,

of Pushkin, Tolstoy, Gogol,
the summer and winter palaces

that were still standing
bright as birthday cakes in their fair country.

Before we slept at night in the big room upstairs, after the
stories he told us, Father would always have us say our prayers,
the most important of which was the prayer to the Guardian
Angels: Oh Angel of God ... ever this night ... to rule and guide.
And there was, of course, *The Deer's Cry*:

> I gather to myself today
> strength in the love of Cherubim,
> strength in the obedience of angels
> and in the service of archangels ...

There came a day when I was home from school, some childhood illness, mumps, perhaps, or measles, or just a 'flu. I must
have been getting over it; I was standing in the warm kitchen
and my beloved grandmother was caring for me. She had a task,
too, and perhaps my illness, whatever it was, had brought me a
little low in myself, because I was petulant, a little cross. She had
a large hank of wool, it was a light green in colour, and she
asked me to stand before her, my arms out as wide as I could
stretch them. She looped the hank about my arms and began to
draw out the wool and gather it into a ball on her lap. I quickly
grew tired, my arms held out like that, and I wished to escape
and read or play, and I know I was exasperating the old woman
whom I loved dearly. Came one of those timeless moments,
those 'epiphanies' one remembers for ever, in its mood, its light,
its dimness. The angelus bell rang from the monastery, the
tolling distant, insistent, morose. Nanna stopped, and took the
skein carefully from my arms, allowing me to bless myself along
with her as she murmured the prayer: *The Angel of the Lord declared unto Mary*, and I replied, though a little carelessly, *and she
conceived of the Holy Ghost*. There was a dog barking somewhere
nearby, a barking that was desultory and unconvincing, as if the
animal, too, were as bored as I was, and as petulant.

We finished the prayer but at once I had to reach my arms
out again and Nanna looped what was left of the hank of wool
over my arms. She was a little cross, now, and I grew still. 'You
know,' she said, quietly, 'the air around us is filled with angels,
and they guard and take care of us, but they also know what's in
our heart and are saddened when we misbehave, or when we
speak to God without due care. Look,' she said, 'look out at that

world outside; there are angels everywhere out there, looking after the world, and they are here, in this kitchen, and watching us. And watching you, and I don't think they're too happy at the moment.'

I was suddenly terrified; I did not like the idea of the air about me filled with watchful angels. I was also a little mortified, for here was this woman, generous and kind to a fault, who had minded and watched over me in all my early years, and I was mean enough to let her know how unhappy I was to be standing there before her, my arms stretched out, instead of sitting in a corner somewhere devouring a book, or playing a game. In that strange mixture of fear and love and sorrow, I remember beginning to cry, very softly. She drew me closer to her, calming me, and we grew, in that moment, to be more quietly near each other from then on. Right up to today. Though she has long been taken by those same angels into Paradise.

There is a most beautiful book, put together by Margaret Barker, called *An Extraordinary Gathering of Angels*. The book is lavishly illustrated with paintings from all over the world and from every era, of angels. There are quotations from studies and sacred books that deal with every aspect of our involvement with angels, especially from the Old Testament and from the New. To read this book, to live with it, is to get a sense that heaven and earth are intimately linked in a skein of care and love and that it is the great fault of human beings that we ignore such a luminosity, and such a love and hopefulness.

Margaret Barker studied theology at the University of Cambridge and has developed her research in an independent capacity. She became President of the Society for Old Testament Study in 1998, and has, to date, written some fourteen books on her chosen subject. Since 1997 she has been part of the Religion, Science and the Environment symposium convened by the Ecumenical Patriarch, Bartholomew I, developing her 'temple theology' as the basis for a Christian environment theology. She was awarded a Doctorate in Divinity by the Archbishop of Canterbury, in 2009, in recognition of her work on the Jerusalem Temple and the origins of Christian Liturgy, which has made a significantly new contribution to our understanding of the New Testament and opened up important fields for research.

Margaret Barker is mother and grandmother, she is a Methodist
Preacher currently living in London.

'Jesus taught that everyone has an angel looking towards God,
and they were shepherd angels' (Barker 366). The most famous
and moving example of the guidance of angels is contained in
the Old Testament story of Raphael and Tobias. In the prayers
for the dead is the lovely prayer, *In Paradisum deducant te Angeli*
… May the angels lead you into Paradise; at your coming may
the martyrs receive you and conduct you home into the holy
city, Jerusalem. May a choir of angels receive you. For Margaret
Barker the study of angels is simply one more strand in the great
story of creation, in the beautiful and ongoing history of God's
dealings with humanity and the earth.

In 'Temple theology' is to be found one of the most serious
views of the covenant made between humankind, creation, and
God. Human beings broke this covenant, bringing with their
own fall the disasters that befell and continue to befall the whole
of creation. Christ's incarnation and the offering of himself in
expiation, was to be the renewal and development of the original covenant, the link and development between the Old and
the New Testaments. Temple theology, based on the building of
the first Temple and the symbolism it contained, advocates a
great deal more than a human stewardship of creation. The Temple
in Jerusalem was the most important focus of Jewish thought
and worship in the time of Christ. The temple, and the tabernacle
of Moses, represented the whole of creation, and so temple theology is also creation theology.

In Margaret Barker's thinking and writing, angels are of vital
and ongoing importance. 'Angels are unseen forces in the creation. They connect the material world of our everyday lives to
the Source of all life whom we call God. They are the means by
which we can know something of God, and the only means by
which we can have complete knowledge of the creation. They
reveal what human minds could not work out for themselves,
and they are also guides along the many paths of human reasoning' (Barker 10). Her book, *An Extraordinary Gathering of
Angels*, published in 2004, is the richest source of the written
tradition of angelology and of references and paintings of angels.
This, for example: 'Isaiah was in the temple, mystically looking

beyond the veil and into the holy of holies itself. He was gazing into the heart of the creation, where he saw fiery seraphim praising the Creator. From their place by the throne the seraphim looked out onto the whole world and saw that it was full of the glory of the Lord' (Barker 138). Here he heard the 'Thrice Holy Hymn': Holy, Holy, Holy … Isaiah 6. Barker's studies outline the notion that the harmony of angels in heaven will be mirrored on the earth, just as the angels appeared to the shepherds on the night of Jesus' birth in the stable and they were singing a form of that 'Thrice Holy Hymn', one of the most wonderful lines being *and peace on earth to men of good will*. Creation theology, then, is an approach to the living out of the most beautiful aspects of the covenant between humanity, creation and God, and the angels act as some of the great forces joining earth to heaven in this great task, now so severely threatened.

In the creation story in Genesis, Adam expressed his dominion over the animals by naming them. But this creation and this naming go on continually from the Creator who holds all of creation together. The Dead Sea Scrolls refer to the 'mystery of existence', meaning the wonder of the source of life, this challenging agreement between humanity, God and creation. Some rabbis have said Day One meant that the Creator was at unity with all of his creation, and St Paul saw this as the goal of all living, when God will be again 'all in all':

> But in fact Christ has been raised from the dead, the first fruits of those who have died. For since death came through a human being, the resurrection of the dead has also come through a human being. For as all die in Adam, so all will be made alive in Christ. But each in his own order: Christ, the first fruits; then, at his coming, those who belong to Christ. Then comes the end, when he hands over the kingdom to God the Father, after he has destroyed every ruler and every authority and power. For he must reign until he has put all his enemies under his feet. The last enemy to be destroyed is death. For 'God has put all things in subjection under his feet.' But when it says, 'All things are put in subjection,' it is plain that this does not include the one who put all things in subjection under him. When all things are subjected to him,

then the Son himself will also be subjected to the one who put all things in subjection under him, so that God may be all in all. (1 Corinthians 15:20-28)

This work will be made possible by the actions of Christ who brings all things into harmony: 'He is before all things, and in him all things hold together' (Colossians 1:17).

The *Benedicite* exhorts the whole of creation to praise the Lord: angels, powers, winds, seasons; and then the visible creation too, the trees, birds and animals. *The Deer's Cry* echoes this exhortation. St Francis called on all creatures to join with humankind and praise their God, their King and their Creator in one great family of creation that includes humankind. When an animal or plant becomes extinct, then that praise is diminished. The bonds of the creation covenant were broken by human sin. Isaiah saw in a vision how the earth was collapsing because the eternal covenant had been broken. A curse was devouring the earth, and its inhabitants were suffering from their own sins: 'The earth dries up and withers, the world languishes and withers, the heavens languish together with the earth. The earth lies polluted under its inhabitants, for they have transgressed laws, violated the statutes, broken the everlasting covenant. Therefore, a curse devours the earth, and its inhabitants suffer for their guilt. Therefore, the inhabitants of the earth dwindled, and few people are left.' (Isaiah 24:4-6).

In *The Merchant of Venice* there is a beautiful passage, spoken by Lorenzo:

How sweet the moonlight sleeps upon this bank!
Here let us sit, and let the sound of music
Creep in our ears: soft stillness and the night
Become the touches of sweet harmony.
Look how the floor of Heaven
Is thick inlaid with patines of bright gold:
There's not the smallest orb which thou behold'st
But in his motion like an angel sings,
Still quiring to the young-eyed cherubins;
Such harmony is in immortal sounds;
In such a night as this,
When the sweet wind did gently kiss the trees

And they did make no noise, in such a night
Troilus, methinks, mounted the Troyan wall,
And sigh'd his soul toward the Grecian tents,
Where Cressid lay that night.

In our own time, we have cast out such notions as the existence of angels, and with the angels we have cast away a sense of
involvement with creation, with the world in which we live. We
have reneged, often and often, on our agreement. Creation was
the original covenant between God and humankind. '... today,
all around us, we witness God's cosmic covenant with us in shreds,
and, along with it, the world and its inhabitants' (McKenna 7).
Perhaps it is time to look again at the work of such writers as
Margaret Barker and gaze around us at the disaster we have created out of creation. 'This is the choice laid before each of us: to
choose now to undo the chaos and to rebuild and replant, to live
as trees planted by running waters, and to obey the Word of the
Lord God Yahweh, or to choose to undo life and to tear down
what is lifegiving and good, and to break faith with the Word of
the Lord' (McKenna 102).

Ever This Night

There was a rose-petal sky all evening
showing from clouds that were turf-shaped and dense;
a full moon lifted behind the pine-grove and four
whooper swans flew low towards the lake,
crying, you would think,
for the familiar wastes of Iceland. I tucked down
into the warmth of the big bed, rosary beads
still curled about my fingers. I thought
how the angel would guard me across the ocean floor
of the night – then wondered, what would my angel do
in her boredom, pent in her God-given cage
of air: be watchful lest I slip into some crevasse?
or step towards the maw of a leviathan, great white
or giant squid? I drifted, bemused
that an angel's bones might be coloured
moon-white, star-blue? feathers colour-patterned
like a goldfinch? Sleep, then, like high tide settling,

I was carried away, sails billowing, to find myself
down amongst the old and harmless wrecks, great
grandfather Ted, great-uncle John. All through the night
I was island, wide spaces opening
off every degree of the compass, life before me, its scenes
already melting into air, into thin air;
and came awake next morning, safe, and dry,
colour-patterned sea-shells in my hands, like dreams.

By Way of a Delayed Introduction

'Beginning a new covenant with the earth absolutely requires a reclamation of the dimension of the sacred' (Cry 115). Leonardo Boff goes on: 'If in recent centuries we have been victims of a model of civilisation that has systematically assaulted the earth and led us to close our ears to the music in things and turn our backs on the majesty of the starry sky, it is because the experience of the sacredness of the universe has been lost.' Without it, all is mechanistic and ecology is merely a technique for management. Creation is tremendous and fascinating, it makes us tremble with awe and it draws us to itself. It is not enough to know all of this; it is necessary to experience the awe, the emotion, the love: hence the focus on Christ, on Eucharist, and on Poetry. It is the aim to develop what Boff calls 'an ethic of unlimited compassion and shared responsibility' (Cry 135).

A great and frightening darkness in our age has been our world's ever-expanding greed and economic ebullience and its near-disastrous effects on our planet's health. Where is poetry when it comes to these questions? It is not my belief that poetry is created to change anything. Rowan Williams, speaking of Jacques Maritain's views, states: 'Virtuous making aims not at the good of humanity but at the good of what is made' (Williams 11). The integrity of the work made is absolutely essential and 'a judgement of beauty cannot as such be morally or metaphysically illuminating' (Williams 13). Poetry may well give our lives a radiance, and what is its relationship to truth? The artist's subjective integrity is not enough; art is not aimed at the will but reaches the intelligence, the emotions, the imagination. 'And the artist as artist is not called on to love God or the world or humanity, but to love what he or she is doing' (Williams 15). The works of love.

My concern is with poetry. But my concerns are also with Christianity and, this being the case, with great Christian poetry. My concerns, too, are with our earth, created by God through the Son, the God incarnate, and with the covenant that is necessarily made between Creator and creature. This covenant has been broken, on our side, and Christ became incarnate to bring us redemption and to bring a new covenant to the fore. My concerns, then, are also to do with the creation, its place in our living and in Christianity, and Christ the Incarnate Word's place in that creation. Our closest touch with Christ is now in Eucharist. And an ongoing and ever-present reality in our lives is the obscenity of war. Do all these concerns cohere? Poetry, Christianity, ecology, Eucharist, and the total abolition of war? The works of love.

There are many who do not understand, nor care for, the spiritual culture out of which some of the poets I love have sprung. Yet they may still enjoy the work as poems. Among today's younger generations words like 'transubstantiation, sacrament, miracle', notions of the 'mysteries of the rosary', feast-days like 'The Assumption' or 'The Immaculate Conception', are utterly irrelevant and without interest in their lives. Take Eliot's *Four Quartets*, for instance; with its references to mystical and other religious themes, shall we have to add note upon note of explanation? There are several issues here, amongst them the poetry itself, and the question of belief. For so long humankind has survived with a decent awareness of mythological deities and metamorphoses, relishing Virgil's works and Dante's, and so many other poems based on these creations, these poems. Will it happen that the same will be said of religion? Shall we have to add note upon note of explanation?

Belief or unbelief ought not to undermine our attitudes to good poetry. If the religious subject of a poem does not stir us it may be that the beauty of the poem as a work of art may yet move us deeply. For too long doctrinal preaching and exhortation, the generalised and clichéd approach of hymns and devotional works, the unquestioning focus on piety, have put us off. In our time one of the great questions is the ecological one: how has it come about that we have placed our own planet in such jeopardy? And can poetry have anything to say about all this? Above all, in the context of the poems presented here, can poetry that has taken Christ as centre, show us anything of worth and pleasure?

As I was growing up the words 'permissive society' and 'libertarianism' were applied only to sexual mores. In recent years it is seen how these words apply much more seriously to the situation in which Europe, and particularly Ireland, has found itself. Angus Sibley, a fellow of the Institute of Actuaries and a former member of the London Stock Exchange, outlines the meanings of the word 'freedom'. Economist libertarianism (Isaiah Berlin, Milton Friedman and others) takes it in a negative sense to mean freedom from restraint or interference: in other words, permissiveness. The positive sense of freedom (the sense of virtue, or moral responsibility, Bernard Häring) takes it as it is understood in Christian terms, the empowerment to do things, the ability to act in a moral way, inseparable from goodness, justice and holiness. Sibley writes: 'In practice, modern economic libertarianism has meant privatising public organisations and cutting public spending; abolishing regulations that restrained abusive competition; weakening trade unions and trade or professional associations, which restrict their members' negative freedom; permitting monstrous mergers where market forces demand them; reducing tax rates, especially the heavy rates that formerly bore upon the very wealthy. The consequences of such policies have been discouraging. We have seen deterioration in public amenities and services; concentration of economic power, with grotesque overpayment of the 'superstars' of capitalism, while earnings of ordinary workers have stagnated; worst of all, the undisciplined conduct of bankers and traders that led to the current crisis' (*Doctrine and Life*: Sept 2009).

If we do not pursue goodness, while, if you wish, pursuing reasonable wealth and contentment at the same time, then our pursuit is immoral and will lead to selfish and evil results. Freedom pursued for one's own gain must not take away the freedom of others. Sibley quotes Benjamin Franklin: 'only a virtuous people is capable of freedom'. Justice and truth require the regulation of contracts and agreements between individuals and groups, where the strength of the individual or group is unequal. Seán McDonagh has written, 'The obsession with economic growth which is a feature of the global economy is impoverishing the majority of peoples of the world and endangering the planet' (McDonagh 1). He wrote this in 1994.

Sibley, in the same article, goes on to show how the state came to be seen as the enemy of the free market when it imposed conditions on that market's 'freedoms'. The market wished to be self-regulating, creating its own 'spontaneous order'; 'but close observers of the recent crash may recall that former president of the US Federal Reserve, Alan Greenspan, questioned by Congressman Henry Waxman in October 2008, admitted that he "made a mistake" in trusting that free markets could regulate themselves without government oversight.' It is clear, from the last years of the twentieth century in Ireland, and the first years of this, that government actually spurred on the self-regulating notion for big business.

True freedom is that spoken of in Romans chapter 8, the true freedom of human beings closely allied to that of the whole of God's sacred creation:

> For the creation was subjected to futility, not of its own will, but by the will of the one who subjected it, in hope that the creation itself will be set free from its bondage to decay and will obtain the freedom of the glory of the children of God. We know that the whole creation has been groaning in labour pains until now; and not only the creation but we ourselves, who have the first fruits of the Spirit, groan inwardly while we wait for adoption, the redemption of our bodies. For in hope we were saved. Now hope that is seen is not hope. For who hopes for what is seen? But if we hope for what we do not see, we wait for it with patience.

Our lives touch their boundaries against emptiness, like islands whose jagged edges stretch themselves away from, or towards, the ocean. Our words are always in conflict with silence, words that are febrile and feeble and yet touch, at times, upon the sublime and upon permanence. At times silence wins out and overwhelms our words, but our hope remains that words can achieve some form of stability, of meaning and lastingness. Space and silence still surround and border our artefacts, our written words, our printed poems. Perhaps out of the ruins of islands, of artefacts, of libraries, a deep and lasting harmony will forever persist in the human consciousness. Our hope remains in the fullness of that harmony, a music of sea against shore, of sky against pillar, of pain a little understood against blind anguish.

That we gather words into sentences to form a bridge between islands, an archway beautiful in itself, though bounded by the reverberating emptiness of both sea and sky. As body after body falls off into dust and oblivion, that there may remain something of articulation in our cries of distress, in our whispered supplications, in our breathed-out prayers of awe before all beauty, in our breathed-in gasps of love. Wisdom piling up along the bounds, as rounded stones pile up along a shore to form a bulwark. Love adding light and peace to the slow procession of creatures, human and animal, across the salt plains oceanwards. Sandcastles falling away against the breeze. Tide rising and the long white lacework of absurdity held against the bulwark's base. Our marks struck deeply into stone. The works of love proclaimed against the works of darkness. Our manuscripts that will never be complete. The works of love.

'That is the glory of poetry, and of secular literature generally, that out of such slight material as the pleasure to be had from the weaving together of words it can make analogues of revelation that can illuminate and affect the whole of our life' (Boyle 127). 'Literature, I think, shows us in words the truth about life. That is not its defining feature, for the defining feature of literature is its non-instrumental use of words, and the defining feature of secular literature is its non-instrumental use of words in order to give pleasure' (Boyle 128).

And that heavy-treading and sometimes light-headed saint, Augustine wrote: 'Thy whole creation ceaseth not, nor is silent in Thy praise: neither the spirit of man directed unto Thee, nor creation animate or inanimate, by the voice of those who meditate thereon: that so our souls may from their weariness arise towards Thee, leaning on those things which Thou hast created, and passing on to Thyself, who madest them wonderfully; and there is refreshment and true strength'.

A suspension of disbelief for the purposes of reading poetry is essential (as it is with other works) and need not disqualify us from an empathy with that religious belief. In good poetry, religious questions are not something fenced off from everyday experience; it is out of religious belief, even religious doubt, deeply engaged with the actual world, that some of the best poetry will come. Formal religions have no monopoly on religious experience and indeed the already formulated and accepted cannons of religious tenets and approaches will often militate against real poetry. Good poetry often arises in unorthodox or secular contexts of religious experience. Even the closest links between a poem's experience and a religious faith will open up horizons beyond the poem's actual surface limits. In good poetry the religious and the aesthetic do not pull against but support each other. The reading of good religious poems is not to be confined to those with religious beliefs. Much of this may seem to be stating the obvious yet the word 'religion' in our time, as even the word 'God', tends immediately to offend the aesthete.

Hence a choice of poems and poetry that bring to the centre of consciousness our need to embrace and not destroy the earth on which we live, the creation of which we are a part, poetry that links the embrace of that creation with the embrace of a Christ more nearly understood, poets that have and continue to explore the relationship between Christian thinking and the individual soul, poetry that takes apart the human proclivity to war and destruction and urges us towards peace: in fact a choice of poems and poets that help elucidate what our existence is all about at its most crucial level of being. The works of love.

Late Have I Loved You

One of the first great Christian thinkers was Augustine, of Tagaste, Algeria, then a Numidian city which became part of the Roman empire. 'Augustine can be called the founder of the Western spirit. No other theologian, apart from St Paul, has been more influential in the West' (Armstrong 119). His influence in so many areas of our thinking extends to our own times and, as well as the fact that he opened up many trains of philosophy and theology that led to good and great developments over the centuries, he has had, in some strands of thinking, a somewhat baleful effect on our outlook.

Augustine was born at Tagaste in 354, his father a pagan but his mother, Monica, a Christian who ensured that her son received a Christian education. 'From my tenderest infancy, I had in a manner sucked with my mother's milk that name of my Saviour, Thy Son; I kept it in the recesses of my heart; and all that presented itself to me without that Divine Name, though it might be elegant, well written, and even replete with truth, did not altogether carry me away' (Confessions, I, iv). He spent much of his early life in a certain licentiousness and even formed a liaison with a woman who bore him a son, Adeodatus, ('Given by God'). For a time he came under the influence of Manichaeism, a material dualism; he was attracted by a philosophy that was unbridled by faith and moral responsibility. He taught grammar and rhetoric, becoming gradually disenchanted with the Manichean outlook. He left for Italy where he came under the influence of Bishop Ambrose in Milan where, at last, he yielded to his inner voices and to the pleading of his mother and, in 386, became a Christian.

In a garden he prayed to be brought to Christ: 'And Thou, O Lord, how long? How long? Is it to be tomorrow and tomorrow? Why not now? Why not this very hour put an end to shame?' Then he heard a child's voice singing 'Tolle lege! Tolle lege!' (Take up and read! Take up and read!). He took up Saint Paul's epistle to the Romans and read the first chapter that met his eyes: 'Let us walk honestly, as in the day; not in rioting and drunkenness, not in chambering and wantonness, not in strife and envying. But put ye on the Lord Jesus Christ, and make not provision for the flesh, to fulfill the lusts thereof.' (Romans 13:13-14) Later he was able to pray: 'Too late, have I loved Thee, O Beauty so ancient and so new, too late have I loved Thee! Thou wast with me, and I was not with Thee; I was abroad, running after those beauties which Thou hast made; those things which could have no being but in Thee kept me away from Thee. Thou hast called, Thou hast cried out, and hast pierced my deafness. Thou hast enlightened, Thou hast shone forth, and my blindness is dispelled. I have tasted Thee, and am hungry of Thee. Thou hast touched me, and I am afire with the desire of thy embraces.'

It is clear that Augustine determined to turn away from the things of flesh, from 'those beauties which Thou hast made'. It was a turn towards Christ, but a particular Christ, Saviour, Son of God, holy, distant, to be loved with a devotion and care that would brook no interference. He received baptism in 387 and set out to devote his great mind to a philosophy that would place reason at the gates of faith and give authority to the Christian message. His confidence in the Platonists grew as he found in them ideas that were in harmony with his faith. He remained a neo-Platonist in so far as this philosophy supported his religious beliefs, reconciling in so far as he could his Christianity with his Platonism. The great dividing points were the mystery of the Word made flesh in Jesus, the mystery of love that was based on humility and grace. Late that same year, 387, his mother Monica died at Ostia and Augustine returned to Africa. He was ordained in 391 and began preaching. He was made Bishop of Hippo and lived in community with his clergy in a form of religious life. He lived a life devoted to preaching, teaching and writing and refuting heresies. His two great books were *The Confessions* and *The City of God*.

Thomas Merton wrote, in his introduction to *The City of God*: 'It is Catholic in the sense that St Augustine's view of history is the view held by the Catholic Church, and by all Catholic tradition since the Apostles' (City xv). The Fall of Rome seemed an impossibility and when it happened, in 410, scapegoats were needed and people turned to the Christians. Augustine's work develops a theology of 'two cities', the human one, Rome being exemplar, and God's city; his work studies the intervention of God into human history. Adam's sin, and the sin of Cain, set up in the world a divided city, one of conflict. And conflict at its worst, war, became one of Augustine's studies. God planned a second city, the City of God, to redeem the first. Merton wrote: 'Even the wars, persecutions, and all the other evils which have made the history of empires terrible to read and more terrible to live through, have had only this one purpose: they have been the flails with which God has separated the wheat from the chaff, the elect from the damned. They have been the tools that have fashioned the living stones which God would set in the walls of his city of vision' (City XVIII).

Elizabeth Jennings writes of the *Confessions IX*, of Augustine, speaking, at Ostia, with his mother: 'He continues: 'Yea, we were soaring higher yet, by inward musing and discourse, and admiring of Thy works'. This phrase (Jennings adds) 'admiring of Thy works,' is vitally important. Augustine sees God shining through all things. What he longs to do is to pierce through things and find the Being who informs them and keeps and balances them both when they are in motion and when they are at rest' (Jennings 23). From this perspective, Augustine developed a theology of praise towards the Creator of these 'works', and praise has become one of the great and serious modes of the Christian's response to the Creator. 'Like many passionate, sensual men, he longed for some experience in which the senses could be overruled and the disorderly emotions be brought into subjection' (Jennings 25).

When it comes to certain other aspects of Augustine's thinking, it is important to remember that he was living and writing through the morning fug of Christianity's early days. A lover of earth and things earthly, a lover, he had yet found (after long resisting) his God and his Trinity deep within his own mind. Later on, however, as he moved closer to God, his sense of what true knowledge is changed; he came to believe that 'the lowest level of knowledge, so far as it can be called knowledge, is sensation, which is common to men and brutes; and the highest level of knowledge, peculiar to man, is the contemplation of eternal things (wisdom) by the mind alone, without the intervention of sensation' (Coplestone 73). While urging humankind to praise God through awareness of the beauty of God's creation, he insists that created things cannot give us complete happiness but must point ever upwards towards God.

How do we come to God? 'The immense distance between God and man cannot be traversed by human effort alone. It is only because God has come to meet us in the person of the incarnate Word that we can restore the image of God within us, which has been damaged and defaced by sin' (Armstrong 122). Augustine lived and wrote during terrible times, barbarian tribes pouring into Europe and bringing down the Roman empire, civilisation in the West appearing to be on the point of disintegration. The fall of Rome influenced Augustine's thinking on man's inherent weakness and his theory of Original Sin would become central to how people viewed our world. Because of Adam's sin, Augustine saw all of humankind condemned to eternal damnation, an inherent guilt passed on through the sexual act. He came to see humanity as ignoble, unworthy of coming close to God, unworthy of the special sacrament of the Eucharist, and to see the sexual side of our being as the most sinful. He wrote:

> Banished after his sin, Adam bound his offspring also with the penalty of death and damnation, that offspring which by sinning he had corrupted in himself, as in a root; so that whatever progeny was born (through carnal concupiscence, by which a fitting retribution for his disobedience was bestowed upon him) from himself and his spouse – who was the cause of his sin and the companion of his damnation – would drag through the ages the burden of Original Sin, by which it would itself be dragged through manifold errors and sorrows, down to that final and never-ending torment with the rebel angels ... So the matter stood; the damned lump of humanity was lying prostrate, no, was wallowing in evil, it was falling headlong from one wickedness to another; and joined to the faction of the angels who had sinned, it was paying the most righteous penalty of its impious treason.'

The denigration of sexuality and of women was already a tendency in the West by Augustine's time; it was he who gave these views credence and an early doctrinal basis. Karen Armstrong has written: 'A religion which looks askance upon half the human race and which regards every involuntary motion of mind, heart and body as a symptom of fatal concupiscence can only alienate men and women from their condition. Western Christianity never fully recovered from this neurotic misogyny, which can still be seen in the unbalanced reaction to the very notion of the ordination of women.' (Armstrong 124). There is, therefore, a certain approach towards the thought of Augustine that can assent fully to his notion of praise, that has taken for granted, over the centuries, his view of Original Sin, and that now needs to re-interpret the limitations of merely 'praising' the Creator for the wonder of his works, the doctrine of Original Sin, and the notion of the perversity of women.

In Book XIII of his *Confessions* Augustine wrote: 'And you saw all that you had made, O God, and found it very good. We, too, see all these things and know that they are very good. In the case of each of your works you first commanded them to be made, and when they had been made you looked at each in turn and saw that it was good. I have counted and found that scripture tells us seven times that you saw that what you had made was good, and when you looked for the eighth time and saw the whole of your creation, we are told that you found it not only good but very good, for you saw all at once as one whole. Each separate work was good, but when they were all seen as one, they were not merely good: they were very good' (Confessions 340).

This is an encouraging paragraph, pointing to one of the central urgencies for ecological practice. The corollary of this is that humankind has a duty to take special care of what God has created and one of the first reactions to such a sense of duty, goodness and wonder must be that praise of which he writes; Book I of the *Confessions* begins with praise: 'Man is one of your creatures, Lord, and his instinct is to praise you. He bears about him the mark of death, the sign of his own sin, to remind him that you thwart the proud. But still, since he is a part of your creation, he wishes to praise you. The thought of you stirs him so deeply that he cannot be content unless he praises you, because you made us for yourself and our hearts find no peace until they rest in you' (Confessions 21).

This is couched in very general terms but it is too easy to
stare back through the dimness of the centuries and impose on
Augustine our own hoped-for sense of caring for creation in its
details and particular crafting. The poet Pádraig J. Daly takes
this thrust of Augustine's urging towards praise and develops
it, calling out the details that he wishes to call out, making
Augustine's implied theology of the worth of creation, shine
forth in its particulars: as Augustine wrote: 'Taken singly, each
thing is good; but collectively they are very good' (Confessions
344).

Then there is the Eucharist. 'That Bread which you see on the
altar, having been sanctified by the word of God is the body of
Christ. That chalice, or rather, what is in that chalice, having
been sanctified by the word of God, is the blood of Christ.
Through that bread and wine the Lord Christ willed to com-
mend his body and blood, which he poured out for us unto the
forgiveness of sins' (Sermons 227). Augustine held that we are
to recognise the Lord Jesus in the breaking of bread; 'For not all
bread, but only that which receives the blessing of Christ, becomes Christ's body' (Sermons 234:2). With Augustine the Real
Presence is undoubted, but the emphasis remains more focused
on sacrifice, on immolation, thus making the giving of his Body
more a personal act of generosity on the part of Christ than a
real participation by the individual in the sacrament. 'Christ is
both the Priest, offering himself, and himself the Victim. He
willed that the sacramental sign of this should be the daily sacrifice of the church, who, since the church is his body and he the
Head, learns to offer herself through him' (City of God 10:20).

He taught that the church as the Body of Christ participates
in the eucharistic Body of Christ, so that they are both identical
and different. 'For Augustine there was no inseparable chasm
between the visible and the spiritual; rather, there was continu-
ity between the two' (Foley 172). At the Last Supper, Christ gave
the disciples the 'figure of his body and blood'; 'what you see is
transitory, but the invisible reality therein signified does not
pass away, but remains' (Sermon 227). The spiritual reality, for
Augustine, was more real than physical realities. Once again, it
is vital to see that Augustine was breaking ground that had not
been developed before, yet his influence was so strong that a

conscious effort is required to understand him in our contemporary concerns. The doctrine of the Real Presence demands an awareness of what the sacrament actually is and does, physically taking the Bread and Wine that have become the Body and Blood of Christ, and consuming it in the normal functioning of the receiver's body.

And who is this Christ? 'For as man, he is our Mediator; but as the Word of God, he is not an intermediary between God and man because he is equal with God, and God with God, and together with him one God' (Confessions 251). 'He who alone was free among the dead, for he was free to lay down his life and free to take it up again, was for us both Victor and Victim in your sight, and it was because he was the Victim that he was also the Victor. In your sight he was for us both Priest and Sacrifice, and it was because he was the Sacrifice that he was also the Priest. By being your Son, yet serving you, he freed us from servitude and made us your sons' (ibid). 'We might have thought that your Word was far distant from union with man, and so we might have despaired of ourselves, if he had not been made flesh and come to dwell among us' (ibid). It is, then, Christ's life that is now within the receiving Christians, physically within the believing church.

On several beautiful, but removed, headlands on the island of Achill, there are Killeens, anonymous graveyards where the unbaptised bodies of children were buried in the guilt and secrecy of night. We are all born, Augustine taught, tainted with the sin of Adam; we are darkened both physically and spiritually, even in the labouring months within the womb, by the black death of Original Sin and it is only baptism, that washing away of inherited guilt, that will free the soul and offer it the possibility of heaven. Augustine held that an unbaptised infant could not be saved. But if there is to be justice and above all love between God and humankind, this simply cannot be the case. We believe in a Creator God that is essentially full of the most generous giving, of an overwhelming love and it is God's love first of all that is our hope and our treasure. Out of love Christ 'was made flesh and dwelt amongst us'. Like mankind, Christ was mortal; like God, we must believe, he was just.

Augustine lived at a time when Rome was being attacked by

the barbarian hordes and he knew that people blamed
Christianity for a failure to defend the city. He also thought that
this may be one of the ways that God chastised humanity for its
immorality. In contrasting the earthly city with what is to be
developed, the City of God, Augustine saw war as sometimes
necessary in defence of the development of this later-to-be City.
'For God's providence constantly uses war to correct and chasten
the corrupt morals of mankind, as it also uses such afflictions to
train men in a righteous and laudable way of life, removing to a
better state those whose life is approved, or else keeping them in
this world for further service'; thus he writes in *The City of God*.
Cruelty, he thought, must have a divine purpose, to chasten and
correct our ways. 'The empire would always have been small
indeed, if neighbouring peoples had been peaceable, had always acted with justice, and had never provoked attack by any
wrong-doing. In that case, human affairs would have been in a
happier state; all kingdoms would have been small and would
have rejoiced in concord with their neighbours ... To make war
and to extend the realm by crushing other peoples is good fortune in the eyes of the wicked; to the good, it is stern necessity.
But since it would be worse that the unjust should lord it over
the just, this stern necessity may be called good fortune without
impropriety' (City of God). He concludes: 'For it is the injustice
of the opposing side that lays on the wise man the duty of wag-
ing wars; and this injustice is assuredly to be deplored by a
human being, since it is the injustice of human beings, even
though no necessity for war should arise from it' (City of God).

It is clear that Saint Augustine had, as the first major philoso-
pher/theologian, a very great influence, both during his lifetime
and down the lightening centuries since then, right up to our
own time. He was, after all, at the dawning of the Christian
thinking and he was probing his own experiences, his own
mind, and his own faith, in order to draw his conclusions and to
teach the Christian news to pagans. His focus on humankind
was anthropocentric, man the centre, the highlight, the master
of all of creation. In later times it is thought, however, that a
basic ethics demands the welfare of the community, the whole,
not just the human community. Humankind must not disfigure
God's image in his creation. God renewed the contract with

humankind, through Noah, after the flood. Genesis 9: 8-17 has it: 'Then God said to Noah and to his sons with him: "I now establish my covenant with you and with your descendants after you and with every living creature that was with you – the birds, the livestock and all the wild animals, all those that came out of the ark with you – every living creature on earth. I establish my covenant with you: Never again will all life be cut off by the waters of a flood; never again will there be a flood to destroy the earth." And God said, "This is the sign of the covenant I am making between me and you and every living creature with you, a covenant for all generations to come: I have set my rainbow in the clouds, and it will be the sign of the covenant between me and the earth. Whenever I bring clouds over the earth and the rainbow appears in the clouds, I will remember my covenant between me and you and all living creatures of every kind. Never again will the waters become a flood to destroy all life. Whenever the rainbow appears in the clouds, I will see it and remember the everlasting covenant between God and all living creatures of every kind on the earth".'

In Thomas Gray's *Elegy Written in a Country Churchyard* there is this stanza:

Full many a gem of purest ray serene
The dark unfathom'd caves of ocean bear:
Full many a flower is born to blush unseen,
And waste its sweetness on the desert air.

There is a presumption here that creation exists for the delight of man, and that whatever is not available to humankind 'wastes its sweetness'. Perhaps the truth is that the whole of creation is of value in and of itself, whether or not a human is by to witness it. 'All creation is bonded together into a single community' (McDonagh 139).

This, then, is Augustine, Church Father, Doctor of the Church, saint, philosopher and theologian and one whose work has filtered down the centuries into even our contemporary view of humankind. Christ. Love. The Just War. The Eucharist. The Works of Love.

Pádraig J. Daly's poem, *Augustine: Letter to God*, moves us lovingly and forgivingly into the vision he attributes to St Augustine:

Augustine: Letter to God

I
Where praise is impossible
I will praise;
And sing where sound faces silence.

I carry death about in me
And inevitable
Cold;

Yet I will sing
Or, failing,
Burst asunder with love.

II
Man cannot evade You:
Every wary mouse,
The ant that builds and climbs,

Each small limpet on a rock,
The waters sucked noisily
Through stones on the shore,

The sleek and watery cormorant
Compel him
To shout You out.

He is the phosphorous sea
Stirred to consciousness,
The cold gravels of the underbed.

From the acids of first time,
From the tepid waters of creation
He draws his voice;

And all creation –
Hills rising out of him
Into sudden seas,

Black shoreline,
The ocean's grit –
Binds him inescapably to praise.

And nowhere but in praise
Can quark or atom
Or any fraction else of mass

Find peace.

III
Each flower
Requires knowledge

And the raindrops
On the curlew's wing

Fall
As questions

There is a curiosity
In every piece of burnt wood.

IV
What am I
That You require me?

And what is my house
That You should come to it?

And what my love that
You demand my loving

And I am lost
Unless I reach and love?

V
I call:
And You are already in my voice

I stretch:
And You are trembling at my fingertips.

You are here and smiling
While I send invitations out.

I draw circles to contain You,
Make clay jars:

But You are
Circle and jar

And the space within
And the space without

And the spacelessness
Without the final space,

Place
Where place has no meaning,

Time
Where all is an endless now.

I call
And I am my own answer;

I stretch
Only to where I have started.

The Monastery, the Mission and the Clock

The Bunnacurry Boys National School has long since crumbled, leaving only bare walls and a floor open to the sky. The wind has long been master here, thistle-dust instead of chalk is blowing about, there are shivering grasses in irregular rows. The lesson has been time and its corollaries. On one of the gable walls, where mouse-eared chickweed grows out of dirt, dust and broken, naked brick, there used to be two wholly fascinating things: one, a large clock, its pendulum visible through a glass doorway, its face browned with age, its minute hand often moving far too slowly for our liking. And a crucifix, large and realistic, with a huge stain across the groin of the suffering, strained body, a stain the colour of lipstick, a stain I could scarcely pull my eyes away from. Time, the Cross, the gable wall. And now I stand, as if forsaken, in the ploshy ground where once there was a wooden floor, among bits of walls where once there was paint, and stone echoing to rote learning.

I hear my name called out, hear that answering call, *anseo*, present, here I am. But that was yesterday, and yesterday was half a century ago. Above me now only the blue sky, clouds passing over, as they have always passed but way back then there were rafters, the schoolroom was big as the world itself, where I would learn everything, know all there is to know of this world; and the next. I was child and innocent back then, sitting among so many others, sing-songing spellings, puzzling over mental arithmetic, learning by rote the history of God, trying to understand that stained figure high on the wall before me. That child is absent now, *as láthair*, flown.

In 1834 the Reverend Edward Nangle set up a Mission Society and a soup kitchen to draw in the poor and starving families of Achill Island to the Protestant faith. He also built a school, a hospital, and a house for the minister. Many of the island boys attended the school and this brought anxiety to the Catholic authorities who sent along a group of Franciscan Brothers who would found their own school to counteract this Protestant

incursion. In 1854 the Bunnacurry Boys National School opened
its doors and the emphasis, as always this emphasis, was on the
teaching of religion, the Catholic religion. The school closed
those doors in 1970, leaving the walls to implode, the furnish-
ings to fall apart, and the memories to flourish. Standing now in
the bitter winds I whisper to the dead in their ordered rows,
anseo, present, Seamus, Thady, Seán, I'm here, I say, still willing,
but slow, as always, and studying still what it may be to live.

Because the emphasis had always been on the studying of religion, I remember well how we spent so many hours over the
old catechism which I knew, cover to cover, by heart, though little
understanding what the heavy and much-articulated words
might mean. We learned, too, whole chunks of Bible history,
stories of exodus and kings, of genesis and wars, of strength incredible and of love betrayed, agreements broken, covenants
cast aside. I have a vivid memory of studying in the kitchen at
home, some task of rote-learning, a passage to be trotted out
word-perfect the next day. I remember the tale, Joseph and his
wonderful coloured coat, but what I remember most is sitting at
that deal table, and falling absent, perhaps gazing beyond myself into the future, with wonder, with hope, with ungrounded
longing. Time past, as T. S. Eliot wrote, and time future, what
might have been and what has been, point to one end, which is
always present. There was a flower-patterned oil-cloth on the
kitchen table; I had my Bible history open before me, I had examined over and over its pictures of deserts, of high mountains
where God thundered out of dark clouds, pictures of oceans
with the high waves parting to reveal dry ground and everywhere there were pictures of those stylised heroes of God's militias. Being there and not there, I was chewing on a pencil-end as
if hunger for knowledge, that ongoing famine, frustrated me
and I was spitting small splinters of that pencil out onto the
stone-flagged floor. Outside, hydrangeas were in bloom, their
sky-blue flowers big as willow-pattern plates; somewhere, not
too far away, a cock crowed and I passed even more deeply into
absence. But on the wall above me was a picture of Jesus,
stylised, his fingers long as tapers pointing to a heart ringed
round with thorns; his ringlets were honey-brown but his eyes
were lifted querulously towards the ceiling. There was a red,

eternal light flickering weakly below the picture. Between him and me, between the Bible history and me, was a vast desert of meaningless words, grains of sand scattered in no fixed pattern and the hunger within me, for that knowledge of the world, of this world and of the next, gnawed at my bones.

But I was truly aware of very little of that in those days. What a difference time makes, and how much we can know of ourselves by standing here, standing in the near-levelled shell of the small school, standing in the present, buffeted by the details of the past. I can remember the stretched body of the Christ on the crucifix on the wall. Now, too, I can imagine the too-perfect eyes of the too-perfect Jesus in the picture at home, I can see them and how saddened they must have been, how they were lowered to where I sat, how those eyes may have been peering down on that restless, stooped-over boy, in anger perhaps, or in mute and trenchant pleading. There was no word spoken, no whisper of love or promise, there was only a summer bee distraught against the window, making a sorry sound. Here, amongst tumbled walls, I hear my name called out, hear that answering call, *anseo*, present, here I am. But that was yesterday, and yesterday was half a century ago.

And Christ was on the Rood

The crucifix, Christ on the Cross, that rust-coloured stain across his groin, the mystery and the presence of it all. It was Good Friday; I was ten years old. I had suffered a good Lent and had put by quite a treasury of sweets and chocolate, given up as a penance (except, of course for St Patrick's Day) for the endless weeks that prepared us for the Easter Triduum. Good Friday. A dreary day, sluggish, with vague expectations and disturbing presences. We had suffered the long Stations of the Cross, rising and kneeling, rising and kneeling, hearing without understanding the lugubrious music and verses of the *Stabat Mater*, and praying for all sorts and kinds of people and places and things. Participating in the long sorrow. Inhaling loss and shadows and darkness in a church denuded of ornament.

Unexpectedly, the later afternoon caused a dramatic change in my attention and my awareness. The Good Friday ceremonies which I had thought sufficient with the Stations, began in a dramatic and memorable fashion. It was in Bunnacurry, and the event was the 'unveiling of the cross'. The priest entered in procession from the back of the church; we all rose, standing in mute expectation, only a very few of us children daring to glance around. There was a pause, and then the priest intoned, singing it in his quavering low-pitched voice, *Ecce lignum Crucis in quo salus mundi pependit*, and the girls in the choir loft responded *Venite adoremus*. We prayed, on our knees again, in quietness. I was moved by the words, by the chant, and as I was training to be an acolyte, I had a vague knowledge of what the words meant: Look! this is the wood of the Cross on which the Saviour of the world was hung. My thoughts were scattered. I was moved. We rose again as the priest moved half-way up the aisle and I could see the great crucifix, held aloft, one of the arms unveiled. The priest sang again, slightly higher, and the choir responded, and we knelt once more. Finally the priest moved to the altar rails, held the crucifix high, both arms now visible, and unveiled the rest, singing once again, higher still, the same call, and there came the same response. It was all very real, very moving, and I exhaled with great emotion, not certain what had been stirred within me, what new awareness had been offered by the dramatic events unfolding in the little, too-familiar village church.

The Venerable Bede completed his great *Ecclesiastical History of Britain* in 731. He tells of vernacular religious songs in England in the early 8th century: he tells of a monk: 'So skilful was he in composing religious and devotional songs that, when any passage of scripture was explained to him by interpreters, he could quickly turn it into delightful and moving poetry in his own English tongue' (Bede: 4.24). He also gives words to a nobleman in Northumbria who tried to get the King, Edwin, to adopt Christianity: 'This is how the present life of man on earth, King, appears to me in comparison with that time which is unknown to us. You are sitting feasting with your ealdormen and thegns in winter time; the fire is burning on the hearth in the middle of the hall and all inside is warm, while outside the wintry storms of rain and snow are raging; and a sparrow flies swiftly through the hall. It enters in at one door and quickly flies out through the other. For the few moments it is inside, the storms and wintry tempest cannot touch it, but after the briefest moment of calm, it flits from your sight, out of the wintry storm and into it again. So this life of man appears but for a moment; what follows or indeed what went before, we know not at all.'

The poem *Beowulf*, a poem written sometime in the eighth century, shows a great deal of the heroic pagan world of that old aristocracy, and it is a pagan world scarcely influenced by Christianity. John Blain, in his chapter 'The Anglo-Saxon Period' (440-1066) writes: 'Until the late sixth century, informed guesswork must make do for history' (History 61). It is known that the invasion of the Germanic tribes, the Angles, Jutes and Saxons, began from about 430 onwards. They brought with them strong social bonds of kinship and its claims of loyalty. Loyalty to the lord or king, just as in Ireland, was vital, as feuds between local lords were common.

'The early Anglo-Saxons were a non-urban people: their important places were important for hierarchical rather than economic reasons' (History 68). The Angles and Saxons were so powerful that they drove out most of the Roman Britons who migrated westwards, many of them into Wales, where they encountered the Irish who had already ravaged that country, and then established their Celtic Christian monasteries.

In England, in the year 597, Pope Gregory the Great knew that King Aethelbert of Kent had a Christian Frankish wife and he sent a monk, Augustine, on a mission to Kent. Augustine was warmly received and he established a monastery at Canterbury. His influence, aided by the king's power, spread rapidly but rather superficially. The Northumbrian rulers Edwin (616-632) and Oswald (633-642) were both Christian and victorious in battle. But here, too, the Christian faith was not soundly based and after Oswald's death his successors quickly apostatised. Augustine, now installed as archbishop of Canterbury, did not get on well with the Welsh bishops and gradually a more strongly founded Christianity had to filter down from Iona, where the Irish monks had established a strong monastery. Oswald's bishop, Aidan, founded the great monastery of Lindisfarne and 'by 660 only the men of Sussex and the Isle of Wight remained pagan, and soon they too were converted' (History 79).

The Christian Church the Irish had developed into monasteries around which small towns developed, provided a model for English society to follow. As that society was even then riddled with feuding lords, loyalty continued to be a virtue of great importance. When one of the old kings died he was buried with great ceremony, and gold and jewelled ornaments were buried along with him, these latter denoting the power and influence of the king. The find at Sutton Hoo, a cemetery of the 6th and 7th century, discovered and excavated in Suffolk in 1939, exemplifies this, along with an elaborate ship burial. Both the sense of heroic loyalty and the ornamentation with gold and jewels of the lord's properties, in life and in death, are significant notions in the poem, *The Dream of the Rood*. 'It is becoming clear that by 750 England contained hundreds of small 'minsters' [monasteries] with genuine and important pastoral functions, serving what may be called the first English parochial system' (History 81). Along with such developments in Christianity in England came literacy.

It is known that Benedict Biscop brought a painting of the

crucifixion from Rome (so Bede tells us) in the year 678 to England. A high 'preaching' cross, The Ruthwell Cross, was discovered in Northumbria, its figurations and runes intended to teach the Christian faith; it dates back to the eighth century and is closely related to some of the contemporary Irish high crosses. The runic alphabet inscription contains excerpts from *The Dream of the Rood*. There are also figurations of Jesus healing the blind, of the Annunciation and of the story of Egypt. The cross was damaged but the poem remained in the Vercelli Book, housed in Vercelli, Italy. By now the whole teaching and dramatic presentation of the contents of the Christian faith were developing in mystery and morality plays, and the unveiling of the Cross on Good Friday may well have been a vital part of the ceremony from the earliest days of Christianity's coming to England.

The word 'rood' comes from the Anglo-Saxon *rod, rode,* 'cross', meaning usually the 'true Cross'. It has come to mean a large crucifix and was placed high on the screen that separated the nave and choir in medieval churches. It was large enough to be seen from everywhere in the church. There are still many churches in England that have such a crucifix, finely carved, gilded and ornamented in several ways. Rood-lights burned before the crucifix in medieval times, using oil in a rood-bowl or other container. It was, and of course remains, a strong and emotive figure at the heart of the Christian faith. During Lent it was kept covered with a rood-cloth, usually violet or black, and larger roods were hung by wrought-iron rood-chains from the chancel arch. Later, feast days devoted to the Rood were established, in Saxon England known as Rood Mass Day, later called the Feast of the Exaltation of the Cross, while the Catholic Church now calls it The Triumph of the Cross. During the Protestant Reformation, when the emphasis was laid more on the pulpit than the altar, most rood screens were removed, but the Catholic Church continued to use the imagery and paintings that had adorned such screens.

Christianity had not long taken root in England when *The Dream of the Rood* was written. Some of the poem retains touches of pagan culture. The dreamer, who appears to be a pagan before the Cross speaks to him, is aware of the crucifixion as a kind of battle, and Christ a warrior. There is then a victory, Christ choosing to die on the cross. It is the decision of the Christ that he will give himself to the battle; he is not forced, he takes it upon himself. The fact that it is the tree that speaks in the dream, is suggestive of an animistic awareness on the part of the author, and the tree, after its enlightenment of the author, itself becomes an object of worship. All of this, whether conscious or unconscious on the part of the poet, would bring the poem closer to the minds of the hearers, those only recently aware of the Christian path. And yet, of course, the poem treats the central focus of the Christian faith, the suffering, death and resurrection of Christ as a triumph over sin. This suffering of Christ, and his triumph, brings about the salvation of the human race.

Atonement was Christ's self-offering to renew the covenant, and this self-offering was the focus of much of St Paul's teaching. In 1 Corinthians he wrote: 'For I resolved to know naught among you save Jesus Christ, and him crucified.' And he goes on (1: 18-25):

> For the message about the cross is foolishness to those who are perishing, but to us who are being saved it is the power of God. For it is written: 'I will destroy the wisdom of the wise and the discernment of the discerning I will thwart.' Where is the one who is wise? Where is the scribe? Where is the debater of this age? Has not God made foolish the wisdom of the world? For since, in the wisdom of God, the world did not know God through wisdom, God decided, through the foolishness of our proclamation, to save those who believe. For Jews demand signs and Greeks desire wisdom, but we proclaim Christ crucified, a stumbling block to Jews and foolishness to Gentiles, but to those who are the called, both Jews and Greeks, Christ the power of God and the wisdom of God. For God's foolishness is wiser than human wisdom, and God's weakness is stronger than human strength.

The poet, then, even if newly turned to Christianity, was deeply versed in his faith. In the poem the Lord and the Cross become one. The tree, like a true retainer, subject to his lord, is willing to serve him faithfully, even to death. They are both pierced by the same nails, both of them are mocked together, and later on, the Cross, too, is resurrected. It is adorned with jewels and is honoured, just as the dead King was honoured in his ship-burial, just as the risen Christ is honoured.

The language was still uninfluenced by the music of Latin though it contained a vigour and immediacy that were rich in their own way. Peter Levi, in his introduction to *The Penguin Book of English Christian Verse* (1984) remarks that 'there have been no completely or thoroughly Christian centuries, and English has never quite become a Christian language. Probably only the dead Latin of the Middle Ages, a half-language, did that.' While wondering exactly what he meant by English never quite becoming a Christian language, with R. S. Thomas and Geoffrey Hill about, not to mention the earlier Herbert and Hopkins, there is little doubt that English at every stage of its development has borne religious poetry very well indeed. Perhaps that influence of Latin, when it passed through the mellifluous tones of religious monastic singing, and through the musical and poetic translations of the King James Bible, gave English a special power. Narrow dogmatic rectitude never sits well with the English language, but dramatic portrayal always does; attempts by poets like John Skelton, even some of the didactic efforts of George Herbert, read forced and leave the reader cold. The very simplicity and urgency of the Anglo-Saxon language helped lead more modern English into the religious sphere, with some success. The dramatic simplicity of *The Dream of the Rood*, its dream-form, its stirring of the dreamer to a change of heart, must have stirred the Anglo-Saxon hearer of the poem as the *Ecce lignum crucis* of the church's ongoing Good Friday liturgy still stirs. And perhaps it is that same rugged strength of language won by Shakespeare and the poets of the seventeenth century that makes religious poetry in the English language so necessary for our own doubting and uncomforted souls.

The Dream of the Rood, which I studied in university, merely construing it with the same lip-in-teeth, puckered effort with which I had worked out Caesar's *Gallic Wars* for my secondary school exams, was the first actual poem that touched me, coming as I did from an island where the images of Christian striving, and particularly the crucifix, dominated every aspect of life.

For some reason that short line that comes strategically, that
sums up musically, rhythmically and thematically all that went
before, all that is still to come, remained firmly in my memory
and surfaces still, unbidden, at strange moments: 'And Christ
was on the Rood.' Christians have been 'glorying in the cross of
Christ' for centuries. The author of this piece was no simpleton;
he knew the purpose and value of such items: 'that they make
their prayers to me as a symbol', that honour should be given to
the Cross only in so far as it leads believers beyond itself and on
to Christ. Christ as hero, a theme taken up quite often in the
poems and devotional writings of Gerard Manley Hopkins,
forms a central part of the work and the hero was, in Anglo-
Saxon times, the warrior who was prepared to give his life in the
service of his lord.

I find the poem central to the fears and needs, indeed the
whole seeking thrust, of our times. It is a poem that stands at the
threshold of the great tradition of poetry, and of religious poetry,
in the English language. Its taking of the wealth of the world's
stones to beautify the 'tree' adds a sense of the labour of the
earth itself to glorify the Christ who stands, in suffering and ultimately in victory, at the centre of our living. Such ornamenting
of the burial sites of the kings also suggested their influence in
the world, and their power over the things of the earth. And
those lines, towards the end, to one who has carried the symbol
of the Cross about with him, or placed it on the wall of a room,
or borne it on the end of a rosary:

> who have borne on your breast this dear, divine
> and best of symbols, have no fear, His blood
> has won you grace over the gravity of earth for ever;

will bring the mind back to the simple though asking faith of
one's youth, and suggest some consolation against our world of
pain.

One of the truly interesting things about the poem is how the
author makes the tree, the cross itself, speak; in this, it seems, all
of creation is represented and the effect is to reverse the 'sin'
that was the fruit of the first tree in Eden. The tree, the rood, becomes in this poem, a kind of priest of creation, standing as
poet, as prophet, between the real, suffering Christ, and the ob-

serving human populace. The 'tree' becomes a beacon, adored by angels, and all the other 'marvels of creation' mused upon it. It is the tree that bleeds for the dying hero of the world, the creature suffering for the pains of the Creator, obeying the Saviour's command to hold him up and not bend down, though the whole earth round about 'shivered' in empathy. This is one of the first, and one of the most powerful, expressions of St Paul's telling of how the whole earth is in labour towards the coming of God's kingdom. The pain of the nails thrust into the tree 'still stings, the open wounds of malice'; creation suffers still, after so many centuries, and appears, in the poem, closer to the Christ than is humankind:

> the heavens all in spate

> above the body of our Ruler, that bright radiance;
> shadows reigned supreme under a thickening cloud;
> all of creation mourned, moaned this cruel chance:

> and Christ was on the rood.

It is time, the 'tree' speaks, that the world 'show honour to me through the whole earth and this broad and marvellous creation', such honour to be shown to the tree, and to all of creation, as symbol of God's love. This symbolism takes the tree of the Cross to reverse the terrible curse that fell on humankind by our first finding ourselves incapable of overcoming our inherent mortality, the 'fall' of our first parents. The poem ends by returning to the author's response, his longing for the day when he, too, will meet the redeeming Hero in heaven. He has been taught by 'the tree' in its absolute closeness to the God who became incarnate in creation through the Son, the Word. It is a hymn to Christ, a hymn to the redemption of all creation. And reads as a wholly contemporary poem, relevant to our times, urgent and moving. It is one of the great, one of the first, 'works of love' of Anglo-Saxon writing.

The Dream of the Rood
(a version of the 7th/6th century Anglo-Saxon poem attributed to
Cynewulf)

Pause with me while I tell the most precious, the best
of dreams, sent to me in the deep silence of night
when men, word mongers, were everywhere at rest.

It seemed that I saw the most marvellous tree
lifted high on the air, and all haloed in light,
most beautiful of all beams of wood; a beacon

bathed in gold; there were breathtaking gems that stood
all around the base, a further five were ablaze
high along the cross-beam. Holy angels of the Lord

looked always on its loveliness, enthralled.
This was no criminal's cross; there came to gaze
the saintliest of spirits, men everywhere and all

marvels of creation mused upon it where it stood.
How strange that tree of victory! and I – steeped in sin,
badly blemished all over – watched that glorious wood

adorned with banners, shining in all its beauty,
garlanded in gold, glorious gems worked in –
the wonderfully wreathed tree of the World's Ruler.

Yet straight through all that gold I could still see
the friend of once-wretched men, how it first began
to bleed on the right-hand side. Sorrow bore in on me,

and fear, before that vision; I saw the beacon change,
become clothed in colours; how at times the blood ran
drenching it in blood-dew, how it bloomed with a strange

beauty. I lay a long while, wretched at heart,
watching my Saviour's tree; until suddenly, most
wonderfully, the wood spoke, uttering these words:

'Long ago – distinctly I remember it! – one day
I was hewn down at the dark edge of the forest
and severed from my stem. Strong enemies seized me,

wrought me into a spectacle for the world to see,
commanding me to hoist their criminals on high;
men carried me on their shoulders and erected me

high on a hill – fixed there by many foes. I saw
the Ruler of mankind rush with real courage to climb
on me and I did not dare (my Lord had warned!)

bend down or break, though I saw the broad
surface of earth shiver. How simple – the Lord knows –
to smite His enemies! but firm and stout I stood,

unmoving. The hero stripped, though He was God Almighty!
robust and resolute, mounting onto the gallows
spirited, in the sight of many, to redeem mankind.

I wavered while the warrior embraced me: clasped me
and I did not dare bend down towards the ground,
fall on the earth's surface, I must stand fast.

I was raised up a Rood, carrying the powerful King,
high Lord of Heaven, and did not dare to bend.
They pierced me with bloody nails, the pain still stings!

the open wounds of malice; they made us fools
together. I was wholly wet with blood
streaming from His side when He gave up His soul

and helpless on that hill I knew a fearful fate:
stretched out in agony the Almighty God
of hosts cruelly wracked; the heavens all in spate

above the body of our Ruler, that bright radiance;
shadows reigned supreme under a thickening cloud;
all of creation mourned, moaned this cruel chance:

and Christ was on the rood.

'Now from afar came virtuous men, hastening
to that solitary Man. I saw it all, my many cares
grievously afflicting me, but I yielded to their chastening

humble and ardent hands. They held the God of Hosts,
took Him down from that dreadful torture; warriors
left me wet with moisture, wounded all over by arrows,

laid Him down, His limbs weary, stood watching at His head;
they looked on the Lord of heaven, resting for a time
weary from a woeful contest. A tomb was already made

in sight of those who slew Him, carved out of stone,
and they laid therein our Saviour, glorious, sublime.
They began to make their songs of sorrow, they mourned

until the fall of evening, then wearily wandered home
from that royal Throne, leaving Him there to rest.
We, however, a long while weeping, stood alone

on our foundations, fearing a dreadful destiny,
while that beautiful body chilled, that treasure chest
of life. Hastening then they hacked us cruelly

to the earth; planted us in a deep pit. Dark. Cold.
But the Lord's retainers, His friends, freed us, and then
set me on high, enhanced with silver and gold.

'Now, dear friend, now it is time that the world know
how I endured the wickedness of evil men
and grievous woes; it is time that the world show

honour to me through the whole earth and this broad
and marvellous creation; that they make their prayers
to me as a symbol. For on me did the Son of God

suffer agonies a while; so I won glory and was raised
high under the heavens, that I may heal the cares
of those who honour me and who offer praise.

Once, I became the most terrible of tortures, of pains
most odious to men, before I opened up for them,
for these word-mongers, life's true way.

See then how the prince of Heaven honoured me beyond
all the trees of the wood, true Keeper of the Kingdom,
as He honoured His mother Mary beyond all womankind.

'Now I require you, dear friend, that you relate
what you have seen to others, reveal in words this vision:
the tree of glory on which God himself had to tolerate

suffering for the ways of men and Adam's ancient sin,
that He tasted death; that He rose truly in great
honour to give help to men, mounted high to Heaven

and will come down on judgement day, angels at His side
to judge, each man and woman in whatsoever way
they have measured out this transitory life. Nor let mankind

be unafraid of what the Ruler of the World will say!
Before the multitudes He will test, and try, to find
where is he who, for the Lord's sake, would taste

death's rancid savour as He did on the Rood!
They shall fear, for there are few who will discover
what to say to Christ that dreadfilled day. But you

who have borne on your breast this dear, divine
and best of symbols, have no fear, His blood
has won you grace over the gravity of earth for ever;

hope then always to dwell with Him in the highest Heaven'.

Oh I prayed then with courage to that happy Cross,
I was alone, no person by, knew powerful longing. My food
now is to love that tree of victory, all else is loss

and forfeiture, to honour it more often than any man yet has.
My will is directed wonderfully towards the rood,
I have no powerful friends in the world, they have passed

from the dreams of earth to the King's glory and dwell
in Heaven now with the High Father. I long
for the day when the royal Rood of the Lord shall

fetch me finally from this transitory life and bring
me where is rapture and revelry in heaven, where all
the people of the Lord shall stand and sing

at the banquet where is bliss perpetual; and I pray
that our God who suffered on the gallows tree
be my friend, who has freed us to the light of day,

the Son and victor, stalwart, successful. He
who came with a glorious consort of spirits to stay
forever within God's kingdom; that I shall see

the Almighty Ruler, risen to where the angels stand,
with the holy company of saints at God's right hand,
the Hero, home with honour to His native land.

Canticle of the Creatures

The monastery of the Third Order of St Francis was situated just a little over half a mile from our house. In my mind, St Francis always stood in quietness, birds roosting on his raised arms, gentle does couched at his feet, and the Devil, bull-shod and horned, glaring from a ring of fire behind him. Sadly, it was this latter figure, this 'foul fiend', that dominated my imagination. In those days we got our milk from the monastery farm and every evening I was sent down with the scoured and shining can to collect the milk. Four pints, I expect, is what I collected.

In brighter times of the year I enjoyed the walk, or run, but in the darker nights I was terrified. There were deep drains either side of the road; beyond the drains there were thorn bushes where anything might lurk; perhaps that steaming figure of the very Devil. Beyond the bushes were open fields sloping away towards the sea. In a child's imagination the world of darkness is densely populated with all sorts of creatures out to harm him. The laneway that left the road and led down to the monastery was a darker tunnel about three hundred yards long, a tunnel made of scraggy old rhododendron bushes that met scraggily overhead. Here the undergrowth was full of noises, short rushes of things, small scuffling sounds, terror, in other words, to a young boy's imagination. I ran, fast as possible, waiting always for that tentacle or slime-wet hand to reach for me, or for that huge shape to loom up before me. When, at last, I knocked on the scullery door I knew a short-lived relief and put on a face of complete bravery before the big monk who opened the door to me. A yellow light flowed out onto the ground from the monastery chapel windows. I could glimpse, through the scullery door and beyond the windows, figures, unshaped and cowled, in an intimate dance with their dark Christ.

I stepped into the scullery; there was a sour silence, smelling of man, of curds, and of wet stone floors. Brother Leo took my can and filled it with milk from the great churn that stood just beside a scrubbed wooden table. Little was said: 'How's the family?' 'Fine'. 'Good, that's good!' That was about it. He had no idea that I was shivering, terrified that I would have to go back up that road in darkness, more slowly this time, as I had to bring my can of milk safely home. 'There now. Mind how you go.' This, followed by a gentle pat on the head, and I was turning back into the tunnels of terror, the impossible road home. The yellow light spilling from the scullery sent shadows shifting through the orchard trees but I was safe still, Brother Leo standing in the doorway, watching me set out. For me the orchard trees with their bitter, arthritic limbs, their boned fingers, their armpits, all of these were the writhing, lost creatures of the drowned ark.

But I always made it home. Up on the road again, the moonlight sometimes, and always the thumping of my own feet on the road, aroused and kept aroused all the irrational rational dread that thudded in my soul and held me petrified, expecting at any moment to be swept away into unmentionable horrors. But very soon a different light in the near distance grew warm for me, that light from home became a music that tuned its strings for me, drowning out the sounds of terror I muttered in my own brain, and I grew certain once more of familial warmth. I longed to run, but had to hold myself back, just a little while longer, a few steps more, and I knew I would enter the warmth and safety of my own kitchen, the familiar and fondling light of the oil lamp and the kindly eyes of Jesus watching out at me from the perpetual red lamp high on the kitchen wall.

Why did I never tell of my dread? Why did I not speak it out at home and see if there was a way to remove such suffering from my young life? I think it must have been that I knew my parents would pooh-pooh such fears, that they would tell me to grow up, there were no such things as ghosts, such words: and yet at other times great and quiet glee would be taken from the recounting of ghost and devil stories in that same kitchen. I think, too, that deep down inside me I also knew that all of my fears were mind-created, that they were no more than projections from my own dreaming, and that one day soon I would grow out of them, I would grow up, I would become an adult, I would send my own children out for milk and tell them not to be so foolish as to fear the darkness, and that the cowled figures

of the monastery were God's good servants, kindly men like St
Francis of Assisi, spreading nothing but blessing all about them.

The Monastery

With its sheds and orchards
an island upon an island;
I was white dough then in many hands.

We drove in the warmth of half sleep to Mass,
the slow, sedate black Anglia
parked on gravel where yellow light

reached from the chapel door;
in overhanging branches
rooks began to grumble.

*

Plaster saints
with plaster lilies in their hands
looked down on polished floors;

Angelo's head was straw;
his sandals slubbered on the parquet floor;
it was he who brought the candleflame

up from the cells to the honey, altar, light;
the flame grew large and welcoming
through the cobalt-blue glass of the door.

The brown coiffed figures on their predieus
were ranks of worker angels;
Angelo's head was straw; I heard him snore

and his head would loll
as if Botticelli's messenger forgot
for a moment his awful declaration.

*

Brother Leo's one glass eye
could penetrate all wickedness
behind the lavatory walls;

his good eye watched you
watching the fixed stare of the other.
There were brass sliding trapdoors

over inkwells on the desks; 'Dip', he would say,
'your filthy fingernails down deep
and write the purity of God into your skulls'.

Those who forgot their Bible History
were made to chew on sour apples;
'the taste of sin', he would say, 'is bitterness'.

*

Away on the road the tankers
ferried shark oil, shark blubber
and the air thickened with the stench;

but sometimes, on our island,
the hillside furze were molten gold
and rhododendron woods at Achill Sound

played hautboy processional music;
the pockets of the monks were deep,
but there was God! among mints

and liquorice and stumps of chalk.

St Francis appears to have envisaged the Third Order as a
middle ground between cloister and world, for those who did
not dare the full rigours of his way of life, or who did not feel
able to take on the responsibilities and dignity of the priesthood.
Indeed, there are those who believe that the humble saint may
have felt more inclined to avoid the dignity of priesthood himself and that this Order is how he would have seen his own
followers, suffering the rigours but without the honour of
priesthood. It may also be the case that progression from the full
and original establishment of the Franciscan Order developed
naturally over time. In Bunnacurry, the Third Order was that
known as The Third Order Regular, as opposed to Secular, as
the latter was to include devout people of both sexes living in
the world. The 'Regular' Order may have come into existence
about 1395, at Foligno, established by one Angelina of Marsciano.

They were accepted as a mendicant order by the Holy See. Its members take the solemn vows.

From the beginning of the nineteenth century, however, many forms of this third order regular were founded, particularly as a basis for establishing such communities in locations where they would provide education and example. Each foundation thus established could have its own particular constitution and could be either autonomous or offer themselves to the jurisdiction of the local bishop. The community in Bunnacurry preserved the original brown habit, the cowl, and the traditional cord of the Franciscan order. In 1852 the Archbishop of Tuam, Dr John McHale, sent monks of the order to Achill to establish a monastery there in order to counteract the work of Protestant colonists from England under the direction of Edward Nangle, who established schools, soup kitchens and a church during the famine years, to inveigle the local people away from the Roman Catholic Church. A 'colony' flourished in Dugort, on the island, and the remnants of it, with the church, still active, can be seen today. The 'work' of the Franciscan Monastery in Bunnacurry was deemed to be finished about 1971 and the area is now a ruin.

I knew little, then, of the saint of poverty and love, of kindliness towards every creature, of his overwhelming and overmastering love of God, and his love for all creatures as they made their own obeisances before God. And in those days I did not know that he, too, had turned his hand, just a bare few times, towards poetry to find out, by naming them, the deepest marches of his own soul, and the rich and savoury delights he took in creation.

From the 7th century onwards the Benedictine rule was established in monasteries throughout western Europe, urging manual work and proper care for the earth, thus ennobling labour for the first time. 'It was very much an extension of the garden tradition of the Bible itself' (Care 130). Good husbandry and responsible stewardship became part of the monk's labouring towards God, a care and love that made a sacrament of working the land.

By the early 12th century, advances were being made throughout Europe, in social organisation, education and technology. People were looking to new ideas, new leaders. Men

like St Bernard of Clairvaux, Henry II of England, Peter Abelard
of Paris, helped bring about a renaissance. The church was still
ordering society though the faith was undergoing its own transformation. A more personal religious experience was sought, as
well as justice in everyday practice instead of resorting to violence and war. Knowledge in theology and jurisprudence increased and texts from other civilisations were sought out, read
and translated. The great universities of Oxford, Paris and
Bologna were born late in the century. Along with all of this
greater independence in everyday living, came a surge towards
personal wealth and status. The church was anxious that so
much in philosophers like Aristotle and in Muslim scholarship
would contradict Christian dogma.

Francis Bernadone was born in 1182 in Assisi. 'God told me I
am to be a new kind of fool in this world' (Bodo 4). His father
was one of the new wealthy merchants in Italy and Francis grew
up as all noble men's sons grow up, in luxury and gaiety. One
day, on giving away to a beggar all he had on him, Francis
found himself mocked and rebuked by his father and his companions. Shortly afterwards he himself became seriously ill and
his father thought he would die. Francis prayed and, on his re-
covery, decided to dedicate his days to the service of humanity.
The details of his life subsequently are a mixture of history and
legend; but it is certain that he began to live a life of abject
poverty and service to the poor. For him, it was a question of rejecting wealth and status and choosing poverty, though it was
poverty-with-a-purpose and the purpose was love. 'I know Christ,
the poor crucified one' (Bodo 6). He wandered Italy, preaching the
love of God. He gathered followers and soon the gospel of kindness and love that they preached had made him famous. He
founded the Order of Mendicant Friars, the Franciscans. He is
supposed to have received the stigmata, the impression on
hands, feet and in the side of the wounds of Christ crucified.
Many of his followers testified to witnessing these wounds, in
his lifetime and after his death. The feast of the Stigmata of St
Francis is kept on 17 September. Because of his love of creatures
and all of creation, he has been heralded as patron saint of animals and of the environment, as well as of Italy. He died in 1226.
He was only forty-four.

Francis, as opposed to the Benedictines, was nomadic. 'For Francis, every creature in the world was a mirror of God's presence and, if approached correctly, a step leading one to God' (Carc 131). It was an approach of fellowship, a distant echo of Amergin, of Taliesin, of Patrick. Francis developed 'the Christian call to love God and the neighbour, to include all creation in a way that heals the split between God, the human and nature so characteristic of much of Christian literature before and since' (Care 133). 'Francis has much to teach us by way of an ecological ethic since our consumer society is obsessed with accumulating wealth to the detriment of the poor and of the earth itself' (Care 133).

The glory of his 'five wounds', his stigmata, is important to Hopkins's poem, *The Wreck of the Deutschland* where the cipher 5 gives him a method of speaking of the death of Franciscan nuns in that shipwreck; Hopkins dedicates *The Wreck of the Deutschland* thus:

To the
happy memory of five Franciscan nuns
exiles by the Falk Laws
drowned between midnight and morning of
Dec 7th 1875

and stanza 23 directly addresses their saint:

Joy fall to thee, father Francis,
    Drawn to the Life that died;
     With the gnarls of the nails in thee, niche of the lance, his
      Lovescape crucifed
  And seal of his seraph-arrival! and these thy daughters
  And five-livèd and leavèd favour and pride,
    Are sisterly sealed in wild waters,
To bathe in his fall-gold mercies, to breathe in his all-fire glances.

A great many stories and legends give rise to the notion of Francis as patron saint of animals and the environment. The *Fioretti* ('Little Flowers') is a collection of such legends. One of these tells that while Francis was travelling with his companions they came to a place where birds filled the trees around them. Francis began to preach to 'my sisters the birds'. The birds came around him, as if they listened. He said: 'My sister birds, you owe much to God, and you must always and in everyplace give praise to Him; for He has given you freedom to wing through the sky and He has clothed you ... you neither sow nor reap, and God feeds you and gives you rivers and fountains for your thirst, and mountains and valleys for shelter, and tall trees for your nests. And although you neither know how to spin or weave, God dresses you and your children, for the Creator loves you greatly and He blesses you abundantly. Therefore ... always seek to praise God.'

A further legend tells that in the city of Gubbio there was a wolf that terrified the district and devoured humans as well as animals. Francis went out to find the wolf which lay down at his feet. He spoke to the animal: 'Brother Wolf, you have caused great harm about here, but I would make peace between you and the people.' He led the wolf into town and because the creature had 'done evil because of hunger', the townspeople agreed to feed the wolf on a regular basis. Francis made peace, too, between the wolf and the dogs and gave both townspeople and the animals his blessing.

Francis wrote his *Canticle of the Sun* around 1224, a poem written in the Umbrian dialect, which tells of his love of creation, every created thing being seen as brother or sister to humanity. The poem expresses his belief that all of creation is good and beautiful but, with humanity, suffers the need for redemption. It is the duty of all creation, as Augustine expressed it, to praise God at all times and Francis, always a lover of the Psalms, writes his poem as an echo of the psalms of praise.

Francis was never ordained, nor did he ever hold an official position. He simply moved around with like-minded companions, through a world similar to our own, filled with people of great wealth and many more in abject poverty. But ever since then the word 'Franciscan' has come to mean a love of God through the most simple and dedicated living. His love of the whole of creation sprang naturally to him and forms a hugely important part of his legacy. Statues and paintings of him are common in every age since his death, most of them associating him with that love. In a world that was turning more and more to the search for personal wealth and honour, Francis turned minds back towards helping others and towards the love of God. The 'Order of Penance' which he conceived was not originally thought of as a separate order, but a way of life. It was a call for people to live by the Bible. The 'Rule' of the Third Order was worked out between 1221 and 1228. One of the early Franciscan Tertiaries summed it up in the phrase, 'The whole world is full of God'.

Canticle of the Creatures

Most high, omnipotent, good Lord!
To you alone all praise, all honour, glory and every blessing.

Only to you, Most High, do they belong, no man
May be found worthy to speak your name.

Praise be to you, my Lord, from all your creatures,
particularly from Master Brother Sun,
he of daylight, through whom you give us light.
How beautiful he is, and radiant in the greatest splendour:
carrying about with him, your likeness, O Most High.

Praise to you, my Lord, through Sister Moon and all the stars:
it is you have made them bright, blessed and beautiful across
        the heavens.

Praise to you, my Lord, through Brother Wind
through air and cloud and storm and every weather,
through whom you deal out sustenance to your creatures.

Praise to you, my Lord, through Sister Water,
so very useful, so humble, so precious and so pure.

Praise to you, my Lord, through Brother Fire,
through whom you brighten up the night:
he is so beautiful, so jocund, so powerful and so strong.

Praise to you, my Lord, through our Sister Mother Earth,
who sustains us and rules over us,
who produces various fruits with coloured flowers and herbs.

Praise to you, my Lord, through those forgiving out of love
        for you
who put up with weaknesses and tribulations.

Blessed are they who endure in peace,
they will receive a crown from you, Most High.
Praise to you, My Lord, through our Sister Bodily Death,
from whom there is no living being will escape
but woe to those who die in mortal sin;
blessed are those whom Death will find in your most holy
    will,
to whom the second death will do no hurt.

Praise then and bless my Lord and give him thanks,
and serve him ever with great humility.

There are echoes throughout the poem of Francis's awareness of the psalms: take, for instance, the beginning of Psalm 19:
'The heavens declare the glory of God; the skies proclaim the
work of his hands.' In the gospel of Matthew, chapter six, a passage outlines God's providential care for all creatures: 'Therefore
I tell you, do not worry about your life, what you will eat or
drink; or about your body, what you will wear. Is not life more
than food, and the body more than clothing? Look at the birds of
the air; they neither sow nor reap nor gather into barns, and yet
your heavenly Father feeds them. Are you not of more value
than they? And can any of you by worrying add a single hour to
the span of life? And why do you worry about clothing?
Consider the lilies of the field how they grow. They neither toil
nor spin, yet I tell you even Solomon in all his glory was not
clothed like one of these. But if God so clothes the grass of the
field, which is alive today and tomorrow is thrown into the
oven, will he not much more clothe you, you of little faith?' This
could be a summary of the whole view of Christian living that
Francis taught and followed.

Towards the end of his life Francis is known to have suffered
greatly with eye problems and indeed underwent, of course
without any anaesthetic or palliative preparations, dreadful operations on his eyes. He finally went blind. As well as his almost
inimitable love of poverty it has always appeared that this saint
lived a life that was in itself a poem; the words he used were always tuned to God's spirit, the world for him was a canticle to
the Lord, the great forces of life and death were to him merely
the friends that were part of the unity of all of God's blessed cre-

ation. There are incidents in his life that, as he predicted, almost make him look a fool, that remind later readers of Don Quixote and his riding forth to help those in distress on a broken horse with a broken lance and a 'broken' mind, as if love for all of humanity could be, in any sense, a foolishness.

In 1982, thinking of this saint, after whom I was named, I wrote a poem:

Francis of Assisi 1182: 1982

Summer has settled in again; ships,
softened to clouds, hang on the horizon;
buttercups, like bubbles, float
on fields of a silver-grey haze; and words
recur, such as light, the sea, and God

the frenzy of crowds jostling towards the sun
contains silence, as eyes contain
blindness; we say, may the Lord
turning his face towards you
give you peace
morning and afternoon the cars moved out
onto the beach and clustered, shimmering,
as silver herring do in a raised net; this
is a raucous canticle to the sun

altissimu, omnipotente, bon Signore

to set up flesh
in images of snow and of white
roses, to preach to the sea
on silence, to man
on love, is to strain towards death
as towards a body without flaw

our poems, too, are gestures of a faith
that words of an undying love
may not be without some substance

words hovered like larks above his head, dropped
like blood from his ruptured hands

tue so'le laude, et onne benedictione

we play, like children, awed and hesitant
at the ocean's edge;
between dusk and dark the sea
as if it were God's long and reaching fingers
appropriates each footprint from the sand

I write down words, such as light, the sea, and God
and a bell rides out across the fields
like a man on a horse with helmet and lance
gesturing foolishly towards night

laudato si, Signore, per sora nostra
morte corporale

at night, the cars project
ballets of brightness and shadow on the trees
and pass, pursuing
darkness at the end of their tunnels of light

the restful voices have been swept by time
beyond that storybook night sky
where silence
drowns them out totally

Why I was given the name of Francis I do not know, nor did I ever think to ask, when I could have received an answer. However, when one bears a name there appears to be a certain compulsion to get to know the life and outlook of the saint involved; poverty on such a scale, and service to others on such a level I could never dream of aspiring to. Having 'enjoyed' my primary education with Franciscans of the Third Order, that saint did, however, seep some influence into my bones. My love for the things of creation has never ceased and to know that Francis is patron saint of animals and the environment has meant a great deal to me. Today the little school I went to is nothing more than a shell; the monastery itself is also falling into ruins. Its work, it appears, is done, but I am not convinced that that is the end of this particular story.

Great Silence

Years ago the monastery died. Now
the roof has fallen through, dangerous beams
are slimed with bird-shit and underneath

are dried cowpats, sheep-droppings, stale
odours, dark-green fungi on the crumbling walls;
there is no way up to the tongueless bell

that waits for the moment of one final clang when it falls.
I stand a long while, shouldered by sorrow,
fretting for the words and firm hands

that built the foundations of a faith; the wind
of the passing of Jesus leaves the air still stirring,
while softest breathings of the Holy Ghost

rattle the steps of the staircase that reaches yet
towards the sky; here astounding news were spoken
and foreign wines as warm as blood consumed.

Crabs now, bitter, hard, litter the orchard grass
where brown-cassocked monks laughed and caught
windfalls in canvas aprons, who were rooting out

ground elder and sexual temptations. Once from the dairy
the chime of an empty churn startled; Angelus
rang out, lifting jackdaws from the sycamores,

and sweetest smoke from just-quenched candles
tickled the nostrils of Almighty God. Now I hear
the purring of pigeons like contented prayers

though in the railed-in graveyard everything
is in order, attending till the Spirit comes again,
the individual cell-doors locked into great silence.

Achill Island is situated some thirty miles from Westport
and, further out along the coast road you come to Croagh
Patrick, the great pilgrim mountain where St Patrick is supposed to have driven the snakes from Ireland. From the western
shores of Achill you could see the pyramid-shaped mountain,
with the chapel on top that appeared like a stipple from where

we stood, on Keem beach, or from Dooega. The mountain dominated the seascape, and with it came the great myth of pilgrimage, of penance and almost every Sunday I saw people leave the island on the trek to Croagh Patrick. Many of them cycled there, the almost forty miles from home to mountain's base, from where many, taking their shoes off, made the difficult and sometimes dangerous climb to the top. There they would attend Mass or repeat their rosaries, going round and round the chapel. Then they worked their way back down, bare feet suffering, they climbed back on their bicycles and made their way homewards.

Penance

They leave their shoes, like signatures, below;
above, their God is waiting. Slowly they rise
along the mountainside where rains and winds go
hissing, slithering across. They are hauling up

the bits and pieces of their lives, infractions
of the petty laws, the little trespasses and
sad transgressions. But this bulked mountain
is not disturbed by their passing, by this mere

trafficking of shale, shifting of its smaller stones.
When they come down, feet blistered and sins
fretted away, their guilt remains and that black
mountain stands against darkness above them.

The simplicity of this faith and the intensity with which it was lived entered my spirit, too, my being gathering an awareness that would seep through my very bones and leave me weltering in the simplicity and immediacy of that faith. This was the faith that was intensified with every class in that small school in Bunnacurry, especially during the half-hour devoted daily to catechism and Bible history. The staging posts of first confession, first communion and confirmation also took on an importance greater than anything else in our young lives, as did the honour and challenge of being an altar boy, an acolyte, answering the Latin phrases with perfect pronunciation and aplomb.

Time and tide, however, do not slow down, nor halt, and the freedom, the joy and the innocence of a young boy brought up in the weathers of old Catholic Ireland, must face the slow and gradual withdrawing of the tide and the harsh storms and chill winters that the ongoing seasons bring with them. I was sent from Achill Island to suffer my secondary education in Mungret College, to spend many long and tedious terms in a boarding school, far away from home, in a climate where I would lose myself into the labyrinths of dismay, confusion, loss and loneliness. There, too, however, I would immerse my mind in new things, some of which would eventually open my spirit to the wonders of the world that was not always regulated and beatified by the consoling, though demanding, tenets of that old-time religion.

Flotsam

Mungret College SJ, Limerick, under the grey-black and sometimes stench-filled smoke from Mungret's cement factory, was a
huge building that to me, as we drove up the long avenue under
trees, seemed threatening and prison-like. It stood far back from
the road, beyond a long row of sycamores. On either side of the
road were fields, great meadows and trampled pasturelands.
When my parents turned the car, waved goodbye and headed
away back down the long driveway, my heart was a rock plung-
ing down into a bottomless well. Behind the building there were
playing fields, the high white poles of goalposts, the hanging
nets of tennis courts. I was overwhelmed by the corridors, the
staircases, the dormitories, the classrooms; I was jostled and
buffeted by so many boys older and larger than I was, boys that
seemed to move in this place with gusto and ease. I was small, I
knew suddenly, very small and lost. I was flotsam amongst a
great high tidal wave that had abandoned so many others, just
like me, high on the churned sand. Many other boys, newly arrived in this place, moved about, lost souls, nervous and shaken
as was I. We were all given supper in a huge refectory, the ordinary boarders to one side, the scholastics separated from us by a
low, wooden partition. I heard the older boys talk and shout to
each other, a certain joy and familiarity in their voices. Many of
the scholastics, already dressed in more sober, dark suits, were
restrained and tense. I was relieved when night prayers were
said in the enormous chapel, prayers that ended with the
singing of the *Salve Regina* to the great thundering music of the
organ, and at last I was shown through a long dormitory with
separate cells divided by wooden partitions, into a smaller room
where there were a dozen beds, without partitions, separated
from one another by curtains.

'This is the new boys' dorm,' an older boy explained to us.
'After a few months some of you will be moved into the bigger
dorm, with partitions and your own space, because some of the
older men will be moving on to the seminary at Grange. But for

the moment, find a bed for yourselves, put your stuff into the locker, your suitcase under the bed. Go to sleep, lights out in ten minutes, and the bell will waken you tomorrow at ten to seven.' He was grinning; he had been here a few years already; he was happy not to be in this dormitory any more, without privacy, among boys who were utter strangers to one another.

I took out my small tin of toothpaste, my new toothbrush. I unfolded a new pair of pyjamas and shoved the suitcase in under the bed. On a locker beside the bed was an enamel basin and an enamel jug sitting in it; I left my toothbrush and tooth-paste on the locker and knew that my life, that had been so blessed with the space and freedom of Achill Island, was now to be confined to this small area, curtained off, Spartan, and cold. What had I done to deserve such punishment? I climbed into bed and lay awake for a long, long time. I prayed my old night prayers, over and over; I prayed to my guardians, *Oh Angel of God* ...

The windows of that dormitory-off-a-dormitory were high and large and without curtains. Uncertain September light kept the room bathed in a faint glow, from moon, or stars, I did not know. I heard shuffling and stirring from the others around me, restless, too, in their small spaces; I thought I heard sighs, and someone sobbing. Gradually the night darkened, gradually I began to doze. I slept, but the sleep was restless and I dreamt I was climbing through tunnels of trees and into sea-caves where everything was dark, where threatening figures loomed out of the branches and reached down from the dripping roofs. I tried to cry out, for help, but my throat would not sound. And then something enormous, black and white, like a bear, came crash-ing loudly through the fuchsia and rhododendron tunnels and a great black paw, the claws sharp and extended, began to reach for me. I came wide awake, terrified. I was sweating.

I found myself sitting on a hard, wooden floor, somewhere. I was in my pyjamas but had a thin eiderdown from the dormitory bed wrapped about my body. I was leaning back against a wall and a pale light glimmered in on me from a high, uncurtained window. I found, too, that I was crying, softly, to myself. For a while I believed I was still in some strange dream; I had no idea where I was, nor even who I was. Only gradually did awareness return. I was frightened and astonished to find myself in the large dormitory, with the separate cubicles, all of them with their curtains drawn across the entrances. I was at the other end of the college from my own small dormitory and had no idea, except that I must have walked in my sleep, how I had come there. For a moment, after I stood up, I felt like shouting for help. But I stopped myself, in time. I gathered the eiderdown around my shivering body and tried to gauge the direction back to my dormitory and bed. Judging by the light of the quarter moon that was low on the sky, I began to move, very slowly, holding my body against the wall. When the darkness fell completely as a cloud came across the moon, I groped along with one hand in front of me, my body gliding against the wall. Eventually I reached a wall that came out at right angles; I turned along with the new wall and continued to move. I came to an opening. I paused. I had no idea if I was right or not. I waited. Soon the moon came out again, shedding the smallest light but sufficient to show me I was back at the archway into the small dormitory. With enormous relief I moved, quickly now, back into my own bed and lay down.

I was very cold, and very frightened. I felt, right then, that I might not be able to last long in this place. It was a world too different to the world I knew. For Achill Island was a place of freedom and space and light, there were wonderful and challengingly beautiful spaces, like that beach at Keel that goes in a graceful curve from low rocks, through miles of perfect sand, extending down to the base of the great Cathedral Cliffs, cliffs that waltz and scurry far out into the sea, their crags and columns lively with fulmar and gull and auk, the sky broad and healthful above, and the ocean stretching away towards a boundless horizon. That, with the high and lovely waves, the gleam of tide-water along the sand, the green, wet foreshore, the mountains ... While here, in this confined and grey-hung place, everything was alien, cramped, overbearing, chill. I had never felt so alone in my life. Around me I could hear some of the others shifting in their sleep. One of the boys was whimpering, softly, like a kitten lost under floorboards. It was, strangely, a comfort to me; at least I was not the only one disturbed by the night, the difference, the unknown. I sat up for a moment and reached to the small locker beside my bed; I had left my precious fob

watch, given to me in a moment of pride and generosity by my
grandfather, in such a way that I might be able to read the time
from my bed, but it was too dark. I took the watch and tried to
read it under the faintest of light still coming through the window but it was no good. I listened for a short while to its gentle
ticking, then left it back on the locker. Soon, I slept again, a deep,
blank sleep, until the sudden shrill scream of the electric bell
tipped me out of the bed into a dark morning. My new life had
begun.

After some weeks I had settled in a little and was beginning
to relish the new subjects: Latin, French, History and English. I
found some of the Jesuit priests to be stiff and angry in themselves and ready to pounce and punish at every opportunity.
Others were gentle and seemed to be at peace with their spirits
and their bodies. Latin I already had a touch of, after my days as
acolyte; father had taught me a little French, some words, some
phrases, and an effort at pronunciation. It was history and
English that I relished most, perhaps because the material was
of interest, partly because the teachers I had for these subjects
appeared interested and excited by them. During my five years
in that Jesuit college, however, I never heard the name Gerard
Manley Hopkins mentioned. There were other names, of course,
the saints, Francis Xavier, Ignatius, Edmund Campion, martyrs,
and one poet, Robert Southwell. Both the teacher of English and
the teacher of history spoke of Southwell and stressed the power
of his faith and the horrors of his martyrdom.

During a three-day retreat in Advent of that year, we were
told of the *Spiritual Exercises* of Saint Ignatius. The afternoon of
the second day was one that would touch me profoundly and
remain with me for ever. It was in the College chapel. Fr
Windermere SJ, a small, dapper priest who had come in from a
Jesuit house in Dublin, gave us a long talk on Ignatius and how
he had shown people how to meditate and pray. This afternoon
we were going to follow Ignatius and make our way through a
meditation on the afterlife of those who die in grave sin. There
was a preparatory prayer; Fr Windermere's voice was high-
pitched, he spoke slowly; there was, at times, a strange glint that
sparked from his spectacles as he happened to turn a little more
towards the grey light coming from a high window of the chapel.

We prayed that we would never die in mortal sin, that we might learn how to avoid hell and damnation. Now, he told us, as we knelt in awed silence, waiting; now we are going to imagine what it would be like to be lost in the caverns of hell. Picture to yourselves ... and he pushed us, our eyes closed, to imagine the length and breadth of hell, its height and depth, and then to think that our wildest imaginings would not even begin to reach the horizons of such a place.

We paused, in silence. Keep your heads down, boys, keep your eyes closed; place yourselves in those caverns, think now of the pains that those around you, and you yourself, must suffer because, through your own sins, through your own fault, you forgot the love of the Eternal Lord and deserve the most impossible pains and sufferings that God can confer on you. My imagination was strong, ready as it was from father's story-telling to us at night. Listen, Fr Windermere went on; can you hear the wailings of those who are suffering all the pains of fire. Impossible pains, in a fire that does not ever die down. Hear the howlings of those around you, hear the cries and blasphemies of those who went through life and did not obey the laws of God. Smell, boys, smell the smoke of those flames, smell the sulphur, the stench of putrid things; can you bear it? You have to bear it. You have deserved it, by your sins. Now taste, taste all you know of bitterness, sourness, all the misery of sin and grief and hope-lessness, for out of here there is no escape, no end, no outcome.

Fr Windermere went on like this, on and on, until I was thrilling with it, thrilling and shivering in a kind of ecstasy of fear and determination. And all around me, in the pews, the other boys, the younger and the older, were silent, too, the high-pitched voice piercing through to the very core of our young lives.

Fr Windermere's argument was very clear to us, and under-lined in a shocking and yet stirring way. We knelt and prayed that we would prefer any suffering on earth in honour of our God and our Lord Jesus Christ to stay pure and steadfast in his laws and orderings, avoiding the temptation of sin and the con-sequences of eternal damnation. And then he introduced Fr Mullan, a giant of a man, some six feet four inches tall and built solidly to match his height, who came striding out of the sac-risty onto the altar, dressed from head to foot in a white habit, as if he were a militant angel, a storm of the purest snow, a breeze of lily-white. He took Fr Windermere's place on the altar and flung back from his head the white cowl that was part of his habit. We saw a strong red face, and a beard as white as his habit and flowing down over his chest. We were stunned. We were awed. We were all attention.

Fr Mullan spoke with a loud, gruff voice, exactly the voice I expected he would have. He told us of his years as a missionary priest, breaking new ground in the African Bush. These were images I had expected to hear and they thrilled me. He spoke of hacking his way through dense forest undergrowth, of finding clearings in the jungle where he began to build a church, using only his own strength and a few ignorant natives. He told of holding trials of power and influence with local witch-doctors and how he always won because he could put his hand into his mouth, take out his teeth, brandish them in the air, and put them back. He demonstrated with a quick gesture, how he could strike fire from his lifted thumb and sure enough, a small flame rose from his lifted arm; he showed us the lighter he could hide in his huge fist and how the miracle of fire out of human flesh won so many souls from paganism to the Christian God. He told how Africa needed men like him, needed them more than ever now, to maintain and develop what had been done by the first Fathers, their ground-breaking, their leading work. Not one word of his passed me by, not a gesture escaped my wrapt attention and when he was finished we all filed up, as if to Communion, and he gave us each a medal, a small silver thing with a picture of the Holy Ghost on one side and an outline map of Africa on the other. It was a treasure. I would not give it away for love or money. And some years later it was the influence of Fr Mullan that made me write a speculative letter, to The White Fathers, Kimmage Manor, Dublin.

Time and Tide: (16th century England)

The population of England grew rapidly during the sixteenth century. As the reign of Elizabeth I drew towards a close, the population had almost doubled. All of this stimulated economic growth. Trade flourished, housing was developed and the arts began to grow in popularity and sophistication. Along with such growth, however, unemployment and poverty, as well as the new phenomenon of urban overcrowding and squalor, also grew. Early enclosures came about, a form of claiming extra land that was sanctioned by government: 'Commons were enclosed, and waste land reclaimed, by landlords or squatters, with consequent extinction of common grazing rights' (History 260). This impacted, too, on the poor, and on the land itself, destroying some natural wildlife shelters and reclaiming swamplands and woods. This effort at 'enclosure' was later to cause great pain to the poet, John Clare.

Along with the growth of trade and commerce, inflation too caused distress. Agricultural prices spiralled during the century. 'The size of the work-force in Tudor England increasingly exceeded available employment opportunities; average wages and living standards declined accordingly' (History 260). There were several years when harvests failed and the swelling population found it difficult even to find food. Yet overall the century saw an increase in economic development and a growth in urban centres, particularly London.

Bosworth Field, in 1485, and the victory of Henry VII over Richard III, brought about a great change in English society. The battle was the penultimate one of the Wars of the Roses, that civil war between the House of Lancaster and the House of York that had raged throughout England in the second half of the fifteenth century. The Lancastrians won and their leader was Henry Tudor who became the first of the Tudor dynasty. Richard III was the last king of the House of York, and he was killed in the battle; it was the end of the Plantagenet dynasty and a period of hesitant stability began. Henry VII inaugurated a new form of

kingship, consolidating the monarchy and drawing more and
more power to the kingship. He developed a form of patronage
which was, in fact, a kind of political control, selecting his own
ministers, awarding and withdrawing land and effects as his
own needs demanded.

Henry VII died in 1509 and, at the age of 18, his son Henry
VIII succeeded. Henry's elder brother, Arthur, had died in 1502.
Henry married Arthur's widow, Katherine of Aragon. Very
soon Henry, in an effort to develop and consolidate the monarchy which his father had built up, showed himself to be a threatening and vindictive character, one who fascinated both the
people and his courtiers, and who determined most things from
his own wholly egotistical standpoint. He saw war as still 'the
sport of kings' and looked to an invasion of France.

His marriage to Katherine was unsatisfactory to Henry; their
sons had died in infancy or were stillborn and only their daughter, Mary, was heiress presumptive. There was no precedent for
a woman on the throne and Henry tried to annul the marriage.
Pope Clement VII would not do so and, after much negotiating
and diplomacy, Henry decided he himself would assume the power
to annul his own marriage. He took to himself the supremacy over
religious matters and married Anne Boleyn, in the hope of
fathering a male heir.

At that time, people were beginning to study their own faith
as the Bible was being translated into the vernacular and widely
published. 'The church authorities believed that the availability
of an English Bible, even an authorised version, would ferment
heresy by permitting Englishmen to form their own opinions'
(History 277). Thomas More, as chancellor, pursued a policy of
strict censorship though he was swimming against the tide. Henry
wanted the Bible to be available, and publication in English at last
appeared in 1535, just before More's death. Erasmus, Dutch hum-
anist and Catholic, was insisting on the worth of human reason
in matters religious; Luther's ideas were becoming popular and
Protestantism was making great advances throughout Europe.
Henry's real challenge was to papal power and, in order to win
his points, there was no alternative save to throw off England's
allegiance to Rome, give himself imperial status and take over
the decisions in all ecclesiastical issues. He had become head of

the Church of England. Thomas Cromwell, who took over from Thomas More (who was executed) helped Henry to dissolve many of the religious houses throughout England and take over their lands and wealth. Henry was effectively almost bankrupt and the annexation of the monasteries' estates brought him in much needed funds. Naturally, vocations declined and abbots were no longer part of the House of Lords.

Anne Boleyn did not give Henry the longed-for son; the future Elizabeth I was born in 1533. Three years later, when Anne had not given birth to a son, Henry had her investigated for high treason; she was found guilty and was beheaded in May of 1536. Henry turned to Jane Seymour and later in that year, they were married. In 1537 she became pregnant and in October of that year, Edward was born. Mary, daughter of Katherine of Aragon, was godmother and Elizabeth, daughter of Anne Boleyn, also had a part to play in the ceremony. Just two weeks later, Jane Seymour died. It appears that Thomas Cromwell sought a foreign bride for Henry, and in January of 1540 he married Anne of Cleves. By June Henry had tired of her and had found another, Kathryn Howard; he divorced Anne and married Kathryn, all in 1540. Henry was 49, Kathryn 19. By November 1541, it seemed clear that Kathryn was flirting, at least, with other men and Archbishop Cranmer informed Henry. She was executed in February of 1542. In 1543 Henry married Katherine Parr who contrived to outlive Henry. He died in 1547 when Edward VI was nine years old.

By now Protestant ideas had gathered strength and Archbishop Cranmer was ordered by the Privy Council to remove all images from places of worship. Much valuable material was seized by the crown. Cranmer's *Book of Common Prayer*, 1552, was in English and unambiguously Protestant. Edward VI was very weak and by 1553 he was dying; by right of birth Mary, Catholic daughter of Katherine of Aragon, was lawful successor. Edward died, July 1553; he had so hated his Catholic sister that he had drafted a 'device' to give Northumberland's daughter-in-law, Jane Grey, the throne. Mary gathered an army and marched on London. Northumberland, Jane and others were sent to the block. In Mary's short reign, some 287 Protestants were burned and many more died in prison. She worked to achieve reconciliation

with Rome and in 1554 Cardinal Pole landed in England and declared that England and the papacy were reunited. When Mary
married Philip, son of Emperor Charles V of Spain, a Protestant
rebellion was planned but came to nothing. Mary died in 1558
and Elizabeth I, daughter of Henry VIII and Anne Boleyn, was
crowned Queen in November of that year.

The reign of Elizabeth I was long and varied, and not without its glories and its wars. She had no dreams of expansion, but
hoped to revive Henry's religious laws and re-establish the
royal supremacy of the church and the break with Rome. In
1563, Convocation approved 39 Articles defining the Anglican
Church's doctrine and by 1571 it was compulsory for all the clergy to assent to these Articles. England had become, officially,
Protestant. Alongside fears of an invasion from Spain, England
grew ever more and more suspicious of priests and laws were
passed that would convict Catholic priests of treason if they
were caught exercising their priesthood. 146 priests had been
executed by the time Elizabeth died. At the same time Puritans
began to take to extremes the popular Protestant teaching and
worked hard to get rid of corruption in church, and all 'popish
rituals'.

A coalition of Catholic forces was formed and plotted to
force the recognition of Mary Stuart's right to the throne. Pope
Pius V issued a bull of excommunication against Elizabeth in
1570 and urged Catholics to depose her. In 1584 William of
Orange was assassinated and fears grew for Elizabeth's personal
safety. The Spanish Armada sailed and was defeated in 1585
and Mary Stuart was executed in 1587. Through all of this the
arts flourished; Elizabeth's Chapel Royal encouraged the com-
posers Tallis and Byrd; Shakespeare and Marlowe produced a
wonderful series of powerful dramas; poets such as Wyatt and
Surrey, Edmund Spenser, Philip Sidney and others grew in
strength and popularity. Yet towards the end of Elizabeth's
reign the kingdom was beginning to slide into great difficulties,
Elizabeth herself appearing to lose her strength and enthusiasm
for the crown. Around 1597: 'Perhaps two-fifths of the population fell below the margin of subsistence: malnutrition reached
the point of starvation in the uplands of Cumbria; disease
spread unchecked; reported crimes against property increased;

and thousands of families were thrown on to parish relief'
(History 317). In March of 1603 Elizabeth died.

Into the turbulent country of such religious stress the Jesuit
priest, Robert Southwell, made his secret entry.

Poet, Priest, Outlaw, Saint
Robert Southwell, Jesuit (1561-1595)

In 1569 a rebellion by Catholics in the north of England sought the restoration of Catholicism and the release of Mary Queen of Scots, in Catholic eyes the rightful heir to the throne. The rebellion was unsuccessful. In 1570 Pope Pius V excommunicated Elizabeth, which automatically released all Catholics from allegiance to her. Soon priests from seminaries across Europe began to come to England, the first Jesuits arriving in 1580. This alarmed parliament which passed severe laws against Catholics and in 1581 made conversion to the Catholic Church a treasonable offence. It was also treasonable for a Catholic priest to work in England, or for anyone to shelter or aid him. Treason was a capital crime. Then the Spanish Armada, sent to invade England and overthrow Elizabeth, set out in 1588. This was the last straw, proving that the Pope and Spain were in league with Catholics and that priests were agents of these foreign powers. The laws were rigorously enforced.

The 'Penal laws' enforced the conformity of all subjects to the Established Church. Many Catholics lost their holdings, and their lives. The celebration of Mass was outlawed, along with the sheltering of priests. While Catholics remained patriotic, as Robert Southwell insisted he was, it was impossible to prove loyalty to monarch and country while remaining a Catholic. Great suffering resulted. 'Persuading to popery' was a treasonable offence and 'An act against Jesuits and seminary priests' was passed in 1585. Treason was punished by the brutal process of hanging, disembowelling and quartering.

'The proclamation of the good news cannot be detached from concern about the natural world in which people are placed: people and planet form an interwoven community that needs to be considered together, rather than separately' (Deane-Drummond 178). For Robert Southwell, the presence of Christ on earth through the incarnation and continuing through the sacrament of the Eucharist, was the hope of life and the life of love. The celebration of the Eucharist, even though it had to be done in secret and under circumstances of extreme, personal danger, was central to Southwell's ministry.

Robert Southwell was born in Norfolk in 1561 and was hanged at Tyburn 34 years later. His grandfather, Sir Richard Southwell, had been a wealthy man and a courtier in the reign of Henry VIII, and had helped bring about the Earl of Surrey's execution. On his mother's side Robert was descended from a Shelley family and a remote connection may be traced forward to Percy Bysshe Shelley. In his very early years legend says he was once stolen by gypsies but was found and recovered by his nurse; later he wrote: 'What, had I remained with the gipsy? How abject, how void of all knowledge and reverence of God! In what shameful vices, in how great danger of infamy, in how certain danger of an unhappy death and eternal punishment!'

Robert was brought up a Catholic and sent to Douai to be educated by the Jesuits. He spent some time in Paris and there asked to be admitted to the Jesuit order. He was only seventeen at that time and, being refused at first, wrote some passionate laments. In 1578, still only seventeen, he was admitted to the order in Rome and took vows in 1580. He did his noviceship at Tournai and was ordained priest in Rome in 1584, when he was barely twenty-three years old. He spent a short time in the English college in Rome, as prefect of studies. He was sent, as per his earnest request, in 1586, to England with a Fr Henry Garnett and took the secret name of 'Cotton' in order to try and move as freely as possible among the souls he had come to serve.

Southwell was worried that many who had been faithful Catholics were now drifting into the Church of England to avoid the fine for every church service from which they absented themselves. Many families held out until they were financially ruined; then they would attempt to make their way to the continent and live on alms. Southwell was made chaplain to the Countess of Arundel for whom his *Hundred Meditations on the love of God* were addressed. He worked zealously for some six years on his missionary work, hiding in various places and under various disguises, pretending an interest in the ways of country gentlemen to distract pursuers. He appears to have remained aloof from controversy, and carried on his missionary work with gentleness and courage. Most of the remaining Catholics were to be found in the countryside. They longed for better days, the most they hoped for being that a priest might be smuggled into their homes to help them in their last hours.

Southwell's urge was to promote the faith and all the virtues through the medium of his verse. This is not to say that he saw poetry merely as a vehicle for preaching and teaching. He took his craft very seriously and became an influence on many of the poets who followed him. In his preface, 'The Author To His Loving Cousin', he writes: 'Poets, by abusing their talent, and making the follies and feignings of love the customary subject of their base endeavours, have so discredited this faculty, that a poet, a lover, and a liar, are by many reckoned but three words of one signification.' As his whole life was a work of love towards his Christ and his fellow-Christians, so his poems were to be an integral part of that love and move with honesty and labour towards their completion. In the poem that serves as preface, he has this stanza: *The Author To The Reader*:

Profane conceits and feigning fits I fly,
Such lawless stuff doth lawless speeches fit:
With David, verse to Virtue I apply,
Whose measure best with measured words doth fit:
It is the sweetest note that man can sing,
When grace in Virtue's key tunes Nature's string.

He is determined, like Herbert after him, to shift the emphasis in poetry from 'profane' love poems to poems written in honour of God and 'Virtue'. But he is also determined to write the best work he can and indeed his poetry was very popular among both Catholics and Anglicans, and went through several editions after his death.

Between 1586 and 1592 he was in England, at permanent risk to his life, and during this period wrote most of his work. The training of the Jesuits made a man sensitive to words and to the possibilities of fine eloquence. But there is, too, much of the work that is the result of personal devotion and thinking. This was the age of Marlowe and of Shakespeare and Southwell fitted well into the great surge of the Renaissance. He had already spent time abroad and was aware of what was going on in Europe. In his verse, too, there is a forward looking sensibility that carries his work powerfully into the period of the Baroque, with Herbert and Donne. For him the birth of Christ, the incarnation, is the central focus and the continuation of that presence in the Eucharist. He sees the incarnation as the beginning of the purification and renewal of the fallen world. And in Southwell, too, as well as in most of the poets under consideration, the sacrament of the Eucharist is paramount. For him it continued the work of incarnation, of Christ's real presence on the earth, purifying and renewing it. He fought hard to counter the Protestant denial of Real Presence. As will be seen later, it was the need to believe in the Real Presence that brought Gerard Manley Hopkins to Catholicism.

There was a strong, though permanently watchful, cohesion among the Catholics in Southwell's age, recalling in ways the early days of the primitive church. Ritual and gathering had to be done in secret, in constant danger from watchful troops, under suspicion always that the gathering might be betrayed. Small groups came together in semi-darkness to celebrate Mass, always wondering if there might be a traitor amongst them. Eventually, through the treachery of a girl, Anne Bellamy, daughter of a house in which he was staying, Southwell was arrested in 1592 and was subjected to very many cruelties and tortures.

He was kept in a dungeon swarming with vermin. He was repeatedly tortured, suffering the rack at least ten times, brought almost to the point of death, revived, and tortured again. He was prodded to inform on the presence of other priests but his steadfastness was remarkable, impressing even his tormentors. There are those for whom religion is a dangerous obsession, there are others whose obsession with danger is a religious thing! After three years in prison he was tried and executed, in 1595. Standing in the cart, he began: 'Whether we live, we live unto the Lord: or whether we die, we die unto the Lord. Therefore, whether we live or whether we die, we are the Lord's ... I am brought hither to perform the last act of this miserable life, and ... I do most humbly desire at the hands of Almighty God for our Saviour Jesus' sake, that he would vouchsafe to pardon and forgive all my sins ...' He had been sentenced to hanging and quartering but was dead before he was cut down. A remarkable man, and a remarkable poet.

Southwell's writings were popular among his contemporaries and circulated in manuscript form; this was a method of preaching the tenets of Catholicism to his flock. It has sometimes been suggested that his poems touched the work of Shakespeare. He was, of necessity, a man of action and adventure in his efforts to remain free among those whom he served but his deepest instincts were towards the mystical life. His poetry was copied by hand and passed around. He wrote in Latin as well as in English, the Latin poems demonstrating a fine and wide literary awareness. His poems in English, given the context of their writing, incorporate the underworld life of risk and danger that he translated into a Catholic tenet. The Catholic Church remembers him as a martyr every year on 21 February.

It was Christ's presence on earth that affected Southwell most and that gave him courage and faith in his calling. If the incarnation had occurred, and Southwell did not doubt that it had, then all our living was enriched and promised liberation from this world and entry into a new. And so, for him, Christmas and the birth of the Saviour became the greatest cause for verse. As with the 'metaphysical' poets after him, paradox was one of his favourite linguistic tools and the presence of God the Creator of the universe in the form of a weakling child on earth is the story that is ultimately filled with paradox:

The Nativity of Christ

Behold the father is his daughter's son,
The bird that built the nest is hatched therein,
The old of years an hour hath not outrun,
Eternal life to live doth now begin,
The Word is dumb, the mirth of heaven doth weep,
Might feeble is, and force doth faintly creep.

O dying souls! behold your living spring!
O dazzled eyes! behold your sun of grace!
Dull ears attend what word this word doth bring!
Up, heavy hearts, with joy your joy embrace!
From death, from dark, from deafness, from despairs,
This life, this light, this word, this joy repairs.

Gift better than Himself God doth not know,
Gift better than his God no man can see;
This gift doth here the giver given bestow,
Gift to this gift let each receiver be:
God is my gift, Himself He freely gave me,
God's gift am I, and none but God shall have me.

Man altered was by sin from man to beast;
Beast's food is hay, hay is all mortal flesh;
Now God is flesh, and lies in manger pressed,
As hay the brutest sinner to refresh:
Oh happy field wherein this fodder grew,
Whose taste doth us from beasts to men renew!

The first stanza of a poem called 'Life is but Loss' is a natural enough view of the world from the perspective of one in constant fear of being taken and tortured and killed. Indeed, Southwell's chosen life was one of such distress, narrow escapes, suffering and the near certainty that he would soon be taken and tortured, that the 'next life' seemed always a thing to be prayed and longed for. This would mean that, in spite of the fact that Christ had taken flesh and come to live amongst us on the earth, the earthly period of our existence was not seen to be of much worth:

By force I live, in will I wish to die.
In plaint I pass the length of lingering days.
Free would my soul from mortal body fly,
And tread the track of death's desired ways!
Life is but loss where death is deemed gain,
And loathed pleasures breed displeasing pain.

As a kind of sequel to this poem, Southwell writes, in 'Lewd Love Is Loss':

If picture move, more should the pattern please;
No shadow can with shadowed thing compare,
And fairest shapes, whereon our loves do cease,
But silly signs of God's high beauties are.
Go, starving sense, feed thou on earthly mast;
True love, in heaven seek thou thy sweet repast.

'Go, starving sense, feed thou on earthly mast': mast is the mixed and mashed-up fruit of the oak, the beech, the chestnut and in those times it was the common food for swine. If his priestly vocation and his constrained circumstances forced him to see his life as wholly dedicated to the love of God, it was inevitable that he would see worldly things in the beauty they did possess as mere shadows of heavenly things. The *Spiritual Exercises* of St Ignatius urged the contemplation, in detail, of place and event, in order to keep the mind focused on actual and real living while moving the mind towards God. The influence of these *Exercises* had to be enormous on one such as Southwell (as, later on, on Hopkins), urging the spirit of an oppressed priest to cast all of his love towards heaven. Southwell, then, is urgent on the value of the incarnation, on the real and continuing presence of the Christ on earth and in his followers, but his natural focus is on heaven and the world to come, this world seen as a place of pain and a mere lading-place for the next world.

In the poem 'Of the Blessed Sacrament of the Altar', Southwell sees all that there is of God's given grace in the bread and wine of that sacrament, and it is through the Eucharist that can be found entrance 'to never-ending grace, types to the truth, dim glimpses to the light';

Christ's final meal was fountain of our good,
For mortal meat He gave immortal food.

Of course, Southwell revels in the further paradoxes of the Last Supper: 'He in His hands Himself did truly lift'. 'The God of hosts in slender Host doth dwell'. The richness of the gift of himself in the sacrament Southwell can express only in terms of sense, as Ignatius would have urged:

To ravish eyes here heavenly beauties are,
To win the ear sweet music's sweetest sound;
To lure the taste the angels' heavenly fare;
To soothe the scent divine perfumes abound;
To please the touch, He in our hearts doth bed,
Whose touch doth cure the deaf, the dumb, the dead.

St Augustine wrote that when one says 'amen' to the receiving of Christ, one is saying amen to becoming as Christ is.

For Southwell, naturally enough, life is exile; the poems were written during his time in England and were intended to convince Catholics that their case was like that of the early Christians and worth their efforts to stand firm. His distribution of the Eucharist to his faithful became an urgency in his life. His poems also offered a preference for death. By his training he was already aware of the power of words and the possibilities of eloquence; this latter penchant mars some of his preaching poems. There is forethought of Donne in 'I live, but such a life as ever dies; I die, but such a death as never ends; My death, to end my dying, life denies, And life, my living death no whit amends'. And it may not be too much to see Hopkins reading a fellow-Jesuit poet, a fellow-sufferer, in later years and relishing his love for words and their emotional resonances as well as his overwhelming emphasis on the Eucharist. Given his love for Christ in his incarnation, it is no strange thing that his most successful poem is a meditation on the nativity:

The Burning Babe

As I in hoary Winter's night stood shivering in the snow,
Surprised I was with sudden heat, which made my heart to
          glow;
And lifting up a fearful eye, to view what fire was near,
A pretty Babe all burning bright did in the air appear;
Who scorchèd with excessive heat, such floods of tears did
          shed,
As though his floods should quench his flames, which with
          his tears were bred:
Alas (quoth he) but newly born, in fiery heats I fry,
Yet none approach to warm their hearts or feel my fire, but I;
My faultless breast the furnace is, the fuel wounding thorns:
Love is the fire, and sighs the smoke, the ashes, shames and
          scorns;
The fuel Justice layeth on, and Mercy blows the coals,
The metal in this furnace wrought, are men's defilèd souls:
For which, as now on fire I am to work them to their good,
So will I melt into a bath, to wash them in my blood.

With this he vanished out of sight, and swiftly shrunk away,
And straight I callèd unto mind, that it was Christmas day.

The poems focus on the person of Christ, and on his sufferings for the benefit of humanity. In this he is a startling contrast to the somewhat later Thomas Traherne whose work focuses on the hope and beauty of this world. Southwell contemplates, too, the innocence and perseverance that Christ displayed in earthly life, in spite of persecution and death. The outlaw Christ is close to the outlaw poet and as long as this is maintained Southwell feels content. Though there was little physical 'delight' in the world in which the poet priest moved, yet that mystical delight in the alignment with Christ remains strong. The key word is 'true': if the Christ remains true to humanity then surely it is humanity's duty to remain true to the Christ, no matter the odds. It is, too, the innocence of the Christ child that Southwell admires, an innocence and a love of humanity that will be put to the ultimate test and will triumph in the blood that will be shed. Southwell was quite aware of the risks he was running, he was certain his own life would end in the shedding of his blood.

A Child My Choice

Let folly praise that fancy loves, I praise and love that Child
Whose heart no thought, whose tongue no word, whose
hand no deed defiled.

I praise Him most, I love Him best, all praise and love is His;
While Him I love, in Him I live, and cannot live amiss.

Love's sweetest mark, laud's highest theme, man's most
desired light,
To love Him life, to leave Him death, to live in Him delight.

He mine by gift, I His by debt, thus each to other due;
First friend He was, best friend He is, all times will try Him
true.

Though young, yet wise; though small, yet strong; though
man, yet God He is:
As wise, He knows; as strong, He can; as God, He loves
to bless.

His knowledge rules, His strength defends, His love doth
        cherish all;
His birth our joy, His life our light, His death our end of
        thrall.

Alas! He weeps, He sighs, He pants, yet do His angels sing;
Out of His tears, His sighs and throbs, doth bud a joyful spring.

This poem erupts out of personal feeling, personal suffering,
personal longing; the broken phrases of the lines combine with
the full rhymes to create a strange effect, the inherent contradictions between the Christ as Man and the Christ as God, allied to
the need humanity has to imitate those contradictions. The ending is dramatically powerful, the last couplets moving with an
easier movement, 'His love doth cherish all: His death our end
of thrall: yet do His angels sing: doth bud a joyful spring.' It is
God's selfless love for humankind that Southwell wants to
preach, this overwhelming love that can urge a man to face
impossible odds to tell others of that love. It is the Counter-
Reformation doctrine of service in spite of suffering and persecution in the response to that love; it is a preaching that works
because the poetry in which it is housed issues from personal
commitment and subtle rhyming, careful mimicry in the movement of the verses, an appeal to the common Christian through
the best-known and most important energies in Christ's life.
And what could be better known and loved among Christians
than Christmas day and the very birth of that Saviour, that loving yet demanding Child come to rescue humanity from suffering by undergoing an even more frightful suffering himself?
Much later on, the Irish poet Patrick Kavanagh, will also be held
in thrall by Christmas and the birth of Christ.

    In Southwell's case, the difficult pleasures of mystical con-
templation were unattainable, but love and the ultimate coming
into the presence of the beloved were not. One poem typifies
this:

I Die Alive

O Life! what lets thee from a quick decease?
O Death! what draws thee from a present prey?
My feast is done, my soul would be at ease,
My grace is said: O Death! come take away.

I live, but such a life as ever dies;
I die, but such a death as never ends;
My death, to end my dying, life denies,
And life, my living death no whit amends.

Thus still I die, yet still I do revive:
My living death by dying life is fed.
Grace, more than nature, keeps my heart alive,
Whose idle hopes and vain desires are dead.

Not where I breathe, but where I love, I live;
Not where I love, but where I am, I die;
The life I wish must future glory give,
The deaths I feel in present dangers lie.

Apart from the sheer delight in the use of paradox evident in this piece also, it is interesting to speculate that John Donne may well have come across poems like this which were circulating amongst Catholics while Donne himself was struggling with his own conscience. Donne's work, of course, bristles with the pleasures of paradox and the self-awareness of the work chimes well with Southwell's verses. Yet there is also a glance backwards in this poem, and in others of Southwell's work, where the use of alliterative words advanced the rhythms of the whole poem. Many of the lines above have fully absorbed that Anglo-Saxon verve and adapted it musically and drawn it with delight into the paradoxes. It is interesting to speculate if Southwell at the end of the sixteenth century in England was aware of, and had read, 'The Dream of the Rood'. Even in the first two lines of 'I Die Alive', the use of the words 'lets' and 'draw' suggest at least an unconscious, and more than likely a fully conscious awareness of the power of such alliterative rhythmic devices as were used in the Anglo-Saxon work. Southwell's poetry, then, frequently moves well beyond the uses of catechism and preachery and takes his religious urges deep into the realms of poetry.

Another fall-back to earlier centuries occurs in those poems
Southwell wrote that retell in verse form the story of the New
Testament. The titles themselves, in this series, give the game
away: 'The Visitation', 'The Nativity of Christ', 'The Flight into
Egypt', and many more. As in the middle ages the method of getting across the story of Christ in memorable form was a worthy
one but in Southwell's case, the staid and serious plodding
along of the verses, without personal intervention and surely
without humour, leaves the reader dry. There is one poem
among these that stands out, however, where the impulse for
deeper movement and understanding through the techniques
of poetry takes over from the preaching impulse.

Christ's Bloody Sweat

Fat soil, full spring, sweet olive, grape of blisse,
That yields, that streams, that pours, that dost distill,
Untilled, undrawn, unstamped, untouched of press,
Dear fruit, clear brooks, fair oil, sweet wine at will!
Thus Christ unforced prevents, in shedding blood,
The whips, the thorns, the nails, the spear, and rood.

He pelican's, He phoenix' fate doth prove,
Whom flames consume, whom streams enforce to die:
How burneth blood, how bleedeth burning love,
Can one in flame and stream both bathe and fry?
How could He join a phoenix' fiery pains
In fainting pelican's still bleeding veins?

Elias once, to prove God's sovereign power,
By prayer procured a fire of wondrous force
That blood and wood and water did devour,
Yea, stones and dust beyond all Nature's course:
Such fire is love, that, fed with gory blood,
Doth burn no less than in the driest wood.

O sacred fire! come show thy force on me,
That sacrifice to Christ I may return.
If withered wood for fuel fittest be,
If stones and dust, if flesh and blood will burn,
I withered am, and stony to all good:
A sack of dust, a mass of flesh and blood.

Here Southwell anticipates one of the strongest images in the work of George Herbert, that of humanity being dust; Herbert will speak of humanity as being 'guilty of dust' as well as sin; here Southwell speaks of himself as 'a sack of dust'. The movement of this poem is from within the poet outwards, not a simple retelling of the gospel narrative. The poet is involved, and deeply so, and the many images and sources of faith in the poem are already familiar from the earlier work. It is also hugely tempting to wonder if Herbert read this poem and drew from it some awareness of a poetry charged with a personal God and an awareness of man as dust! Here again is the commitment to self-sacrifice that this poet-priest-outlaw laid out for himself; here, too, that imagery of fire so frequent in Southwell's view of suffering, and its contrast with images of streams and blood. The opening lines offer a sense of generous giving, and the broken sentences stress the awe of the poet aware of this extravagance. The movement to the Christ and his free giving of himself for love of the Father, crowns this first stanza beautifully.

The second stanza offers strange yet effective imagery and contrast, the pelican giving her blood for her young, the phoenix being destroyed by fire but glorying in resurrection. The extravagance of the lines is wonderful: 'How burneth blood, how bleedeth burning love, / Can one in flame and stream both bathe and fry?' The delight in language and paradox moves side by side with a deeply religious sentiment and the phrases are put in the form of questions to make the reader (or the author himself) probe the truth more deeply. Then he kindly, as preacher cum teacher cum poet, answers his own questions, urging the reader to see how Elias, through prayer, could call down a saving fire from heaven and Elias, as we know, was taken up to heaven in a chariot of fire. Southwell equates this fire with love, the power of Divine love answering to the sufferings of humankind. We have moved far and wonderfully and yet gently from the awed and hesitant opening of this poem to the final stanza that stands back in glad amazement from what the poem itself has revealed: 'O sacred fire!' The poem shifts directly into prayer, thus mirroring the poem's movement and drawing both poet and reader into immediate contact with what the poem speaks of, the demands of love that result in a loving fire to consume the soul and turn all that is noxious and transitory into ash.

W. B. Yeats wrote: 'Too long a sacrifice can make a stone of the heart. O when may it suffice?' In the case of Robert Southwell the question may be answered, 'only at death'. It was essential for Southwell to lie low, to be an outlaw in his own country, for his faith's sake. It was important, he felt, that his gift for poetry be used to forward his vocation as a missionary and that he use his talents to teach his frightened flock. But his aim always appears to have been martyrdom and it is this desire for self-sacrifice that dominates his work and that, too often, draws the poetry into avenues where it becomes verse only, though even that verse is well-achieved. He held up before his own eyes, and before the eyes of his flock, the examples of martyrs; but he also holds up Mary Stuart, Queen of Scots, as a saint and a martyr. He speaks of her troubles and, of course, he is thinking of his own, and how they are transfigured only in the afterlife. We are back to the Christian paradox of death bringing life, of life being death. As Hans Urs von Balthasar points out, Christ's own life was oriented towards martyrdom, he was fully conscious of where the path he was following must lead him. So, too, with Southwell. If Queen Mary did not dread death because it would bring her closer to Christ, then, Southwell reasons, English Catholics should not fear death either, mortal life being little more than restricting their contact with the Lord. Here, finally, is the glory of suffering, here is the ultimate example of purific-ation being no more than the method by which one leaves this life and is welcomed into God's life.

Decease Release
Dum morior orior

The pounded spice both taste and scent doth please,
In fading smoke the force doth incense show,
The perished kernel springeth with increase,
The loppèd tree doth best and soonest grow.

God's spice I was and pounding was my due,
In fading breath my incense savoured best,
Death was the mean, my kernel to renew,
By lopping shot I up to heavenly rest.

Some things more perfect are in their decay,
Like spark that going out gives clearest light,
Such was my hap, whose doleful dying day
Began my joy and termed fortune's spite.

Alive a Queen, now dead I am a Saint,
Once Mary called, my name now Martyr is,
From earthly reign debarrèd by restraint,
In lieu whereof I reign in heavenly bliss.

My life my grief, my death hath wrought my joy,
My friends my foil, my foes my weal procured,
My speedy death hath shortened long annoy,
And loss of life an endless life assured.

My scaffold was the bed where ease I found,
The block a pillow of Eternal rest,
My headman cast me in a blissful swound,
His axe cut off my cares from combered breast.

Rue not my death, rejoice at my repose,
It was no death to me but to my woe,
The bud was opened to let out the Rose,
The chains unloosed to let the captive go.

A prince by birth, a prisoner by mishap,
From Crown to cross, from throne to thrall I fell,
My right my ruth, my titles wrought my trap,
My weal my woe, my worldly heaven my hell.

By death from prisoner to a prince enhanced,
From Cross to Crown, from thrall to throne again,
My ruth my right, my trap my style advanced,
From woe to weal, from hell to heavenly reign.

Southwell's life and writing are a heroic testimony to faith in Christ and in the Eucharist. There is a personal courage to live what he saw as the truth that is a continuing factor in the lives of those who still suffer. Gustavo Gutierrez says: 'Fidelity unto death is a wellspring of life' (Gutierrez 23), and this is in the context of his book, *We Drink from Our Own Wells*, written about the struggles of the suffering in Latin America in the second half of the twentieth century. He speaks of those who suffer martyr-

dom for their truth: 'The present-day Latin American experience of martyrdom bids us all turn back to one of the major
sources of all spirituality: the blood-stained experience of the
early Christian community, which was so weak in the face of the
imperial power of that day.' Down so many centuries there
have been martyrs, and as well as Southwell under Elizabeth, all
the Protestant martyrs under 'Bloody' Mary must form part of
this remembrance. Gutierrez quotes the psalms: (42:11 and 43:3-
4)

> Why are you downcast, O my soul?
> Why so disturbed within me?
> Put your hope in God,
> for I will yet praise him,
> my Savior and my God.
> O send out Your light and Your truth,
> let them lead me;
> Let them bring me to Your holy hill
> And to Your dwelling places.
>
> Then I will go to the altar of God,
> To God my exceeding joy;
> And upon the lyre I shall praise You,
> O God, my God.

In Southwell then, many of the great Christian themes are
already enunciated: the incarnation, the Eucharist, an unquestioning love. Indeed, all the trials and sufferings that Southwell
underwent may be described as 'works of love', the greatest of
all being his self-giving for the sake of his Master, Christ.
However, there is of necessity in this poet, a rejection of the
earth itself, creation is to be suffered through on the way to the
saving of one's soul in the next life. This viewing of the world as,
in the words of the great poem, the *Salve Regina*, a place where
we are 'mourning and weeping in this valley of tears', is one
that permeated a great deal of Christian thinking down the centuries. Not all poets, however, were distracted by such a view.

The Works of Love

This is, perhaps, the moment to continue with the interrupted Introduction to this book. In the Book of Tobias, when the son has returned from his difficult journey, his father asks him what they can offer to the man, the angel Raphael, who had helped him on his way. 'Then Tobias called his son to him and said: What can we give to this holy man, who has come with you? Tobias answering, said to his father: Father, what wages can we give him? or what can be worthy of his benefits? He conducted me and brought me safe again, he received the money of Gabelus, he caused me to have my wife, and he chased from her the evil spirit, he gave joy to her parents, myself he delivered from being devoured by the fish, you too he has made to see the light of heaven, and we are filled with all good things through him. What can we give him sufficient for these things? But I beseech you, father, to desire him that he would vouchsafe to accept of one half of all things that have been brought. So the father and the son calling him, took him aside; and began to desire him that he would agree to accept half of all things that they had brought. Then he said to them secretly, Bless the God of heaven, give glory to him in the sight of all that live, because he has shown his mercy to you. For it is good to hide the secret of a king: but to reveal and confess the works of God … I discover then the truth to you, and I will not hide the secret from you. When you prayed with tears, and buried the dead, and left your dinner, and hid the dead by day in your house, and buried them by night, I offered your prayer to the Lord. And because you were acceptable to God, it was necessary that temptation should prove you. And now the Lord has sent me to heal you, and to deliver Sara your son's wife from the devil. For I am the angel Raphael, one of the seven, who stand before the Lord. And when they had heard these things, they were troubled, and being seized with fear they fell upon the ground on their face. And the angel said to them: Peace be to you, fear not. For when I was with you, I was there by the will of God: bless him, and sing praises to him. I seemed indeed to eat and to drink with you but I use an invisible meat and drink, which cannot be seen by men. It is time therefore that I return to him that sent me: but bless God, and publish all his wonderful works. And when he had said these things, he was taken from their sight, and they could see him no more. Then they lying prostrate for three hours upon their face, blessed God, and rising up, they told all his wonderful works.'

The aged Tobias had, according to the story, done a great deal of good, helping those who suffered, burying the dead, giving alms ... but it appeared necessary, too, to God to test him, not as severely as he was to test Job. Tobias had come through all of this and God, out of his overwhelming and gratuitous love, sent Raphael to help. The works of love are performed, in this story, by Tobias and by God.

The works of love, then, are the good deeds that humanity does, for its own development, for the benefit of all, or for the love of God. The works of love are anything done in the pursuit of one's livelihood or one's duty. These are activities of whatever kind that are positive works, not destructive of the human endeavour. A road well built, without exploitation of worker or council; a meal well cooked; the iris, the sunflower paintings of Vincent Van Gogh; Brahm's *German Requiem*; Alberto Giacometti's *Woman of Venice*; John Banville's *The Sea*; Milton's *Lycidas* ... all of these are amongst the works of love.

Ivan V. Lalić was born in 1931 in Belgrade and died there in 1996. He was one of Serbia's finest poets. Here is one of his poems, translated from Serbian by Francis R. Jones:

Of the Works of Love

The works of love are scattered through the world
Like the scars of war;
                           grass grows fast
Over the battlefield, and the wet ember of earth
Bursts into flame to restore the terrible virginity,
As before the embrace, before the remembering, before the
                           voices
At dawn, with lips just parting:
The works of love are in dispute –

And when the wall crumbles, and when the garden grows
          wild,
When the word is erased, when the ring is broken,
Love loses out;
                    but listen to the screams of the birds
Over the cove where the sea learns from lovers
A different tenderness: time is impartial
And the world is love's task,
                                    the long rehearsal
Of immature gods.

Love is, of course, the greatest of the 'works of love', God's
love for the earth and for humanity, human love for God and for
all of creation. What opposes the works of love is war and destruction, violence and hatred, selfishness and greed. If love is
'grace', anything that lifts us up from the mire of our sinfulness
and evil, then its opposite is 'gravity', anything that brings us
down. In Lalić's poem he sees that 'the world is love's task', and
creation itself learns tenderness from lovers, lovers who are yet,
in this life, immature gods. War is destruction, and evil is in war
with love, there is dispute, but in the crumbling of walls and the
neglect of gardens, in the loss of language and languages, and
the breaking of agreements, then it is destruction that is the win-
ner. Our task therefore is to place on the balance all the works of
love we can achieve in order to be part of God's original creation
of love, wholeness and beauty.

Julian of Norwich wrote: 'And he showed me ... a little
thing, the size of a hazelnut, on the palm of my hand, round like
a ball. I looked at it thoughtfully and wondered, "What is this?"
And the answer came, "It is all that is made." I marvelled that it
continued to exist and did not suddenly disintegrate, it was so
small. And again my mind supplied the answer: "It exists, both
now and for ever, because God loves it." In this "little thing" I
saw three truths. The first is that God made it; the second is that
God loves it; and the third is that God sustains it' (Julian 67-68).

This is the greatest of the works of love: The 'prior and un-
conditioned divine love towards human kind caused God to
send for our redemption his Son, whose free and obedient
acceptance of a violent death at the hands of a wicked world

revealed, as nothing else could, God's loving self-giving on our behalf' (O'Collins 108)

St Paul puts the question that rises from this, in Romans 8: 31-2: 'What, then, shall we say in response to this? If God is for us, who can be against us? He who did not spare his own Son, but gave him up for us all – how will he not also, along with him, graciously give us all things?'

And in 2 Corinthians 5:18-19: 'All this is from God, who reconciled us to himself through Christ and gave us the ministry of reconciliation.'

John wrote: (1 John 4:8-12) 'Whoever does not love does not know God, because God is love. This is how God showed his love among us: He sent his one and only Son into the world that we might live through him. This is love: not that we loved God, but that he loved us and sent his Son as an atoning sacrifice for our sins. Dear friends, since God so loved us, we also ought to love one another. No one has ever seen God; but if we love one another, God lives in us and his love is made complete in us.'

Love, love of God and love of neighbour. But the works of love go further; there is the world, the whole of creation in which humanity lives and breathes and works, that creation which comes from the loving Creator. In the first book of the Old Testament, after his work of creation, Genesis states: 'and God saw everything that he had made, and indeed, it was very good'. It is not only humankind that God finds pleasure in, but 'everything he had made'. If creation is placed in humankind's keeping, then there is a duty of care, of development, of love. Later, in Genesis 9:8-17 we read: 'Then God said to Noah and to his sons with him: "I now establish my covenant with you and with your descendants after you and with every living creature that was with you – the birds, the livestock and all the wild animals, all those that came out of the ark with you – every living creature on earth. I establish my covenant with you: Never again will all life be cut off by the waters of a flood; never again will there be a flood to destroy the earth." And God said, "This is the sign of the covenant I am making between me and you and every living creature with you, a covenant for all generations to come: I have set my rainbow in the clouds, and it will be the sign of the covenant between me and the earth. Whenever I bring clouds over the earth and the rainbow appears in the clouds, I will remember my covenant between me and you and all living creatures of every kind. Never again will the waters become a flood to destroy all life. Whenever the rainbow appears in the clouds, I will see it and remember the everlasting covenant between God and all living creatures of every kind on the earth".' A covenant, an agreement, is a two-way thing; the covenant between God and all of creation, including humankind, has been upheld and renewed on one side. On the other side, humankind has been rapidly destroying the creation, both human (through wars and omnipresent violence) and the earth itself. Humankind has been destroying the works of love.

Ecological awareness is new to humankind because it has been put at the forefront of our consciousness over the past destructive decades. Love of the earth and awareness of its beauty and importance to human living have always been present but taken for granted until the realisation that real damage has been, and is increasingly being, caused. 'On the one hand scientific knowledge of the way different ecosystems work and are interconnected can lead to a profound sense of awe, wonder and beauty reflected in natural wisdom. One might suggest it leads to the threshold of a vision of God, reflecting God, as it were, in the mirror of God's works. On the other hand our lack of appropriate use of science and technology through the project of modernity itself with its drive towards progress and consumption has led to an arrogant disregard for the natural world and its workings, putting us on the brink of ecological collapse. Human knowledge has itself become corrupting, as it has disregarded the wisdom that is implicit in the natural world' (Deane-Drummond 165).

Therefore the focus of this study of Christ, Eucharist, Incarnation, Poetry ... must also be on ecology and how the other themes work necessarily on the greatest threat to existence that has ever come upon us. 'With Jesus, we are sent into the world to love all that has been created, and to live with the specificity and limitedness of being human beings, in a community, in time' (McKenna 135). 'We are to imitate God and repair the world, restore earth, make it all whole and holy again, so that its inherent life becomes ever more abundant and available, shared with every human being in communion and passed on to the next generations' (McKenna 142). Secular sciences have brought about this mess, but it has also been caused by the failure of the Christian churches to hold on to the truth and love that Christ brought, with his 'new covenant', into our lives. The problems we are faced with are clear: population growth, the careless use of resources, pollution, climate change, increase in sea level rise, availability of water, food distribution, health, economic disasters, environmental impacts, biodiversity loss. It would be depressing to enumerate all the difficulties. It is useful to remember that if present market economies foster these spiralling habits of over-consumption, thereby turning every value into a commodity, yet a renewed wonder at the miracle of the world and the human place in that world must help us back towards responsible behaviour.

Naming, knowing and caring for the earth, all of this is richly present, though as a sub-text, in the work of the poets presented in this study, in Hopkins, Clare, Herbert, and many more ... It is still present among indigenous peoples, such as the Indians. The answer, however, is not a return to the mechanics of the past but a return to a consideration of the human covenant with God and with creation. 'It is a sad fact of recent history that the churches have been slow to recognise the gravity of the ecological problems facing the earth' (McDonagh 103). 'In recent centuries the Catholic Church tended to cut itself off from the wider European intellectual ferment which it could no longer control' (McDonagh 104), indeed often portraying the proponents of modern science as enemies of the faith. Exclusions and blame are not the answer. Love is the answer, that invitation to love that was offered by Christ in his incarnation, that is so perfectly presented in the work of George Herbert, particularly in his magnificently simple and immediate poem 'Love'.

The Seventeenth Century

Elizabeth I was succeeded by James VI of Scotland, son of Mary Queen of Scots, and inaugurated as James I of England. Though James was a convinced Protestant, at the beginning of his reign the Catholics had great hopes of more tolerance, but these soon proved to be illusory. In 1605 came the Gunpowder Plot, a conspiracy by a number of hotheaded Catholics (the best known being Guy Fawkes) to blow up the Houses of Parliament when the King and the members of Parliament were present. The plot was discovered before it could be carried out and the conspirators were subsequently executed, but strong anti-Catholic feeling was aroused and the penal laws were strengthened and again strictly enforced. During these years Anglicanism achieved a measure of peace and confidence in itself and its clergy were content to pursue their parochial careers and enjoy a time of growth and consolidation.

'Towering above the Stuart age were the two decades of civil war, revolution, and republican experiment which ought to have changed fundamentally the course of English history but did so, if at all, very elusively' (History 327). The population grew rapidly and by mid-century it peaked, dropped back a little and levelled off. But there was a good deal of poverty as food-prices had soared. A decline in living standards as a result of this brought some unease to the country. Late in the century this changed; the population was more stable, agricultural production improved. 'Almost all the ideas which were to transform English agriculture down to the early nineteenth century were known about 1660' (History 333).

The century saw the most serious emigration from England; many went to the West Indies, some went to Virginia and Catholic Maryland, and some to Puritan New England; many of these were hoping for freedom from religious persecution and to set up their own religious establishments. Many more were forcibly transported as punishment for various transgressions. Several from Catholic families fled to Europe, where they could enter religious houses. Some Protestants went to join military mercenary groups and later returned to fight in the Civil War. During the latter part of Elizabeth's reign, civil war had been looming over the uncertain succession, over the rival religious factions, over the threats from the continent. By 1620 or thereabouts, these threats had eased: the Stuarts were securely on the throne; Catholics had settled for deprived status and minimal persecution, though they suffered discriminatory taxes and charges and were denied public office. Puritan piety and zeal was widespread but accepted the essence of the Prayer Book, seeking to spiritualise the household and supplement worship. The period 1569-1642 is the longest period of domestic peace England had ever known. George Herbert died in 1633 so he was one of the rare poets and priests of that period whose life, thinking and poetry, developed in a settled time.

Poor Cabinet of Bone
George Herbert (1593-1633)
who found himself, and us, too, guilty of dust

George Herbert was born in Montgomery, Wales in 1593. He was born when the great religious trials of the end of Elizabeth's reign were beginning to calm down. He lived through a period of relative peace and died before the rush towards Civil War in England that altered the face of that country for ever. His father died when George was very young and he and his six brothers and three sisters were raised by their mother, the wonderful Magdalene, patron to, and honoured by John Donne who dedicated his 'Holy Sonnets' to her and delivered her funeral sermon. George studied at Trinity College, Cambridge. He took his degrees and was elected a major fellow of Trinity, and in 1618 was appointed Reader in Rhetoric at Cambridge, and in 1620 elected public orator. This was a special honour and, in an attempt to serve his king, Charles I, whom he saw as promoting peace and justice, he had himself elected, in 1624, to represent Montgomery in parliament. He was quickly disillusioned with parliament and appears to have suffered a period of hesitancy and confusion before he found he could serve his God better in the priesthood. In 1629, Herbert married his step-father's cousin Jane Danvers.

He took holy orders in the Church of England in 1630 and spent the rest of his life as rector in Bemerton near Salisbury. Here he preached and wrote poetry, helped rebuild the church out of his own funds and cared deeply for his parishioners. He came to be known as 'Holy Mr Herbert' around the countryside in the three years before his death of consumption, at the too-early age of forty, in 1633. Reading his poems over and over, one gets the impression that here is a man whose every thought focuses on his God, whose every mood is examined in the light of God's love, God's presence or seeming absence, a man whose every sense of failing blames the self as a being composed merely of dust, yet whose every hope is that this dust will be resurrected by a God who becomes, not a remote and angry figure, but a friend, closer than any human being can ever be. His unwavering thrust towards the love of Christ, his ordering of that love as central to his living, placed the created world in second place. But it was love, love, love, that Herbert sought, fought for, and embraced.

Anthony Thwaite called Herbert 'the chief ornament of the Anglican Church'. Elizabeth Jennings wrote: 'Almost every poem is a record of a relationship of reciprocity between God and himself' (Jennings 77). His writings were not published in his lifetime but he left them to the care of his friend and fellow parson, Nicholas Ferrar of Little Gidding, asking him to publish the poems only if he thought they might do good to 'any dejected poor soul.' He was friendly with Ferrar and this friendship moved Herbert closer to the celebration of communion. In those times the taking of communion was a rare event, perhaps only once a year; Ferrar, in his community, celebrated communion at least once a month. For Herbert, communion with the Christ became one of the deepest needs of his being and the most urgent expression of mutual love between an individual and his Creator.

W. H. Auden said of him that 'One does not get the impression from his work that the temptations of the flesh were a serious spiritual menace to him, as they were to Donne.' This, of course, we do not know but it seems clear from the poems and from his prose passages outlining the ideals he had for the parson, 'The Country Pastor', that he did attempt to keep his life in perfect order. Nor did he seem to suffer from religious doubts: in the seventeenth century very few people did. Herbert was High Anglican and the great troubles of the faith and the Civil War were yet to come so Herbert's struggles were interior ones, debating in his own heart with God and with his own human appetites. Above all the awareness was one of human frailty and hopelessness without the intervention of a loving God. Michael Schmidt says of him: 'A medieval quality, different from Donne's new scholasticism, survives in the work' (Schmidt 213). Perhaps it was this surety, this certainty and inward-gazing urge that sent Herbert's work, after an initial popularity, into such a decline that Samuel Taylor Coleridge was able to write, in his *Biographia Literaria*, that his works 'are comparatively but little known'.

George Herbert comes across, then, as someone who has worked it all out. It is he, perhaps, who best exemplifies the dangers and the successes of writing out of a generally shared store of images and references, and out of a widely accepted and understood set of beliefs. The dangers are mainly those of sermonising, banality, of repeating oneself, of speaking out of a sense of belonging to a church that has the monopoly of truth. In several of the poems, an assertive piety overcomes the poetry but may be redeemed in Herbert's wish that his work be ever exemplary and uplifting. His successes, and they are very many, come when he takes off his priestly robes, the masks of preacher, the make-up and costume of guide, and faces his God with direct intent, focusing on his own experience as suffering man face to face with a God who is undoubtedly there but fades too often behind the dust-grimed windows of the human soul. How touchingly honest these lines: 'Thou that has given so much to me, / Give one thing more, a grateful heart.' The poetry touches the sublime when Herbert shows us the drama inherent in his struggle to find love, and to accept that the love that Christ has come on earth to offer, is real and tendered to one 'guilty of dust and sin'. His Christ is a real, a human person, close to the sufferings of humanity and close to the author's heart and mind, dining with thieves, laying tables for meals, and to whom Herbert refers as 'my dear'. This at times easy intimacy is a delight in religious verse and surfaces again in Hopkins, centuries later, in both its delightful and terrible forms.

Apart from the decorum and decency of his fine verses, Herbert's ongoing appeal lies in his argument, not with God or with himself, but with an inherent 'guilt' in humankind that leads men and women inevitably to destruction. This is the 'entropy' that Teilhard de Chardin later took to its extremes; it is what Herbert calls being 'guilty of dust', and it is that phrase, and the poem in which it abides, that appears to me to help create one of the most compelling of all religious poems. Its shortness hides the depth and range of its thought and experience; its perfect form hides the deep and ongoing experience the author brings to the work. And from this, his finest poem, Herbert catches perfectly the Christian certainty that God is the initiator and sustainer of love and that it is the task of humankind to accept that love and to respond to it, in spite of sin, in spite of 'dust' and our proclivity towards failure.

And here's a passage from *The Country Parson*, not too cheerful, nor too promising: 'The Country Parson is generally sad, because he knows nothing but the Cross of Christ, his mind being defixed on it with those nails wherewith his Master was: or if he have any leisure to look off from thence, he meets continually with two most sad spectacles, Sin, and Misery; God dishonoured every day, and man afflicted.' This sense of guilt and misery leads the poet to view the earth as merely a distraction. Ecology, the need to take care of our world, was not in any way a question in the seventeenth century, at least in the first part of it; it was a time when the Protestant ethic was growing in strength and assertion, and the notion that election and concentration on scripture were all in all. Creation, then, for Herbert, was merely a stepping-stone towards the next life; as Schmidt writes, 'He looks through or beyond manifest nature towards God' (Schmidt: 213).

God's act in creating is an act of renunciation and abdication, an act of love most fully pronounced in the incarnation. In the fullness of God's vision, Christ the Son would need to suffer and die, so to enter most completely into the living, suffering and dying of human beings, thereby sharing everything and thereby, too, redeeming everything to that creating God. Simone Weil says, 'The crucifixion of God is an eternal thing.' It is not God's power, but his love, that fuels the universe, the diminution of self when he creates being nothing less than a perfect act of love. As renunciation then God is love; as might and power, in the creation of the material universe, its ongoing thrust and development and its necessary entropy and construction/destruction – his movement towards 'dust' – he remains undiminished. There exists a space therefore between God and God, between love and transcendence; it is this space that must be filled by a loving humanity. Christ stands like a beggar imploring humanity for this love. The works of love!

'God created because he was good, but the creature let itself be created because it was evil. It redeemed itself by persuading

God through endless entreaties to destroy it' (Simone Weil). In creating human beings, God gave them something unique: free will and autonomy. He created us with the freedom to accept and return, or to reject his love. For what is love if it is not given freely? Weil sees this autonomy as the great sorrow in human living because the human will is weak, it is not obedient to God as the growth of a flower is obedient to God's creating ordinance. Hence, in failing in obedience, man fails in love; he is, then, guilty of sin. If, however, man's autonomy is renounced, if it is given back to God in a free gesture of total obedience, then man becomes fully in tune with God's love in creating.

Herbert is aware of the great generosity of the creating God. Many of his poems tell of the need for man to respond to that generosity. As in the following poem where the title suggests 'reprise' of a theme, the theme of gratitude to God for what he has done for us.

The Reprisal

I have consider'd it, and find
There is no dealing with thy mighty passion:
For though I die for thee, I am behind;
My sins deserve the condemnation.

Oh make me innocent, that I
May give a disentangled state and free:
And yet thy wounds still my attempts defy,
For by thy death I die for thee.

Ah! was it not enough that thou
By thy eternal glory didst outgo me?
Couldst thou not grief's sad conquests me allow,
But in all vict'ries overthrow me?

Yet by confession will I come
Into the conquest. Though I can do nought
Against thee, in thee I will overcome
The man, who once against thee fought.

Herbert sees humanity as guilty, and deserving of punishment and death. It is the overwhelming love of God that throws humans down, suggesting both the paucity of our response, and

the generosity of that same God that gives some hope. He begins his prose treatise, *The Country Pastor*, by saying: 'A Pastor is
the Deputy of Christ for the reducing of Man to the Obedience
of God.' It is this failure in obedience that brings man to sin. R. S.
Thomas says of Herbert's own and frequent illnesses: 'In fact
Herbert like a good Anglican equates sickness with sin, and
good health with holiness, believing implicitly in God's power
to heal, if it be also his will'.

In the poem 'Man's Medley', Herbert writes:

Hark, how the birds do sing,
And woods do ring.
All creatures have their joy: and man hath his.
Yet if we rightly measure,
Man's joy and pleasure
Rather hereafter, than in present, is.

This is clear enough in determining the value Herbert placed
on earthly things. This view was, up to quite recent times, the
'valley of tears' view, that we must pass cautiously through the
world in order to arrive at the next world, hacking our way
through the briars and thick brush of temptation and sin. It was
not, indeed, that this world did not offer its attractions, and that
Herbert found the restrictions of his labouring towards the love
of Christ burdensome. The finest achievements of this poet are
those where he makes a mini-drama of his struggle with himself, with his willing himself towards love. He enjoyed food and
wine before he placed such restraints upon himself; he has determined to fling off his ties and bands and walk free through
the world, yet one whisper of love from his Christ, and he is
won back to his sacred calling.

The Collar

I Struck the board, and cried No more.
I will abroad.
What? shall I ever sigh and pine?
My lines and life are free; free as the rode,
Loose as the winde, as large as store.
Shall I be still in suit?
Have I no harvest but a thorn

To let me bloud, and not restore
What I have lost with cordiall fruit?
Sure there was wine
Before my sighs did drie it: there was corn
Before my tears did drown it.
Is the yeare onely lost to me?
Have I no bayes to crown it?
No flowers, no garlands gay? all blasted?
All wasted?
Not so, my heart: but there is fruit,
And thou hast hands.
Recover all thy sigh-blown age
On double pleasures: leave thy cold dispute
Of what is fit, and not. Forsake thy cage,
Thy rope of sands,
Which pettie thoughts have made, and made to thee
Good cable, to enforce and draw,
And be thy law,
While thou didst wink and wouldst not see.
Away; take heed:
I will abroad.
Call in thy deaths head there: tie up thy fears.
He that forbears
To suit and serve his need,
Deserves his load.
But as I rav'd and grew more fierce and wilde
At every word,
Me thoughts I heard one calling, Childe:
And I reply'd, My Lord.

Herbert wrote out of the wide meadow of tradition, but his
grasp of it was imaginative, each poem carefully wrought, well-
proportioned, and finely structured. This very structuring into
carefully crafted forms fitting each individual poem, echoes in
itself an ordering imagination that works out of surety and the
delights of constraint; some poems are didactic, arguments with
others, but the best are interior arguments with self and not on
doubts but on self-doubt. Those poems, like 'Love', which are
fully achieved, have about them a sense of the special love of

Christ for the soul in their very many song-like qualities. If
Aaron was the great high priest of the early books of the Old
Testament, Herbert would wish himself, as a priest of the Lord,
to emulate that holy man. But how is he to do that? Here again
we see the centrality of Christ to Herbert, and not only that but
the human need to be absorbed by the freely-given and overwhelming love of that Lord. The first stanza outlines the ideals
for priesthood, the second shows his own unworthiness; yet he
has Christ, and by dressing himself in the love of Christ, he becomes more worthy.

Aaron

Holiness on the head,
Light and perfection on the breast,
Harmonious bells below raising the dead
To lead them unto life and rest.
Thus are true Aarons drest.

Profaneness in my head,
Defects and darkness in my breast,
A noise of passions ringing me for dead
Unto a place where is no rest:
Poor priest! thus am I drest.

Only another head
I have another heart and breast,
Another music, making live, not dead,
Without whom I could have no rest:
In Him I am well drest.

Christ is my only head,
My alone only heart and breast,
My only music, striking me e'en dead;
That to the old man I may rest,
And be in Him new drest.

So holy in my Head,
Perfect and light in my dear Breast,
My doctrine tuned by Christ (who is not dead,
But lives in me while I do rest),
Come, people; Aaron's drest.

Herbert knew, then, a lifelong struggle to subject his will to that of his Lord. There are moments of rebellion, periods of doubt, times of deadness. During all of this he strove to keep his life conscious of God. Always aware of priesthood, its demands, its graces, he saw the world as offering a sacramental view of living:

Man

For us the winds do blow,
The earth doth rest, heav'n move, and fountains flow.
Nothing we see but means our good,
As our delight, or as our treasure;
The whole is either our cupboard of food,
Or cabinet of pleasure.

The stars have us to bed;
Night draws the curtain, which the sun withdraws;
Music and light attend our head;
All things unto our flesh are kind
In their descent and being; to our mind
In their ascent and cause.

Each thing is full of duty;
Waters united are our navigation;
Distinguished, our habitation;
Below, our drink; above, our meat;
Both are our cleanliness. Hath one such beauty?
Then how are all things neat!

More servants wait on man
Than he'll take notice of; in ev'ry path
He treads down that which doth befriend him,
When sickness makes him pale and wan.
Oh mighty love! Man is one world, and hath
Another to attend him.

Since then, my God, thou hast
So brave a palace built, O dwell in it,
That it may dwell with thee at last!
Till then, afford us so much wit,
That, as the world serves us, we may serve thee,
And both thy servants be.

This view of the world has greatly altered and yet, in many aspects, the deepest value of such a view has been preserved. 'The cross-bias in Herbert's life was his smouldering love for God, and his commitment to ambition and worldly pleasures. It was in the tension between worldly honours and the disciple-ship of the humble Christ that the poems were forged' (Scott: 53). 'The love that Herbert writes about, and what he would have understood by the word, from the Christian teaching he ab-sorbed, would have been firmly based on the idea that love is something which comes from God, and has been shown us most vividly and instructively in the life of Jesus' (Scott: 57). As an Anglican minister he revelled in the certainty that his church then enjoyed; he did not live to see the destruction of that cer-tainty. As David Scott writes: 'Anglican spirituality is tied by its roots to the earth of the regular sacrament. There, in the experi-ence of the church, the divine and human meet. Christ becomes a reality among us. In it we are taken by the hand to heaven' (Scott: 61). For Herbert, too, the Christ was most closely to be met in the sacrament of communion. It is here that mankind shares most fully in the life of God. 'Bread becomes body, wine becomes blood, God becomes human and humanity is drawn up into participation in God' (Scott: 61).

The Agony

Philosophers have measur'd mountains,
Fathom'd the depths of the seas, of states, and kings,
Walk'd with a staff to heav'n, and traced fountains:
But there are two vast, spacious things,
The which to measure it doth more behove:
Yet few there are that sound them; Sin and Love.

Who would know Sin, let him repair
Unto mount Olivet; there shall he see
A man so wrung with pains, that all his hair,
His skin, his garments bloody be.
Sin is that press and vice, which forceth pain
To hunt his cruel food through ev'ry vein.

Who knows not Love, let him assay

And taste that juice, which on the cross a pike
Did set again abroach, then let him say
If ever he did taste the like.
Love is that liquor sweet and most divine,
Which my God feels as blood; but I, as wine.

There is, then, the question of dust! In the poem 'Easter',
speaking to his own heart that it should sing the Lord's praise he
says:

That, as his death calcined thee to dust,
His life may make thee gold, and much more just.

Christ's death is seen as burning down to ashes the heart of
man, yet out of these ashes, this dust, gold may be retrieved. The
natural progress of man, then, is to die, as Jesus did, to become
dust, but because of Jesus's resurrection, dust is no longer the
final end of man's life. In 'Easter Wings' mankind is seen as
'Decaying more and more'; if, however, a human being can
grow in harmony with the Christ, and rise in praise at his resurrection, then the impetus towards destruction can become its
opposite through grace. 'Then shall the fall further the flight in
me.' For this reason, when Herbert uses the word 'dust' at the
end of a line, seeking a rhyme, he will most often use the word
'trust'. The opposite seems true, also; when the sense of sin pre-
vails, then he will rhyme 'dust' with 'lust' which often takes the
place, in Herbert's language, of the generic term 'sin'. He will
see 'sicknesses and shame' as God's punishment for sin, and in
this case being guilty of dust and guilty of sin are close aligned:
yet, turning to God again a similar line will prevail: 'Affliction
shall advance the flight in me.' Previews of Hopkins in all of
this!

The way towards trust is to go with the will of God; 'Let me
be soft and supple to thy will.' In a poem called 'Holy Baptism'
Herbert writes:

The growth of flesh is but a blister,
    Childhood is health.

Apart from its possible influence on the thinking of Henry

Vaughan, this too shows how closely Herbert equated physical and spiritual well-being. All through the poetry it is the undeserved love Christ offers the soul that carries the soul through to eternal life: the individual, without God's grace, cannot succeed. A human being's natural inclination is to 'die, or fight, or travel, or deny'; man's heart is naturally filled with 'venom':

> Oh smooth my rugged heart, and there
> Engrave thy rev'rend law and fear;
> Or make a new one, since the old
>   Is sapless grown,
>   And a much fitter stone
> To hide my dust, than thee to hold.

In the poem 'Sin', he outlines the ways and means God has devised to guide the soul, from the care of parents, through the methods the church herself employs, to angels and grace: 'Yet all these fences, and their whole array/One cunning bosom-sin blows quite away'. One cunning bosom-sin! For Herbert, a man properly ordered in every aspect of his life, from his health, through his manner of dress, to his reverent approach to God in prayer, has the greatest hope of countering the disorder of sin and dust.

Prayer

> Prayer the Church's banquet, Angels' age,
> God's breath in man returning to his birth,
> The soul in paraphrase, heart in pilgrimage,
> The Christian plummet sounding heav'n and earth;
>
> Engine against th'Almighty, sinners' tower,
> Reversed thunder, Christ-side-piercing spear,
> The six-days world transposing in an hour,
> A kind of tune, which all things hear and fear;
>
> Softness, and peace, and joy, and love, and bliss,
> Exalted Manna, gladness of the best,
> Heaven in ordinary, man well drest,
> The milky way, the bird of Paradise,
>
> Church-bells beyond the stars heard, the soul's blood,
> The land of spices, something understood.

It is the sense of undeserved grace, the awareness of God's freely offered and unconditional love that touches Herbert to the core. Can man's response, in spite of his sin, in spite of his thundering towards dust, be to love in return? And what kind of love is that to be? In the poem 'Christmas' Herbert speaks of Christ as 'my dear'. In the poem 'Love' (I) he contrasts Love with 'that dust which thou hast made'. God made the great universe out of love, humankind has offered this 'dust' its love, giving to the creation what it should give to the creator. In 'Love' (II), if Immortal Love is Heat, this poem develops the image of love as fire; if we are consumed then 'Our eyes shall see thee, which before saw dust'. Both these sonnets in some form contrast God's great creating impulse out of love with man's offering his love to the material side of creation; man, being 'a crumb of dust' ('The Temper') offers his love to dust, instead of to Love himself. While the soul is at its devotions, the flesh is in close proximity to tombs in the poem called 'Church Monuments'; 'that it betimes / May take acquaintance of this heap of dust', to which 'school' all will at last be driven. Here the earth itself is seen merely as a monument to 'death's incessant motion',

> Which dissolution sure death best discern,
> Comparing dust with dust, and earth with earth.

This view of God's blessed creation is one that must, in later years, lead to the destruction of our world. The great duty of our own times is to bring this created 'dust' back into its original harmony with the Creator and with humankind who were created to take care of this world, a world the God, out of his overwhelming love, entrusted to our love.

We all share, then, in this good fellowship of dust. By acquainting the body, through the mind's urgings, with its inevitable end, 'thou mayest know / That flesh is but the glass, which holds the dust, / That measures all our time; which also shall / Be crumbled into dust'. The image of the hourglass here is the perfect one for de Chardin's idea of 'entropy'. Twice in this poem the word 'dust' is made to rhyme with 'trust'; in the final stanza it rhymes again, this time with 'lust'. In several other poems these same rhymes recur; as already noted, it is when the emphasis is on man's sinfulness then it will rhyme with lust; when, however, there is hope in the Christ's redeeming powers, the word will rhyme with 'trust'.

Virtue

Sweet day, so cool, so calm, so bright,
The bridal of the earth and sky:
The dew shall weep thy fall tonight;
    For thou must die.

Sweet rose, whose hue angry and brave
Bids the rash gazer wipe his eye:
Thy root is ever in its grave,
    And thou must die.

Sweet spring, full of sweet days and roses,
A box where sweets compacted lie;
My music shows ye have your closes,
    And all must die.

Only a sweet and virtuous soul,
Like season'd timber, never gives;
But though the whole world turn to coal,
    Then chiefly lives.

Here the word 'coal' must be seen as cinders, ashes, dust. The poem is itself a full disclosure of how we are 'guilty of dust'. The guilt comes because we have turned our love to the created thing and not the creator. All of this is subsumed in Simone Weil's consciousness of the human condition though here it is expressed instinctively and with different emphases. If Weil's sense is of the difference of God and of man's inadequacies, how the human must move away from self into 'decreation', Herbert indeed urges man, himself, to come closer in affection and love to Christ, the great Lover. So many poems begin as familiar conversations or have lines within them that speak directly to God as a close, a very close, friend: 'My love, my sweetness, hear!'; 'My God, I read this day ...' 'Ah my dear angry Lord ...' 'My God, if writings may ...' This easy confidence in the presence of his God underlines Herbert's sense of God as love, Love, close and concerned. 'Oh my Redeemer dear,/After all this canst thou be strange?' In the great poem to which I have been leading, all of these movements and ideas come together in overwhelming, yet simple majesty, a simplicity and directness that Simone Weil herself must have treasured. Humanity is guilty, of dust and of sin, yet it is God's very urging that insists that the response of humanity, even under such drawbacks, must be love, an un-guilty love.

George Herbert, then, is central to the view, in poetry as well as in his faith practice, that Christ is the focus of our hope and our living in the world, although his stress on that focus turns towards heaven, bypassing – while not despising – the world of God's creation. Christ is in the heart and in the will and the sensual world must be relentlessly held under control.

An addendum: Jesus 'sat down and dined' with sinners, with the outcast of Jewish society, with beggars, the poor, the crippled, the blind, the lame, with the despised and ostracised, the tax collectors, the prostitutes. He entertained sinners in his home, and was entertained by them. There is the rich parable of the wedding feast to which the wealthy refused to come; it may well have been a distinct memory from Jesus's own life, knowing they would not come because the outcast might also be there. There is the story of Jesus inviting himself to the home of Zacchaeus, the tax collector, the most maligned of them all. This dining with sinners set Jesus apart at once and showed how God himself forgave sinners, indeed went further and sought them out. The invitation to sup with Christ, then, is a very special one, relevant as background to this most dramatic poem of Herbert's, relevant, too, to all those invitations to the table of the Lord that Christians of all denominations are party to. Down all the ages, this inviting of the poor and sinners to one's table has been and remains a very uncommon thing; no doubt it was so in Herbert's time, too. The more unusual the invitation, the more powerful looms this poem.

Love

Love bade me welcome, yet my soul drew back,
    Guilty of dust and sin.
But quick-ey'd Love, observing me grow slack
    From my first entrance in,
Drew nearer to me, sweetly questioning,
    If I lack'd anything.

A guest, I answer'd, worthy to be here.
    Love said, You shall be he.
I the unkind, ungrateful? Ah my dear,
    I cannot look on thee.
Love took my hand, and smiling did reply,
    Who made the eyes but I?

Truth Lord, but I have marr'd them: let my shame
    Go where it doth deserve.
And know you not, says Love, who bore the blame?
    My dear, then I will serve.
You must sit down, says Love, and taste my meat:
    So I did sit and eat.

It is wonderful how Herbert reached such a firm sense of the overwhelming love and closeness of God. The sense of sin and unworthiness, of the human distancing from God, had been great for centuries, shown in the development of eucharistic trends. 'By the fourth century bread intended for eucharistic worship was often stamped, marked, or shaped in a particular way, setting it apart from ordinary table fare' (Foley 166). The moving of the altar behind a screen, keeping the common laity out, was a strong development, the people seeing themselves as 'unworthy', either to receive communion or to bring gifts to the offertory. 'After the ninth century there is a significant shift in the recipe for eucharistic bread, with unleavened bread becoming customary and eventually mandatory in the Christian West' (Foley 166/7); this served to remind people of Christ's actual bread during the Passover feast, but also removed communion even further from the people. Communion, when given, was given on the tongue, a further distancing, and 'Drinking through a tube (of the consecrated wine) replaced drinking from the cup, and eventually the cup was completely withdrawn from the laity' (Foley 171). Herbert, in his great writing towards the clarification and demonstration of God's overwhelming love for humankind, brought Eucharist closer to the grasp of human hope and longing.

The Pandy-Bat

There were no poems by George Herbert on any course in Mungret College. Indeed, during my five years of struggle in that institution, I gathered no care for, or true awareness of, poetry. I was in a continual state of mute rebellion, doing the minimum of work, getting away with whatever pieces of mischief I could devise. Once or twice I escaped, with two other rebels, and thumbed a lift into Limerick city where I could go and see a movie, eat liquorice allsorts, peppermint creams, read the newest editions of the comics, and slip back into college before evening study when we all had our given places in the large Study Hall. I just about got away with it though two or three times I was caught *flagrante delicto* and, but for the fact that my elder brother, Declan, had been working his way through the college some two years ahead of me and leaving a trail of academic and behavioural distinction behind him, and more! he was fully expected to (and eventually did) head for Emo and the Jesuit novitiate, I would have been dumped out of college without ceremony, without references, without my Leaving Certificate.

In that way I laboured long and hard through my years under the remote shadow of St Ignatius, through Elements and Rudiments which, being then enthusiastic and innocent, I put together into one year, *summa cum laude*, through Grammar, Rhetoric and the other classically named rooms that led one through to Leaving Certificate.

One of the Jesuits, a small priest, cold and distant, many of us took a fierce dislike to. He walked the corridors and the grounds of the college, hands thrust into the pockets of his soutane, his eyes watching greedily for 'someone to devour'; we knew he delighted in the use of the pandy-bat, that punishment machine made of lengths of leather stitched together, that fitted neatly into the inside pocket of that same soutane. We baited him.

In my next-to-final year in Mungret College, things came to a head between this tightly-clenched priest and us, his unwilling pupils, his suffering subjects. For some small misdemeanor by some boys – smoking in the toilets, perhaps, or was it sneaking out to the playing-fields one evening for a game of poker? – our priest had banned the entire college from heading into town on one of the 'play-days', a feastday, 3 December, the holiday of the great Jesuit martyr, Francis Xavier. We had to hang about the corridors all day, mumbling, morose, our mood darkening as the day darkened. But we planned our revenge.

I will call him Fr Pandy Bat, for ease of writing. He was in charge of one of the big dormitories, fifth year and sixth years combined. He had his own room off the dormitory, up at the top end, a green curtain drawn back before the door. We had our in-dividual cubicles, divided into units by three wooden parti-tions, the opening with a curtain that could be drawn over for privacy. We each had our enamel basin and enamel jug for washing. Lights out, night prayers said, our lost day buzzing like wasps still about our ears, we kept ourselves awake, listen-ing, waiting. When at last Fr Pandy Bat ceased prowling about the dormitory and we heard the door of his own room open and close quietly after him, we began to count: fifteen minutes pre-cisely, to allow him time to get into his pyjamas and get to his own bed.

The fifteen minutes up, one of the boys shouted the com-mand: 'War!' and we began. Curtains closed over the cubicles we began to bang our enamel basins against the wooden parti-tions, bang the enamel jugs against the enamel basins, fling water from the jugs up into the air, over the curtain and out onto the open spaces of the dormitory. The noise was magnificent! the noise of battle, the clamour of war. And we carried on, re-lentlessly, with our crashing and clashing and banging, for at least five, maybe even ten minutes. One thing, however, we had forgotten, namely that we would not hear, through the noise of battle, the door of Fr Pandy Bat's room open, nor the patter of the priest's slippered feet as he set out to discover and name the culprits. We forged ahead, shaking the welkin, shattering the night until, quite suddenly, all the lights in the dormitory were switched on. Silence fell, at once. Fr Pandy Bat called out that all the curtains were to be opened and he would come around and speak with us.

He did. He had a list of names. Some twenty of us he had

chosen for exemplary punishment. I was one of the chosen. We were lined up, in our pyjamas, outside the green curtain of Fr Pandy Bat's door. He drew aside the curtain, opened the door of his room, beckoned the first boy inside. We heard the awful slap of the leather down on the pyjama'ed flesh of the buttocks of the first boy, four terrible thumps, a pause, another four. Eight severe slaps on the bottom. Unheard-of punishment. One by one we were brought in, one by one we had to bend down over a large travelling chest in that room, one by one we suffered the indignity and pain brought to us by that piece of leather. One by one we came back out and made our way to our cubicles, and not one of us was able to hold back the tears of pain and humiliation. Fr Pandy Bat may have worn himself stupid with his lifting and falling of leather, but we, rebels and miscreants, spent a long time in our beds, suffering real pain, eventually crying ourselves into some sort of unrestful sleep.

About a month after that Fr Pandy Bat left the college. I never heard of him again. But our victory, if that is what it was, left a hollowness in me that summed up all my weary time in boarding school, far from home, far from the spaces and places I loved so well.

At the end of each term, urgent to get the hell out of there and home to Achill, we all sang the *Te Deum* with enormous gusto. Apart from morning Mass which I attended in a semi-comatose state at 7.30 every morning, apart from rosary which was rushed through at about 2.30 every afternoon, religious matters passed me by as surely as lessons in algebra and trigonometry left me utterly indifferent. All in all, I missed God's beautiful world of outdoor things, the air, the sea, the sky, the rivers and when I got home on holidays I often meandered down along the small river in Cashel, from its source in the low hills to its broadening out into the sea.

Riverdown

It begins somewhere high in the hills, somewhere impossible to pinpoint with complete accuracy, the way the soul begins, perhaps, the way hope might begin, or faith. There must be a source, a wellspring, fed with the many rains that come in off the Atlantic and cross the island like spirits on some great migration. It begins as little more than a dribble out of peatlands, out of innocent places, marshy hollows, from under the high mist-clouds that take over these heather uplands where sheep shrug out shelters for themselves against bogbanks and cower low from the winds that pass through all the way from the frozen wastes thousands of miles away. The water comes to trickle out of mossy places, under the secret tracks of foxes and the rending-places of the hooded crow. Slowly it gathers, forging its tiny gorge, invisible at first, then gurgling so that you can hear it, like a presence somewhere in the darkness of night, and then it is found making its way down towards the white-washed gable-ends of outhouses.

It becomes a stream, almost before you are aware of it, where wheatears thrive along its margins and little golden eels find their living in it, hiding under half-buried stones and in under the dripping banks. It swells, the way a young life swells, garnering strength and a little pride in itself. Until it touches one of the old roads, manmade and inhibiting, where a bridge is built, where a child can crouch and hide, touch the flaking masonry of the underarch, be lonely and at peace, listening to the occasional car passing over. It is a place to listen to the small murmurings of the stream, to the jittering calls of the wren; it is a place, solitary there under the bridge, to stay for ever, perfect, useless, desire stilled. A place, too, where a child can drop a tiny stick on one side of the bridge and run to watch it emerge on the other side, can know a small triumph, the learning of the forces that make this earth of ours continue on its way, a triumph as if a victory has been won, as if a three-masted schooner has been launched, successfully, into the flow.

But the stream moves on, without waiting; it moves through

more human sounds, by the edges of a village, through cultivated
fields, deepening all the time, the landscape flattening out and
becoming dull, the river, for now it is a river, deepening betimes
to a pool where small brown trout hold their bodies against the
flow. Now it is time for the wandering child, absent from the
real flurries of what too many people call the real world, to stop
and hear the distant bell from the monastery call out Angelus,
announce noon, the turning point, the angel-mystery where, in
the time of man's believing, a small genuflection would be made
and people would touch their knee, humbly, to the sustaining
earth. Now the afternoon takes on its own breadth and greyness, all the rivers of the world flow down into the sea and yet
the sea will not overflow. Admire, here, by the river that works
to be called majestic, the beautiful bog-iris, the furze-bush blos-
somings, the rushes thriving in the marsh acres; now and then a
donkey brays, or cows plash into muddying water. Nearer the
sea there are houses, some old and rickety in the winds, some
squat and new and scarcely lived in; dogs bark, and you are
forced to climb out of the river's way into someone's meadow.
Your pilgrimage down from high places has begun to weary
you, because the pleasure has been in the travelling and now the
tide has reached upriver, turning the world to slobland with its
stench of decay, its mud-bubbles, mullet sluppering in the shallows and your spring has vanished into sea-rot. Still, you have
grown knowledgeable, something has been achieved, you gather yourself still for the ongoing endeavour, you hold onto your
longing that you will yet find the centre and source, the life-
force, the mystery, home.

Old Testament, the Covenant

A broadening of moral vision is part, and an essential part, of a developing humanity and, in our disjointed and distracted age, such a broadening and strengthening is essential; '... it seems that humanity progresses to truth through a process of trial and error, a process that is going on within the pages of scripture as well' (Duffy 105). Joseph O'Leary has written: 'Biblical triumphalism is at the root of the evils of sectarianism that have blighted Christian history' (Duffy 104). For so long, Christians were discouraged from reading the Old Testament and in sixteenth century England, so many Christians were burned to death because they dared to read the Bible in the vernacular. So, fear and misunderstanding attended the study of the Old Testament when it was actually read. It is essential to realise that the authors of the individual texts of the Old Testament were writing out of the very primitive conditions in which they lived, and from the undeveloped viewpoint of the society they moved through. 'The Bible is a record of growth in the understanding of God from a primitive beginning, but the continuation of that growth depends on our own mature and responsible reading of the Bible' (Duffy 112). It is important to beware of traditionalism and absolutism.

In simple terms, Christians have been distraught by the violence of Exodus, for example, by the story of the 'Passover' when God struck down the firstborn of the Egyptians, human and animal: 'At midnight the Lord struck down all the firstborn in the land of Egypt, from the firstborn of Pharaoh who sat on his throne to the firstborn of the prisoner who was in the dungeon, and all the firstborn of the livestock' (Exodus 12:29). When the Israelites crossed through the Red Sea and the Egyptians followed, the Lord closed up the sea again: 'The waters returned and covered the chariots and the chariot drivers, the entire army of Pharaoh that had followed them into the sea; not one of them remained' (Exodus 14:28). But there was worse than this, worse than the innocent of the Passover being slain, worse than a whole army being wiped out, and most cruel and dastardly deeds abound throughout those early books. For instance, in Judges: 'Abimelech was told that all the lords of the Tower of Shechem were gathered together. So Abimelech went up to Mount Zalmon, he and all the troops that were with him. Abimelech took an axe in his hand, cut down a bundle of brushwood, and took it up and laid it on his shoulder. Then he said to the troops with him, 'What you have seen me do, do quickly, as I have done'. So every one of the troops cut down a bundle and following Abimelech put it against the stronghold, and they set the stronghold on fire over them, so that all the people of the Tower of Shechem also died, about a thousand men and women.'

Literature is the expression of the spirit of a nation; the books of the Bible are like an anthology of the literature of Israel in its pilgrimage to find a lasting dwelling-place and a home for worship of their God. The books are written in different ages, from the most primitive to the time of Christ. Many of the books of the Old Testament are poems, an individual's response to the circumstances of his times, some of them, as with David, the work of one man facing his God. But these are poems that make demands on our lives; the works of Herbert, Hopkins, Marvell, are poems, but do not make such demands. And the words that make demands on our lives come from the original Covenant between God and humankind.

'In the beginning ...' As God created he looked at what was done and 'saw that it was good'. And on the sixth day God created humankind; 'and let them have dominion over the fish of the sea, and over the birds of the air, and over the cattle, and over all the wild animals of the earth, and over every creeping thing that creeps upon the earth' (Genesis 1:26). 'And God saw everything that he had made, and indeed, it was very good' (Genesis 1:31). And on the seventh day, on the Sabbath, God rested. Genesis is a cosmic covenant between God and all living creatures. God placed humankind in the 'garden' to till it and to keep it. What humankind, in its breaking the agreement to take care of the earth, has for so long forgotten, is that 'the creative response of the earth to God's will and Word is one that is participatory in the creative process – in other words, it is empowered by God to act in an intermediary way in order to bring

forth particular creatures' (Deane-Drummond 87) so, the whole
of creation and not just humankind, participates in evolution
and 'it also suggests that non-human life from the beginning
participates with the divine in creativity' (Deane-Drummond
87). This goes much further than a belief in human 'stewardship'; humanity is a participator in creation, alongside created
things, part of evolution, part of creation and a partner in creation. 'Creation itself is seen as bringing order out of chaos –
pushing back the wilderness and creating a garden. God himself takes delight in the garden. In Gen 3:8 he walks in the garden at the time of the evening breeze' (Care 121).

Humanity broke the agreement almost at once. The first 'sin'
was to disobey God's command to leave the 'fruit of knowledge' on the bough of the tree. And in no time, after breaking
that covenant, one man killed another, Cain destroying Abel,
and setting humankind on its awful and difficult journey back
towards love. 'Just as faithfulness to the Covenant or walking in
the way of the Lord brings about order and harmony between
people and in the cosmos itself, sin destroys the human friendship with the Divine, induces human misery and brings about
cosmic chaos' (Care 125). It is the myth of the human journey,
the 'garden' an image of the possible perfection of humankind,
the 'sin' the inherent negativity in human living, the 'entropy',
and the death of Abel the propensity of humankind towards violence and murder. This journey, through the Old Testament, brings
humanity to its one great hope, the birth of Christ, the incarnation.
Of ourselves, humanity would be incapable of saving the covenant,
of renewing the agreement between earth, human beings, and God.
'Salvation involves the total human and earth reality and thus it has
a social, political, economic, ecological as well as an other-worldly
dimension' (Care 126). Paul sees Christ as reconciling the whole
universe: 'He is the head of the body, the church; he is the beginning, the firstborn from the dead, so that he might come to have
first place in everything. For in him all the fullness of God was
pleased to dwell, and through him God was pleased to reconcile
to himself all things, whether on earth or in heaven, by making
peace through the blood of his cross' (Colossians 1:20). Hence:
'The Redemption of the human body and the redemption of the
universe are bound together' (Care 128).

Back to the unutterable violence of those early times. Take Chapter 6 of Joshua and the taking and destruction of Jericho; after the walls came tumbling down 'they devoted to destruction by the edge of the sword all in the city, both men and women, young and old, oxen, sheep, and donkeys'. And then 'they burned down the city, and everything in it'. The chapter ends, 'So the Lord was with Joshua; and his fame was in all the land.' Primitive values indeed, but part of the ongoing covenant between humans and God, a covenant that had to be renewed over and over because of the defection of the humans. So Joshua has to renew the covenant once more; in chapter 24: 'Then Joshua said to the people, 'You are witnesses against yourselves that you have chosen the Lord, to serve him,' and they said, 'We are witnesses'. So Joshua made a covenant with the people that day, and made statutes and ordinances for them at Shechem. Joshua wrote these words in the book of the law of God; and he took a large stone, and set it up there under the oak in the sanctuary of the Lord. Joshua said to all the people, 'See, this stone shall be a witness against us; for it has heard all the words of the Lord that he spoke to us; therefore it shall be a witness against you, if you deal falsely with your God.' So once again, an agreement has been made, a testament renewed, a covenant re-registered. It is the image of humanity calling itself to attention, to the wrong turns made on the great journey.

There had been a major breakdown already, long after Adam and Eve had messed up on the first covenant. Genesis 6 begins: 'When people began to multiply on the face of the ground, and daughters were born to them, the sons of God saw that they were fair; and they took wives for themselves of all that they chose'. But the Lord saw the wickedness of humankind and 'that every inclination of the thoughts of their hearts was only evil continually'. This was not the agreement, the covenant between God and humanity and God decided to wipe out his creation, saving only a pair of every kind of living thing. After the flood, however, when Noah offered a pleasing sacrifice to God, the covenant was renewed. Chapter 9 of Genesis tells how 'God said to Noah and to his sons with him, 'As for me, I am establishing my covenant with you and your descendants after you, and with every living creature that is with you, the birds, the domestic animals, and every animal of the earth with you, as many as came out of the ark. When I bring clouds over the earth and the bow is seen in the clouds, I will remember my covenant that is between me and you and every living creature of all flesh that is on the earth.' The covenant restored, then, is not just between God and humankind, but between God and humankind and all creation.

Therefore Luke in chapter 12 of his gospel, has Jesus say: 'Are not five sparrows sold for two pennies? Yet not one of them is forgotten in God's sight.' The relationship of humanity to God, then, extends far beyond the merely human to the whole of God's creation. 'Christianity is a message of life, a message based on the gratuitous love of the Father for us' (Gutierrez 1), and this love is to be reciprocated, not just between humans and the Father, but between all of creation and the Father. If the non-human praises God by its very existence, and cannot but do so, it is humankind that loves consciously and willingly and that offers a voice and a will on behalf of all of creation. The wanton destruction and carelessness of humanity towards the earth is therefore utterly reprehensible, and is to be deemed sinful.

In Thomas Gray's 'Elegy Written in a Country Churchyard' there is this stanza:

Full many a gem of purest ray serene
The dark unfathom'd caves of ocean bear:
Full many a flower is born to blush unseen,
And waste its sweetness on the desert air.

There is a presumption here that creation exists for the delight of man, and that whatever is not available to humankind 'wastes its sweetness'. Perhaps the truth is that the whole of creation is of value in and of itself, whether or not a human is by to witness it.

Here, then, for the first time and not the last, is the focal text from St Paul that brings home to us the importance of that original covenant between God and creation: it is in Romans, chapter 8: 'I consider that the sufferings of the present time are not worth comparing with the glory about to be revealed to us. For the creation waits with eager longing for the revealing of the children of God; for the creation was subjected to futility, not of its own will but by the will of the one who subjected it, in hope that the creation itself will be set free from its bondage to decay and will obtain the freedom of the glory of the children of God. We know that the whole creation has been groaning in labour pains until now; and not only the creation, but we ourselves, who have the first fruits of the Spirit, groan inwardly while we wait for adoption, the redemption of our bodies.'

The second half of the Seventeenth Century

James I was an intellectual and believed that kings were divinely appointed and only answerable to God. He often fought with his parliament and was not very wise in many of his practical decisions. He was undignified in himself and a latent homosexual whose affair with a young courtier who rose to be Duke of Buckingham did nothing for his reputation. Buckingham took over government from the ailing James who died of smallpox when his son, Charles, was just 12. Buckingham remained in control until his assassination in 1628. James had had a 'plantation policy' in Ulster, dispossessing native Irish Catholic landowners and replacing them with thousands of families from England, thus creating the roots of a conflict that would last for hundreds of years.

After George Herbert, three more poets saw out the seventeenth century with its confusion of religious and worldly beliefs: Andrew Marvell, Henry Vaughan and Thomas Traherne. Their poetry differs greatly from one to another but the questions and longings remain the same. Charles I succeeded his father in 1625, taking over fully at the death of Buckingham, and the early years of his reign were a time of relative peace for English Catholics. His French Catholic Queen consort had Catholic chaplains, religious houses and schools founded on the continent by English Catholic exiles flourished, and even for a time papal agents returned. Meanwhile the penal laws were largely held in abeyance through the king's favour and only two martyrs suffered between 1625 and 1640.

John Calvin developed and refined Reformation ideas to inspire the Puritan revolution in England under Oliver Cromwell in 1645 and the colonisation of New England in the 1620s. The Puritans were an extreme Protestant party in England, who sought further reform of the English church in accordance with Calvinist theology, and they were very hostile to Catholics. Persecution recommenced; two priests were executed in 1641 and several more in the first half of 1642 and, with the outbreak of the Civil War between king and parliament in August 1642, persecution continued under the parliament alone after the king had left London: thirteen priests put to death between August 1642 and August 1646. Of some eighty-five martyrs, six priests (including four Franciscans) suffered during the years of the Civil War, all under the Act of 1585.

'Where James was an informal, scruffy, approachable man, Charles was glacial, prudish, withdrawn, shifty' (History 354). However, he was willing to live chastely and presided over a chaste court. He pursued war weakly and between 1625 and 1630 England was at war with Spain and with France but parliament failed to supply the means to make these wars a success. In 1629 Charles I had a major confrontation with parliament over foreign policy, while parliament was feeling impotent and frustrated. This mood of confrontation did not allow any unity of purpose and in the 1630s the king ruled without parliament. He further alienated many people by his support of Archbishop William Laud whose religious ideas approached Roman Catholic beliefs and ritual, wholly anathema to strict Protestantism and the Puritan beliefs. People also believed that popery was being tolerated again, and even welcomed.

Then in 1637 Charles blundered into war with his Scots subjects and was easily outmanoeuvred, losing face and money. A parliament was called that demanded the king's compliance with its work and Civil War broke out in 1642. The massacre of some 3,000 Protestants in the North of Ireland helped rumours grow that Charles was scheming with the Irish Catholics. Parliament dreaded the king's control over the militia. So, in 1642 the country was severely divided and once again religion was playing a crucial part in the struggle. Puritan militancy rose against Archbishop Laud, there were outbreaks of popular iconoclasm, Anglicans divided against Laud and the king. The struggle lasted from 1642 to 1646, a battle at Edgehill settling nothing in October of 1642 but in 1643 it was all-out Civil War.

By late 1645 parliament was paying its troops, and the unpaid royalist armies began to fade away: 'The Civil War was won by attrition' (History 365). But parliament had established a number of committees with arbitrary powers to raise funds so that by 1648 parliament appeared more oppressive than the king. Parliament decided the new national church would be based on a new service book, 'Directory of Public Worship', new catechism, new articles of faith, all in a very Puritan spirit. Many refused to accept and began to call for liberty of conscience for themselves and a right of free religious assembly outside the national church. This was a new beginning in religious thinking and developed rapidly as people had grown tired and deeply hurt by the long and impossible religious conflicts. Above all it is the poetry of Thomas Traherne that reflected most this change, though his work did not become known until centuries after his death.

'The Puritan experiment was ineffective but added to popular hatred of an arbitrary parliament' (History 370). At this stage it was again religious notions that drove the war further; after all the sufferings of God's people it would not do to return to earlier times; one final thrust towards domination was demanded. Parliament, having no money left, was not keen to try and raise more taxes so the army now prevented parliament from surrendering. An attempt to establish a democratic state failed. So a second Civil War began, a revolt against centralisation and military rule. The army put down the revolts that sprang up and late in 1648 the war ground to a halt. A minority from the army forced parliament to arraign the king who was tried in 1649 and he was beheaded in public, suffering his death with the dignity becoming a martyr. This was the first English monarch who had been executed and this, too, was anathema to the English mind. From 1649 to 1660 England attempted to be a republic. Monarchy was abolished as well as the House of Lords and the Anglican Church as the main national faith. From 1649 to 1653 a 'Rump Parliament' governed, selling crown and church lands to raise funds, and also former royalist lands to finance Cromwell's violent conquest of Ireland.

John Milton, poet, wrote tracts on behalf of the Puritan and parliamentary cause and attacking the high-church leanings of Archbishop Laud and the Church of England; after the Civil War he wrote in defence of the republic, implicitly endorsing the execution of Charles I. He was made 'Secretary for Foreign Tongues' in 1649. In a further tract he praised Oliver Cromwell, urging him to remain true to the 'revolution'. The gradual onset of blindness forced Milton to dictate further work to secretaries, one of whom was Andrew Marvell. After the Restoration Milton had to go into hiding, a warrant having been issued for his arrest. But he was arrested and imprisoned and was in great danger until his influential friends, including Marvell, helped to have him released. In 1658 he had begun the great work of 'Paradise Lost'; he was deeply disappointed at the failure of the revolution, at the certainty that the kingdom of heaven was not to be found on English soil, and he now felt there was a need 'to justify the ways of God to men'. Later he followed this with the flat, unprepossessing tomes of 'Paradise Regained', a somewhat dispirited attempt to show how someone like Job can resist all the temptations of Satan and remain true to God.

By 1653 Oliver Cromwell, commander of the army, demanded further reform. Cromwell was a convinced Calvinist, seeing himself as a second Moses who would lead his people to a new, promised land. Many people rallied to his side, too many of them believing that Cromwell was the John-the-Baptist forerunner to the new Eden, the final Revelation when England would be the green and fertile land of the heavenly kingdom. Cromwell called an 'assembly of saints', hand-picked men who thought as he did to morally regenerate the people and to bring God back. Cromwell took power into his own hands and the army became responsible for government. He ruled as Lord Protector until his death in September 1658, a death that threw his supporters into despair and a distress that, after all, the Promised Land was not about to appear. A great number of people threw up their hands in frustration, turning away from the promises of religion to more secular concerns. With Cromwell's death the unconvinced republic faded out. In 1660 Charles II was restored to the throne and was declared to have reigned since his father's death, as if there had been no interregnum. Charles II set out to restore harmony and harmonies, agreeing a general Act of Indemnity and Oblivion. He tried to restore the Church of England but wished to grant freedom of religious assembly; even after all the trials, these measures towards harmony were defeated by parliament and the Puritan leaders. The Act of Uniformity was restored. Charles II was sympathetic to Catholicism and was received into the Catholic Church on his deathbed. Nothing had yet been truly resolved.

In the late 1660s Charles' younger brother James, Duke of York and heir presumptive to the throne, became a Catholic and then married the Catholic Mary of Modena in 1673. Protestants now became really alarmed at the prospect of a Catholic king in England. They were ready and willing to accept the fabrication that a Catholic conspiracy existed to assassinate Charles, put Catholic James on the throne and begin the massacre of Protestants. Titus Oates, who spread the rumour, was later convicted of perjury, flogged and sent to prison, but his allegations had caused widespread panic and the beginning of a further persecution of Catholics. Between 1678 and 1681, a bishop, several priests and brothers were executed, some of them charged with involvement in the Oates plot. Parliament tried to bar James from the throne but Charles dissolved parliament. Charles spent his last years in comparative peace and in 1685 was succeeded by James II. James was childless from a second marriage and, expecting his Protestant daughter, Mary and her Dutch husband William of Orange, to succeed him, he tried to ensure religious freedom and civil equality for Catholics. In 1688 a son and heir was born to James and the possibility of a Catholic dynasty appeared very real indeed. William was invited in to England and marched to meet James at Salisbury; James, however, became manically ill and no battle ensued. William and Mary were jointly offered the throne. 'An age which derived its momentum from Christian humanism, from chivalry, from a reverential antiquarianism, gave way to an age of pragmatism and individualism' (History 398). We are reeling away from that age yet.

An isle far kinder than our own
Andrew Marvell (1621-1678)

Marvell's life spans the reign and execution of Charles I, the Commonwealth, and the Restoration of Charles II. It appears that his innate wisdom, his gentle and gentlemanly concerns, saw him through all the difficult variations. He leaned a good deal towards Puritanism. He championed John Milton and was part cause of keeping that genius from gaol for his work with parliament. He also praised Oliver Cromwell, though not vociferously. While in university he converted, for a short while, to Catholicism; he was non-committal during the Civil War and went abroad for several years. Back in England he was well accepted amongst royalists. In 1650 he composed his 'Horatian Ode upon Cromwell's Return from Ireland'. He supported Cromwell and for a time tutored a ward of Cromwell's; he held his seat as MP until his death. He also supported the Restoration, campaigned for religious toleration, and satirised the court. The general thrust of his living is that of a reed, honest in its being, but capable of withstanding gales from whichever side they come. As a poet, he was also gentlemanly, learned, cautious and swayable.

Born in Yorkshire in 1621, Andrew Marvell's family moved to Hull where his father, the Rev Andrew Marvell, was made a lecturer in Holy Trinity Church. He studied in Trinity College, Cambridge, where he wrote poems in Latin and Greek. He received his BA in 1638 and shortly after that his mother died. In 1640 his father was drowned and Andrew left Cambridge. He travelled in Europe for several years and in 1650 became tutor to Mary Fairfax, daughter of the retired Lord General of the parliamentary forces. He appears to have done a great deal of writing at the Fairfax family home, Nun Appleton House, examining, in a poem titled 'Upon Appleton House', the claims of public versus private life. By 1653 he had become a friend of John Milton who recommended him for the post of Assistant Latin Secretary to the Council of State. Marvell joined the Cromwellian side and tutored Cromwell's nephew at Eton. For a time he saw Cromwell as a force under God's guidance, saw him 'as the harbinger of the latter days, the divinely appointed hero who is to preside over the elect nation in conformity with God's will and to prepare for the Second Coming of Christ and the Millennium of the Earthly Paradise' (David Scott, 232). Cromwell died 1658 and such hopes died with him.

After the Restoration and still in favour, Marvell was instrumental in saving Milton from an extended jail sentence, and perhaps even from execution. In 1659 Marvell was elected MP for Hull. His work, as his living, embodies the classical virtues of poise and elegance, though his overuse of 'does' and 'do' etc to fill out lines in the poems, somewhat detracts from their power. He remained an MP until his death and was deeply engaged in political activities. His poise was a European poise, the simplicity of his work being a studied effect, particularly in the poem quoted here, 'Bermudas'. Poetry as artifice keeps the ego and poetry separate from one another and Marvell's religious poems move outside and around his own being. Later generations have largely forgotten his political activities while remaining smitten by the grace of his finest lyrics. His range is wide, his sophistication notable; his imagination, from being highly introspective, turned later to satire and commentary on the foibles of his fellow humans. With Marvell, poetry in England moves into a more sophisticated stage, more highly wrought verse forms and a polished, intellectual awareness of the world. It was this polish and intellect that brought him through so many crises, the same polish and intellect that underlined his poetry. He died suddenly of a fever in 1678.

Much of Marvell's poetry is based on religious thinking, and a great deal of that still favours escape from worldly things in favour of heavenly. As yet, in English poetry, there is little awareness of creation as worth something in itself. Southwell, Herbert, now Marvell, all of them keep their eyes turned heavenward, even though the conventions for much secular poetry faced earthward, but not towards the actual earth but an imagined one of nymphs and shepherds and abstract notions of roses and cream and strawberry lips. Marvell's poetry, too, is highly

self-conscious and reads like a truly clever sermon whose ending we may foresee, but not how that ending will be achieved.
His 'dialogue poems' set up imaginary confrontations between
opposing notions; it is a form conventional for the time, in alter-
nating stanzas, creating a vaguely dramatic atmosphere, loosely
reminiscent of medieval Morality Plays. As in those plays, the
outcome is already known, as is the debate between Body and
Soul, and 'A Dialogue Between the Resolved Soul and Created
Pleasure'; the Soul, setting out as 'resolved', will undoubtedly
win the vote over 'created pleasure'. There is no contest.

'Bermudas' is something else entirely!

Bermudas

Where the remote Bermudas ride
In th'ocean's bosom unespied,
From a small boat, that rowed along,
The listening winds received this song.
'What should we do but sing his praise
That led us through the watery maze,
Unto an isle so long unknown,
And yet far kinder than our own?
Where he the huge sea-monsters wracks,
That lift the deep upon their backs,
He lands us on a grassy stage,
Safe from the storms, and prelate's rage.
He gave us this eternal spring,
Which here enamels everything,
And sends the fowl to us in care,
On daily visits through the air.
He hangs in shades the orange bright,
Like golden lamps in a green night,
And does in the pom'grantes close
Jewels more rich than Ormus shows.
He makes the figs our mouths to meet,
And throws the melons at our feet,
But apples plants of such a price,
No tree could ever bear them twice.
With cedars, chosen by his hand,
From Lebanon, he stores the land,

And makes the hollow seas, that roar,
Proclaim the ambergris on shore.
He cast (of which we rather boast)
The Gospel's pearl upon our coast,
And in these rocks for us did frame
A temple where to sound His name.
Oh! let our voice His praise exalt,
Till it arrive at Heaven's vault,
Which, thence (perhaps) rebounding, may
Echo beyond the Mexique Bay.'

Thus sung they, in the English boat,
An holy and a cheerful note;
And all the way, to guide their chime,
With falling oars they kept the time.

This is a poem that floats out from the difficult times in the mid-seventeenth century. On the surface everything seems plain: a group of English sailors has left the storms of religious controversy to find somewhere they may practise their puritan beliefs without persecution; they find a sort of Paradise, a new island 'far kinder than our own'. The sailors sing a song of praise to God for leading them here. In the first place, it is not easy to believe that ordinary English sailors would have chanted such a song; nevertheless, the sense of what's going on is clear enough, people driven from England by religious intolerance find, not only a place of peace where they can practise their own faith, but that God has been even more generous in presenting them with a kind of Eden. The poem is spoken from a strange perspective; it is a song 'overheard', not a personal response therefore, but more a longing and so the ideal conditions can be seen to be more credible. Have they found Utopia? Is it a song of praise, a psalm of thanks, a celebration of the physical world (against the thrust of the other works), is it a sea shanty? There are many questions to be asked and this, of course, is not accidental in such an accomplished poet as Marvell. What, then, is his purpose?

Firstly the poem begins in the present tense with 'ride', then goes into the past with 'rowed'. Apart from the strange association of sound between those two words, 'ride, rode and row, rowed') there ought not to be a sense of the past tense of 'ride'. The Bermudas are remote and 'unespied', yet the details offered with such authority in the poem make it seem that they have been long 'espied'. Further, the boat is still on the ocean, rowing along; and indeed the sailors seem at first to be a little grudging of their singing task: 'What should we do but ...?' Not a lot else one can do rowing along towards the islands.

Marvell has clearly found some references to the Bermudas and uses his rich imagination to fill out the concept of a new Jerusalem, a place of beauty and peace, overflowing with the generosity of the Creator. It is in the outline of this generosity, in the clear admiration and love of the more-or-less exotica of the islands, that Marvell's imagination here really takes off and gives the poem its wealth and memorability, as well as its sens-uous richness. In the years 1613 and 1624 books appeared re-porting on the Bermudas and Marvell must have perused them; these were works hoping to persuade other English Puritans to come and join the growing commonwealth in the islands. However, Marvell's vision omits the problems and some of the more ugly details suggested in these works. His notion of an eternal spring was not mentioned, nor is it actual. The islands had been discovered long before by a Spaniard, Juan Bermudez, and an attempt to change the name to The Summer Islands, for the English, when Captain Summers was shipwrecked there in 1609, did not succeed.

From all of which it becomes clear that Marvell is simply writing about the longing for movement, for escape from English turmoil, for journeying, for 'rowing along' and if the hoped-for paradise is not reached, yet the going towards it is what matters. For this reason songs of praise must be raised; 'we have here no lasting city' and must keep journeying onwards to find the per-fect place. We may never actually come ashore to relish this abundance of God's generosity, save in the next life. It is the journeying that matters, the seeking, and the singing of God's praises.

Hence there are several somewhat disturbing notes in the poem: jewels and ambergris and pineapples of great price sug-gest trade already and even piracy; the praise the travellers sing may well, but only may, touch other coasts as well. And through it all is the sense of time, the rowing, the rhythms of the seasons, the tides, time, time, time. Marvell's language creates a wonderful Edenic view, particularly those magic lines: 'He hangs in shades the orange bright, Like golden lamps in a green night'; but underneath the magic is a strong realism, even the negative view of the physical world that has always captured Marvell's mind. The poem, in spite of the surface definition, hints rather than states, hints towards a promised land and God's special protection for Englishmen. Green was the colour of spiritual restoration, to contrast, perhaps, with orange and the looming William. Apples are mentioned, suggesting the Fall and the garden of Eden, the fall, the restoration, the Leviathan slain before Christ's triumph. Marvell's poem shines a light on the English dream of the time for the coming at last of the kingdom, for that peace and prosperity of a promised land, the dream that Cromwell's presence gave, for a time, some hope of coming to pass.

A Seminary Dream

Sometimes, late into Autumn, the rains persist for days. There is little sunshine, less warmth to dry out the land. The countryside becomes saturated. Then there may come winds from the Atlantic and days of the heaviest rain. The countryside cannot absorb so much water and it flows off the surface of the land too quickly, down into the rivers. The rivers swell and flow with unusual power, bursting their banks, flooding village and town and city, and large tracts of water lie for days, like lakes, over the earth.

This is a metaphor, perhaps not too perfect, for my life at the still tender age of seventeen. As a child I had washed in the warmth of religious things, graced, before and after meals, by the gift of God's bounty, porridge, crusty bread, and bacon. As I grew I had been groomed in the salons of God's mercy, taught in the classrooms of God's laws, worshipped in the great bright halls of God's churches. I was saturated in God's watchful presence, I had breathed God in with every breath I drew. During all the years of my delighted, enriching dalliance with the beauty and wildering extent, the free-flowing and sometimes drastic life and love of Achill's natural landscapes, I know myself to have been moving always through the fields of God's being, I was awash with God, the river of his presence was swollen within me, the banks would break, there would need to be some form of release. For what else was possible but to be instinct with God and the things of God, coloured by the catechism of God's cares and demands, walking in the ways of the valley of caution, onwards and upwards in the direction of the restored garden that was Eden.

My last year in college was a quiet one. Perhaps I had matured a little. Perhaps I was uncertain where I would be heading next. Perhaps I settled down to study and prepare for that vital, final examination, the Leaving Certificate. My elder brother had already spent his first year in the Jesuit Novitiate in Emo, and we had, as a family, visited him in that sacred space. I had been moved by his certainties, his quiet determination, his obvious contentment. I had been impressed.

Then, on my final day in Mungret College, the last examination over (I think it was in mechanical drawing, in which subject
I expected to do well) there were very few of us left in the house.
I moved out, alone, that early summer evening and stood a long
while in the abandoned rugby field, goalposts rising white and
still at either end, like footmen left with no-one to wait upon,
and the air replete with thrushes' songs. Tomorrow I would be
heading home and my secondary schooling would be completed.
I felt a great sense of freedom and something, too, of loss. I grew
aware, for the first time, that I had held myself tense against my
schooling, tending to reject the authority of the priests, pining
for the width and openness of my island and the freedom of
childhood. Now, gently, like a long, slow sigh, something young
and independent yielded in me, something passed in the dusk
above me, as if a spirit had left me, ruffling my hair in its passing. I was taken by an incorrigible sorrow that I had not known
before as I stood there, perhaps allowing myself to be aware at
last that I stood at the last white line of childhood, that I needed
to grasp my life and make something of it. Perhaps it had to do
with endings, with my first affect of lonesomeness and I knew,
standing away at the field's edge, hands in my trouser pockets
and my suitcase, back up in the dormitory, packed for home,
that I would seek out this God that had saturated my being, I
would seek him out by name and nature, this God that was already chalk in my ignorant bones, already erratic in my untried
flesh.

When I got home I told my parents my decision. University,
no; I had no wish for, nor knowledge of, chemistry, doctoring,
teaching, lawyering ... It seemed obvious to me that, after my
upbringing, after some of the finer Jesuits in Mungret urging me
to ask myself if I had a 'vocation', that I would follow my elder
brother. I think my parents were a little dubious. That made me
the more determined, but I was determined, too, that I would
not follow into the Jesuit order. Wasn't there that wonderful
great priest all dressed in white, who spoke of the missions ...
yes, the White Fathers. I asked my father if he knew how I could
get in contact with them. We worked out the address: The White
Fathers, Kimmage Manor, Dublin. I got a letter back within days,
a warm and welcoming letter, from The Holy Ghost Fathers,

Kimmage Manor, Dublin. I was given an outline of their life and mission; they seemed just like those of the White Fathers. They invited me to visit them. I did. I would become a Holy Ghost missionary to Africa. I was given my list of things to get, given a date on which to turn up at the novitiate in Kilshane, Co Tipperary, and it was all settled. I relaxed into a warm summer.

The Chime and Symphony of nature: Henry Vaughan (1621-1695)

Between 1642 and 1646 England was torn apart by civil war. On the one hand the supporters of King Charles I – the Royalists, known to the other side as 'Cavaliers', from the Spanish *Caballeros*, horsemen, but also 'gentlemen'. On the other stood the supporters of parliament, known as 'Roundheads', because of the shaven heads of London apprentices who had supported parliament. A large cause of the division was religion, a cover, really, for worries about nationhood and ethnicity. Parliament stressed their Englishness; a reaction consisted of the 'Celtic' Cornwall and Wales. Many of the other Royalist forces had been mercenaries brought over from Ireland, strengthening the parliament's 'patriotic' stance.

Henry Vaughan was born in 1621 to Thomas Vaughan and Denise Morgan in Newton-upon-Usk in Breconshire, in Wales. He studied at Oxford with Thomas, his twin brother. Later, Henry studied law in London but the Civil War broke out and, as did so many other Welsh young men, he joined on the side of the king and served in South Wales for a time.

Vaughan returned to Breconshire in 1642 as secretary to Judge Lloyd, and later began to practice medicine. In 1650 he published the first part of a collection of poems, *'Silex Scintillans'*. The title, 'The Flaming Flint', suggests the hardness of the human heart which needs God or tragedy to strike fire from it. The book was enlarged and reprinted in 1655. Vaughan's first wife died and he married again about this time. After 1655, however, he published nothing of real interest and died in 1695 and was buried in Llansantffraed churchyard in Wales.

Silex Scintillans: flint flashing, looks forward to one of the great themes of Gerard Manley Hopkins, how the heart, in hiding, needs to be brought out into the world of love and service by God's gift of suffering. Vaughan's poetry took fire from his reading of George Herbert, though Vaughan's God does not come so personally close as Herbert's. There are many differences between the two poets yet the echoes are several and real. 'Herbert's work was a point of departure for Vaughan and not a dominating influence' (Jennings 73). Vaughan is the poet of white in all its physical and moral implications. 'He lived in a spectrum between the pure white of infancy and a recovered whiteness of eternity' (Schmidt 243). Unlike Herbert, he moved close to the things of the earth, to a love of creation which he saw as valuable and uplifting. Along with this, the great interest in Vaughan is that the poetry also moved into realms far beyond the senses. 'Vaughan is, perhaps, more than anything else, the poet of innocence; his sense of sin, or at least the way he writes about it, is general and theoretical rather than particular and concrete as it is with Herbert' (Jennings 79). His experiences of war did not canker him, yet alongside the misery of the war, Vaughan suffered some personal bereavements, including the death of his beloved brother Thomas. If the poetry looks at life with a longing for the innocence that early childhood knows, there may be a hint, too, that here is a committed Royalist looking back to a lost age.

In Vaughan's poetry, alongside the language of Anglican Christianity, the created world is presented in real and emotive terms. If Vaughan was the last of the 'metaphysical poets' of that great century of poets, then he, alongside Thomas Traherne, may well be seen to open a new age for poetry. 'His achievement is to bring the transcendent almost within reach of the senses' (Schmidt 244). He called himself a 'Silurist', the Roman name for the British tribe from his part of Wales, so he wished to associate himself with that area, its beauty, its created lushness. Alongside this faithfulness to creation, Vaughan found in Herbert a means of praising the things of God, the parliamentarians having done away with the finer things of the Anglican faith, and the Puritans having destroyed so much of the emotional response to God that had helped the ordinary believer into faith. In the poem 'Regeneration', he speaks of a primrosed spring day when he went abroad, 'Yet was it frost within': it is a mini-pilgrimage poem where he sets out in grief, reaches a pinnacle where he hears a voice urging him onwards; he heads 'full east, a fair, fresh field could spy' (very reminiscent of Bunyan's book,

Pilgrim's Progress) and finds only prophets and friends of God.
Vaughan wished to find, out of the present turmoil, a world
where humans move with God and amidst the angels. He finds
a new grove where

> The unthrift sun shot vital gold
> A thousand pieces,
> And heaven its azure did unfold
> Checker'd with snowy fleeces,
> The air was all in spice
> And every bush
> A garland wore; thus fed my eyes
> But all the ear lay hush.

He comes upon a bank of flowers that lay unmoving though
a loud wind blew. He wishes it would blow on him and bring
him an easeful death. Vaughan sensed the presence of the
Creator in the fields of Wales. His basic metaphorical work is
that of light, here on earth only a glimmering light, but the full
light shines in paradise. This light suffuses the whole of the created world and he tended to shift Herbert's loved theme (of
order in everything) to the unorthodox idea that the natural
creation remains unfallen, and that it instinctively performs the
rites of praise and thanksgiving due to the Creator. Out of the
murderous chaos of war, he hoped to find a way of reconciling
creation to its Creator.

The Star

> Whatever 'tis, whose beauty here below
> Attracts thee thus and makes thee stream and flow,
> And wind and curl, and wink and smile,
> Shifting thy gate and guile;
>
> Though thy close commerce nought at all imbars
> My present search, for eagles eye not stars,
> And still the lesser by the best
> And highest good is blest;
>
> Yet, seeing all things that subsist and be,
> Have their commissions from divinity,
> And teach us duty, I will see
> What man may learn from thee.

First, I am sure, the subject so respected
Is well dispos'd, for bodies once infected,
Deprav'd, or dead, can have with thee
No hold, nor sympathy.

Next, there's in it a restless, pure desire
And longing for thy bright and vital fire,
Desire that never will be quench'd,
Nor can be writh'd, nor wrench'd.

These are the magnets which so strongly move
And work all night upon thy light and love,
As beauteous shapes, we know not why,
Command and guide the eye.

For where desire, celestial, pure desire
Hath taken root, and grows, and doth not tire,
There God a commerce states, and sheds
His secret on their heads.

This is the heart he craves, and who so will
But give it him, and grudge not, he shall feel
That God is true, as herbs unseen
Put on their youth and green.

Yet, seeing all things that subsist and be,
Have their commissions from divinity,
And teach us duty, I will see
What man may learn from thee.

In that central stanza, Vaughan sets the star as an example of
'duty' to the Creator: and this is true of 'all things'; humanity
may well, and must, learn from the creation: 'Yet, seeing all things
that subsist and be,/Have their commissions from divinity,/
And teach us duty, I will see/What man may learn from thee.'
At last, this is a new and fresh note in English poetry. Vaughan
touches here on the doctrine of 'correspondences', the belief that
there is in the heavens a force that runs through all things, based
on light, and even the humblest object on the earth bears kinship
with the heavens. By the study of the star and its shifting lights,
he hopes to find the God that is behind all of that force and
stress. Is this the first time in poetry in English that God, creation

and human beings, the movement of the soul and the movement of the earth and heavens, all come together in a unified vision?

The word 'mystic' and its adjective 'mystical' are perhaps the most misused words when it comes to poets who immerse their work in religious thought and imagery, and Henry Vaughan is probably the most subject to this too-facile way of classifying work. If he stretches his being away from this world towards God, it is not in the way of sheer love or devotion; it is urged from a basis of distaste for the world of humans with its propensity to sin, suffering and misery. A true mystic takes God as friend, even as lover, and sighs to be with God for God's sake, not out of distaste for this world. The great focus of Vaughan's poetry is on the innocence of children and childhood, combined with the notion that the child comes from the hand of God the Creator and moves away further and further from that God as life develops. The same can be said of human kind as a whole; as men and women were expelled from the Garden of Paradise and forced into the misery of human history, gradually humanity moved further from that same God and from the covenant of mutual care that was God's creating. Vaughan's notion is that it would be wonderful to find a way of recovering a life of innocence once more. As with Traherne, he is not to be seen as utterly naïve, he was not foolish enough to believe one could return to such an age, but he hoped that adults could learn from such innocence. From these ideas there spring some wonderfully beautiful poems but taken on its own merit this is not a mystical poetry, indeed it often smacks of a wish to move away from the responsibilities a person has to the self and to humanity as a whole.

That world of childhood, he believes, is close to the world of the angels who, in turn, are the closest to God. Vaughan would wish to be an angel, but again it is to escape the misery that this world of humans dumps on humankind: 'Since all that age doth teach, is ill ...' From all of this, too, spring the images he will employ, the basic one being that the world is darkness, the next world and God are light. There is a sympathy with creatures who do not harm the world, but rather bring joy into it, and give praise to the Creator. After his experience of war, and as he practised as a doctor, there was no doubt that human nature in itself offered no great appeal to Vaughan. Thinking back to the innocence, the light, the truth of Eden, he knows that creatures have remained true to God's covenant.

The Bird

Hither thou com'st; the busy wind all night
Blew through thy lodging, where thy own warm wing
Thy pillow was. Many a sullen storm
(For which course man seems much the fitter born)
    Rained on thy bed
    And harmless head.

And now as fresh and cheerful as the light
Thy little heart in early hymns doth sing
Unto that providence, whose unseen arm
Curbed them, and clothed thee well and warm.
    All things that be, praise him; and had
    Their lesson taught them, when first made.

    So hills and valleys into singing break
And though poor stones have neither speech nor tongue
While active winds and streams both run and speak,
    Yet stones are deep in admiration.
Thus Praise and Prayer here beneath the sun
    Make lesser mornings, when the great are done.

For each enclosèd spirit is a star
    Inlighting his own little sphere,
Whose light, though fetched and borrowed from afar,
    Both mornings makes and evenings there.

A great deal of Vaughan's verse displays this spirit of loving fellowship with the natural world, and what links humanity and creation as a whole is the aspiration towards the light that gives life and the divine Life that is the source of all light. For Vaughan, then, the earth we inhabit is source and promise of everlasting light and life, it is exemplar of praise and prayer and yet he is fully conscious that our true and lasting life is elsewhere.

In the preface to the 1655 edition of his book, he complains of poems written merely for wit's sake: 'Where the sun is busy upon a dung-hill, the issue is always some unclean vermin.' He gives credit to George Herbert with turning his own work away from mere worldly thoughts to divine things. The influence is obvious and pervasive, in phrase and image, yet Vaughan moves in a very different direction. This is a poetry of awe – more addressed to God the Father and Creator, and the One who draws all things to himself, than to his Son, a personal friend and soul-mate. Vaughan is poet of innocence: not poet guilty of dust and sin. Perhaps because the religious longing and the almost complete disheartening he knew before the world of humans, pushed his work to take more care over the religious aspect than the poetic; therefore many of his poems are dull and repetitive, and the metaphorical fabric becomes a little threadbare from overuse. Yet the influence of Herbert is every-where palpable, in so many ways, both formal, in metaphor, and in many of his abrupt openings. Compare, for instance, the opening of his poem 'The Resolve':

> I have considered it; and find
> > A longer stay
> Is but excused neglect.

with Herbert's opening to his poem 'The Reprisal':

> I have considered it, and find
> There is no dealing with thy mighty passion:

There is a poem written to Herbert, 'The Match':

> Dear friend! whose holy, ever-living lines
> > Have done much good
> > To many, and have checked my blood,
> My fierce, wild blood that still heaves, and inclines,
> > But is still tamed
> > By those bright fires which thee inflamed;
> Here I join hands, and thrust my stubborn heart
> > Into thy deed,
> > There from no duties to be freed,
> And if hereafter youth, or folly thwart
> > And claim their share,
> > Here I renounce the poisonous ware.

The influence of Herbert does occasionally too much intrude

but it is important for Vaughan that this be continually set aside as both poets part company in so many other ways. Now and again he uses a phrase of some endearment when touching on God, such as 'Haste, haste my dear', but it does not have the same sense of genuine closeness that Herbert achieves. Herbert lives far more contentedly in, and committed to, the actual world, though without paying it much attention; Vaughan despises the world inhabited by human beings and lives also for the next:

> Rise to prevent the sun; sleep doth sins glut,
>   And heaven's gate opens, when this world's is shut.
> ('Rules and Lessons')

In the poem 'Corruption' he sees humankind in its early years as being still so close to creation and the Creator, and to the Eden from which it was expelled, that everywhere about him, humans may catch glimpses of that glory;

> Angels lay leiger here; each bush, and cell,
>   Each oak, and high-way knew them,
> Walk but the fields, or sit down at some well,
>   And he was sure to view them.

The word 'leiger' is now obsolete, but meant a minister or ambassador resident in his court or seat of government. A poem called 'Child-hood' has these lines:

> An age of mysteries! which he
> Must live twice, that would God's face see;
> Which Angels guard, and with it play,
> Angels! which foul men drive away.

David Scott says of Vaughan, 'There is a sadness and a melancholy lurking underneath much of what he writes, which the consolations of the natural world, the hills, the stars, the rivers, strive to heal' (Scott 103). Vaughan's vision is, of course, close to the words of Christ who said 'Suffer the little children to come to me and do not forbid them, for of such is the kingdom of God.' From here, and from Vaughan's intention of holding his place until he reaches death, comes that great longing for innocence and childhood that echoes later on in Blake and in Wordsworth, and nowhere does Vaughan achieve a higher and

more rhythmically perfect expression of this desire than in his
great poem:

The Retreat

Happy those early days, when I
Shin'd in my angel-infancy!
Before I understood this place
Appointed for my second race,
Or taught my soul to fancy ought
But a white, celestial thought;
When yet I had not walk'd above
A mile or two from my first love,
And looking back – at that short space –
Could see a glimpse of His bright face;
When on some gilded cloud, or flow'r,
My gazing soul would dwell an hour,
And in those weaker glories spy
Some shadows of eternity;
Before I taught my tongue to wound
My conscience with a sinful sound,
Or had the black art to dispense
A sev'ral sin to ev'ry sense,
But felt through all this fleshly dress
Bright shoots of everlastingness.
O how I long to travel back,
And tread again that ancient track!
That I might once more reach that plain,
Where first I left my glorious train ;
From whence th' enlighten'd spirit sees
That shady City of palm-trees.
But ah! my soul with too much stay
Is drunk, and staggers in the way!
Some men a forward motion love,
But I by backward steps would move;
And when this dust falls to the urn,
In that state I came, return.

The soul comes wholly innocent and clean from its previous
life which appears to have been one of potency within the

thought of the Creator; but it is life itself, the world of human sin
(and perhaps he remembers Herbert's 'dust') which pollutes,
blackens the white soul, darkens the light until it flounders
hopelessly, leaving only fading memories of that whiteness, that
light. The poem itself is memorable, holding as it does the sense
that he simply allows his deepest emotion here to flow forth,
controlled by rhyme and its focus on the central thought. There
is no doubt that the 'I' here is the poet himself at his most true,
vulnerable and honest. The very perfection of the poem in its
formal glory, combined with the colouring of loss and longing
within, that almost breathless rush of the poem towards what
the soul desires, all of this wholly mirrors the loss of the perfection the suffering spirit feels itself capable of, if not in the future,
then somehow in the past.

The loss of his brother, Thomas, at the age of about 27, had a
strong and darkening effect on his own life and feeling. Now the
world seems an even darker and emptier place:

> Come, come, what do I here?
>   Since he is gone
> Each day is grown a dozen year,
>   And each hour, one;
>   Come come!
> Cut off the sum,
> By these soiled tears!

And another poem reads thus:

> Silence, and stealth of days! 'tis now
>   Since thou art gone,
> Twelve hundred hours, and not a brow
>   But clouds hang on.
> As he that in some cave's thick damp
>   Locked from the light,
> Fixeth a solitary lamp,
>   To brave the night ...

where Plato's image of the cave comes to mind.

Many of the great themes of Christian hope and love, of
longing and desire, of the awareness of human foibles and the
perpetual charging of armies here and there to secure some form

of peace, some form of commonwealth, meet in Vaughan's poem, 'Peace';

Peace

My soul, there is a country,
Afar beyond the stars,
Where stands a wingèd sentry,
All skillful in the wars.

There, above noise and danger,
Sweet Peace sits crowned with smiles,
And One born in a manger
Commands the beauteous files.

He is thy gracious Friend
And (O my soul, awake!)
Did in pure love descend,
To die here for thy sake.

If thou canst get but thither,
There grows the flower of peace,
The rose that cannot wither,
Thy fortress, and thy ease.

Leave, then, thy foolish ranges;
For none can thee secure
But One, who never changes,
Thy God, thy Life, thy Cure.

This delightful and delighting poem links that source of light and life with the incarnate Son of God, the Christ. Vaughan, lacking the supports, the sacraments, the festivals, the rituals of a church, took Herbert's poems as church and borrowed heavily on his poems. Because his heart longed to celebrate the earth and heavens in the context of his faith in Christ, he wished himself back in a time and place where angels walked amongst men. He creates, in his poems, a primitive Welsh world where nature was alive and alert to, and diffused with, divinity. Holding such beliefs, Vaughan inevitably came to see the world of humans, as opposed to that of God's creation formed in love, as corrupt and corrupting and this, unfortunately, has been a tenet of Christian belief for far too long, right up into our own

age, though other poets have tried to refute it. The world is corrupting because humanity is foul and evil:

> Thus thou all day a thankless weed dost dress,
> And when th'hast done, a stench, or fog is all
>   The odour I bequeath.
> ('Unprofitableness')

> Sweet Jesu! will then; let no more
> This leper haunt, and soil thy door.
> ('Christ's Nativity')

Many more instances of this can be found through the poetry
of Henry Vaughan. There is, of course, the same awareness of
man's state as being compounded of soul and dust as there is in
Herbert, but in Vaughan it tends more to be clay, and a putrid
clay at that. This being the case, it is inevitable that poetry itself,
in Vaughan's mind, be portioned only towards things beyond
this earth, to faith, to God, to pleading.

> And for his sake
>   Who died to stake
>   His life for mine, tune to thy will
>   My heart, my verse.
> ('Disorder and Frailty')

For Vaughan then, man is a creature of vile clay, yet in that
clay God has planted a seed which is his own spirit of light; this
seed stirs in the darkness which it must cast off and grow high
into the light. The use of the imagery of light and darkness is the
most obvious one in Vaughan, almost every poem using it in
some form. This leads to a longing for that last day, that final
call, the great judgement when Christ's kingdom will dawn,
when the night will be forever expelled and humanity shall at
last reach fulfilment, out of vile clay into eternal light. For this
Vaughan is waiting; dressed, and ready to go;

> Yet let my course, my aim, my love,
> And chief acquaintance be above;
> So when that day, and hour shall come
> In which thy self will be the Sun,

Thou'lt find me dressed and on my way,
Watching the break of thy great day.
('The Dawning')

If humankind is made out of vile clay then it is suffering that
kills off the weeds and tares that surround the growing plant.
This, too, is part of the old Christian myth that is still widely
held. Here we are struggling through our 'vale of tears', struggling to get across a marshy ground, the whole purpose being to
reach the other side and come out as unscathed as possible.

And since these biting frosts but kill
Some tares in me which choke or spill
That seed thou sow'st, blest be thy skill!
('Love and Discipline')

                              Thou art
Refining fire, oh then refine my heart,
        My foul, foul heart
('Love-Sick')

Vaughan's store of images is limited but he has ransacked
that store to such effect that the poetry works by a strange, almost unwilling and cumulative power, and a great many of those
images and ideas are contained in that fine poem, 'The World':

The World

I saw Eternity the other night,
Like a great ring of pure and endless light,
All calm, as it was bright;
And round beneath it, Time in hours, days, years,
Driv'n by the spheres
Like a vast shadow mov'd; in which the world
And all her train were hurl'd.
The doting lover in his quaintest strain
Did there complain;
Near him, his lute, his fancy, and his flights,
Wit's sour delights,
With gloves, and knots, the silly snares of pleasure,
Yet his dear treasure
All scatter'd lay, while he his eyes did pour
Upon a flow'r.

The darksome statesman hung with weights and woe,
Like a thick midnight-fog mov'd there so slow,
He did not stay, nor go;
Condemning thoughts (like sad eclipses) scowl
Upon his soul,
And clouds of crying witnesses without
Pursued him with one shout.
Yet digg'd the mole, and lest his ways be found,
Work'd under ground,
Where he did clutch his prey; but one did see
That policy;
Churches and altars fed him; perjuries
Were gnats and flies;
It rain'd about him blood and tears, but he
Drank them as free.

The fearful miser on a heap of rust
Sate pining all his life there, did scarce trust
His own hands with the dust,
Yet would not place one piece above, but lives
In fear of thieves;
Thousands there were as frantic as himself,
And hugg'd each one his pelf;
The downright epicure plac'd heav'n in sense,
And scorn'd pretence,
While others, slipp'd into a wide excess,
Said little less;
The weaker sort slight, trivial wares enslave,
Who think them brave;
And poor despised Truth sate counting by
Their victory.

Yet some, who all this while did weep and sing,
And sing, and weep, soar'd up into the ring;
But most would use no wing.
O fools (said I) thus to prefer dark night
Before true light,
To live in grots and caves, and hate the day
Because it shews the way,
The way, which from this dead and dark abode

Leads up to God,
A way where you might tread the sun, and be
More bright than he.
But as I did their madness so discuss
One whisperd thus,
'This ring the Bridegroom did for none provide,
But for his bride.'

The politician, like the rest of us, lives in this world of darkness but Vaughan sees him as being within a deeper darkness,
digging, like the mole, and shifting his life even further off from
the main course of light. The rest of us weep and sing, but sometimes find the light. The distaste for the actual world in which a
human lives was, of course, strengthened by the belief that here
we are in a shadow-world, born alienated from our true world,
that we live in darkness and misery on this earth. While in this
world of darkness, a human may turn towards God's creation
and seek consolation, yet be aware, too, that all of creation is blighted
by humanity's original fall. As yet, even though Vaughan is content
amongst the beauty of creation, it remains a vague and abstracted
place in the poetry: 'flowers, bowers, banks, groves,' and it will
be some time before the actual naming of creation takes its place
in poetry:

I walked the other day
    Into a field
Where I sometimes had seen the soil to yield
    A gallant flower,
But winter now had ruffled all the bower
    And curious store
I knew there heretofore.

'Curious store', 'gallant', 'ruffled'… such terms. 'A gallant
flower' is so vague as to be of no interest in itself, leading at once
away from actuality into Vaughan's treatise. As we have lived
long after the Romantic era we have been schooled to see an actual
daffodil with its breeze-blown loveliness, or a bank of primroses
touched into exquisite beauty by speedwell or bluebell. Yet in
the next poem there is a foretaste of what might have been possible, side by side with a blankness that is also vague; Vaughan

talks about 'some gloomy grove' but then goes on to be almost precise:

> Or those faint beams in which this hill is dress'd
> After the sun's remove.

The image is accurate and moving, perhaps all because of the use of the word 'this', the poet thinking of a precise place and time. This poem was one of the very first to reach me when I was still a child, and it came to me in this way: my grandmother had a fat Missal, which she brought with her to every Mass. As she looked after us as children a great deal, I often found myself kneeling, fidgeting, trying to pass the time, in the pew beside her. Her Missal intrigued me, as I occasionally saw her in tears as she poured over it. Fat in itself, it was made fatter still by the number of Mass cards which packed it. On several of these memorial cards were written the lines: 'They are all gone into the world of light/And I alone sit lingering here.' I wondered who 'they' were, and where this world of light was; I wondered, too, what this loneliness and lingering were all about. I would look up into the old woman's gentle face, hurt with sorrow, then gaze up at the great blaze of candles about the altar and the dim sunlight made more bright and colourful by the glazed and coloured windows. But the power of the music in the words and, of course, the strength of the statement and the imagery, brought the lines deeply into my soul where they nestled, waiting. Waiting until I came across the whole poem many, many years later and at once fell in love all over again with the whole thing ...

They Are All Gone ...

They are all gone into the world of light!
And I alone sit ling'ring here;
Their very memory is fair and bright,
And my sad thoughts doth clear.
It glows and glitters in my cloudy breast,
Like stars upon some gloomy grove,
Or those faint beams in which this hill is dress'd,
After the sun's remove.
I see them walking in an air of glory,

Whose light doth trample on my days:
My days, which are at best but dull and hoary,
Mere glimmering and decays.
O holy Hope! and high Humility,
High as the heavens above!
These are your walks, and you have show'd them me,
To kindle my cold love.
Dear, beauteous Death! the jewel of the just,
Shining nowhere, but in the dark;
What mysteries do lie beyond thy dust,
Could man outlook that mark!
He that hath found some fledg'd bird's nest, may know
At first sight, if the bird be flown;
But what fair well or grove he sings in now,
That is to him unknown.
And yet, as angels in some brighter dreams
Call to the soul when man doth sleep,
So some strange thoughts transcend our wonted themes,
And into glory peep.
If a star were confin'd into a tomb,
Her captive flames must needs burn there;
But when the hand that lock'd her up, gives room,
She'll shine through all the sphere.
O Father of eternal life, and all
Created glories under Thee!
Resume Thy spirit from this world of thrall
Into true liberty.
Either disperse these mists, which blot and fill
My perspective still as they pass:
Or else remove me hence unto that hill
Where I shall need no glass.

This is one of Vaughan's poems where the imagery of light
and darkness is most succinctly employed. Everything that is
good and glorious awaits us elsewhere, not in this world! As a
corollary death becomes the most desired thing; in this world
are gloom and sorrow, darkness and decay, thrall and dust; in
the next are brightness and joy, light and fullness, liberty and
love. Yet now and again, though as we grow older in life and

our 'memory' of that other world grows ever dimmer, still angels in our dreams may occasionally touch us with the glimmering of that far-off light. Yet he speaks, too, of those 'created glories', creation in itself, without the cussedness of humankind. Henry Vaughan saw himself as 'dressed, and on my way'.

The poetry of Henry Vaughan is a poetry that finds this world alien to humankind, that revels in traces of a 'memory' of a better world and longs for and moves always to find that better world. It is to be found only in death, and it is God's way and will to bring the cautious and prayerful soul to that world. The troubles of the times, the wars and strife that were common, the religious bickering and the doubts about practice and ritual, all contributed, no doubt, to his approach. But it is an approach to the relationship between this world and the next that lasted far too long in the poetry of religion, and the religion of poetry. If peace is only to be found in the next world, what point is there in striving to make anything perfect in this? Why worry about the works of love? Yet now and again Vaughan gets the poetry so rich that these poems exemplify what is creatively best in humankind: when the poem shifts from a pleading or a complaining mode into a quick cry of personal distress or longing, when the imagery is not forced and thinned out by overuse, then his skill in verse form and rhyming lifts the work to another level.

Dressed, and on My Way

I, too, found myself dressed and on my way. It was September 1961 and I had stepped, at last, out of childhood and was moving in a direction that threatened and awed me, that delighted and bemused me and, to this day, I remain wholly uncertain as to why exactly I was making the move. I can only put it down to the immersion in Roman Catholic imagery and emphases over my childhood years and through my misdirected teenage years. Perhaps I was making up for something, some guilt deep down within me; perhaps, somewhere, I truly believed that this was the way I would make it through the valley of tears. Perhaps I was enamoured of the Middle Ages, their religious crises, their atmosphere of God-ness, their miracles and wonders and glories. Perhaps, as yet, I was merely a drifter. Whatever were the reasons, and all of this was before the liberating storms of the Second Vatican Council, my parents, and my grandmother, drove me from my island, Achill, to the new island of religious life, to the novitiate in Kilshane, a fine old mansion close to the village of Bansha in County Tipperary.

We turned in off the main road and the car moved slowly, in through the opened gate between high pillars and undisturbed, aristocratic trees, the fug of silence thickening between us after the long voyage across Ireland. There was a long, meandering driveway, crossing through rich meadowlands towards an island of trees, terror rising in me as the car rounded on a gravel foreshore. The house was, indeed, a mansion and I could see a great glass conservatory to one side, an archway leading into what appeared to be a yard with farm buildings and, standing about in front of the mansion's open door, others stirred restlessly, there at the shuddering end of boyhood, all of us presented, and received, at the Lord's door. I took out my small, brown suitcase that contained my new life. Nanna held me awhile, in silence, at a loss, though taut with pride and loneliness. Pray for me, she whispered. I had come here to gather myself together, to become all Ariel. Now I know that it was she and all my family who ought to pray for us who formed the rearguard generation, aground, washed up by the last high tide of medieval Catholicism. I watched the small red tail lights of the old Ford Prefect as father negotiated the driveway back into the world.

Novice master

He came in through the top door –
moody, mantled, Lord of our strange isle –
and stood behind the table, watching us;
at once a shiver of guilt ran in my blood.

He sat; we sat; and he began:
the company of men ...
Of fixed purpose, wing-dip, swoop,
he was a harrier, pitched high

and haughty, with some disdain
testing and troubling us,
urging us, starlings, one from the other
into our own untrusted loneliness;

each time I go out among mankind
I return a lesser man ...

Postulant first, then novice, dressed in black soutane, white-rope cincture, white collar above a blue stock in honour of the Virgin Mary, I was turned, at once, into a serious young man, my eyes and years focused on becoming a full Holy Ghost Father. Novitiate, a full year, silence, loneliness, and a deeply contented sense of being contained, directed and approved. I loved the Holy Office, reading 'Lauds' in Latin while I walked the beautifully kept and extensive grounds, under the trees, by the flower beds with their carefully manicured grass edges, or singing Vespers in choir in the soothing, beautiful Gregorian chant, singing in four-part male-voice harmony some of the works of Thomas Tallis, or Orlando Lassus or Giovanni Pierluigi da Palestrina.

Exercise, he told us,
the small, stiff muscle of holiness;
and day after day we came

in threes, through the cloister door,
taking our places,
black figures, pacing

the cinder track around a field,
hurrying in the chase,
wisdom always disappearing

ahead of us, and our God,
from his high vantage-point,
cheering us on.

Master of novices. Custody of the eyes. Silence at all times. Rising at 5.50 every morning to come down to the chapel for meditation, followed by the singing of Matins. Study of the Rules and Constitution. Outdoor manual labour. The saying, in silence and in Latin, of the hours, prime, terce, sext, none …

After the soft noctem of the Latin chant
we faced, till dawn, into a Great Silence;
we were a flock of isolated starlings
settling in the rich foliage of an oak;

all day a small brass crucifix lay heavily
on the pillow; I held and kissed it, then
folding my hands across my breast,
lay down again into medieval darkness.

At the end of the year we took first vows, 'simple' vows of poverty, chastity and obedience. We had entered the novitiate forty-eight in number; some thirty-two of us were put aboard a bus and driven to the seminary in Kimmage Manor, Dublin, for the next stage of our formation. I was set to study philosophy, through Latin, for two years in the seminary. Philosophy, theodicy, cosmology – such subjects, and throughout the day silence continued, save for breaktime after lunch when we walked three by three, discussing *'ens ut sic'* or Thomas Aquinas …

The seminary, still as a village before the dawn.
Hunched figures come, rummaging through our dreams.
When the bell has called for the third time

we will unhook huge shadows from the door and tie them on.

We shift and sigh in choir like an avenue of trees.
When the world stirs we will be still again,
shivering and solitary on exposed headlands.

Tell of His Wonderful Works

Psalm 105 has the lines: 'O give thanks to the Lord, call on his name, make known his deeds among the peoples. Sing to him, sing praises to him; tell of his wonderful works.' As yet, I simply saw the wonderful works as the Christ, coming to save us all, to bring the whole world to heaven. I had not even begun to dream of 'the works of love' as something other alongside God's redemptive movements. As novices, and later as seminarians, we had our own Divine Office to recite and we had a weekly cycle of psalms, readings, prayers, that followed the route of the major Office. Ours was known as 'The Little Office of the Blessed Virgin Mary'. There were mid-mornings or late afternoons when I would stop under an old oak tree, listening to thrush or blackbird, and recite to myself one of the psalms of praise, in Latin of course, the music of the language and the richness of the images moving me deeply. I had no awareness yet that my love for such praises stemmed from a love of physical creation; after all, I had grown up in the beauty of Achill Island, an Ireland in miniature, with all the variety of the Atlantic wildness on the western side and the more gentle straits of Blacksod Bay to the east. I breathed forth the Lauds of the psalms with fervour. Now I read the psalms as poems, great, though sometimes repetitive, religious poems. And I read them too as prayers, more conscious now of the creation in peril, of the covenant made between all humanity and this beloved earth, more humble too in the faith that I am struggling to contain, maintain and develop.

Psalm 8

O Lord, our Sovereign,
how majestic is your name in all the earth!
You have set your glory above the heavens.
Out of the mouths of babes and infants
you have founded a bulwark because of your foes,
to silence the enemy and the avenger.
When I look at your heavens, the work of your fingers,

the moon and the stars that you have established;
what are human beings that you are mindful of them,
mortals that you care for them?
You have made them a little lower than God,
and crowned them with glory and honour.
You have given them dominion over the works
    of your hands;
you have put all things under their feet,
all sheep and oxen,
and also the beasts of the field,
the birds of the air, and the fish of the sea,
whatever passes along the paths of the seas.
O Lord, our Sovereign,
how majestic is your name in all the earth!

This is a psalm that reiterates the covenant between humanity and God, God giving dominion to humanity over all the wonderful things that God has created. Humanity being such a poor, forked thing, what a great honour and wonder it is that God has been so generous to us. 'John's gospel is a reminder that in the form of the *Logos*, Christ exists in relationship with all created things, but at the incarnation Christ becomes one with all flesh – that is, exists in kinship with all created beings' (Deane-Drummond 100). This must lead towards a wider identification with the needs of human beings alongside the needs of the whole of creation. Creation speaks the praises of God; humanity gives those praises voice. But is there not a further necessity laid upon us, to love, care for and cherish that creation? and to do so in the name of Christ, incarnate, made flesh in that creation?

Psalm 19

The heavens are telling the glory of God;
and the firmament proclaims his handiwork.
Day to day pours forth speech,
and night to night declares knowledge.
There is no speech, nor are there words;
their voice is not heard;
yet their voice goes out through all the earth,
and their words to the end of the world.

In the heavens he has set a tent for the sun,
which comes out like a bridegroom
     from his wedding canopy
and like a strong man runs its course with joy.
Its rising is from the end of the heavens,
and its circuit to the end of them;
and nothing is hid from its heat.

The law of the Lord is perfect,
reviving the soul;
the decrees of the Lord are sure,
making wise the simple;
the precepts of the Lord are right,
rejoicing the hearth;
the commandment of the Lord is clear,
enlightening the eyes;
the fear of the Lord is pure,
enduring forever;
the ordinances of the Lord are true
and righteous altogether.
More to be desired are they than gold,
even much fine gold;
sweeter also than honey,
and drippings of the honeycomb.

Moreover by them is your servant warned;
in keeping them there is great reward.
But who can detect their errors?
Clear me from hidden faults.
Keep back your servant also from the insolent;
do not let them have dominion over me.
Then I shall be blameless,
and innocent of great transgression.

Let the words of my mouth and the meditations of my heart
be acceptable to you, O Lord,
my rock and my redeemer.

Creator of all and lawgiver; both relate to each other; the
works of his love.

There are many Old Testament songs of victory: God as saviour from slavery (and here there's a link to the Passover and Eucharist). But does God need our praise, or the praise of creation? God owns them: 50:8-12. It's 'a wondrous, joyful way of recognising the wonders of God's powerful love in our regard' (Psalm 28). The psalms bring the love of the past into the present and the future. For instance, Psalm 19 leads to Romans 10:14-18, the passage on the Presence of God across all creation.

There is constant reiteration of the notion of the earth giving praise to God: Psalm 89: 'The heavens are yours, the earth also is yours: the world, and all that is in it – you have founded them. The north and the south, you created them.' Psalm 95 speaks of the dominion of God over all things: 'In his hand are the depths of the earth; the heights of the mountains are his also. The sea is his, for he made it, and the dry land, which his hands have formed.' And Psalm 96 begins: 'O sing to the Lord a new song; sing to the Lord all the earth, Sing to the Lord, bless his name, Tell of his salvation from day to day.' And later in the same psalm: 'Let the heavens be glad, and let the earth rejoice; let the sea roar and all that fills it; let the field exult, and everything in it. Then shall all the trees of the forest sing for joy before the Lord; for he is coming, for he is coming to judge the earth.' Such psalms, repeated day upon day, fill the soul with a sense of communion with the earth, a sense of belonging, of praise and of fellowship with all creation.

Other matters, of course, fill the psalms as well as the awareness of the wonders of the earth. In Psalm 103 the singer juxtaposes creation with covenant, and with mortality: 'As for mortals, their days are like grass; they flourish like a flower of the field; for the wind passes over it and it is gone and its place knows it no more. But the steadfast love of the Lord is from everlasting to everlasting on those who fear him, and his righteousness to children's children, to those who keep his covenant and remember to do his commandments.'

Psalm 104 is a psalm central to this thinking. As Thomas Berry writes: 'If the earth grows inhospitable toward human presence, it is primarily because we have lost our sense of courtesy toward the earth and its inhabitants, our sense of gratitude, our willingness to recognise the sacred character of habitat, our capacity for the awesome, for the luminous quality of every earthly reality' (Dream 2). Psalm 104 opens with a call to the soul to praise God as creator of all things:

> Bless the Lord, O my soul.
> O Lord my God, you are very great,
> You are clothed with honour and majesty,
> wrapped in light as with a garment.
> You stretch out the heavens like a tent,
> you set the beams of your chambers on the waters,
> you make the clouds your chariot,
> you ride on the wings of the wind,
> you make the winds your messengers,
> fire and flame your ministers.

Our Creator God is great and wonderful, creating and commanding, guiding and directing the overwhelming powers of his creation, in charge, overseeing all and using created glories as his ministers. He is creator of the earth on which we and all creatures live:

> You set the earth on its foundations,
> so that it shall never be shaken.
> You cover it with the deep as with a garment;
> the waters stood above the mountains.
> At your rebuke they flee;
> at the sound of your thunder they take to flight.
> They rose up to the mountains, ran down to the valleys
> to the place that you appointed for them.
> You set a boundary that they may not pass,
> so that they might not again cover the earth.

God's hand works intimately on the earth and controls and directs all the waters of the earth, holding them back from once more destroying the earth as they did in the time of Noah; this, too, recalls the renewal of the covenant made between God and creatures after that first and overwhelming flood. Thus far the writer is outlining God's complete involvement and mastery over the whole of his creation, a little like God's outlining of the position of God towards Job and all of humanity. He goes on:

> You make springs gush forth in the valleys;
> they flow between the hills,

giving drink to every wild animal
the wild asses quench their thirst.
By the streams the birds of the air have their habitation;
they sing among the branches.
From your lofty abode you water the mountains;
the earth is satisfied with the fruit of your work.

Being in control of all the waters of creation, God takes care of the inhabitants of the earth; how necessary water is to all life, and how the earth responds, quenching thirst, singing, and being satisfied. And not only water:

You cause the grass to grow for the cattle,
and plants for people to use,
to bring forth food from the earth,
and wine to gladden the human heart,
oil to make the face shine,
and bread to strengthen the human heart.
The trees of the Lord are watered abundantly,
the cedars of Lebanon that he planted.
In them the birds build their nests;
the stork has its home in the fir trees.
The high mountains are for the wild goats;
the rocks are a refuge for the coneys.

Over the centuries humanity has stressed the transcendence of God, God seen as beyond us, unreachable in his great glory, and all of this is true to some degree but the emphasis has been too much, and now, with the earth in crisis, with economics and power and greed dominating human living and threatening the very existence of the planet, it is vital that we see our God as immanent, as concerned not only with human safety and growth, but with the safety and growth of all physical creation. The trap of pantheism, where everything is seen as God, has been avoided and this psalm leads us to the certainty of God's care for the earth, his close concern in its wellbeing. Other religions have always been more clear and overt about the human relationship with creation, the Vedas, for example, urging close ties between humanity and the world in which we live and move; the *Upanishads* declare all things in creation to be interrelated and

Buddhism insists on concern for the life of all creatures, the monk being forbidden to take any life. 'A new spirituality which sees the earth as permeated with the divine presence would undoubtedly provide the basis for worldwide co-operation among religious people today to respect and care for the earth. I believe that this new religious sense, especially among Christians, must permeate our concern for the earth' (Care 152). The sense is new for Christians, though the spirituality we yearn for has always been present, and the great Indian tribes, scattered in their freedom once across the plains of North America, were aware of such a spirituality. Psalm 104 goes on:

> You have made the moon to mark the seasons;
> the sun knows its time for setting.
> You make darkness, and it is night,
> when all the animals of the forest come creeping out.
> The young lions roar for their prey,
> seeking their food from God.
> When the sun rises, they withdraw
> and lie down in their dens.
> People go out to their work
> and to their labour until the evening.

Perhaps if Christians had taken poetry like this from the Old Testament more seriously, then we would not be stressing this spirituality as 'new'. Thomas Berry has written: 'We have a new story of the universe. Our own presence to the universe depends on our human identity with the entire cosmic process' (Dream 17). Look again at the great poem of St Francis of Assisi, or even at the poetry of 'The Deer's Cry' attributed to St Patrick. The instinct of the early Christian saints appeared much closer and more intimate across created things. The psalmist sees how God has ordered not only the great powers of creation but the lives of all creatures, including humankind, within the park of that creation. Our response must be awe, delight and praise; and, of course, respect, care and courtesy.

> O Lord, how manifold are your works!
> In wisdom you have made them all
> the earth is full of your creatures.

> Yonder is the sea, great and wide,
> creeping things innumerable are there,
> living things both small and great.
> There go the ships,
> and Leviathan that you formed to sport in it.

The 'works' of God are manifold, created out of wisdom, all kinds of creatures, from the smallest creeping things, the ant, the scorpion, the flea, to the Leviathan, the whale, the sunfish, the basking shark, also created for the pleasure to be found in being part of that creation. And all creatures look to God in their utter dependence on him:

> These all look to you
> to give them their food in due season;
> when you give to them, they gather it up;
> when you open your hand, they are filled with good things.
> When you hide your face, they are dismayed;
> when you take away their breath, they die
> and return to their dust.
> When you send forth your spirit, they are created;
> and you renew the face of the ground.

Not only the fish of the sea, the birds of the air, the creeping creatures of the plains and woods and forest are thus wholly dependent on their Creator for their living, but humankind, too. These, of course, are the ultimate 'works of love'. The works of God throughout the universe are created out of love, as the incarnation will show in due time. Therefore humankind, as the only creatures that can verbally express their gratitude, their worship, their praise, must offer such homage on behalf of humankind, and of all of creation:

> May the glory of the Lord endure forever;
> may the Lord rejoice in his works –
> who looks on the earth and it trembles,
> who touches the mountains and they smoke.
> I will sing to the Lord as long as I live;
> I will sing praise to my God while I have being.
> May my meditation be pleasing to him,
> for I rejoice in the Lord.

Let sinners be consumed from the earth,
and let the wicked be no more.
Bless the Lord, O my soul.
Praise the Lord!

It is sin that perverts the course of creation which, without humankind, would flourish and grow unthwarted in its original covenant. 'Deep Ecology', a thinking that offers equal value to human and non-human creation and the importance of those systems that sustain and develop our planet, states that created things have value in themselves, independent of their use as human resources. Recent trends in economics, in multinational companies, in huge and impersonal corporations, have made humans act almost as robots, without individual responsibility for their actions on the earth. Even governments tend to stand numb before globalisation. All of this brings about severe poverty amongst those beyond the vast economic forces, and the whole earth suffers without individual attention to its parts. Military conflicts have become enormous destroyers of people and environment, witness the recent irruptions of Israeli forces in The Lebanon and Gaza. The works of love demand the responsible use of the earth's resources in creating the stability, the harmony, the interdependent relationships, between human and human, between human and planet. The works of God's love need the responses of love, respect and admiration for all of creation.

Psalm 148 is another psalm that brings all of this together:

Praise the Lord!
Praise the Lord from the heavens;
praise him in the heights!
Praise him, all his angels;
praise him, all his host!
Praise him, sun and moon;
praise him, all you shining stars!
Praise him, you highest heavens,
and you waters above the heavens!
Let them praise the name of the Lord,
for he commanded and they were created.
He established them forever and ever;
he fixed their bounds, which cannot be passed.

Praise the Lord from the earth,
you sea monsters and all deeps,
fire and hail, snow and frost,
stormy wind fulfilling his command!
Mountains and all hills,
fruit trees and all cedars!
Wild animals and all cattle,
creeping things and flying birds!

Kings of the earth and all peoples,
princes and all rulers of the earth!
Young men and women alike,
old and young together.
Let them praise the name of the Lord,
for his name alone is exalted;
his glory is above earth and heaven.
He has raised up a horn for his people,
praise for all his faithful,
for the people of Israel who are close to him.
Praise the Lord!

Brother Sun and Sister Moon, as Francis of Assisi would have called them, praise the Lord. All of the earth, and the whole of creation praises the Lord. The psalm tells that this will go on forever, and that the Lord has set the creation as immovable. Long had we believed so, and long, still, do we hope.

A short, intense psalm is Psalm 117, one that insists on praise because God's love is steadfast:

Praise the Lord, all you nations!
Extol him, all you peoples!
For great is his steadfast love toward us,
and the faithfulness of the Lord endures forever.
Praise the Lord!

So when I stood, alert, young, enthusiastic, filled with peace and joy, a child of God born and raised under his watchful eye, and kept in the care of his wings spread over me, and when I read my Little Office, when I stood there in the lush grounds of Kilshane and watched out over the rich valleys of Tipperary, my heart soared with such songs of praise, such certainty in my life, such order. And when I prayed in my small cell in Kimmage Manor, Dublin, and a busy seminary life moved and grew all about me, there under the snow-covered hills of the city, it was still all praise, all wonder, and all safe, sure and promising. It was many years later before any thought that this great creation which I knew was praising God as I had praised him, was in any trouble. I read, in the work of Leonardo Boff, liberation theologian, the sentence: 'Since 1990 a species a day is disappearing.' And further on, 'Earth was thought to be inexhaustible in its resources and it was assumed that humanity could progress indefinitely toward the future. Both infinites are illusory' (Cry 2). The last verse of the final Psalm, number 150, reads: 'Let everything that breathes praise the Lord!'

Angel
Thomas Traherne (1637-1674)

Thomas Traherne was born in Herefordshire. His father was a shoe-maker who died when Thomas was still quite young. The boy was brought up by an uncle amidst a poverty which always remained vivid in his mind. He won an MA in arts and divinity in Brasenose College, Oxford, and in 1657 was given the rectory of Credenhill, near Hereford, where he served as parish priest for ten years. In 1667 he was appointed private chaplain to the Lord Keeper of the Seals under Charles II but still appears to have spent most of his life in humble parish duties. He was described as 'a good and Godly man, well learned, a good preacher, a very devout liver'. He died in his patron's house at Teddington, Hampton, and was buried in the church there.

After his death his manuscripts disappeared and were not found until they turned up in street bookstalls in 1897, more than two hundred years later. The person who found them thought the poems were by Henry Vaughan but, as they were eventually bought by Bertram Dobell, an expert on the poetry of that time, he recognised the work of Traherne. Dobell edited the work, publishing *Poems* in 1903 and the prose work *Centuries of Meditations* in 1908. Study of these works seemed to indicate that Traherne was a simple, naïve thinker whose only real theme was 'felicity', the happiness one knows even on earth and will discover all the greater in heaven. In the late 1960s *Commentaries of Heaven* was found on a burning rubbish heap and just about rescued. *Select Meditations* was found in 1997, severely mutilated; again in 1997 a manuscript was discovered in the Library in Lambeth Palace and that same year the very fine essays, *The Kingdom of God* and *Love* were discovered. Also in 1997 another manuscript, *The Ceremonial Law* was found in Washington DC.

Apart from the astonishing discoveries, it is a great wonder and delight that the work of Traherne has survived at all. After these new discoveries, 'A new Traherne emerges, no naïve optimist or rural songster but a serious thinker, debater, theologian and visionary. Here we see a man of his time, not only grappling with issues of his day, theological and political discussions that were shaping the future of his church and his society, but also open to questions that concern us now, deep questions about who we are, about what it means to be human, our place in the universe, about our hopes and aspirations, our insatiable demands, our destinies.' (Inge 262)

Traherne is seen as one of the last of the so-called Metaphysical poets, though very little of his work was published in his lifetime. His work has so often been compared to Henry Vaughan's that the mistaken attribution of the re-discovered mss is understandable. Yet the poets are vastly different. If Vaughan's emphasis is on looking back to a time of innocence, Traherne prefers to look to the present and to take delight in the works of the Creator. This would be a better homage to him, Traherne holds, than the continual nostalgia for better times long past. Yet he shares, with Vaughan, the wish that mankind should remain childlike, holding on to as much of the innocence in which he was born as possible. Traherne did not marry; he devoted himself to prayer and good works and left after him some houses devoted to the help of the poor in Hereford. A good man, then and, if not one of the greatest of poets, yet a good poet and a dedicated and serious Christian.

Traherne lived through an era of terrifying religious controversies. At a moment when he was struggling with agnosticism the following occurred (Traherne has written it in *Centuries of Meditation*): 'Another time, in a lowering and sad evening, being alone in the field, when all things were dead and quiet, a certain want and horror fell upon me, beyond imagination. The unprofitableness and silence of the place dissatisfied me, its wideness terrified me, from the utmost ends of the earth fears surrounded me. How did I know but dangers might suddenly arise from the east, and invade me from the unknown regions beyond the seas? I was a weak and little child, and had forgotten there was a man alive in the earth. Yet something also of hope and expectation comforted me from every border. This taught me that I was concerned in all the world, and that in the remotest borders the causes of peace delight me; and the beauties of the earth when seen were made to entertain me; that I was made to hold a communion with the secrets of divine providence in all the world ... The comfort of houses and friends, and the clear assurance of treasures everywhere, God's care and love, his goodness, wisdom and power, his presence and watchfulness in all the ends of the earth were my strength and assurance forever.'

It is a moment of extraordinary epiphany, yet we need read nothing unique into the experience, such epiphanies being common to young men of intellect and integrity everywhere. What may be remarkable is that it affected Traherne's life and work so deeply from that day on. His giving of himself, in his life and in his poetry, to the interior conviction he discovered at that time, was quite exemplary, matched perhaps only by the unswerving devotion of a George Herbert. The lately discovered manuscripts show how he wrote and thought deeply and widely about his experience.

Many claims have been made on Traherne's behalf, efforts to draw him into all sorts of esoteric sects and movements, using a phrase like 'Teach me, O Lord, these mysterious ascensions. By descending into Hell for the sake of others, let me ascend into the glory of the Highest Heavens', again from *Centuries*. This is little more than a prayer that, through suffering, he might rise to the love of God. The fact that he was familiar with Platonic thought and the work of thinkers like Plotinus, does not move him beyond a mild Christian mysticism into secret societies of any kind. Traherne was a searcher for truth, and he was a poet, expressing his deepest emotional life through the medium of rhyme, rhythm and metaphor. None of this makes him a crank. None of this makes him a 'mystic'. However, it is important to understand aright his notion of joy and light in his concept of happiness on earth and in relation to God; otherwise he can be seen as a rather naïve innocent in this harsh world.

He wrote in *Centuries*: 'I was entertained like an angel with the works of God in their splendour and glory.' If he sought and studied the roots of lasting happiness, he was yet not unaware of the wars of the times, of the deep dread and suffering they caused; as a priest he visited the poor and the sick. Some of the poems touch on the notion of Eden rediscovered. If, like Vaughan, he had no sense of a supporting church about him, he tried to lay a solid foundation to his thinking. At the Restoration he confessed allegiance to the restored Church of England. He turned to nature, the things of God's marvellous creation, for affirmation of his beliefs.

Eden

A learned and a happy ignorance
Divided me
From all the vanity,
From all the sloth, care, pain, and sorrow that advance
The madness and the misery
Of men. No error, no distraction I
Saw soil the earth, or overcloud the sky.

I knew not that there was a serpent's sting,
Whose poison shed
On men, did overspread
The world; nor did I dream of such a thing
As sin, in which mankind lay dead.
They all were brisk and living wights to me,
Yea, pure and full of immortality.

Joy, pleasure, beauty, kindness, glory, love,
Sleep, day, life, light,
Peace, melody, my sight,
My ears and heart did fill and freely move.
All that I saw did me delight.
The Universe was then a world of treasure,
To me an universal world of pleasure.

Unwelcome penitence was then unknown,
Vain costly toys,
Swearing and roaring boys,
Shops, markets, taverns, coaches, were unshown;
So all things were that drown'd my joys:
No thorns chok'd up my path, nor hid the face
Of bliss and beauty, nor eclips'd the place.

Only what Adam in his first estate,
Did I behold;
Hard silver and dry gold

As yet lay under ground; my blessed fate
Was more acquainted with the old
And innocent delights which he did see
In his original simplicity.

Those things which first his Eden did adorn,
My infancy
Did crown. Simplicity
Was my protection when I first was born.
Mine eyes those treasures first did see
Which God first made. The first effects of love
My first enjoyments upon earth did prove;

And were so great, and so divine, so pure;
So fair and sweet,
So true; when I did meet
Them here at first, they did my soul allure,
And drew away my infant feet
Quite from the works of men; that I might see
The glorious wonders of the Deity.

The first stanza may be misleading; he was never unaware of the sorrows that surround us, save, perhaps in his childhood, nor was he unaware that creation could be soiled and the sky 'overclouded'. To us all, in childhood, Eden seems real; we live our first years in a type of Eden; we will spend our lifetime longing for a new Eden to be revealed to us, beyond the sorrowing, the grief, the pains. There will be 'swearing and roaring boys'; the 'as yet' of the presence of silver and gold is a warning; also the phrase 'at first' signals dangers to come. Yet the 'glorious wonders of the Deity' will never fade.

And the question of evil? His writings move cautiously and thoughtfully through humanity's tendencies towards greed and evil, yet as a priest he appears to have moved with a warm reasonableness and charity through his parish. 'At a practical level Traherne's response to the demands of poverty and deprivation are found not so much in his writings as in his life, in his recorded generosity and in his final testimonial will. In this he models for his readers a life tuned to the needs of others. Theologically, the question of unanswered need is addressed by Traherne in the illogicality of the Christian cross on which the most powerful is crucified. Life is killed and love continues to hope in the face of utter loss' (Inge 265). It is also the memory of the innocence, the untainted purity, the joy of childhood that keeps him searching; there is no longing to go back to those times, what must be done is to find the same sort of innocence and purity again, by facing up to, and understanding, what life is, and what the life to come: 'I must become a child again' is the last line in a poem called 'Innocence'.

Traherne willed to have no nonsense in his work, no special shows nor tricks of language or metaphor, wishing only to show 'the naked truth', to use 'A simple light, transparent words ...' And the object of the exercise would be to allow the soul to see its 'great felicity' and know the bliss to which it is heir. He will, then, avoid all 'curling metaphors' and 'painted eloquence'. His will be 'An easy style drawn from a native vein' in an effort to find true wisdom. His simple metaphor is that of a man richly dressed in 'woven silks and well-made suits', with gems and polished flesh; how men notice such but are not aware of God's work, nor the soul where God abides:

> Even thus do idle fancies, toys and words,
> (Like gilded scabbards hiding rusty swords)
> Take vulgar souls, who gaze on rich attire
> But God's diviner works do ne'er admire.

The poet Elizabeth Jennings wrote of Traherne's 'intense delight in the natural world: 'Traherne is an innocent writer in the only valuable sense that a writer can be innocent – that is to say, the sheer momentum of his experience carries him beyond any tendencies towards self-consciousness.' But she complains: 'The poems are often lovely artifacts, certainly, but they are artifacts – sealed off, separate, curiously unattainable. And the delight appears to have diminished, the joy to be diluted. We admire but do not participate.' (Jennings 83ff). It had been thought that Traherne was a Christian Platonist, believing in the pre-existence of the soul that partook of the divine nature and so the soul, in life, will hold on to the primal ideas evoked in images of nature. Traherne wrote: 'to conceive aright and to enjoy the world, is to conceive the Holy Ghost, and to see his Love; which is the Mind of the Father.' This, however, is not Platonism; in Traherne's mind, all of creation is permeated by the sustaining hand of God and therefore all things in that creation are sacred. This is a view he held strongly and expanded on in his newly-discovered works; indeed so convinced was he of the value of physical creation that he saw humans as superior to angels, humans having bodies and therefore capable of enjoying God's creation.

An early poem expresses the wonder of being born, a notion common to us all, that we are alive in this place at this time, surrounded by these created things, but here well expressed in the sense of amazement at the gift of living:

> Long time before
> I in my mother's womb was born,
> A God preparing did this glorious store,
> The world, for me adorn.
> Into this Eden so divine and fair,
> So wide and bright, I come His son and heir.
> ('The Salutation')

Traherne, then, rather than being a simpleton drunk on unfounded happiness, sees this world as a prelude to another where everything is filled with light and joy, and because we are already heirs to this wonderful existence, what is needed is to maintain awareness of that world and exult in our awareness of it. This awareness is best expressed, according to Traherne, through the eyes of a child that is still unconscious of wickedness. There are multitudes who might not see this world as an 'Eden so divine and fair' but that is not the point here, the emphasis is on the free gift of God's creating. And this is one of the first statements of such a notion, the world up to this time being regarded as a source of sin, to be avoided in favour of purely spiritual notions. If Vaughan sees our arrival on earth as a loss and our growth as a gradually diminishing memory of great times into a miserably sinful living, Traherne prefers to concentrate on the actual moment:

Wonder

How like an Angel came I down!
How bright are all things here!
When first among His works I did appear

O how their glory me did crown!
The world resembled His Eternity,
In which my soul did walk;
And every thing that I did see
Did with me talk.

The skies in their magnificence,
The lively, lovely air,
Oh how divine, how soft, how sweet, how fair!
The stars did entertain my sense,
And all the works of God, so bright and pure,
So rich and great did seem,
As if they ever must endure
In my esteem.

A native health and innocence
Within my bones did grow,
And while my God did all his Glories show,
I felt a vigour in my sense
That was all Spirit. I within did flow
With seas of life, like wine;
I nothing in the world did know
But 'twas divine.

Harsh ragged objects were concealed,
Oppressions, tears and cries,
Sins, griefs, complaints, dissensions, weeping eyes
Were hid, and only things revealed
Which heavenly Spirits and the Angels prize.
The state of Innocence
And bliss, not trades and poverties,
Did fill my sense.

The streets were paved with golden stones,
The boys and girls were mine,
Oh how did all their lovely faces shine!
The sons of men were holy ones,
In joy and beauty they appeared to me,
And every thing which here I found,
While like an Angel I did see,
Adorned the ground.

Rich diamond and pearl and gold
In every place was seen;
Rare splendours, yellow, blue, red, white and green,
Mine eyes did everywhere behold.
Great wonders clothed with glory did appear,
Amazement was my bliss,
That and my wealth was everywhere;
No joy to this!

Cursed and devised proprieties,
With envy, avarice
And fraud, those fiends that spoil even Paradise,
Flew from the splendour of mine eyes,
And so did hedges, ditches, limits, bounds,
I dreamed not aught of those,
But wandered over all men's grounds,
And found repose.

Proprieties themselves were mine,
And hedges ornaments;
Walls, boxes, coffers, and their rich contents
Did not divide my joys, but all combine.
Clothes, ribbons, jewels, laces, I esteemed
My joys by others worn:
For me they all to wear them seemed
When I was born.

Traherne wished to know no limits, no borders, no boxes that might contain and divide the glory of the world in which we live. We come from the realm of angels and, as Vaughan insists, we remember that realm although it gradually fades from memory; Traherne is aware of a 'native health and innocence' and, as the poem progresses through its delicately modulated rhymes, its steady rhythmic flow, one keeps expecting a 'but' … There is none, at least not in this poem. And therefore it is a uniquely refreshing work, one of the very first in the great cannon of poetry in English to betray such pleasure in things of earth. Seen through the prism of God's creating will, the world in its innocence and sinlessness is a cause of unutterable joy. Humanity has, however, muddied that world by sin, but it is Christ's

redemption that has bought back that innocence and sinlessness
and our life now is to long for that renewal of God's kingdom
and to desire it with all our heart. 'Desire is not just one theme
among many in Traherne but the backbone of his writing, and
the consistency of his vision of a desiring God is unusual if not
unique for his period' (Inge 4).

Traherne was a child when the Civil War broke out and
Hereford, where he lived, suffered a great deal; it had sheltered
Charles I and had suffered siege for a time. Traherne welcomed
the stability promised by the restoration. 'Far from being a man
with his head in the clouds, Traherne was grounded both in the
nuts and bolts of parish work and in the burgeoning intellectual
life of his day' (Inge 15). After the shocks of the execution of
their monarch, the hatreds and deaths of the Civil War, the
abandoning of the dream of England as the New Jerusalem,
people turned to new ideas, new discoveries, new freedoms.
Traherne followed and understood the new discoveries in science
though his reverence for creation and the beauty and worth of the
natural world continued to grow. And always, through God's
magnificent creation, humanity is in longing mode; 'His purpose is always to show the desire that exists in God for the
human soul, and in the human soul for God and the process by
which these two may be united in love' (Inge 36). The whole
purpose of creation is love. 'For Traherne's God is a passionate
God whose desire for the human soul is beautified by its own
excess' (Inge 39). It is the Divine Lover in pursuit of the soul, this
is God's 'want' – both in terms of lack and desire – and it must
be humanity's response, too. There is an echo of Augustine here:
'The infinite aspiration with which we reach infinitely towards
the infinite end – that is the love of God – is mirrored in God's
infinite reaching towards us. And the insatiability of our hungers
and thirsts echoes the great hunger for souls in the heart of God'
(Inge 71). The beauty and praise offered to God by creation 'al-
lures' humanity towards their Creator and human beings join
with created things in their Hallelujahs and Lauds.

Traherne's individual poems are linked to one another in a
process of ratiocination and conversation with self and God, so
that his work reads as one long sequence of poems. He is, then,
better read as a whole rather than in individual pieces.

... Whether it be that nature is so pure
And custom only vicious, or that sure
God did by miracle the guilt remove
And make my soul to feel his love

So early; or that 'twas one day
Where in this happiness I found,
Whose strength and brightness so do ray
That still it seemeth to surround:

What e'er it is, it is a light
So endless unto me
That I a world of true delight
Did then and to this day do see.

The imagery of light permeates the poetry along with that of being an Adam in Eden before any sense of sin entered the souls of mortals. Before awareness – 'I was an inward sphere of light'. In a poem called 'The Preparative', he is close to echoing Vaughan:

Unbodied and devoid of care,
Just as in heaven the holy angels are.
    For simple sense
Is lord of all created excellence.

Man is born 'as free / As if there were nor sin, nor misery'. And all happiness on earth is bound up with vision, with light, with an awareness of that great life to which we are heirs: 'Felicity / Appears to none but them that purely see.' Traherne spent his life seeking that felicity, that vision of the Divine permeating all of creation, that awareness of 'the Jesus body, the Jesus bones' that St Paul outlined as the mystical body of the universe, where God wills the happiness of all creation. The light of a man's living is to be trained towards this vision, this awareness; and the poetry reflects and highlights the progress towards felicity.

Traherne was not so naïve and foolish that he would not admit the darkness of the world, and the forces that continually work to destroy that felicity. But, he states, that awareness will not shake the deepest roots of his vision:

The first impressions are immortal all;
And let mine enemies hoop, cry, roar, call,
Yet these will whisper if I will but hear,
And penetrate the heart if not the ear.

It is the heart, then, that matters to the work of Traherne, and
in his life he exemplified the Christian sense of charity and service. At times the poetry tends to labour this theme of innocence
and complicity with the world, and the rhymes and rhythms
tend to remain rather repetitive and dull. But the ongoing work
examines the self, for understanding of the human place in the
grand scheme of things. 'Nature teacheth nothing but the truth',
and by an awareness of nature man comes to a knowledge of
God: 'The world's fair beauty set my soul on fire.'

He writes, in *The Select Meditations*: 'The Skies and the Rivers,
the sun and the stars, the Beauty of the world, their Dominion
over Beasts and Fowls and Fishes, the Dignity of their Nature
and the Image of God which none could Deface, but each man
Himselfe; these were permanent and stable Treasures ...' He
speaks of the treasures of Eden: 'These simple, great and illustri-
ous treasures of Eden are not just elemental treasures of earth
and air and water, energies and organisms from atom to Adam'
(Inge 94). In so many ways, then, Traherne calls to the contemporary concern with conservation and the preservation of the
whole of God's creation. In his admiration for nature, he calls
out, too, to the Romantics of the late eighteenth and early nineteenth century.

A Serious and Pathetical Contemplation
of the Mercies of God
For all the mysteries, engines, instruments, wherewith the
world is filled, which we are able to frame and use to thy
glory.
For all the trades, variety of operations, cities, temples,
streets, bridges, mariner's compass, admirable picture,
sculpture, writing, printing, songs and music; wherewith the
world is beautified and adorned.

Much more for the regent life,
And power of perception,
Which rules within.

That secret depth of fathomless consideration
That receives the information
Of all our senses,
That makes our centre equal to the heavens,
And comprehendeth in itself the magnitude of the world;
The involv'd mysteries
Of our common sense;
The inaccessible secret
Of perceptive fancy;
The repository and treasury
Of things that are past;
The presentation of things to come;
Thy name be glorified
For evermore.

*

O miracle
Of divine goodness!
O fire! O flame of zeal, and love, and joy!
Ev'n for our earthly bodies, hast thou created all things.
All things
Animals,
Vegetables,
Minerals,
Bodies celestial,
Bodies terrestrial,
The four elements,
Volatile spirits,
Trees, herbs, and flowers,
The influences of heaven,
Clouds, vapours, wind,
Dew, rain, hail and snow,
Light and darkness, night and day,
The seasons of the year.
Springs, rivers, fountains, oceans,
Gold, silver, and precious stones.
Corn, wine, and oil,
The sun, moon, and stars,
Cities, nations, kingdoms.

And the bodies of men, the greatest treasures of all,
For each other.
What then, O Lord, hast thou intended for our
Souls, who givest to our bodies such glorious things!

This strangely-formed poem is almost a litany of the wonders of creation, and in *Centuries* Traherne writes: 'I wonder much, (the World being so Beautiful and Glorious in every Eye, so really deep and valuable in Worth, so peculiarly applied to the use and service of every person;) that the Heathens did miss the fruition of it, and fail to measure themselves and their Felicity, by the Greatness of its Beauty ... For the Earth is really better than if all its Globe were of beaten Gold, the Seas are better than if all their Abysses were full of Diamonds ... and the Sun alone a greater Treasure than all the wealthy Mines in the Indies: every man is surrounded with all the Light of their Advantages, and so much served by them, as if no man but himself were alive in the World'. Traherne, then, falls outside the limits of Neo-Platonism because he sees God revealed, sensed and perceived profoundly in the created world ... 'where Plotinus denies the essential enduring reality of the physical world, Traherne affirms the physical with his whole heart' (Inge 105).

Friend of the Restoration, Traherne was somewhat aghast at some of the changes England was going through. He saw that the needs of the marketplace were beginning to take precedence over questions of faith. It was a time when the Puritans were insisting that wealth was a sign of God's favour. Traherne's comment was 'That anything may be found to be an infinite treasure, its place must be found in Eternity and in God's esteem'. Traherne was adamant that any constraint on humans, any withdrawal of the possibilities of free choice, would dishonour those who were made in the image and likeness of God. Hence his strong hatred of the Roman Church which he saw as usurping freedom and developing ambition in religion. The gunpowder plot he saw as one of the efforts of Rome to curb freedom. For him, then, the Pope was Antichrist. 'All creatures,' he wrote, 'stand in expectation what will result of our liberty,' a clear echo of St Paul's letter to the Romans. Hence he was against enclosures of any sort, against the imposition of limitations on freedom of choice.

His view of Eucharist was clarified in *Sacred Meditations* when he wrote: 'Those that think our union with God so incredible, are taught more in the Sacrament. He gives Himself to be our food, is united to us. Incorporated in us. For what doth he intimate by the Bread and wine, but the Bread and wine are mingled with our flesh, and is nourishment diffused through all our members, so he is Love mingling with our Love as flame with flame. Knowledge sharing in our knowledge as Light with Light, an omnipresent sphere within our sphere.'

The rediscovery of innocence in childhood is perhaps the closest Traherne comes to the poetry of Vaughan yet it is clear from the rest of the work that Traherne is following his own course and that this view of childhood, of man's initial innocence, is his own and part of his overall concerns. Men, he writes, are 'More fools at twenty years than ten'. Out of all of this his vision of a perfect world to which we may aspire forms the heart of Traherne's work. A poem called 'Christendom' outlines his vision of a perfectly attuned city, in harmony with itself and with each inhabitant:

> Beneath the lofty trees
> I saw, of all degrees,
> Folk calmly sitting in their doors, while some
> Did standing with them kindly talk,
> Some smile, some sing, or what was done
> Observe, while others by did walk;
> They viewed the boys
> And girls, their joys,
> The streets adorning with their angel-faces,
> Themselves diverting in those pleasant places.

This is a more down-to-earth vision of the Heavenly City than is offered in the Book of Revelation, it is the town next county uplifted to an ideal place. The people who dwell in this town are perfected, they are innocent like children, they are 'incarnate cherubin':

> In fresh and cooler rooms
> Retired they dine; perfumes
> They wanted not, having the pleasant shade
> And peace to bless their house within,

By sprinkled waters cooler made
For those incarnate cherubin.
  This happy place
  With all the grace,
The joy and beauty which it did beseem,
Did ravish me and heighten my esteem.

One of the strangest poems in Traherne's output, one that joins itself most obviously to the age in which he was writing, that famous 'metaphysical' age, is the following:

On Leaping Over the Moon

I saw new worlds beneath the water lie,
New people; yea, another sky
And sun, which seen by day
Might things more clear display.
Just such another
Of late my brother
Did in his travel see, and saw by night,
A much more strange and wondrous sight:
Nor could the world exhibit such another,
So great a sight, but in a brother.

Adventure strange! No such in story we,
New or old, true or feigned, see.
On earth he seemed to move
Yet heaven went above;
Up in the skies
His body flies
In open, visible, yet magic, sort:
As he along the way did sport,
Like Icarus over the flood he soars
Without the help of wings or oars.

As he went tripping o'er the king's high-way,
A little pearly river lay
O'er which, without a wing
Or oar, he dared to swim,
Swim through the air
On body fair;
He would not use or trust Icarian wings

Lest they should prove deceitful things;
For had he fallen, it had been wondrous high,
Not from, but from above, the sky:

He might have dropt through that thin element
Into a fathomless descent;
Unto the nether sky
That did beneath him lie,
And there might tell
What wonders dwell
On earth above. Yet doth he briskly run,
And bold the danger overcome;
Who, as he leapt, with joy related soon
How happy he o'er-leapt the moon.

What wondrous things upon the earth are done
Beneath, and yet above the sun?
Deeds all appear again
In higher spheres; remain
In clouds as yet:
But there they get
Another light, and in another way
Themselves to us above display.
The skies themselves this earthly globe surround;
We are even here within them found.

On heavenly ground within the skies we walk,
And in this middle centre talk:
Did we but wisely move,
On earth in heaven above,
Then soon should we
Exalted be
Above the sky: from whence whoever falls,
Through the long dismal precipice,
Sinks to the deep abyss where Satan crawls
Where horrid death and despair lies.

As much as others thought themselves to lie
Beneath the moon, so much more high
Himself and thought to fly
Above the starry sky,

As that he spied
Below the tide.
Thus did he yield me in the shady night
A wondrous and instructive light,
Which taught me that under our feet there is
As o'er our heads, a place of bliss.

                    * * *

To the same purpose; he, not long before
Brought home from nurse, going to the door
To do some little thing
He must not do within,
With wonder cries,
As in the skies
He saw the moon, 'O yonder is the moon
Newly come after me to town,
That shined at Lugwardin but yesternight,
Where I enjoyed the self-same light.'

As if it had even twenty thousand faces,
It shined at once in many places;
To all the earth so wide
God doth the stars divide
With so much art
The moon impart,
They serve us all; serve wholly every one
As if they served him alone.
While every single person hath such store,
'Tis want of sense that makes us poor.

The poem is quite carefully constructed, beginning with the
poet's vision of day, followed by his brother's vision of the
moon, back to the poet's wisdom and ending once more with
the brother and the moon. We start with an experience of sunlight in which the poet sees beyond what mere sunlight on the
earth will display; his brother, then, in leaping over the moon
reflected in a stream of water, gets another view of creation. The
image of Icarus is cleverly used and developed for it is the sunlight that destroyed the wings in the original myth and the fall
of Icarus was a disaster. If the poet's brother had fallen into the

water he would have fallen through, as far as the moon itself; a beautiful 'conceit', the fall being down and up at the same time, painful and revealing, a vision and a hurt. And always it is the existence of another view of the world that is in question. If he had fallen through into the reflected sky, he could have described to the inhabitants what it was like on the earth above them, thus once again turning our physical world on its head.

There are echoes of phrases from the Bible, 'What wondrous things upon the earth are done ... on earth as it is in heaven ...' There are worlds held within worlds. While we are on earth we are in heaven and while in heaven we are on earth and how rightly does the first conclusion come: 'Did we but wisely move, On earth in heaven above, We then should be Exalted high Above the sky'. The lovely word 'tripping' along the King's highway, suggests the danger and the joy of moving in the actual world, all of which eventually comes down to the use of neither oar nor wing, but 'swimming', and in this case swimming in the air; the cleverness of this is admirable. All of this 'unreasonable' and highly imaginative work, is yet fully earthed, particularly in the final two stanzas where the brother, after a stint in hospital, 'brought home from nurse', has to go outside to use the toilet: 'To do some little thing He must not do within'; even the name of the village where Thomas and Philip lived is used. Like the moon and the stars, that shine always somewhere in the world, God too is available to everyone and it is our poor minds alone that are unwilling to open up to the wonder and mercy of God's presence.

The special grace of Traherne's poetry, then, is its positive response to the story of Christ's revelation of God and of human destiny, a destiny that grows and finds its greatest richness alongside the ordinary things of creation. Reading this poet almost inevitably arouses an answering hope, almost a conviction, in the reader. The surface innocence of the verse, with its often repeated memories of childhood integrity, is still carefully focused on his theme, and the individual poems are constructed with intelligence and purpose. And overall, Traherne touches on the extraordinarily new notion for that time that the physical creation is God's body. God inhabits creation: as he writes in 'The Kingdom of God': 'He dwelleth in his Kingdom, not as in other

Temples, where he is the object of the Adorer's Thoughts and Affections only. But as the Skill of an Architect dwells in his Work, and the Face of a Spectator in the Mirror he beholds. As the virtue of the Sun dwells in the Trees and Herbs it inspireth, and a fountain in the Stream, so does the Fullness of the Godhead lodge in his Kingdom'. Traherne is an intriguing poet, a poet of his own time and place, using language and poetry as the late seventeenth century employed it, yet singing his way into our own twenty-first century with messages of meaning and of hope.

A Seminary Dream II

In St Joseph's Church, Bunnacurry, Achill Island, I was acolyte. After early morning Mass I came out onto the sanctuary to quench the six high candles behind the altar. I had a quencher long as a billiard cue; I swung my starched-white surplice, raised my cue, cupped each candle and sent fragrant ghosts whispering among the rafters. Light, coloured whey and honey and cobalt, played on the wall through the simplest of stained windows, and soon only dust-motes were left drifting across the light. I felt born to the task of acolyte, competent, and yet indifferent. I was gangly then, slow-witted perhaps, but willing, and God was playing games around my ignorance, wheedling me already through my senses till he had kindled a small indigenous flame within me that would become spur, and irritant, as yet unquenchable, though there was something forced about it, something over-subtle, a thing un-pure.

I was taught God's laws from my first days, how love is the same as obedience. I lived, while wind off the hills came scarifying the lake, Nanna's fingers raw from a washing rock at the lake's edge. All else was shown to me as the hopeful ways of pilgrimage, the undefined distances, the teasing of those fabulous names: Zebulon, and Naphtali, and all the legendary disasters of God's stopping-places. Sometimes God lurked among the kitchen scents, Nanna in a whirlwind of flour while, from the range, came the swelling of soda farl, potato bread or rhubarb pie. Grandfather was there then, restless, as if he were always setting out, consulting an old fob-watch, ticking us off, preparing always for that evening ritual of rosary, lamp and pipe.

At last, still growing up, I lived the seminary dream. Because it *was* a dream, and I floated through it, happy there, in a dazed way. I thought it must be there that God would be, that inland island among the suburbs, *hospitium* of trees and shrubbery, low hills beyond, blackbirds and silence. There I would find him, incarnate, God mattering, the matter beautiful. I see it now as a snare of loveliness, and I a bee lured into the orchid cave for nectar; trapped. But for those – almost five – full years, how I loved him, how I tended book and breviary and philosophy, treading every track and path and highway that the ministers of God's care would point out to me. Holy Ghost, I would become a spirit-bird lifting from the earth into God's close.

In pre-dawn darkness, always, in my room apart, I whispered *laudetur Jesus Christus*. I was now embodied spiritan, sure of myself, sure of God, solitary, like God, though among peers, a never fully understood impulse holding me, in the prescribed place, at the prescribed time. By rule and regulation every breath I took was glory to my God; I wore God's smell and carried about my person the darkness of my God. *In aeternum. Amen.* By day I set to study him, his dealings with the fathers, theirs with him; I sat absorbed, all my concentration on my God. The dry, black figures of my superiors moved like living statues and all was medieval, silent and obtuse. I learned another language in which to speak to him and knew the certainties of a many-layered security. Love was the word reiterated everywhere and I could decline it: *amor, amoris* ... my body held, and cinctured, my spirit burning, *ignis fatuus*.

It was the music, too, that lifted me, male voices raised into the sacred chant, a wood of poplars blown this way by the breeze, then that, following rites the way the poplars yield to necessary force. So many of us, making a fair field, surpliced and in choir, and I imagined God, sitting like grandfather in his comfort chair, eyes closed and hands resting across his paunch, delighting in it, dispensing grace and glory to us privileged – though now I know it was my own elated being relishing the music and relishing it mostly beyond his listening.

It was beautiful, but it was a dream. I prayed, kindle in me the fires of holy love; I would go up in flames and leave a charred patch on the earth. Evening, Now I lay me down to sleep ... I folded my arms over my heart: prayed: Oh Lover crucified! and eased my soul to a blessed metaphysical darkness, entering original, essential loneliness. Sometimes, deepest dark, body sweats the day's failures into the mesh of the sheets; I dream of my final end, this body, this companion/lover sweating my life's spirit into the mesh of the earth. Exhausted from exercises of the soul I prayed *nunc dimittis servum tuum, Domine*

… Time came when I lay sleepless, breathing a loneliness not spoken of in the texts, and though intelligent of the ordered mechanisms of God's universe, in my own soul some disorder began to swell and I began to find silence in mind or body where I was trying to ask questions I could not find the words to frame.

Nanna, I wrote, you'd laugh to see me, sometimes, ring the seminary bell announcing angel-time, or festival High Mass. I have to swing my weight on the long rope, three draws without a muttering from the bell, building-up, like preparation for prayer, and then a surge and I'm hoisted high, the bell calling, I in flight, like Icarus, three times three and nine, a music ever-so-slightly off its key, but it brings me back to Bunnacurry grove when I'd climb, grandchild, among the pine-trees towards the windy top and sit, part of it, and then the chapel bell would ring the Angelus and three minutes later the bell from the monastery would call and I'd see you, there in the yard, praying, you'd strike your breast and the Word was made flesh and you'd genuflect and hold yourself, head bowed, a long time in reflection …

Jackie, she replied, thanks for your always welcome letter. It's as ever good to hear from you, I know you can write only once a month. I take up my pen to tell you all is well and quiet here, DG. Father Tiernan has complained off the altar about the dance-hall back the road. The monastery in Bunnacurry is being closed. Doesn't that say something about the times that are in it? The foxes have been in the chicken-run again. I am lonesome, between times. I have not been feeling all that well, pains in my chest, tiredness. Pray for me …

Nanna was brought, at length, to spend her last sorry weeks in the Hospice for the Dying, as it was then called, in Harold's Cross, near Kimmage Manor. I called in, a few times, cycling from university where they had sent me to do a degree. I was in my black, clerical suit, my clerical collar, my stock; I had clips around my trouser legs and I took my black hat off when I entered the wards. The good nurses and sisters smiled at me, and deferred. But Nanna was lying hurt and lost, and only sometimes knew where she was and who I was. My sorrow grew like a great tumour within me. And when I left her, and returned to the seminary, there was truly nobody to whom I could turn, nobody but that God to whom I had dedicated myself, body and soul, and for the first time in my life I began to long for a female companion who would take me, body and soul, in her elemental arms and comfort me, hush me, and explain what love might be. For I had come to see and study with so many fine young women in the university who walked about in a lovely freedom, smiling, chatting, their skirts swinging about them and so many, many times my heart quite simply lurched, and could not find relief.

Nanna died. I was sent to stand over her plot in stole and surplice, sprinkling water. I was told I must hold myself detached in sacred ceremony, as if love could not have scope and human tears were failure; Nanna, treasure in heaven; childhood over and the dim ages, my eyes opening. It was as if, standing over the plot my beloved grandmother was lying in, I knew at last that I had need of the earth, I had need of womanlove, of sharing, that celibacy was not for me, nor the whole, long hardness of solitary prayer. Mid-morning then, a few fraught weeks later, when the others were at Lauds, I crept away, a small suitcase in my hand, down the marble stairway and out beneath yew trees to wait, under a high wall, for a bus into the city. I saw it then, not as failure, but as God's way of weaning me to the dry mathematics of the concerns of the whole of creation. And I was welcomed home. Strange place. Strange comforts. A stranger on the bleak island of the world and in its rhythms God faded back into a dim, almost medieval legend. And I was held again by the mysteries of ocean, woman, sky, of city street, of kittiwake, puffin, auk.

I had been studying in university, English and French, which would leave me with little choice but to seek a job as a teacher somewhere. One of my companions, cycling in from Kimmage Manor every day, and cycling back, was another seminarian who had come from Mauritius to be with us in Kilshane and Kimmage. He was a native French speaker and together we spoke to each other, teaching one another our several languages. And one special day, as we waited in a lecture room for the lecturer to turn up, he produced a small, a beautiful book, *La messe sur le monde*, by someone with the difficult name of Pierre Teilhard de Chardin. The French was beautiful. The thought was beautiful. I read it, and was enamoured, finding again, while the Second Vatican Council in Rome was just beginning to open new bright avenues in Catholic thought, a link between the earth I loved and the God I had tried to find.

I remember, as I read this book, this poem, beginning for the first time in my life to have a sense that there was no reason to fear, as a follower of Christ, anything that science or the 'real world out there' might throw up in the way of knowledge, certainty or fact. I remember thinking, perhaps for the first time, in a mode wider than mere religious life had ever, so far, offered me, wider than that self-wrought, heaven-preoccupied way of being that had held me fast for so very long. And every now and then, growing aware that our lecturer was not going to show up at all this morning, I cast a glance about me and was taken again and again by the loveliness of the young women who were scattered through the lecture hall, chatting and eager and sure.

Pierre Teilhard de Chardin SJ

Teilhard de Chardin was born in 1881 and entered the Jesuit novitiate at Aix-en-Provence in 1902, at a time when the religious orders were being expelled from France. He was sent into refuge in Jersey. In 1905 he was sent to teach physics and chemistry in Cairo and here he developed his knowledge of and interest in geology and paleontology. His father had brought him to an appreciation of the beauties of his native Provence and he came to love its richness and diversity. He finished his training as a Jesuit in England. His central awareness was of the world in evolution, not a once-off and finished phenomenon. He saw it as progressing towards spiritualisation. He was witness to both World Wars and won the *Médaille Militaire* and the *Légion d'Honneur*, yet his outlook remained full of optimism, a Christian optimism that is beguiling and heartening. He saw Christ, the centre of creation, as the prototype of love, and evolution as developing towards fullness in Christ as the Omega Point, the pleroma, new heaven and new earth. Teilhard 'claimed that evolution was not simply a process; it was holy, "a light illuminating all facts", by which he meant that it was God's way of creating' (Deane-Drummond 105). He saw Christ as 'the one Omega to which the universe points in its fulfilment' (ibid 105). 'Love is creative, saving and redemptive, and it is through love that Jesus Christ acts as the world's loving and animating centre' (ibid 105). He has often been criticised for not seeing Christ as a fully human figure, a criticism that is unfounded for, as a Jesuit, he believed unreservedly in the full incarnation of the Divine Word, in the physical and actual presence of Jesus on the earth.

In 1923 he travelled to Tientsin to begin his serious field work. It was in the East that his thinking developed, based on his scientific researches into the evolution of the world, combining this with his love of Christ in the flesh. He got back to France in 1924 to find that his religious superiors were already anxious about some of his philosophical views and ordered him to stop teaching. Hurt, but obedient, he went back to China, to Peking.

His discoveries, and the theories developed from these discoveries, were of great importance. He also travelled in India and America. In August 1939 he was again in Peking and during the war in Europe he was stagnating in China; when Japan occupied China he was again unable to leave. In 1951 he went to live in New York where he was able to devote himself to his anthropological studies. He died there in April 1955. His life exemplified a devotion to Christ through his priesthood, and the study of the physical, evolving world in which he lived. His view of Christianity was widened because of his studies and his view of the developing world and its relationship to Christ was unique and fruitful in many ways. Towards the end of his life he was able to write, 'Today, my faith in God is sounder, and my faith in the world stronger than ever.'

His *Le Milieu Divin* ('The Divine Milieu'), though written in 1926 and 1927, was not published until 1957. 'La messe sur le monde' was written in 1918 and reworked in 1923.

He wrote: 'Is the Christ of the gospels, imagined and loved within the dimensions of a Mediterranean world, capable of still embracing and still forming the centre of our prodigiously expanded universe? Is the world not in the process of becoming more vast, more close, more dazzling than Jehovah? Will it not burst our religion asunder? Eclipse our God?' (Milieu 8). In the middle of the twentieth century it appeared that scientific knowledge was urging the supremacy of reason, that all of the universe would eventually be classified, clarified and understood by scientific research. In contrast to this, and yet emerging from scientific research, Teilhard maintained that God is the centre, Christ is at the centre of the centre, and creation is nothing apart from this centre. The whole of creation, as Teilhard saw it, is permeated with Christ, 'the divine presses in upon us and seeks to enter our lives' (Milieu 12). So he saw all human endeavour as being part of the development, expansion and value of all of creation. Instead of eschewing the things of the world, then, 'our spiritual being is continually nourished by the countless energies of the perceptible world' (Milieu 21). Teilhard sees humanity's aim as producing an *opus* in one's life, and 'at the same time he collaborates in another work, in another *opus*, which infinitely transcends, while at the same time it narrowly determines, the perspectives of his individual achievement: the completing of the world' (Milieu 24). This *opus*, this work of love, is a participation in the development of matter, creation expanding and developing to become, ultimately, the new earth, the heavenly Jerusalem.

'All the processes of nature, from the emergence of life itself to the cycle of the seasons and the metabolic process of living forms, are intimately related' (Care 78). Teilhard helped to bridge the gap between scientific study and Christian understanding; McDonagh quotes Mircea Eliade who said that Teilhard was 'the first Christian author to present his faith in terms accessible and meaningful to the agnostic scientist and to the religiously illiterate in general' (Care 79). Creation forms a single whole and over it the great sun of Christ the King is rising, the universal Christ. Teilhard holds that the power of the incarnate Word penetrates matter, going down into the depths and up into the heights of creation. The wonderful grace of this truth is that 'Owing to the interrelation between nature, soul and Christ, we bring part of the being which he desires back to God in whatever we do' (Milieu 26). In this way, Teilhard can speak of our works, our labours that go to build the *pleroma*; and thus are we engaged in the works of love in response to the love-work that was the original creation.

The works of love are found throughout the world, at all times and in all places, enriching the physical world in which we live and move, urging our care for that physical world, and in enriching it we enrich our souls. It is a vision of great hope and consolation, bringing us to a 'sense of the close bond linking all the movements of this world in the single, all-embracing work of the incarnation ... so we shall be unable to give ourselves to any one of our tasks without illuminating it with the clear vision that our work – however elementary it may be – is received and put to good use by a Centre of the universe' (Milieu 32). Teilhard goes on to speak of the forces in the world that help creation towards growth, and to the forces of diminishment that tend to hold us back. In this way, he echoes often the thought of Simone Weil. His is not a vision of untrammeled good and growth, it is a vision fully aware of the dark element in the world, though in outlining his view of life, this aspect of the creation may not have been treated fully enough. The problem of evil is common to all systems of thought and faith but Teilhard's theology is focused on the Omega, the Pleroma, the new heaven and the new earth. We overcome evil, and death, by finding God in it: 'By virtue of Christ's rising again, nothing any longer kills inevitably but everything is capable of becoming the blessed touch of the divine hands, the blessed influence of the will of God upon our lives' (Milieu 49).

Teilhard offers humanity a holistic perspective. Matter grows into complexity and consciousness, in humans; and goes on to form a unit in Christ. God is transcendent. Humanity finds its place in the evolutionary process. Humanity lives on this one planet – all connected; there is interaction of biosphere and noosphere, the latter the realm of the spirit and the mind, and it was this interaction that the Roman Catholic Church found questionable and condemned. But Teilhard held Eucharist in high regard and saw it as the way Christ unites matter and spirit in human beings. This is, of course, the opposite of world-denying. Teilhard saw already, after the two world wars, at a time of globalisation, of market economy – all of this he saw as good, as a development towards the unification of earth and humanity. Perhaps he was not wrong; perhaps all this may yet come to pass, though it has seemed a little foolish in the light of later developments and before environmental issues came to the fore. Evolution, he claimed, is God's way of creating. Christ 'embedded' God in evolution. A resurrected, exalted Christ of the *parousia* will be the Omega Point. Love is the energy of evolution: 'His vision was one where the love of the risen Christ was vividly present to all creatures and the whole creation, rather than in any way detached from material reality' (Deane-Drummond 105).

Teilhard shifted thinking away from a Fall/Redemption theology traceable back to Augustine, that had no real theology of creation. Teilhard 'is convinced that religion in the twentieth century needs to be grounded on our new understanding of cosmic evolution if it is to be meaningful to men and women of our time' (Care 82). If taken apart from his personal devotion to Christ, then it may seem that the Christ of Teilhard's evolution is difficult to identify with; but the holistic way he looked at the world must be remembered. The difficulties of evil, of suffering and death in the world, form part of his notion of how evolution moves on; it entails the growth of being through the entropy that is part of all of creation. There is the 'original fall' which he defines as the forces of diminishment in the world that make things fall apart, in failure, in destruction, in death. It is this force of entropy that hollows us out, that makes space in which we may find our God, in which we may work without rest until we find Christ in everything. Death itself is the final entrance into the care of God, and on God and the incarnate Christ we have to rely.

Evolution, then, appears cruel. Yet through its ever-greater complexity it will come, Teilhard holds, to a great unity. Finally, in his thinking, it is Eucharist, the personal closeness to the real, resurrected Christ, that prolongs the incarnation and maintains Christ's connection to all the elements of creation. There is, in 'The Divine Milieu', a paean of praise reminiscent of 'The Deer's Cry'. Teilhard writes, 'All around us, to right and left, in front and behind, above and below, we have only had to go a little beyond the frontier of sensible appearances in order to see the divine welling up and showing through. But it is not only close to us, in front of us, that the divine presence has revealed itself. It has sprung up so universally, and we find ourselves so surrounded and transfixed by it, that there is no room left to fall down and adore it, even within ourselves' (Milieu 84). Because of the incarnation, all of creation has become 'Christified'; we, humanity, may consciously develop the presence of Christ within ourselves and within creation, thus working towards the Omega point, and it is Eucharist that is the main strength offered to us: 'As our humanity assimilates the material world, and as the Host assimilates our humanity, the Eucharistic transformation goes beyond and completes the transubstantiation of the bread on the altar' (Milieu 98), sentiments beautifully expressed in his poem, 'La messe sur le monde'. Here is part of that hymn, that prayer, in my own version:

'La Messe sur le monde'
Offertory:

And since, O Lord, once more,
not in the forests of the Aisne, but in the Asian steppes,
I have neither bread, nor wine, nor altar,

I will raise my being above symbols to the Pure Majesty of
what's real
and I, your priest, will offer you
on the altar of the whole earth

the labour and the suffering of the world ...
I will place upon my paten, oh my God,
the expected harvest of each day's effort;
I will place within my chalice the sap of all fruits
that will today be poured out ...

Let them come to me, then, the memory and mystical
Presence of those
whom Light awakens to enter into a new day! One by one,
Lord,
I see them, and love them, those you have given me
as sustenance and as natural charm of my existence ...
Those who surround and support me without my knowing,
those who come and those who go, those, above all who,
in Truth or error, at their office, laboratory, factory
believe in the Progress of all things,
and pursue with passion today the Light ...
This human ocean whose slow, monotonous oscillations
fling trouble into the most believing of souls ...
I would that now my being may resonate to their deep murmuring. This
the matter of my sacrifice, this
the offering you are waiting for, to appease your Hunger,
to stanch your Thirst ... this the growth of our World.

This bread, our effort, is only in itself a vast disintegration ...
This wine, our suffering, is only in itself, alas, a dissolving
drink.

Lord, make us one!

* * *

This was the text, in French, which I relished that morning
while waiting for my lecturer, in University College, Dublin. I
expect the year would have been 1965, the Second Vatican Council
letting gusts of fresh air sweep through the Catholic Church, and
ultimately sweeping me off my feet and out into the world

again. It was years later, at a time when, at last, poetry was beginning to mean something to me, that I worked with The
Chieftains to compose a Mass in the hope of continuing the
great work done by Seán Ó Riada, a Mass performed by The
Chieftains and the Whitehall Choir of which I was then director,
on television, at Listowel Writers' Week, and in some of the
churches around Dublin city. The words I wrote for the
Offertory, clearly stirred by the work of Teilhard de Chardin,
were set to music and still ring true to me. It was, in fact, the first
poem I ever had published and it appeared in a journal called
Aquarius, edited from the Servite Priory in Benburb, Co Tyrone.

Offertory

We offer you, Lord, in our strong, our sensitive hands
to-day this bread:
this plough and plod, soft coaxing, collecting,
the mixing and moulding, dull rumbling of trucks
till the crates all are named for those countless lands;
from our proud, proud hands, o Christ, accept this bread.

We offer you, Lord, in our soil-cracked, our swollen hands
to-day this wine:
this fall, this crush, the strain, the pain
o crumbling collapsing of flesh and the fierce
dizzy dash of the blood of those countless lands;
from our weary, weary hearts, o Christ, accept this wine.

Then give into our hands
your flesh
to melt and merge with the soil and stones,

and give into our hearts
your blood
to seep through the sweat when the world groans;

that our earth may grow through its brightest blackest parts
a sight well pleasing to the Lord of lands.

Revolutions and Rebellions

The 'Glorious Revolution' of 1688 shifted a great deal in the minds and hearts of the population of England, left Ireland in a pool of blood after the Battle of the Boyne, with a heritage of hatred and sectarianism that trickles through the country still. William of Orange, saviour of the Protestant cause, would accept no less that being made king, and Mary his queen. At the end of the seventeenth century, Anglican orthodoxy had become widespread. England was still in conflict, the Nine Years War, 1688-1697, was followed by the War of Spanish Succession, 1702-13. Antagonism with the French was uppermost but the wars made England a major force in continental politics. In 1689 the Toleration Act gave limited freedom of worship to Protestant non-conformists. William III died in 1702 and was succeeded by Anne, William's sister-in-law, daughter of her Catholic Father, James II. She had little impact and died without surviving issue and so was the last monarch of the House of Stuart. She was succeeded by George I, her second cousin, of the House of Hanover, in 1714.

A Jacobite rebellion, in 1715, an attempt to restore James and some measure of toleration for Catholicism, failed. The first half of the eighteenth century had many financial problems; along with these there were infections, such as small-pox, that reduced the population. Many lost money in speculation, and through corruption that was rife in the Hanover court. There was a sense of greed, crime was more common, and the mid-century turned to a foppish attempt towards prosperity, vulgarity and commercialism. Religious issues remained muted though unchanging. All through this the Anglican monopoly remained. Late in the century the industrial revolution began to change England. Many people began to move into the cities, and into mining and manufacturing industries. The invention of the steam engine was important in the drive for greater material success.

The eighteenth was the century of the rise of the 'gentry', wealthy middle-class landowners. Furniture was catered for,

with people like Chippendale, Hepplewhite and Sheraton producing wonderful pieces for those who could afford them. The
visiting of spas became popular amongst the well-to-do and
seaside resorts became popular, amongst both the well-off and
the poorer. At this period, too, the habit of wealthy young men
setting off on a 'grand tour' of Europe began to develop. Yet a
great many lived still at the level of subsistence. Towns grew
larger as people came in from the countryside seeking work.
London grew enormously. Land enclosure began to take over
again and, though it allowed more efficient use of the ground, it
deprived the poor and travellers of some of their space.

There was some stability during the reigns of George II and
George III, great developments in roadways and turnpikes.
Society was growing ever more polarised with wages for the
labouring classes getting even worse. The anti-papist Gordon
riots of 1780 produced a real state of terror in London, and
marked a further stage in the display of an unashamed religious
prejudice. The later French revolution helped destroy any tolerance that was left. In 1738 John Wesley founded the Methodists,
and they became a separate denomination from the Church of
England. Wesley preached widely throughout the country and
offered the poor the possibility of doing all right in heaven.
Technology advanced at great speed with many other inventions
leading to an age of reason, a sophisticated and determined exploration of the physical world.

The eighteenth century, with its application of Newtonian
scientific methods to Christian faith, attempting to purge it of
any mystery and establish religion on a purely rational basis,
turned Christ to the scrutiny of reason; our late age had begun.
Reason proposed alternative Christs: it ignored the metaphorical
nature of faith. 'Western Christians were so committed to a literal
understanding of their faith and had taken an irrevocable step
back from myth; a story was either factually true or it was a
delusion' (Armstrong 307). This large, somewhat wealthy and
pretentious middle class dominated the century and it was at
the end of this period that John Clare, poet, was born into a poor
and labouring family. George II died in 1760 and was succeeded
by George III. Dominions abroad were developed, Quebec, the
American Colonies, the West Indies and more exploration into

the East and Asia, particularly India, sending wealth home, yet costing a great deal of money. The War of Independence, ending in 1776 with America's Declaration of Independence, cost Britain dearly in its attempt to wage war at such a great distance.

By 1815 the reversal of fortunes between Britain and France was visible; over twenty years of war culminated in the victory of Waterloo, but consistent industrial development and the winning of wealthy dominions gave Britain, as a nation, a fine economic edge. The French seaports had been damaged and England had won a great deal more of international trade. 'Trade and distribution provided the central impulses for industrialisation. No other European country had 30 per cent of its population in towns, to be fed, clothed, and warmed, or controlled such vast overseas markets' (History 478). England forged ahead with agriculture, coal, iron and textiles. The early nineteenth century also saw an Evangelical revival, emphasising the availability of grace to all who lived by the words of the Bible. It was 'a faith of crisis, valid against atheistic revolution, unfeeling industrial relationships, and brutal personal behaviour'. (History 484). It was also politically conservative.

England welcomed with enthusiasm the French Revolution though Edmund Burke complained loudly in his *Reflections on the Revolution in France*, published in 1790. It was followed by Tom Paine's reply, *The Rights of Man*, urging individualistic, democratic reform. Authorities feared 'the contagion of ideas'. In 1793 England was at war with France. These wars cost England dearly in terms of finance and manpower, drafts into the militia, taxes. In the towns the post-war poverty threatened the outbreak of unrest. By 1881 about two thirds of the population lived in towns. There was a severe cholera epidemic throughout Europe in 1832, taking some 31,000 English souls. As the century developed so did poverty, crowding in the towns and cities, squalid circumstances, drastically dangerous sanitary conditions. In 1820 George III died and was succeeded by George IV who was followed in 1830 by William IV. In 1829 the Catholic Emancipation Act, greatly influenced by the work of Daniel O'Connell, brought an end to much of the official discrimination against Catholics.

The century began with great political and social unrest. In

1812 the Tory prime minister Spencer Perceval was assassinated. In 1820 a plot to kill the entire cabinet failed. Between 1811 and 1816 textile workers broke the new machines as they thought they would take over their jobs and unemployment would follow; they were known as Luddites. Then in 1817 workers marching with a petition to London were stopped by soldiers. In 1819, 11 people were killed and hundreds wounded in 'The Peterloo Massacre' when soldiers shot at an unarmed crowd. John Clare, poet, may have been unaffected by these industrial troubles, but he came to have sufficient troubles of his own.

Where flowers are, God is, and I am free
(John Clare 1793-1864)

John Clare, and a twin sister, were born in the village of Helpston, Northamptonshire, in 1793. Both children were weak at birth, and the girl died within a matter of weeks. It appears that this fact later haunted John, though at a deep level within himself. Many years later he wrote lines for her:

Bessey – I call thee by that earthly name
That but a little while belonged to thee –
Thou left me growing up to sin and shame
And kept thy innocence untained and free
To meet the refuge of a heaven above
Where life's bud opens in eternity.

As with Hopkins later on, it is the sense of the loss of innocence in life that brings a certain sadness to the soul. In Clare's poetry 'childhood is represented as a lost paradise that can be regained only in eternity' (Bate 18). As a child he spent much time wandering on Emmonsales Heath and loved its flora and fauna which he came to know intimately; from a poem of that title:

The birds still find their summer shade
To build their nests again
And the poor hare its rushy glade
To hide from savage men

'The Enclosures'; between about 1809 and 1820, Helpston and its surrounds were gradually enclosed, open fields were fenced off, setting up a new disposition of lands for greater production, rights of way were closed, more divisions with fences and hedges were created; trees came down, *No Trespassing* signs went up. Streams were stopped so ditches could be made straight. Clare saw it all as giving unrestricted power to big landowners: gypsies, loved by Clare, were amongst those greatly affected. Commonages and waste grounds were also restricted and all of this infringed on Clare's right to wander.

In those early years he caused damage, innocent and child-ish, and came, later in life to regret that; but his horror of adult destruction continues in this same poem:

> He that can meet the morning wind
> And o'er such places roam
> Nor leave a lingering wish behind
> To make their peace his home –
>
> His heart is dead to quiet hours
> No love his mind employs
> Poesy with him ne'er shares its flowers
> Nor solitude its joys

'He has a deep respect, even a reverence, for other forms of life, delighting in their integrity, and troubled by the spread of cultivation that ravaged their hitherto neglected territories.' The poems he wrote later on 'raise in an entirely unforced manner most serious questions about the human use of the non-human natural world' (Summerville 98).

John Clare was born into the home of an agricultural labourer and had little or no formal education, being forced from an early age to skip schooling to help out in the fields. However, he was no mere simpleton, no ignorant genius: he was a quick learner and an avid reader, and was endowed with an acute memory. He knew the Bible well and the Psalms by heart. As he grew he bought books that he could ill afford and built up quite a sub-stantial library. He balked, however, at learning Latin and grammar, finding these unnatural and unnecessary. There is a poem Clare wrote that is deeply influenced by the Psalms, and is one much more formal than Clare's usual work (a Clare touch, however, is that he sees his 'bones like hearthstones burning away'):

> Lord hear my prayer when trouble glooms
> Let sorrow find a way
> And when the day of trouble comes
> Turn not thy face away
> My bones like hearthstones burn away
> My life like vapoury smoke decays

My heart is smitten like the grass
That withered lies and dead
And I so lost to what I was
Forget to eat my bread
My voice is groaning all the day
My bones prick through this skin of clay ...

But thou Lord shalt endure forever
All generations through
Thou shalt to Zion be the giver
Of joy and mercy too
Her very stones are in their trust
Thy servants reverence her dust

While he was still quite young he fell in love with one Mary
Joyce and it appears that he never spoke his love. She remained in
his mind as his first true love and he fantasised always about her,
the fantasy taking over in later years that he had, in fact, married
her. But he wrote: 'It was platonic affection, nothing else but love
in idea.' He seems never to have been shy with other women and
his real loves and his fantasies blurred and merged as he grew
less stable in mind. Even after Mary Joyce died, still a spinster,
Clare did not accept her death and continued to write to her and
about her, believing for a time that he had two wives, Mary and
Patty, his actual wife. Love of books isolated him from others but
his joy continued in his solitary roaming around the countryside.
'Gardening, birding and botanising were as central to his life as
reading, writing and loving' (Bate 281).

The Morning Wind

There's more than music in this early wind
Awaking like a bird refreshed from sleep
And joy what Adam might in Eden find
When he with angels did communion keep
It breathes all balm and incense from the sky
Blessing the husbandman with freshening powers
Joy's manna from its wings doth fall and lie
Harvests for early wakers with the flowers
The very grass in joy's devotion moves
Cowslaps in adoration and delight

This way and that bow to the breath they love
Of the young winds that with the dew pearls play
Till smoking chimneys sicken the young light
And feeling's fairy visions fade away

His religious sensibility already associated such joy in the countryside with Eden and Adam, such prelapsarian glory, and it is the presence of the 'smoking chimneys' that begin to destroy the scene. In his later depressions and madness he sometimes thought himself damned and sought reassurance; he had once tried a primitive Methodist movement: 'my feelings are so unstrung in their company that I can scarcely refrain from shedding tears and when I went to church I could scarcely refrain from sleep' (quote in Bate 255). He needed enthusiasm, simplicity and freshness though his inborn sense of restraint drew him back. Clare was not fond of going to church; he preferred to read his Bible or a religious treatise. He had little trust in priests, indeed, he gradually lost his trust in people in general. Like Hopkins he kept notes on his observations in the fields, and did drawings, too, detailed and delicately observed. Indeed, his later mental difficulties sometimes make one think of Hopkins, depressions, symptoms of physical distress.

Trying to find labour he tried his hand at all kinds of odd jobs, even joining the militia for a time, in expectation (all England was on tenterhooks) of an invasion by Napoleon's armies; he was given some training but was quickly dismissed, being small and seemingly weak, an 'odds and sods man', with a uniform too big for him and a helmet too small. What made his life worth living, then, he came to find in poetry, and in his mind he later associated poetry with love unfulfilled, Mary Joyce and her absence tormenting him. Gradually, the love of poetry took him over though he enjoyed drinking (often far too much) with his friends: 'Despite his weak constitution, he sought to keep up with their drinking, especially on Saturday nights. These were known as "randy nights", when they all met in the pub to drink and sing 'and every new beginner had to spend a larger portion than the rest, which they called "colting"' (Bate 75). Yet he tended to despise those very same co-revellers' lack of awareness of the glories of creation. The poem 'The Robin's Nest' shows how he wishes to be

> Far from the ruder world's inglorious din
> Who see no glory but in sordid pelf
> And nought of greatness but its little self
> Scorning the splendid gift that nature gives
> Where nature's glory ever breathes and lives

This is where he finds comfort and relief, even in memory and imagination later on:

> there is no curb
> Of interest, industry, or slavish gain
> To war with nature, so the weeds remain
> And wear an ancient passion that arrays
> One's feelings with the shadows of old days
> The rest of peace the sacredness of mind
> In such deep solitude we seek and find.

His sheer delight in nature is unfeigned, as is his wish to capture this as fully as he can in verse: and he writes

> – my heart aches for the dower

> The pencil gives to soften and infuse
> The brown luxuriance of unfolding hues
> This living luscious tinting woodlands give
> Into a landscape that might breathe and live

Out in the countryside he is found gathering joy from the bounty of summer:

> And here I gather by the world forgot
> Harvests of comfort from their happy mood
> Feeling God's blessing dwells in every spot
> And nothing lives but owes him gratitude

So many of the poems and parts of poems contain the phrase 'I love ...' and he goes on to describe in delightful and moving detail what has stirred him. 'His pathos, unheard of elsewhere in English poetry, draws on his sense of the vulnerability of natural things, of the rural order, and, obliquely, his own vulnerability' (Schmidt 389). All too often, in Clare, 'the act of loving description is the poem' (Schmidt 392), but in much of this his sheer immersion in creation and his exquisite use of language to

capture both the detail of what he experiences and his sense of
the innocence and fragility of beauty around him, make him
unique in English poetic work. There is much pre-figuring of a
poet like Hopkins here:

Pleasant Spots

There is a wild and beautiful neglect
About the fields that so delights and cheers
Where nature her own feelings to effect
Is left at her own silent work for years
The simplest thing thrown in our way delights
From the wild careless feature that it wears
The very road that wanders out of sight
Crooked and free is pleasant to behold
And such the very weeds left free to flower
Corn poppys red and carlock gleaming gold   (charlock)
That makes the cornfields shine in summer hour
Like painted skys – and fancy's distant eye
May well imagine armys marching bye
In all the grand array of pomp and power

And here is a stanza from 'The Moorhen's Nest':

And man the only object that disdains
Earth's garden into deserts for his gains
Leave him his schemes of gain – 'tis wealth to me
Wild heaths to trace –

Gradually Clare came to realise that few people seemed to
share his love of nature; and when 'the enclosures' came, he was
greatly upset. As he grew older and more mature, he became
more and more conscious of heritage, of the gifts of nature that
were spiritually important to humankind, how love of environment mattered to him but seemed to matter so little to the great
world about him, and he was hurt by the greed and cant he
noticed everywhere. Between about 1800 and 1825 a great deal
of what had been public land became 'enclosed' around the
Helpston area, fields were fenced off, new roads marked out,
new allotments of land set out, with much of the road edges and
wild heathlands blocked from public access. Clare saw all of this
as the long reaching of human greed into the free realms of

creation. A poem he called 'The Eternity of Nature' begins like this:

Leaves from eternity are simple things
To the world's gaze – whereto a spirit clings
Sublime and lasting – trampled underfoot
The daisy lives and strikes its little root
Into the lap of time – centurys may come
And pass away into the silent tomb
And still the child hid in the womb of time
Shall smile and pluck them when this simple rhyme
Shall be forgotten like a churchyard-stone

One almost foresees the Hopkins line: 'there lives the dearest freshness deep down things ...'

Further along in 'The Eternity of Nature':

And the small bumble bee shall hum as long
As nightingales, for time protects the song
And nature is their soul to whom all clings
Of fair or beautiful in lasting things
The little robin in the quiet glen
Hidden from fame and all the strifes of men
Sings unto time a pastoral and gives
A music that lives on and ever lives
Both spring and autumn, years rich bloom and fade
Longer than songs that poets ever made

There is in all this a great deal more than the literate bump-kin who sees and marvels at nature without giving thought to where the marvel comes from: and the poem ends:

'Tis nature's wonder and her maker's will
Who bade earth be and order owns him still
As that superior power who keeps the key
Of wisdom, power, and might through all eternity

There is quite a late poem, written during his final years in the asylum; he has retained, all through his life, his love of nature, and has, of course, lost all faith in humanity. His fidelity to nature, to the details and sense of belonging, is quite extraordinary, given his physical and mental problems; the wisdom he has acquired over his frustrated longings and his long sufferings comes across in this poem, as well in its statements as in its perfectly flowing language, rhymes and rhythms; it is the work of a wise man, perfectly wrought, not what one would expect from a man in his condition;

Would'st thou but know

Would'st thou but know where Nature clings
That cannot pass away
Stand not to look on human things
For they shall all decay:
False hearts shall change and rot to dust
While truth exerts her powers
Love lives with Nature, not with lust.
Go find her in the flowers.

Dost dream o'er faces once so fair,
Unwilling to forget?
Seek Nature in the fields and there
The first-loved face is met
The native gales are lovers' voices
As nature's self can prove
The wild field-flowers are lovers' choices
And Nature's self is Love.

His hurt continues when he sees how humans treat nature: this is made very clear in the following excerpt from a poem called 'Summer Evening':

Prone to mischief boys are met
Gen the eaves the ladder's set
Sly they climb and softly tread
To catch the sparrow on his bed
And kill 'em O in cruel pride
Knocking gen the ladderside
Cursed barbarians pass me by
Come not, turks, my cottage nigh
Sure my sparrows are my own
Let ye then my birds alone
Sparrows, come from foes severe,
Fearless come, ye're welcome here
My heart years for fates like thine

A sparrow's life's as sweet as mine
To my cottage then resort
Much I love your chirping note
Wi' my own hands to form a nest
Ill gi' ye shelter peace and rest
Trifling are the deeds ye do
Great the pains ye undergo
Cruel man would Justice serve
Their cruelty's as they deserve
And justest punishment pursue
And do as they to others do
Ye mourning chirpers fluttering here
They would no doubt be less severe
Foolhardy clown ne'er grudge the wheat
Which hunger forces them to eat
Your blinded eyes, worst foes to you,
Ne'er see the good which sparrows do
Did not the sparrows watching round
Pick up the insect from your grounds
Did not they tend your rising grain
You vain might sow – to reap in vain
Thus providence when understood
Her end and aim is doing good
Sends nothing here without its use
Which Ignorance loads with its abuse
Thus fools despise the blessing sent
And mocks the giver's good intent
O God let me the best pursue
As I'd have other do to me
Let me the same to others do
And learn at least Humanity

'A sparrow's life's as sweet as mine'. There may well be some irony in this line; he did not view his life in any sense as 'sweet', and so is linking himself with the suffering and humility that others impose on the bird. Even when he met Martha Turner, a nineteen-year-old girl, he found it hard to pluck up his courage and 'succeeded so far as have the liberty to go home with her to her cottage about 4 miles off'. He was six years older than

Martha, whom he called Patty and they married as Patty was expecting a child; he wrote several love poems but it is never quite clear whether they are addressed to his wife or to his other real, or imagined, loves. Patty remained with him through all their vicissitudes, and they were many, and they had several children, even while John's parents, both elderly and in poor health, lived in the small cottage with them.

Perhaps his views on 'love' were not the usual views; his awareness of Spring and how creatures come together in their own form of 'love' seemed a model for him, while he also appears to have indulged his own 'lusts' whenever he got the opportunity. Here is the second part of a duet of sonnets called 'First Sight Of Spring':

> Spring cometh in with all her hues and smells
> In freshness breathing over hills and dells
> O'er woods where May her gorgeous drapery flings
> And meads washed fragrant with their laughing springs
> Fresh as new-opened flowers untouched and free
> From the bold rifling of the amorous bee
> The happy time of singing birds is come
> And love's lone pilgrimage now finds a home
> Among the mossy oaks now coos the dove
> And the hoarse crow finds softer notes for love
> The foxes play around their dens and bark
> In joy's excess mid woodland shadows dark
> And flowers join lips below and leaves above
> And every sound that meets the ear is love

There were many who came to know, love and greatly admire the poems John Clare was writing and many friends and sponsors worked to have them published. Clare's indifference to spelling and grammar made the task of editing and publishing quite difficult and caused Clare many periods of anxiety and frustration. Eventually his first book, *Poems Descriptive of Rural Life and Scenery* was published in London by Taylor and Hessey, Fleet Street, the publisher of John Keats. The book was an enormous success and ran quickly through several editions. Meanwhile Clare continued to make a poor living by doing odd jobs, such as lime-burner, gardener, haymaker, jack-of-all-trades.

For a short while he became, for the literary society of London to which he was introduced by John Taylor, the publisher, a fine curiosity. He was delighted, for a while, with his fame but it continued to be his poetry that made life meaningful for him, that gave him some form of confidence in himself, that moved him occasionally into the realms of joy.

The Peasant Poet

He loved the brook's soft sound
The swallows swimming by
He loved the daisy-covered ground
The cloud-bedappled sky
To him the dismal storm appeared
The very voice of God
And where the Evening rock was reared
Stood Moses with his rod
And every thing his eyes surveyed
The insects i' the brake
Were creatures God almighty made
He loved them for his sake
A silent man in life's affairs
A thinker from a Boy
A Peasant in his daily cares –
The Poet in his joy.

Clare's love of landscape, particularly in his childhood, re-mained an emblem of paradise to him, and is associated in his mind with childhood innocence, a trait in this poet, this lover of nature, this long-suffering peasant who was deeply aware of his God through the beauty of the world about him. Centuries later, Patrick Kavanagh will echo Clare. Indeed, with its biblical refer-ence and its intense delight in the countryside and the solitude that gives space and mood for thinking, 'The Peasant Poet' could well have been written by Kavanagh. There is a real bond of love between both poets and nature, a true sense of belonging and even the language both use to express this, brings it more to life. Indeed, for Clare, it is almost a love-affair and its destruction brought about the destruction of his mind. He became, naturally, very angry at those who would use the world for economic gain. In such a world he would feel alien and lost.

One of the great delights of Clare's work is the occasional use of Northamptonshire dialect, as in the lines 'the sailing puddock's shrill peelew'. This kind of language much amused the English literati and this, together with his accurate and loving description of the countryside about him, added to the sense of curiosity and weirdness so beloved of the literary hangers-on. The sheer immersion of Clare's senses in the world about him, the richness and local immediacy of the language he uses, are startling and unforgettable. In his *Oxford Essay Lectures*, Seamus Heaney has a chapter on Clare which he calls 'John Clare's Prog'. Because of Clare's use of language and dialect Heaney speaks of 'the here-and-nowness, or there-and-thenness' of the work' (Heaney 66).

Clare was trying to support his wife and seven children. His strange fame called him away from home too often; he visited London where he met writers like Hazlitt, De Quincey, Coleridge, who liked him but could not make him a permanent part of their company. His fellow villagers began to grow suspicious of his fame and contacts and Clare felt ever more and more sidelined in life. Clare's liking for strong drink also began to cause further troubles. He spent most of his income on food for his family, often depriving himself and yet drinking to excess. He suffered from occasional 'swoonings', a kind of panic attack. By 1823 a heavy depression began to settle on him and he never recovered fully. Whatever the nature of his disorder, it is clear that Clare really suffered greatly. His mental confusions were serious and hurtful, as he lost a sense of who he was and what life was about. And yet, when he carries his self-awareness and his simplicity of thought and language into an honest appraisal of life, his poetry touches deeply. Underneath his unsophisticated forms, though rarely expressed, is a strong and unshaken sense of God's existence as the ultimate arbiter of truth, of the certainty that his frustrated love and his frustrated dreams will at last be fulfilled. He placed himself wholly in God's care.

> And he who studies nature's volume through
> And reads it with a pure unselfish mind
> Will find God's power all round in every view
> As one bright vision of the almighty mind

His eyes are open though the world is blind
No ill from him creation's works deform
The high and lofty one is great and kind
Evil may cause the blight and crushing storm
His is the sunny glory and the calm

For John Clare, self-knowledge and humility held together whatever strands of sanity he was left with. And it is a self-knowledge in touch with and sustained by God, not the God of theologians, of pastors or mystics, but the God of the country-side that Clare loved and longed to live in. 'Though he professed himself an Anglican, Clare's attendance at church was most irregular. His deepest feelings of a religious kind were re-served for his experience of nature and his memories of child-hood innocence and joy' (Bate 59). Clare's poem 'Childhood' is quite simply a delight in its nostalgia, language and detail:

By Langley Bush I roam but the bush hath left its hill
On Cowper Green I stray, 'tis a desert strange and chill
And spreading Lea Close Oak ere decay had penned its will
To the axe of the spoiler and self-interest fell a pray
And Crossberry Way and old Round Oak's narrow lane
With its hollow trees like pulpits I shall never see again
Inclosure like Buonaparte let not a thing remain
It levelled every bush and tree and levelled every hill
And hung the moles for traitors
     – though the brook is running still
It runs a naked stream cold and chill

His poetry strengthened as the distractions of his popularity faded and he melted back, older and wiser, into himself. As the poems regain their freedom, the personal conversational tone absorbs more easily the quaint words. In 1821 the death of a son who died within 24 hours caused him great pain; he consoled himself that the child had avoided all the sufferings that growing to manhood would entail and that he was at rest 'with nature that is all divine', a phrase that he mulled over and later changed to 'with cherubs that are all divine'. Perhaps in the case of a child's death, Clare felt somewhat diffident about moving away from the strict tenets with which he had been brought up in school, at home and in church. 'Clare seems torn between a sense of the divinity of nature and a more orthodox belief in Christian salvation. And he cannot suppress the darker thought that his baby might not have found peace, in which case religion would be nothing but a cruel joke' (Bate 212). In a piece composed in June of 1844 he wrote:

> Infants' graves are steps of angels where
> Earth's brightest gems of innocence repose,
> God is their parent, they need no tear,
> He takes them to his bosom from earth's woes;
> A bud their life-time and a flower their close
> Their spirits are an iris of the skies
> Needing no prayers – a sunset's happy close.
> Gone are the bright rays of their soft blue eyes,
> Dews on flowers mourn them and the gale that sighs.

By now, Clare had absorbed more wisdom and cynicism than perhaps he cared for, but it all enlivens the poems and makes the man more aware of himself and his loves and difficulties. His joy in nature was unabated and it was here he found his only real solace, from the world of those who would impose on him, and from the twitchings of his own mind. At this stage in his life he associates the innocence, the freedom, the beauty of the natural world with the kindliness of God, and with his own greatest hope.

> Poets love nature and themselves are love,
> The scorn of fools and mock of idle pride
> The vile in nature worthless deeds approve
> They court the vile and spurn all good beside
> Poets love nature like the calm of heaven
> Her gifts like heaven's love spared far and wide
> In all her works there are no signs of leaven
> Sorrow abashes from her simple pride
> Her flowers like pleasures have their season's birth
> And bloom through regions here below
> They are her very scriptures upon earth
> And teach us simple mirth where e'er we go
> Even in prison they can solace me
> For where they bloom God is, and I am free.

A stanza from a poem 'To a Lark Singing in Winter' has this delightful piece:

> The god of nature guides her well
> To choose best dwellings for hersel'
> And in the spring her nest we'll tell
> Her choice at least
> For God loves little larks as well
> As man or beast

A letter written in 1832 to his friend Henry Cary gives a further idea of how important poetry was to him: 'If you laugh at my ambitions I am ready to laugh with you at my own vanity for I sit sometimes and wonder over the little noise I have made in the world until I think I have written nothing as yet to deserve any praise at all – so the spirit of fame, of living a little after life like a name on a conspicuous place, urges my blood upward into unconscious melodys and striding down my orchard and homestead I hum and sing inwardly those little madrigals and then go in and pen them down, thinking them much better things than they are until I look over them again and then the charm vanishes into the vanity that I shall do something better ere I die and so in spite of myself I rhyme on.'

By now the mental and physical problems that Clare suffered were gathering pace and intensity. Speculation may well continue for ever on the precise nature of these sufferings but the symptoms all seem to point to what we now know as manic depression or 'bipolar affective disorder'. In July 1837 he was admitted 'by authority of his wife', to Matthew Allen's private asylum in Epping Forest, northeast of London, being then about 44 years old. 'He suffered from a distressing array of physical and mental symptoms' (Bate 409), but even here poetry was a relief and a release to him, his only lasting source of joy – and of torment.

There is a passage in Shakespeare's 'A Midsummer-Night's Dream' in which Theseus says:

> The lunatic, the lover and the poet
> Are of imagination all compact:
> One sees more devils than vast hell can hold,

That is, the madman: the lover, all as frantic,
Sees Helen's beauty in a brow of Egypt;
The poet's eye in a fine frenzy rolling,
Doth glance from heaven to earth, from earth to heaven;
And as imagination bodies forth
The form of things unknown, the poet's pen
Turns them to shapes, and gives to airy nothing
A local habitation and a name.

Clare often spoke of 'the blue devils' that bothered him and his great love, Mary Joyce, he never even touched. And yet here is a man whose soul gave itself to the things of nature, and who watched with care where the Divine Providence seemed to offer some redemption: 'The poet's eye in a fine frenzy rolling, Doth glance from heaven to earth, from earth to heaven.' Seamus Heaney wrote: 'For all his reputation as a peasant poet, Clare had mastered the repertoire of prescribed styles and skills: nowadays a poet as capable and informed as this would probably be headhunted to teach a graduate workshop in versification' (Heaney 69). This was a poet who was confined to Bedlam, and Heaney goes on to state that 'What distinguishes it is an unspectacular joy and totally alert love for the one-thing-after-anotherness of the world' (Heaney 70). The level of engagement with his world gives the poems their life. Heaney sees the theme of Clare's work as 'the awful necessity of the gift of keeping going and the lovely wonder that it can be maintained – a gift which is tutored by the instinctive cheer and courage of living creatures, and heartened by every fresh turn and return of things in the natural world' (Heaney 78).

In his first stint in the asylum, Clare seems to have been allowed a good deal of freedom of movement and he eventually simply walked away from the place. But his sorrow and sometime despair at his condition brought him to write one of his most famous poems:

I Am

I am – yet what I am, none cares or knows;
My friends forsake me like a memory lost:
I am the self-consumer of my woes –

They rise and vanish in oblivion's host
Like shadows in love-frenzied stifled throes
And yet I am, and live – like vapours tossed

Into the nothingness of scorn and noise,
Into the living sea of waking dreams,
Where there is neither sense of life or joys,
But the vast shipwreck of my life's esteems;
Even the dearest that I love the best
Are strange – nay, rather, stranger than the rest.

I long for scenes where man hath never trod
A place where woman never smiled or wept
There to abide with my Creator, God,
And sleep as I in childhood sweetly slept,
Untroubling and untroubled where I lie
The grass below – above, the vaulted sky.

Again the simplicity, the humility of that one word
'Untroubling', leaves us gasping at the sheer genius of this man.
Clare was aware that his life caused difficulties to others, to his
wife, his children, even his carers in the asylum. He knew in his
deepest core that he was not made for human companionship
and longed for, and found peace only in solitude and amid the
loveliness of creation. Here is a poet, troubled beyond what
most of us will ever know, who yet peers out of his darkness
now and again and grasps with the naturalness of his birth and
station the energies of life and creation that he knows are real.
His faith continues unquestioning, even in the depths of his
wrecking and being wrecked. But his faith is not that of church
or sect, it is the faith in the creator who has wrought such wonders that, as Hopkins will write, 'the world is charged with the
grandeur of God'. Clare wrote:

God looks on nature with a glorious eye
    And blesses all creation with the sun
    Its drapery of green and brown, earth, ocean, he
    In morning as Creation just begun
    That saffron East foretells the rising sun
    And who can look upon that majesty
    Of light brightness and splendour nor feel won

With love of him whose bright all-seeing eye
Feeds the day's light with Immortality?

This peasant poet, this lost and grieving soul, did not keep his sorrowing out of the poetry. There is a poem where this suffering is given its place and because of the immediacy of his writing and his awareness, the suffering is brought home to the reader, and we feel it in phrases like 'My bones like hearthstones burn away', and 'But thou hast held me up awhile and thou hast cast me down.' This poem reads powerfully as it takes into itself all Clare's poetic achievement, all his self-knowledge, all his acute observation, not only of nature and himself, but of the attitude of other people towards him. And the poem ends again with the unquestioning acceptance of his fate under the watchful eye of the Creator who has laid all things out:

Lord hear my prayer when trouble glooms

> Let sorrow find a way
> And when the day of trouble comes
> Turn not thy face away
> My bones like hearth-stones burn away
> My life like vapoury smoke decays
>
> My heart is smitten like the grass
> That withered lies and dead
> And I so lost to what I was
> Forget to eat my bread
> My voice is groaning all the day
> My bones prick through this skin of clay
>
> The wilderness's pelican
> The desert's lonely owl
> I am their like, a desert man
> In ways as lone and foul
> As sparrows on the cottage top
> I wait till I with faintness drop
>
> I hear my enemies' reproach
> All silently I mourn
> They on my private peace encroach
> Against me they are sworn

Ashes as bread my trouble shares
And mix my food with weeping cares

Yet not for them is sorrow's toil
I fear no mortal's frown
But thou hast held me up awhile
And thou hast cast me down
My days like shadows waste from view
I mourn like withered grass in dew

But thou Lord shalt endure forever
All generations through
Thou shalt to Zion be the giver
Of joy and mercy too
Her very stones are in their trust
Thy servants reverence her dust

Heathens shall hear and fear thy name
All kings of earth thy glory know
When thou shalt build up Zion's fame
And live in glory there below
He'll not despise their prayers though mute
But still regard the destitute

Perhaps one of the saddest and most disturbing journeys a poet ever undertook is when, in July 1841, Clare set off through Epping Forest to find the Great York Road and walk home. For him it was an 'escape' from an asylum that had become intolerable to him, as had the absence of, and from, his family. He suffered great cold, hunger, thirst, at one stage dining on grass at the side of the road; he lost direction, he slept in sheds and ditches, waking to find himself soaked through; his shoes were poor and his feet suffered greatly. This for four days, and almost one hundred miles. Yet he was scarcely in the door of his own home before it was clear that his mind was in a worse condition than ever, and five months later, in December of 1841, he was admitted to Northampton General Lunatic Asylum where he was to die some 23 years later.

A late poem gathers a great deal of John Clare together, though the poems he wrote in the asylum were few and far between, and very scattered, as he imagined himself to be, now

Lord Byron, now Robert Burns, indeed anybody and everybody who crossed his mind. Yet his fame out in the world was growing and people came occasionally to see and speak with him. He was happy to sit in an alcove and talk with anybody, provided he had his tobacco to hand. Right to the last his love of creation was untouched, his love of language and his love for God remained strong and clear in his occasional moments of lucidity:

> The wind blows happily on everything
> The very weeds that shake beside the fold
> Bowing they dance – do anything but sing
> And all the scene is lovely to behold
> Blue mists of morning evenings of gold
> How beautiful the wind will play with spring
> Flowers beam with every colour light beholds
> Showers o'er the landscape flye on wet pearl wings
> And winds stir up unnumbered pleasant things
>
> I love the luscious green before the bloom
> The leaves and grass and even beds of moss
> When leaves 'gin bud and spring prepares to come
> The Ivy's evergreen the brown-green gorse
> Plots of green weeds that barest roads engross
> In fact I love the youth of each green thing
> The grass, the trees, the bushes, and the moss
> That pleases little birds and makes them sing
> I love the green before the blooms of spring
>
> Sorrow is felt not seen – the grief of verse
> Is writ by those who share not in our pain
> The pall embroidered and the sable hearse
> Are symbols not of sorrow but of gain
> What of the scutcheoned hears and pall remain
> When all is past – there sorrow is nor more
> Sorrow's heart aches – and burning scars will stain
> As morning dews – as April showers is o'er
> Some tears fall on their graves again …
>
> False time what is it but a rogue's account
> Of books wrong-kept – time's keystone is the sun

WHERE FLOWERS ARE ...

True nature's wronged – and what is the amount
But death's diseases – that their circuit run
Through error and through deeds that fate has done
Religion is the health – the sun's bright ray
By which the goal of Love and Freedom's won
The ocean's tide will flow its natural way
And none its speed and none its course will stay

All nature has a feeling: wood, brooks, fields
Are life eternal – and in silence they
Speak happiness – beyond the reach of books
There's nothing mortal in them – their decay
Is the green life of change to pass away
And come again in blooms revivified
Its birth was heaven, eternal is its stay
And with the sun and moon shall still abide
Beneath their night and day and heaven wide

Clare identified himself and his living with the places and animals that inhabit his poems, often in their fragility combined with their labours at survival. In the final years in the asylum 'Clare was withdrawing into non-identity' (Bate 494). No poems survive from the years 1852-1859. 'To continue in self-belief was his perpetual struggle in the asylum' (Bate 499).

I am quite certain that John Clare never heard of ecology, or of christology, nor of bi-polar affective disorder ... yet in his life and poetry, he is a great exemplar of all of these concepts and affects ...

Early in 1864 he was 'very helpless and quite childish', and on 20 May 'he simply ceased to breathe'. Clare had at last stepped out of the constrictions of his life into the wide meadows of light; he had gone home, to the Creator and the original Eden of his dreams.

* * *

Moved and hurt for the sufferings of John Clare, I wrote this
piece for him:

John Clare's Bedlam

What do they pack for you in that battered suitcase
as they leave you to the madhouse door? How do they say

'goodbye'? how turn away? And how do you
turn from them, from the finches, from the sloe-

blossoms and music of the rainclouds – how do you face
towards that scanting cell? How may the warm sun's rays

discover where you are, all this not in the scheme
of God's devising? Can you sing while you suffer the severe

processes they have planned for your purgation?
– bleedings, chemicals – to turn the runnels of your brain

to oozings? And all the while the unfazed robin
calls you to rake for her the good, black earth again,

the fox would lead you down his trodden path, through
fragrances of pine, the tough-branched undergrowth you
        know

out to the heather marches where you would hymn, apart,
God and made-things, Christ and abundance, because the
        heart

is a shire too great to be fenced off, and the sky above is
        chaste
and shiftful as divinity, life-giving as the dark blood of the
        Christ.

Disturbing beyond belief

After leaving the Holy Ghost Fathers (now known as Spiritans) I searched for my place in the world. It was not easy to discover a world that I had been taught to beware of, instinctively, and for a while I tried to have a foot in either camp. At last I married Barbara Sheridan, daughter of the comedian Cecil Sheridan, and we settled down in a small house in Dublin. I was teaching, so was she. A child was expected. The world looked real and good. However, after the birth, Barbara was not recovering her strength. There were weeks when she appeared to be diminishing in body and spirit and the doctors sought to find the cause. She was suffering acute pains in all her joints, joints that were knotted and twisted in agony. Eventually, SLE was diagnosed, systemic lupus erythematosus, a disease in which the immune system attacks the cells and tissues of the body and can attack any and every part of the human body. The name 'lupus', wolf, was a terrifying one, as was the word 'systemic', which I did understand. Her entire body was wracked with pain and I prayed with an intensity and sincerity I had never known before, even in the seminary. Eventually they announced they had found the cure: she was heavily treated with cortisone, steroids, and a swift and remarkable improvement took place. Everything seemed to be going well again. But I was not to forget, how could I? the suffering and pain she had endured, a woman whom I loved, a kind and generous spirit, attacked with such ferocity my very faith in a benign God began to waver, slightly, ever so slightly.

Barbara also suffered from depression and had done so all her life, an illness known as endogenous depression, not a depression as such, but a chemical imbalance in the brain that can be treated, balanced and she had lived a fairly normal life until then. Indeed, in the fervour of my love, I considered myself capable of helping her through such bouts that seemed to occur with a form of seasonal return. Now, however, the steroids began to do damage in this area and, while her bodily health improved, her mental health began to slide. After some weeks, she had to be

hospitalised for depression and this was a cycle of some six
weeks. Sadly, it was to be a recurring cycle.

Life began to move on a difficult track, physical suffering followed by mental problems and the doctors seemed incapable
then of finding a balance of medication that would ease the ebb
and flow of pain and suffering. We had some very, very hard
times. I was still thinking in terms of faith and wrote this piece
after a sorry event at home; it is a poem wholly influenced by St
John of The Cross, his work *En una noche oscura* … which in turn
was a love-poem between the soul and God, based on the 'Song
of Songs':

On a Dark Night

On a dark night
When all the street was hushed, you crept
Out of our bed and down the carpeted stair.
I stirred, unknowing that some light
Within you had gone out, and still I slept.
As if, out of the dark air

Of night, some call
Drew you, you moved in the silent street
Where cars were white in frost. Beyond the gate
You were your shadow on a garage-wall.
Mud on our laneway touched your naked feet.
The dying elms of our estate

Became your bower
And on your neck the chilling airs
Moved freely. I was not there when you kept
Such a hopeless tryst. At this most silent hour
You walked distracted with your heavy cares
On a dark night while I slept.

Barbara showed me a book someone had given her in the
ward in hospital; I remember it as a slim, well-fingered paper-
back, Penguin I think, about the life and work of Hildegard of
Bingen, of whom I knew nothing. Barbara had been moved to
see how much this twelfth-century nun had suffered herself,
and how she had still turned to God with love, and to the works
of creation with devotion. I was introduced to a concept I had

never before averted to, the feminine God, the feminine side of God, indeed the whole relationship of woman to church, to that church of which I was a member. We discussed, often, in the quiet ward of the hospital, how the Catholic Church had moved women aside from service in the church, though it was women who stayed closest to Christ in his most awful moments, who had first discovered the empty tomb, who had first celebrated and offered Eucharist in their homes after the death of Christ. I could not see why this should be the case, was it that the hierarchy were afraid of women, of property rights, of losing their hegemony of power in the church? In the early part of this century, it has become clear that the ordination of women in the Roman Catholic Church is a matter of necessity and inevitability, and that their absence at the core of ministry has been a major cause in the male destruction and abuse of children over so many years.

Hildegard of Bingen, 1098-1178, was born last child of ten, to a noble family. At the age of eight she was 'given to God as a tithe'; she was placed in the care of a woman who lived a solitary and secluded life. This woman, Jutta, taught Hildegard how to read and led her deeply into the spiritual life. Hildegard tells how she had visions from early childhood, once witnessing 'a brightness so great that [her] soul trembled'. All through her life, this concept of light and brightness stayed with her as a blessed light that illuminated the world for her. She grew celebrated as healer and herbalist though she suffered many illnesses herself, as woman and as nun. The women who had been directed around Jutta, eventually became part of the Benedictine order. On Jutta's death in 1136, Hildegard was elected to lead the community. Mary T. Malone calls her 'one of the most accomplished persons, male or female, in the whole western Christian tradition' (Malone 109).

Throughout her life, she suffered illness. At the same time she was experiencing 'visions', which she began to write down. She produced a work known as *Scivias*, a description of a cycle of visions about the relationship of humanity and creation with God. She also composed a collection of music and poetry called the *Symphonia*. She gained fame as a herbalist and people came to her searching for cures for their ailments. She also moved around Germany, teaching and telling her visions and poetry.

Initially, she was approved by the church authorities but later on ran into difficulties after she, out of human compassion, allowed an excommunicated person to be buried in consecrated ground. She was forbidden the Eucharist for a long time. The ban was lifted only a short while before she died. Hildegard celebrated the feminine, the fertility dimension of creation: 'There is no ambiguity towards creation in Hildegard, no revulsion at the mention of earthly, bodily or inanimate nature. She does not see the world as evil or corrupting, to be subdued and tamed through ascetical practices' (Care 134). This was highly unusual in the twelfth century and disapproved of by church and religious congregations. 'Nature evokes joy, wonder, praise, awe and especially love. She is so beautifully adorned that even her creator approaches her in the guise of a lover to embrace her with a kiss' (Care 135). The 'Song of Songs' from the Old Testament was with her constantly, a book filled with the imagery of sensual love, of caring and abiding in love. 'With her we can leave aside the gloom, pessimism and guilt that commonly haunt Christian spirituality and joyfully recognise God's presence in the world around us' (Care 136), but again one must ask what about the dark and murderous and cruel side of creation?

> To the Trinity be praise!
> God is music, God is life
> that nurtures every creature in its kind.
> Our God is the song of the angel throng
> and the splendour of secret ways
> hid from all humankind,
> But God our life is the life of all.
> *(Version: Barbara Newman)*

Yet Hildegard's views were somewhat paradoxical, too, supporting orthodox reforms within the church and agreeing that women were indeed the weaker sex and owed support and obedience to their masters. On the other hand, 'her writings on women are entirely revolutionary and her own ecclesial life is marked, not so much by obedience as by a profound self-confidence in her own prophetic role' (Malone 109). In those times it was seriously dangerous for a woman to claim divine guidance and even more so to write down her thoughts and intend them to be teachings. The philosophy of Aristotle was growing in importance at this time and Hildegard's own work was pushed into the background. She suggested that men were composed of fire and earth, not fire and air, as Aristotle proposed, and that women were of water and air whereas Aristotle had them of water and earth. This was a fundamental difference in medieval thinking. 'Both women and men are created in the image of God and hence she frequently reflects on the feminine aspects of the Divine. Conversely, since God contains both feminine and masculine elements, the images of God, men and women, each contain both of these elements' (Malone 116). A great strength, therefore, in women and one lacking to the church is the feminine quality of mercy.

What, then, has our human life become? Among machines, industrial giants, offices with dried flowers and air-conditioning, computers, appliances at home, traffic jams, cars in the driveways, what has our life become? Instinctively we pursue our own human perfection. 'If we seek to work out a new covenant with nature, one of integration and harmony, we find sources of inspiration in woman and the feminine' (Cry 27). But the church has dismally failed, both in terms of fidelity to women and fidelity to creation itself. And the consequences have been dire. Hildegard had written: 'The earth which sustains humanity must not be injured, it must not be destroyed. The soul is a breath of living spirit that with excellent sensitivity, permeates the entire body to give it life. Just so, the breath of the air makes the earth fruitful. Thus the air is the soul of the earth, moistening it, greening it.' 'God Hugs you! You are encircled by the arms of the mystery of God!' Along with this love of God, this closeness, there is always the real experience of suffering, finitude and sin. Creation itself appears to progress through breakages, upset, destruction, killing. As we sat and talked together, Barbara and I, we were very much aware of it.

After seven years, Barbara died, on the eve of the eve of Christmas. She had been in the hospital for some six weeks before her death yet that death came as a sudden shock to all of us, and to the medical staff. It left me shattered. I felt that God himself, or herself, had shut a door against me. I placed a photograph of our wedding day on the mantelpiece and wrote:

Sacrament

You, pictured for ever, before me;
I stand in black
and wear a white carnation;
you, holding an array of golden roses, maidenhair,
smile up at me, and you are beautiful;
your body washed for me
and gently scented;
you, set apart in white,
a mystery, all sacred;

we are holding hands forever, dedicated;
such the signs of a deep abiding grace.

Another image graven on my mind:
you lie, again in white;
on your breast a silken picture of the Virgin;
they have washed your body,
closed your eyes,
you hold no flowers;
there are vein-blue traces of suffering on your skin,
your fingers locked together,
away from me.

But it is I who have loved you,
have known the deepest secrets of your grace;
I take the golden ring from your finger,
I kiss the bride –

and they close the heavy doors against me
of that silent, vast, cathedral.

By taking back the ring from her finger I felt that I was not letting God have the satisfaction of taking her from me, that I was still the one who was to care for her, that she was mine, as the sacrament of matrimony had stated. The truth is, I was lost, lost to faith, lost to normal living, lost to myself. Lost, for the moment, to God.

Coral Strand

I see her figure stooping on the sand
in winter cold, with the wild sea
behind her, she is held in the history
of shells – cowrie, periwinkle, whelk –
in their white disintegration on the strand;

how could I, loving her, imagine then
her dying, where I stood on rocks at the shore
of her mystery? Now, on a train, I pass
over a causeway where men have been channelling
tides; from our flanged hurrying the shorebirds –

shell-duck, oystercatcher, gull – shear
away; I see them in their countless generations
stab at living things on the shore
of a changing ocean; my face, perplexed,
is staring back at me from the window.

James Mackey, in his book on Jesus Christ, speaks of 'our ever renewed creation eternally wandering on its way, making whole again and renewing through all unavailing destruction and death whether natural or malicious' (Mackey 198), but it was not as easy as that. 'Faith in the goodness of creation is a way of affirming the certainty that the cosmos is more powerful than chaos, because God its Creator has dominion over the absurd and over death' (Cry 36). For some time I lived in a form of chaos; the fact that I had two young children to care for helped me a great deal to keep my eye and mind on the path, though the faith side of that path had virtually disappeared.

Years later I was to visit my sorrowing again, to try and fit it more snugly into the patterning of my living, the trajectory of my passage across the world. I found the searing pain, the accuracy of colouring, the immediacy of shape in the paintings of Edvard Munch and his work moved me to a poem of my own, 'The Instruments of Art'. Part-way through that poem I visited Barbara's sorrowing, and my own, once more, beginning in the seminary, moving past her death:

Life-

drawing, with naked girl, half-light of inherited faith,
colour it in, and rhyme it, blue. In the long library, stooped
over the desks, we read cosmology, the reasoning
of Aquinas; we would hold

the knowledge of the whole world within us. The dawn
chorus: *laudetur Jesus Christus*; and the smothered,
smothering answer: *in aeternum. Amen*. Loneliness
hanging about our frames, like cassocks. New

world, new day. It is hard to shake off darkness, the black
habit. The sky at sunset – fire-red, opening its mouth
to scream; questions of adulthood, exploration of the belly-
        flesh
of a lover. It was like

the rubbling of revered buildings, the moulding of words
into new shapes. In the cramped cab of a truck she, first time,
        fleshed
across his knees; the kiss, two separate, not singular,
alive. It was death already, prowling

at the dark edge of the wood, fangs bared, saliva-white.
Sometimes you fear insanity, the bridge humming to your
        scream
(oil, casein, pastel) but there is nobody to hear, the streaming
        river
only, and the streaming sky; soon

on a dark night, the woman tearing dumbly at her hair while
        you
gaze uselessly onto ashes. Helpless again you fear
woman: saint and whore and hapless devotee. Paint your
        words
deep violet, pale yellow,

the fear, Winter in Meath, Fugue, The Apotheosis of Desire.
The terror is not to be able to write. Naked and virginal
she embraced the skeleton and was gone.

Where now the 'Faith of our Fathers'? where the Love that neither height nor depth nor any other thing may separate us from the love of God?

Stone

Landscape without figures, no breeze,
and barely light; no birds sing,
no hare or rabbit shapes;
trees stand, threatened, their branches numbed.

Stone dominates, not just those
rocks piled into a cairn's shape
nor the one huge stone that stands
almost upright; the early mist

is the colour of stone, and has obscured
the sky. Now, should a man appear
he would move as a spectre might, pass
and leave no trace. A deeper blackness

among the rocks may be a cave-mouth,
or an illusion of shadow, holding
a memory of colour, like washed-out blood.
A train screams in the distance.

Landscape, disturbing beyond belief.

Around this time I discovered the poetry of Gerard Manley Hopkins. I immersed myself in it. It moved me with such power that I spent an entire night sitting at the kitchen table until the dawn light was already greying the window, trying to understand why that magnificent poem, 'The Wreck of the Deutschland', which then I did not fully grasp, was sending shivers up and down my spine. I spent so long over it that it left me exhausted, and left me also with a small rekindling of faith, a distant murmuring of hope, and a certain love for poetry above all.

Gerard Manley Hopkins
Earth, sweet Earth, sweet landscape ...

As a young man Hopkins made many sketches in his note-books, detailed examinations delicately wrought, of flowers, trees clouds: he called these sketches 'My treasury of explored beauty'. From an early age, then, he loved the beauty and won-der of the earth in its detail and in its grander aspects. Speaking of the summer of 1866, Paddy Kitchen writes: 'At no time did Hopkins look more carefully than during that chilly early sum-mer; but although the forefront of his mind was scientifically recording details of landscape and weather, the middle area – so to speak – was responding with emotion to the beauty of nature's proliferation, while the deepest, over-riding response of his mind was a philosophic one – a desire to find unity' (Kitchen 87). The poems echo the observations he made in his journals and notebooks, some of which are: speaking of a fall of snow – 'It tufted and toed the firs and yews and went on to load them till they were taxed beyond their spring. The limes, elms, and Turkey-oaks it crisped beautifully as with young leaf. Looking at the elms from underneath you saw every wave in every twig'; of bluebells – 'I do not think I have ever seen anything more beautiful than the bluebell I have been looking at. I know the beauty of our Lord by it.' He watched waves foam 'into long chains of suds, while the strength of the back-draught shrugged the stones together and clocked them one against another.' In April 1873 he was reading in his room when he heard noises and looked out to witness the felling of a beautiful ash tree; 'there came at that moment a great pang and I wished to die and not to see the inscapes of the world destroyed any more.' He writes of 'swifts rounding and scurling under the clouds'. This close consciousness and love of creation leave him vulnerable to despair when the actualities of presence leave him, or when he sees the destruction of what is beautiful, and in many of these ways Hopkins shares in the sensibility of John Clare.

So many years before the word 'ecology' came into anyone's mind, this poet was urging the absolute beauty of creation and how such a beauty leads inevitably to the love of Christ. He was born and brought up an Anglican and the Eucharist, from the beginning, was central to his thinking. In an early poem, again dwelling on the suffering of Christ and of our response to that suffering, he writes of our sharing in that sacred life, a response similar to that in Herbert's great poem 'Love':

Barnfloor and Winepress
   And he said, If the Lord do not help thee, whence shall I help thee?
   out of the barnfloor, or out of the winepress? 2 Kings VI: 27

Thou that on sin's wages starvest,
Behold we have the joy in harvest:
For us was gather'd the first fruits,
For us was lifted from the roots,
Sheaved in cruel bands, bruised sore,
Scourged upon the threshing-floor;
Where the upper mill-stone roof'd His head,
At morn we found the heavenly Bread,
And, on a thousand altars laid,
Christ our Sacrifice is made!

Thou whose dry plot for moisture gapes,
We shout with them that tread the grapes:
For us the Vine was fenced with thorn,
Five ways the precious branches torn;
Terrible fruit was on the tree
In the acre of Gethsemane;
For us by Calvary's distress
The wine was racked from the press;
Now in our altar-vessels stored
Is the sweet Vintage of our Lord.

In Joseph's garden they threw by
The riv'n Vine, leafless, lifeless, dry:
On Easter morn the Tree was forth,
In forty days reach'd heaven from earth;
Soon the whole world is overspread;
Ye weary, come into the shade.

The field where He has planted us
Shall shake her fruit as Libanus,
When He has sheaved us in His sheaf,
When He has made us bear his leaf. -
We scarcely call that banquet food,
But even our Saviour's and our blood,
We are so grafted on His wood.

The poem may be derivative but it is seminal to the late
Hopkins. The full thrust of his poetry is Christ, the need to be
close to Christ who will rescue us, through his death and resurrection, into life; the need to be aware of Christ, too, as the suffering Lord whom we have to follow, through our own suffering and dismay, our efforts and failures. And the need for
Eucharist, that we share physically in that banquet food, we becoming the fruitful tree, the suffering vine, sharing in the blood
of Christ. And further, to know that Christ in his creation, in the
wonder and awe and indeed in the pain that nature herself endures, to know the Christ through the physical universe and to
remain close to him there. All this develops through the poetry
and gives the energy and motive for his writing. All this, too, is
dependent on the strength of the heart, its optimism, its sense of
self-growth, and its intellectual underground. When any of these
props to his living and his work fails, then the poetry drops into
the gloom and suffering of the 'terrible sonnets' and requires a
great act of will to lift the writer out of his gloom. The great marvel
is how Hopkins succeeded in writing sonnets that themselves
are wonders of poetry while he was in the depths of despair in
Dublin in the last years of his life.

The 'Oxford Movement', most of whose members were at
Oxford, a movement also known as 'Tractarianism' after a series
of Tracts written between 1833 and 1841, wished to show how
Anglicanism was the direct descendant of the Church of the
Apostles; it was a conservative, intellectual appeal to Anglican
tradition, very much against making the church a partner of the
state with its consequent move towards secularisation; there
was a fear, after the Reform Act of 1832, that atheism would
gather force. This movement was at its height and controversy
raged while Hopkins was in Oxford. Clerical resistance to any

move towards secularisation was announced, liberalism in theology was attacked. The movement also hoped to incorporate
some of the doctrines of the Roman Church and the Orthodox
Church, most notably aspects of the liturgy and ceremonial,
thereby wishing to bring more energy and symbolism into the
Anglican Church. It was a time when theology was the main
subject of conversation on campus. There was a greater emphasis
on the doctrine of the Eucharist.

Several of the Tractarians complained that all of this was
merely an effort to Romanise the church and indeed the movement split in 1845 with those, like John Henry Newman, saying
that as nothing separated them from Rome they would 'go over'.
Newman had a profound influence on Hopkins and Hopkins
stayed in touch with him all his life. Otherwise the Oxford
Movement, also known as Anglo-Catholicism, gave Anglicanism
an added and sustaining strength. The focus on the Eucharist,
however, influenced many to take up belief in the 'Real Presence'
and it was this aspect of the movement that gave Hopkins his impetus to follow Newman into the Roman Church. This, he knew,
would alienate him from his family who remained staunch
Anglicans and there was hurt between them right to the end of
Gerard's life. In Dublin he found himself even further removed
from his family, in distance, faith and politics.

Denis Donoghue, in his review of Paddy Kitchen's book,
quotes Hopkins' note of August 7, 1882: 'God's utterance of himself in himself is God the Word, outside himself is this world. This
world then is word, expression, news of God. Therefore its end,
its purpose, its purport, its meaning, is God and its life or work to
name and praise him.' In his poetry Hopkins succeeded beyond
all hope in creating an oeuvre utterly in tune with this objective,
to name and praise Christ in his creation. In his life he found it
drastically difficult to continue against all the suffering and dis-
appointment which came his way. In several of the later poems
he urged himself to be more gentle on his own heart:

> My own heart let me have more pity on; let
> Me live to my sad self hereafter kind,
> Charitable; not live this tormented mind
> With this tormented mind tormenting yet.

I cast for comfort I can no more get
By groping round my comfortless, than blind
Eyes in their dark can day or thirst can find
Thirst's all-in-all in all a world of wet.

Soul, self; come, poor Jackself, I do advise
You, jaded, let be; call off thoughts awhile
Elsewhere; leave comfort root-room; let joy size

At God knows when to God knows what; whose smile
's not wrung, see you; unforeseen times rather – as skies
Betweenpie mountains – lights a lovely mile.

'The English language that Hopkins needed had to be a sinewy
vernacular, gathering up its history with particular care for experiences otherwise lost; having root room instead of mere space; stirring forgotten meaning in the verb 'to size'; and allowing a poet to
use 'betweenpie' as a verb. Bright sky seen between two mountains makes each dappled or pied; another sign of God's grandeur'.
(Donoghue 227). 'Poor Jackself!' speaking to his own being, to the
depth of sorrow and distraught emotions he experienced in being
sent to Dublin where the work he was given was overwhelming,
dull, tedious and, as he thought, pointless.

How did he come to such a sorry pass in his life while the
poetry soars, deepens, thickens and sings? The details of his life
are given, perhaps in almost too great a measure, in the work of
Paddy Kitchen and Paul Marinari. For me the excitement with
the poetry, and with the vision that the poetry develops, began
with the great early work that seems to have burst forth from him
like contained floods released: 'The Wreck of the Deutschland'.

The central focus of the poem is Christ, Christ the hero that
climbed onto the Rood to save suffering humanity, Christ the
Tormentor who torments those he loves so that they find the
purity that will allow them bask in his presence, Christ the
lover, who has given himself in Eucharist for the health and redemption of the entire creation. It is a poem of immense breadth
and beauty, its rhythms and music, its language, rush and slow-
fall, its torrential downpouring and still pools, and exhibits
what Nicholas Boyle says of the greatest writing: 'No secular literature can show us life as it is in itself, what it is that presents

itself in an unrepeatable way to every new human child, but the greatest literature, that in which the most distinctive mood is united with the greatest degree of detachment from the author's historically contingent personality, can bring us to the point where we can understand the possibility that the lost Atlantis of Being may reveal itself in words' (Boyle 137).

It is Christ who is master of the universe, the One, the Exemplar, the Omega, to whom all human beauty bows; the suffering and evil in creation is the unChrist. The allowing of the mastering of Christ over the soul is the same as the theme of Herbert's poem 'Love'. This is almost forced upon the soul, the Creator must 'unmake', and this echoes forward to Simone Weil's concept of uncreating. The burn of God's touch insists that the response is to be as a child's towards its father: 'Over again I feel thy finger and find thee.' This touch of Christ is twofold, demanding, and tenderly encouraging. The sense that life is riffled through with moments, periods, of suffering, physical and mental, is God's way of pushing the soul. Hopkins uses 'lightning and lashed rod' when speaking of his own suffering, the 'terror' of presenting before Christ, the 'swoon of a heart' trodden down and the stress the midriff knows. As Herbert's poem portrays the sudden yielding to the demands of love, so Hopkins yields 'with a fling of the heart to the heart of the Host' and can almost boast of that yielding, as Herbert's poem ends with a sign of complacent acceptance. The 'Host' in Hopkins's phrase is both Christ's presence in the sacrament and the host who invites Herbert to the banquet. On a grander scale, the same overwhelming demands of the wreck bring about the yielding of the sisters to the crushing demands of Christ, offers the central tragedy that is the subject of the poem.

We are all 'soft sift in an hourglass', but Hopkins is aware that a vein of what is true and lasting runs through us all, 'Christ's gift'. The stars speak him, the sunset – but these are not always before our eyes and we must develop this vein within us, because we are such sift, 'His mystery must be instressed, stressed.' This mystery is Christ's incarnation, from the womb-life through to the passion and beyond; it is through suffering, when the heart is 'hard at bay' that we turn to Christ, we come 'To hero of Calvary, Christ's, feet'. (Echoes here of the great

'Dream of the Rood'). Hopkins's prayer is that Christ push the
heart, through 'wrecking and storm', to acknowledge this presence, this mercy, this 'Father and fondler of heart thou hast
wrung'. The narrative of the second part of the poem extends
and clarifies this incarnation awareness. Though the writing of
the poem began with the second stanza of this second part, the
actual narrative, the laying out of the poem begins with Hopkins's
deep reflection, from the experience of his own life and dealings
with Christ.

> I kiss my hand
> > To the stars, lovely-asunder
> > Starlight, wafting him out of it; and
> > > Glow, glory in thunder;
> > Kiss my hand to the dappled-with-damson west:
> > Since, tho' he is under the world's splendour and wonder,
> > > His mystery must be instressed, stressed;
> For I greet him the days I meet him, and bless when I
> understand.

Hopkins tells the story of the wreck with fine narrative skill.
The nun is 'a lioness', a 'prophetess' and his admiration for her
faith, for gathering all her will and strength together, overwhelms him. This is of course a foretaste of the poem 'The
Windhover', and in stanza 18 he writes:

> Ah, Touched in your bower of bone,
> > Are you! Turned for an exquisite smart,
> > Have you! make words break from me here all alone,
> > > Do you! – mother of being in me, heart.
> > O unteachably after evil, but uttering truth,
> > Why, tears! is it? tears; such a melting, a madrigal start!
> > > Never-eldering revel and river of youth,
> What can it be, this glee? the good you have there of your own?

Here he speaks to his own heart, admiring her, almost envious
of her, as he will be addressing his own heart in 'The Windhover'.
Her eye is pure, focused, concentrated, and it is on Christ. In the
later poem 'Henry Purcell', there is again this gathering of self
into focus:

It is the forgèd feature finds me; it is the rehearsal
Of own, of abrupt self there so thrusts on, so throngs the ear.

Let him Oh! with his air of angels then lift me, lay me! only I'll
Have an eye to the sakes of him, quaint moonmarks, to his
    pelted plumage under
Wings: so some great stormfowl, whenever he has walked
    his while

The thunder-purple seabeach plumèd purple-of-thunder,
If a wuthering of his palmy snow-pinions scatter a colossal
    smile
Off him, but meaning motion fans fresh our wits with
    wonder.

As in 'The Windhover', as the 'stormfowl' here: Christ is the judge, 'weighing the worth', he is an 'Orion of light' and 'martyr-master'. What Christ did was to redeem us by Sacrifice and asks those whom he loves, 'his own bespoken, / Before-time-taken, dearest prized and priced', to follow in his footsteps.

In Stanza 25, the nun 'Was calling "O Christ, Christ, come quickly!"' and Hopkins asks what she meant: did she wish to die as Christ, her 'lover' had? or seek 'the crown' of martyrdom quickly, that glory and reward we cannot imagine? Hopkins knows it was not ease that she was seeking: there is an intervention in the poem as Hopkins addresses his own heart again, the writing echoing the urgency and excitement of the revelation he makes towards himself: 'the Master, Ipse, the only one, Christ, King, Head' – Stanza 29, and he returns to the nun who has got it all together, as he will later envy the kestrel who has mastered all its powers to action. Hopkins knew a life of pain and patience but the reward is the obtaining of Christ; and 'is the shipwreck then a harvest?' This leads to the question of suffering being a good because of the end. He ends the poem with a prayer to this nun, not only to enlighten the poet but all of England; stanza 35 ends the poem with a climax of names for Christ, including the 'hero of us', the roodmaster, Hopkins himself so convinced that it is Christ who is close to us, leading us, calling us:

Pride, rose, prince, hero of us, high-priest,
Our heart's charity's hearth's fire, our thoughts' chivalry's
    throng's Lord.

He was studying theology at St Beuno's when he wrote 'The Wreck of the Deutschland' and the poem streams out of his thinking and longing at the time. 'Hopkins's Christ is not the humane but static figure of a pre-Raphaelite painting. He is the active divinity whose agonised and loving life he had frequently relived (in the Ignatian exercises), and he is also the being to whom all his strongest emotions were now directed' (Kitchen 167). Indeed it was the coming as close as possible to Christ that finally persuaded Hopkins to abandon the Anglican Church and join the Catholics, the Real Presence in the Eucharist was what he needed and struggled towards: Kitchen: 'The Half-Way House shows how difficult it was for him to find this Love, how the established church had not fulfilled his needs, and how it was only the revelation of the Real Presence at communion that enabled him to "o'ertake Thee" and not be stranded and left behind as Love swept by on wings' (Kitchen79).

Commenting on Hopkins's sermons, Devlin writes: 'The Eucharistic Sacrifice was the great purpose of his life and his own chosen redemption: perhaps he would have instituted it and into it have disappeared – as at Emmaus' (Devlin 162).

Indeed, in some ways this approach to the Catholic Church and the regime of the Jesuits was to distance him from the strict directions of that order, whose theological and philosophical reliance remained on the *Summa* of St Thomas of Aquinas. As Thomas Pick wrote: 'This emphasis on the God-Man as the pattern, the hero, for each of us is one of Hopkins's most attractive themes. He may have been influenced by Scotus, who in his christology liked to stress the human element, while in general St Thomas liked to stress the divine' (Pick 84). The centrality of Christ's actual presence in Hopkins's life cannot be overstressed; when he feels he has lost this sense, his being crumbles.

So many of Hopkins's poems, particularly after the great resurgence of his work when 'The Wreck of the Deutschland' had liberated his powers, are simple revelling in the glory and worth of nature, each poem leading on from this to a glorying of God, the creator. Hopkins sees God as master, nature as fresh and fruitful, and man in need of redemption. The implication, inevitably, is that nature is not in need of this form of redemption but partakes already of that dear freshness and renewal that leads the human being who is aware of it, directly to God. The world itself, the physical universe, is shot through with sanctity; it is the bones of God, the body of Christ, it is the atmosphere we breathe in and breathe out.

God's Grandeur

The world is charged with the grandeur of God.
    It will flame out, like shining from shook foil;
    It gathers to a greatness, like the ooze of oil
Crushed. Why do men then now not reck his rod?
Generations have trod, have trod, have trod;
    And all is seared with trade; bleared, smeared with toil;
    And wears man's smudge and shares man's smell: the soil
Is bare now, nor can foot feel, being shod.

And for all this, nature is never spent;
    There lives the dearest freshness deep down things;
And though the last lights off the black West went
    Oh, morning, at the brown brink eastward, springs –
Because the Holy Ghost over the bent
    World broods with warm breast and with ah! bright wings.

This poem was written in the fervour and joy of his time in St Beuno's when he was setting out on the challenging but blessed life of his vocation. The fact that the poem is a definite statement suggests there is absolutely no doubt in the poet's mind of the truth of what he declares: 'The world is charged with the grandeur of God'. The word 'charged' is typically rich; the world has been given the duty of proclaiming the grandeur of God, and it is alert with the electricity that displays such grandeur. It is man alone that can destroy such a charge, the blearing and smearing that the industrial age has caused to the earth. And now, in Hopkins's time, humanity has come to a mood of atheism that does not recognise, does not pay attention to, does not 'reck' God's rule. The 'association of the experience of beauty with a religious experience becomes increasingly more and more central for Hopkins' (Pick 32). Hopkins has now put God at the forefront of his thought and living; his awareness of the things of creation must be conjoined to such a fervour; hence the strength of the statement of the poem. Yet it is not all simply joy and light; the idea of 'shook' foil, of oil 'crushed' retains the notion that glory is revealed only through suffering.

With humankind about to damage nature, Hopkins's further statement, his reason why 'nature is never spent', is not easy for non-believers to understand or accept. Hopkins believes it is so because, between God and humanity, and between God and creation, there is an ongoing contract, an agreement and it is the way of creation to show forth God's grandeur and it will not fail its contract, though humankind may. In our present century, Hopkins's statement might not have been so blithely made in the context of our current near-destruction of the planet.

The Starlight Night

Look at the stars! Look, look up at the skies!
  O look at all the fire-folk sitting in the air!
  The Bright boroughs, the circle-citadels there!
Down in dim woods the diamond delves! The elves'-eyes
The grey lawns cold where gold, where quickgold lies!
  Wind-beat whitebeam! Airy abeles set on a flare!
  Flake-doves sent floating forth at a farmyard scare! –
Ah well! It is all a purchase, all is a prize.
Buy then! Bid then! – What? – Prayer, patience, alms, vows.
Look, look: a May-mess, like on orchard boughs!
  Look! March-boom, like on mealed-with-yellow sallows!
These are indeed the barn; withindoors house
The shocks. This piece-bright paling shuts the spouse
  Christ home, Christ and his mother and all his hallows.

This poem, too, is filled with the ecstasy and immediacy of complete faith. Ruskin had associated such acute physical perception of nature with a high moral awareness and this has permeated Hopkins's thinking about creation. In his case, however, Hopkins associated all of this with the presence of Christ in creation. He had also discovered the work of Duns Scotus, the thirteenth century Franciscan philosopher and theologian. Scotus had given him a framework for his faith which is not a strictly Thomist nor Jesuit view, that Christ's incarnation was not an act of reparation for the original 'Fall', but was a free act of love which would have taken place with or without the Fall. With the developing idea in our time, after the work of Teilhard de Chardin and others, the notion of a static 'cosmos' has given way to a 'cosmogenesis', an ongoing evolution towards the fullness of Christ in the final coming of God's kingdom, and this notion is implicit in Hopkins's view of Christ's relationship to creation.

Scotus had also prompted Hopkins to his awareness of 'inscape', the individual difference that makes each thing and each human distinct in itself, with its own life, its own special and unique being. Hopkins took 'inscape' to be a thing of beauty which is distinctive and patterned, the inner kernel of being; and beauty as the 'inner form', the essence of a thing exposed in pattern and design as its 'outer form'. In Stonyhurst Hopkins wrote of a day when 'The ashtree growing in the corner of the garden was felled ... a great pang and I wished to die and not to see the inscapes of the world destroyed any more.'

Hopkins wrote in his Journal: 'As we drove home the stars came out thick; I leant back to look at them and my heart opening more than usual praised our Lord to and in whom all that beauty comes home.' The music and linguistic wizardry of the poem 'The Starlight Night' tell of this heart opening with wonder and joy in Christ. Hopkins wrote: 'God's utterance of himself in himself is God the Word, outside himself is this world. This world then is word, expression, news, of God. Therefore its end, its purpose, its purport, its meaning, is God, and its life or work to name and praise him.' And humanity's response to this naming and praising? It must be to honour and preserve creation, to give creation a voice in praise, and to see the hand of the Creator, the spirit of God, through it all. All celebration and gratitude for the overwhelming bounty of God, but it is not merely a given, it must be earned by humans through prayer and suffering, and then, through it all, as held in a barn, what is to be found but Christ?

The poem retains touches of the Pre-Raphaelite language and focus; Hopkins illustrates the 'love of plentitude in nature' by picking a subject that is plenitude in the extreme: there are millions of stars and this allows the awe, the many calls to 'Look!' The language, too, reflects this plenitude. The language effectively creates the excitement Hopkins himself felt at the sight. The poem is alive with colour and light: 'fire-folk,' 'quick-gold,' 'whitebeam,' 'diamond delves'. The stars are 'folk', living in 'citadels' and Christ is linked to all of this, these fire-folk are one with 'Christ and his mother and all his hallows.' It is a poem in which his love of creation and his love of language are one, and one with his love of, and awareness of Christ.

Spring

Nothing is so beautiful as Spring –
   When weeds, in wheels, shoot long and lovely and lush;
   Thrush's eggs look little low heavens, and thrush
Through the echoing timber does so rinse and wring
The ear, it strikes like lightnings to hear him sing;
   The glassy peartree leaves and blooms, they brush
   The descending blue; that blue is all in a rush
With richness; the racing lambs too have fair their fling.

What is all this juice and all this joy?
   A strain of the earth's sweet being in the beginning
In Eden garden. – Have, get, before it cloy,

   Before it cloud, Christ, lord, and sour with sinning,
Innocent mind and Mayday in girl and boy,
   Most, O maid's child, thy choice and worthy the winning.

Spring, of course, is the time of rebirth, of resurrection, and the Lamb may be a part of that. But the poem moves back to the original spring of the world, the 'Eden garden' when the covenant was unbroken and all the juice and joy of growth and hope were unspoilt; sin had not yet happened and Hopkins longs for that original innocence and purity. It is Christ who is urged to hold on to that purity in 'Innocent mind and Mayday' in children before it is cloyed. 'I do not think I have ever seen anything more beautiful than the bluebell I have been looking at. I know the beauty of our Lord by it. Its inscape is mixed of strength and grace.' It is this unsullied strength and grace Hopkins admires most, and it is Christ who is the touchstone and urgency of all this beauty and freshness. And John Pick has written: 'While many of the mystics have closed their eyes the better to concentrate on the things of the spirit (the Curé d'Ars feared that even the sight of a rose would distract him), Hopkins opened them wide to find the One ablaze in the many' (Pick 36).

In the Valley of the Elwy

I remember a house where all were good
To me, God knows, deserving no such thing:
Comforting smell breathed at very entering,
Fetched fresh, as I suppose, off some sweet wood.

That cordial air made those kind people a hood
All over, as a bevy of eggs the mothering wing
Will, or mild nights the new morsels of Spring:
Why, it seemed of course; seemed of right it should.

Lovely the woods, waters, meadows, combes, vales,
All the air things wear that build this world of Wales;
Only the inmate does not correspond:

God, lover of souls, swaying considerate scales,
Complete thy creature dear O where it fails,
Being mighty a master, being a father and fond.

St Beuno's is situated in the heart of a most beautiful area of Wales and Hopkins relished his time there. His welcome into a home has also touched him dearly and the scent of the woodsmoke on his entering the house he associates with the kindness of the people. He sees this as natural to these people as the very air they breathe is a gift of kindness to them, they are nourished by it, cared for and Hopkins's favourite image of care is that of the bird that shelters her brood or eggs under her wing. Yet not all the people are like that: 'Only the inmate does not correspond'. His plea, then, is to God the creator, the master and father, that he 'complete thy creature' by giving them the grace to correspond with creation. This is a clear statement of Hopkins's view that creation itself is good, that it is necessary that humanity focus themselves on the beauty and worth of creation and that thereby God is served and humanity elevated to holiness. 'It was as if he had concretely apprehended in the warmth of his aesthetic intuition that, as St Thomas said, the beauty of creatures is nothing else than the likeness of the beauty of God' (Pick

35). It was perhaps Scotus who deepened this sense in Hopkins, and his belief that any destruction of beauty is evil.

The Sea and the Skylark

On ear and ear two noises too old to end
Trench—right, the tide that ramps against the shore;
With a flood or a fall, low lull-off or all roar,
Frequenting there while moon shall wear and wend.

Left hand, off land, I hear the lark ascend,
His rash-fresh re-winded new-skeinèd score
In crisps of curl off wild winch whirl, and pour
And pelt music, till none 's to spill nor spend.

How these two shame this shallow and frail town!
How ring right out our sordid turbid time,
Being pure! We, life's pride and cared-for crown,

Have lost that cheer and charm of earth's past prime:
Our make and making break, are breaking, down
To man's last dust, drain fast towards man's first slime.

Among creation's glories, the tide, the skylark, 'shame this shallow and frail town'. Hopkins worked in some of the poorer parts of England, in Liverpool, in Bedford Leigh and in London. He was deeply aware of the industrial growth throughout England, the poverty it brought to some parts of the overcrowded cities and towns, and the way that the world of nature was being destroyed in its wake. Yet human beings were created guardians and carers of the created world, supposed to be 'life's pride and cared-for crown' yet compared with the purity of the original creation we have lost cheer and charm and are draining 'fast towards man's first slime'. It is a bleak portrait of humanity, as is the previous poem, yet it must be remembered that for Hopkins humanity is destined to be part of the great kingdom of God, to become more and more Christlike, to partake in Christ's body and blood through the Eucharist, to glow in the glories of nature, and reality was something quite different. The younger Hopkins, although he seems to have suffered pains and illnesses all his life, has been hurt by the failure to reconcile suffering humanity with its destruction of nature. From a man who wrote in his journal: 'Wonderful downpour of leaf: when the morning sun began to melt the frost they fell at one touch and in a few minutes a whole tree was flung of them; they lay masking and papering the ground at the foot. Then the tree seems to be looking down on its cast self.' Such detailed and loving observation brought about a sense of almost personal affront at the human degradation of created things.

Pied Beauty

Glory be to God for dappled things –
  For skies of couple-colour as a brinded cow;
    For rose-moles all in stipple upon trout that swim;
Fresh-firecoal chestnut-falls; finches' wings;
  Landscape plotted and pieced – fold, fallow, and plough;
    And all trades, their gear and tackle and trim.
All things counter, original, spare, strange;
  Whatever is fickle, freckled (who knows how?)
    With swift, slow; sweet, sour; adazzle, dim;
He fathers-forth whose beauty is past change:
                        Praise him.

If the covenant of Eden is offered between humanity, God and creation, then it is important for humanity to note the absolute wonder of that creation. The wonder, as Hopkins sees it, is in the 'dapple', how creation is both ever-changing and ever-the-same. And that creation, in its magnificent difference, has been created by a never-changing, never-different Creator, a creation electric with beauty created by a God whose beauty never alters. And that beauty is made flesh, is incarnated in Christ. Praise is our natural response, as it was for St Augustine, for St Francis of Assisi, for St Patrick ...

Hurrahing in Harvest

Summer ends now; now, barbarous in beauty, the stooks rise
Around; up above, what wind-walks! what lovely behaviour
Of silk-sack clouds! has wilder, wilful-wavier
Meal-drift moulded ever and melted across skies?

I walk, I lift up, I lift up heart, eyes,
Down all that glory in the heavens to glean our Saviour;
And, eyes, heart, what looks, what lips yet gave you a
Rapturous love's greeting of realer, of rounder replies?

And the azurous hung hills are his world-wielding shoulder
Majestic – as a stallion stalwart, very-violet-sweet! –
These things, these things were here and but the beholder
Wanting; which two when they once meet,
The heart rears wings bold and bolder
And hurls for him, O half hurls earth for him off under his feet.

John Pick writes of this poem: 'It bears the stamp of an almost
ecstatic experience of the sacramental operation of nature upon
him' (Pick 58). It is yet another poem of sheer joy in the beauty of
creation at the fullness of harvest and inevitably leads Hopkins
to glory in the creator of such beauty. His own 'harvesting', his
'gleaning', is to savour Christ, the saviour and redeemer of the
world. The 'reply' of creation is one of love, simple and unwavering love that should exist between beholder and beheld. He
was upset and almost personally hurt when he saw destruction
done to natural things:

Binsey Poplars
felled 1879

My aspens dear, whose airy cages quelled,
Quelled or quenched in leaves the leaping sun,
All felled, felled, are all felled;
   Of a fresh and following folded rank
            Not spared, not one
            That dandled a sandaled
      Shadow that swam or sank
On meadow and river and wind-wandering weed-winding bank.

O if we but knew what we do
      When we delve or hew –
   Hack and rack the growing green!
      Since country is so tender
To touch, her being so slender,
That, like this sleek and seeing ball
But a prick will make no eye at all.

Where we, even where we mean
    To mend her we end her,
  When we hew or delve:
After-comers cannot guess the beauty been.
    Ten or twelve, only ten or twelve
      Strokes of havoc unselve
          The sweet especial scene,
  Rural scene, a rural scene,
  Sweet especial rural scene.

Hopkins wished the wildness of creation to be preserved, in the face of all the destruction and 'development' of the second half of the nineteenth century. On a walk in Scotland he came across a waterfall, where the water came rushing down from the hills and flowed on into Loch Lomond:

Inversnaid

This darksome burn, horseback brown,
His rollrock highroad roaring down,
In coop and in comb the fleece of his foam
Flutes and low to the lake falls home.

A windpuff-bonnet of fawn-fróth
Turns and twindles over the broth
Of a pool so pitchblack, fell-frowning,
It rounds and rounds Despair to drowning.

Degged with dew, dappled with dew
Are the groins of the braes that the brook treads through,
Wiry heathpacks, flitches of fern,
And the beadbonny ash that sits over the burn.

What would the world be, once bereft
Of wet and of wildness? Let them be left,
O let them be left, wildness and wet;
Long live the weeds and the wilderness yet.

The richness of the language captures the wealth of joy and delight that the burn offered to Hopkins, a place where despair itself, faced with such beauty, must vanish. The last two lines could well have become the slogan of ecologists in our own time. 'Ribblesdale', written in 1882, takes this love of creation to its conclusion, outlining how nature glorifies God, how it is humanity's care and duty to give it tongue, as it simply exists, God's care originally. As he says in the Sermons: 'God is holiness, loves only holiness, cares only for it, created the world for it (which, without man, if churned or pressed would yield God none)', that is, no voice to utter that praise. Ribblesdale is in Lancashire, and the poem echoes the passage from Paul, (Romans chapter 8): 'For the creation was subjected to futility, not of its own will, but by the will of the one who subjected it, in hope that the creation itself will be set free from its bondage to decay and will obtain the freedom of the glory of the children of God. We know that the whole creation has been groaning in labour pains until now; and not only the creation but we ourselves, who have the first fruits of the Spirit, groan inwardly while we wait for adoption, the redemption of our bodies. For in hope we were saved. Now hope that is seen is not hope. For who hopes for what is seen? But if we hope for what we do not see, we wait for it with patience.' Hopkins found, during his time in Lancashire, places that were severely overcrowded, the rivers polluted, and he could see all the damage already inflicted on creation by the Industrial Age. Instead of being able, then, to offer praise, the world that Hopkins saw was already bearing the signs of care and concern on its brow.

Ribblesdale

Earth, sweet Earth, sweet landscape, with leaves throng
And louchèd low grass, heaven that dost appeal
To, with no tongue to plead, no heart to feel;
That canst but only be, but dost that long –

Thou canst but be, but that thou well dost; strong
Thy plea with him who dealt, nay does now deal,
Thy lovely dale down thus and thus bids reel
Thy river, and o'er gives all to rack or wrong.

And what is Earth's eye, tongue, or heart else, where
Else, but in dear and dogged man? – Ah, the heir
To his own selfbent so bound, so tied to his turn,
To thriftless reave both our rich round world bare
And none reck of world after, this bids wear
Earth brows of such care, care and dear concern.

To return to Christ, the incarnation, and Eucharist, which, together with the beauty of creation, are the main thrusts of the
work of Hopkins. All of this was well announced in 'The Wreck
of the Deutschland' but he returned again and again to these
themes, the incredible gift of the incarnation that has raised humans and all created things to levels of hope and wonder. As he
prayed in that great early poem, Christ is the one who is to save
us from the final floundering of our lives. If the works of Christ
were works of love, the works of Hopkins, too, stayed ever as his
own works of love, finally offered under terrible strain and suffering. He wrote: 'the influx of grace within us is the birth of
Christ within man, a re-incarnation of the Incarnation. Man becomes Christ through going with grace, the life of Christ within
him.' In a poem called 'The Bugler's First Communion', Hopkins
shows two special traits of his character: firstly his Victorian
sense of pride in the soldiery and, more importantly, his faith in
and need for Christ's real presence in the Eucharist:

Here he knelt in regimental red.
Forth Christ from cupboard fetched, how fain I of feet
To his youngster take his treat!
Low-latched in leaf-light housel his too huge godhead.

John Pick comments: 'Here is the potent young perfection that
Hopkins had long adored in man and nature – can the Eucharist
arrest it for ever?' (Pick 193). The poem prays: 'Though this
child's drift/Seems by a divine boom channelled, nor do I cry/
Disaster there; but may he not rankle and roam/In backwheels
though bound home?/That left to the Lord of the Eucharist, I
here lie by.' The beauty and innocence of youth, Hopkins hopes
will remain firm, now that the young soldier is joined to Christ.
The boy was sent to Afghanistan where Hopkins almost hoped
he might be killed before that innocence was destroyed! In a sermon delivered in 1879 in Bedford Leigh, Hopkins said: 'There
met in Jesus Christ all things that can make man lovely and love-
able', and he goes on to reason this through; he believed, for
instance, that not even a hair of his head could fall: 'for myself I
make no secret I look forward with eager desire to seeing the
matchless beauty of Christ's body in the heavenly light.'
Christ, then, is Hero for Hopkins, hero and focus and centre

of living and he sees Christ, through the incarnation, as his dearest friend. In the Sermons he wrote: 'Our Lord Jesus Christ is our hero, a hero all the world wants ... Often mothers make a hero of a son; girls of a sweetheart and good wives of a husband ... but Christ, he is the hero'.

Up to this point, life seemed good and sacred to Hopkins, even though he suffered illnesses and weakness all his life. By now his reputation among his fellow Jesuits was that he was, at best, 'eccentric' and at worst 'stark raving mad'. 'No doubt thinking of his own fate as he prepares to leave for Ireland, deemed dispensable for his perceived eccentricities, he notes that real excellence is too often overlooked' (Marinari 313). On February 18, 1884 Hopkins arrives, 'reluctant and apprehensive' at 85-86 St Stephens Green, as Professor of Greek and Examiner in Classics for the Royal University of Ireland. The great and terrifying test of all his hopes, beliefs and dreams was upon him. In Dublin, his faith remains fixed on Christ and, as he suffers distance from all he loves back in England, he writes on Christ: 'Wish to crown him King of England, of English hearts and of Ireland and all Christendom and all the world' (Devlin 255).

'Enter Hopkins, sent to Dublin to teach what is perceived as two all-but-dead languages to an Irish Catholic population far more interested in gaining what has been so long denied them: positions of economic and political power. For most of them – from the Catholic clergy on down through his own students – Hopkins, with his Oxford background and moreover an English convert to Catholicism, will remain under suspicion and an anomaly at best' (Marinari 320). Under all the constraints he knew he kept reminding himself of the importance of focusing on Christ, trying to lay himself down into God's keeping. He was suffering more and more often from a 'debilitation weakness'.

It is one of the great sadnesses that Hopkins was subjected to the sufferings and futility of his last years. He was in Dublin and wished to be back in England but it appears to have been the job he was given that drove him to distraction: 'I was continuing this train of thought this evening when I began to enter on that course of loathing and hopelessness which I have so often felt before, which made me fear madness ...' The correcting of so many examination papers offered by students who were scarcely interested in their subject did not help. His retreat notes for January 1888, made in Dublin, contain the following: 'This morning I made the meditation on the Three Sins, with nothing to enter but loathing of my life and a barren submission to God's will. The body cannot rest when it is in pain nor the mind be at peace as long as something bitter distils in it and it aches'. He writes: 'Our lives and in particular those of religious, as mine, are in their whole direction, not only inwardly but most visibly and outwardly, shaped by Christ's' ... 'And my life is deter-mined by the incarnation down to most of the details of the day' ... 'The incarnation was for my salvation and that of the world: the work goes on in a great system and machinery which even drags me on with the collar round my neck though I could and do neglect my duty in it.' Even his poetry began to abandon him, and his hopes that he might ever find proper publication; in his Notes in 1883 he wrote: 'I earnestly asked our Lord to watch over my compositions, not to preserve them from being lost or coming to nothing, for that I am very willing they should be, but they might not do me harm through the enmity or im-prudence of any man or my own; that he should have them as his own and employ or not employ them as he should see fit. And this I believe is heard.'

His first effort in Dublin was unfinished:

The times are nightfall, look, their light grows less;
The times are winter, watch, a world undone:
They waste, they wither worse; they as they run
Or bring more or more blazon man's distress.
And I not help. Nor word now of success:
All is from wreck, here, there, to rescue one –
Work which to see scarce so much as begun
Makes welcome death, does dear forgetfulness.

Christ is still the focus, but there is greater stress on suffering and how, as the Nun in the 'Wreck of the Deutschland' knew, it is through suffering that Christ draws humanity closer to him-self: this is now the Christ, the peace and parting Christ, the hid-den Christ:

To seem the stranger lies my lot, my life
Among strangers. Father and mother dear,
Brothers and sisters are in Christ not near
And he my peace my parting, sword and strife.
England, whose honour O all my heart woos, wife
To my creating thought, would neither hear
Me, were I pleading, plead nor do I: I wear-
y of idle a being but by where wars are rife.

I am in Ireland now; now I am at a third
Remove. Not but in all removes I can
Kind love both give and get. Only what word
Wisest my heart breeds dark heaven's baffling ban
Bars or hell's spell thwarts. This to hoard unheard,
Heard unheeded, leaves me a lonely began.

Thinking back again to the Deutschland, this is a passage
from the Book of Job, chapter 10: 'Your hands shaped me and
made me. Will you now turn and destroy me? Remember that
you moulded me like clay. Will you now turn me to dust again?
Did you not pour me out like milk and curdle me like cheese,
clothe me with skin and flesh and knit me together with bones
and sinews?' The fact that the inspiration is from Job adds to the
sense of God's nearness, that burning presence his power, either
to save or to purify.

'Carrion Comfort'

Not, I'll not, carrion comfort, Despair, not feast on thee;
Not untwist – slack they may be – these last strands of man
In me ór, most weary, cry I can no more. I can;
Can something, hope, wish day come, not choose not to be.
But ah, but O thou terrible, why wouldst thou rude on me
Thy wring-world right foot rock? lay a lionlimb against me?
    scan
With darksome devouring eyes my bruisèd bones? and fan,
O in turns of tempest, me heaped there; me frantic to avoid
    thee and flee?

Why? That my chaff might fly; my grain lie, sheer and clear.
Nay in all that toil, that coil, since (seems) I kissed the rod,

Hand rather, my heart lo! lapped strength, stole joy, would
      laugh, chéer.
Cheer whom though? the hero whose heaven-handling flung
      me, fóot tród
Me? or me that fought him? O which one? is it each one? That
      night, that year
Of now done darkness I wretch lay wrestling with (my God!)
      my God.

One of the unfinished pieces: tentatively titled 'Ash-Boughs',
was written in Dublin in September 1887:

Not of all my eyes see, wandering on the world,
Is anything a milk to the mind so, so sighs deep
Poetry to it, as a tree whose boughs break in the sky.
Say it is ashboughs: whether on a December day and furled
Fast or they in clammyish lashtender combs creep
Apart wide and new-nestle at heaven most high.
They touch heaven, tabour on it; how their talons sweep
The smouldering enormous winter welkin! May
Mells blue and snowwhite through them, a fringe and fray
Of greenery: it is old earth's groping towards the steep
Heaven whom she childs us by.

'Thousand-fingered branches, as if reaching, clawing, for the
very heavens they were once childed by, the inscape of the trees
in winter or in early spring, showing themselves as they are:
part of fallen nature's great procession out from and back to
their Creator, old earth groping and pining, like himself, for his
heavenly Father' (Marinari 381). So we go back to 'The Wreck of
the Deutschland' where God's physical and spiritual nearness is
manifest, not only in the individual soul's labouring towards
God, but in the presence of nature itself:

Thou hast bound bones and veins in me, fastened me flesh,
And after it almost unmade, what with dread,
Thy doing: and dost thou touch me afresh?
Over again I feel thy finger and find thee.

After a long period of almost unbearable suffering and near
despair during which all he could write were the 'terrible sonnets', so called because they are filled with anguish, though

wonderfully accomplished, he called on all his strength of will and all his deeply held beliefs, to pull him through that awful time. In July 1888 he wrote a strange, though very rich sonnet, and he is once again aware of the wonder of the world in which we live and have our being, and it is this wonder that offers him an opportunity to lift himself out of the misery in which he has been living. It bears the form of the sonnet, with codas, the switch coming in the second line of the first coda with that cry 'Enough! the Resurrection', after deciding on the misery of humanity's condition in the world. It is not a sudden lifting of depression or pain, not a sudden revelation, but a reminder to himself of what the Christian message is all about, and how it is the will that seeks to forge ahead, in spite of pain and desolation:

That Nature is a Heraclitean Fire
    and of the Comfort of the Universe

Cloud-puffball, torn tufts, tossed pillows ' flaunt forth, then
        chevy on an air-
built thoroughfare: heaven-roysterers, in gay-gangs ' they
        throng; they glitter in marches.
Down roughcast, down dazzling whitewash, ' wherever an
        elm arches,
Shivelights and shadowtackle in long ' lashes lace, lance, and pair.
Delightfully the bright wind boisterous ' ropes, wrestles,
    beats earth bare
Of yestertempest's creases; in pool and rut peel parches
Squandering ooze to squeezed ' dough, crust, dust; stanches,
    starches
Squadroned masks and manmarks ' treadmire toil there
Footfretted in it. Million-fuelèd, ' nature's bonfire burns on.
But quench her bonniest, dearest ' to her, her clearest-selvèd spark
Man, how fast his firedint, ' his mark on mind, is gone!
Both are in an unfathomable, all is in an enormous dark
Drowned. O pity and indig ' nation! Manshape, that shone
Sheer off, disseveral, a star, ' death blots black out; nor mark
        Is any of him at all so stark
But vastness blurs and time ' beats level. Enough! the
        Resurrection,
A heart's-clarion! Away grief's gasping, ' joyless days, dejection.

> Across my foundering deck shone
A beacon, an eternal beam. ' Flesh fade, and mortal trash
Fall to the residuary worm; ' world's wildfire, leave but ash:
>> In a flash, at a trumpet crash,
I am all at once what Christ is, ' since he was what I am, and
This Jack, joke, poor potsherd, ' patch, matchwood, immortal
diamond,
>> Is immortal diamond.

Back to a passage from St Paul, in Romans, 8:18: 'For I reckon that the sufferings of the present time are not worthy to be compared with the glory which shall be revealed in us. For the earnest expectation of the creature waits for the manifestation of the sons of God. For the creature was made subject to vanity, not willingly, but by reason of him who has subjected the same in hope, because the creature itself also shall be delivered from the bondage of corruption into the glorious liberty of the children of God. For we know that the whole creation groans and labours in pain together until now. And not only they, but ourselves also, who have the first fruits of the Spirit, even we ourselves groan within ourselves, waiting for the adoption, namely, the redemption of our body.'

Hopkins, in his notebooks, sermons and devotional writings, and of course in his poems, had this passage deep within his spirit and his great, his central poems, are filled with the basic themes of this passage: that humanity fell and caused the 'fall' of all creation; that humanity now works for the restoration of the original kingdom of God and that all of creation waits along with humanity for this 'redemption'. Creation, for Hopkins, is a signal and sign of God's wonder, grandeur and love and the beauty and well-being of creation must remain in the hands of human beings to be marvelled at, cared for and loved.

There is no doubt that his love of beauty, of the physical things and patterns of the world, took on more than a sacramental force for him. The world outside the self in its redemptive quality and its loveliness praises God; hence it is all a question of incarnation: of being in the Flesh. In that strange and wonderful poem, 'That Nature is a Heraclitean Fire and of the comfort of the Resurrection' this is manifest: 'Million-fuelèd, nature's bonfire burns on.' And if humanity is the glory of this creation, then all the more so must creation be cherished in its detail and its growth. Hopkins goes on to consider the sad fact of the death of the human: 'nor mark/Is any of him at all so stark/But vastness blurs and time beats level.' At this point in the poem and indeed in his life, his technique flexes all its muscles, then falls to simplicity until the will takes over in 'Enough! the Resurrection'. The fact of his faith in the Christ leads him to the conclusion that man will be 'Immortal diamond'. This applies, too, to all of creation, as Paul outlined in the above passage. After all it is humanity who has sullied the face and fact of creation's beauty:

> Generations have trod, have trod, have trod;
> And all is seared with trade; bleared, smeared with toil;
> And wears man's smudge and shares man's smell: the soil
> Is bare now, nor can foot feel, being shod.
> And for all this, nature is never spent;
> There lives the dearest freshness deep down things ...

And how does this occur?

> Because the Holy Ghost over the bent
> World broods with warm breast and with ah! bright wings.
> ('God's Grandeur')

It is certain that Christ was the centre of Hopkins's world; and it is the unity of creation and what it may achieve when perfectly in action and in harmony with itself, and when men are also in harmony with nature, that another fine, though earlier, poem, 'The Windhover', celebrates. The basis for this 'oneness' of the whole world is, in Hopkins's view, the Real Presence in the Eucharist. In a letter to his old schoolfriend, E. H. Coleridge, on 1 June 1864, Hopkins said that the main object of Christian belief was the doctrine of the Real Presence: that is belief in the actual presence of Christ's body and blood in the Eucharist. It was this that brought him to Catholicism. In the summer of 1872 Hopkins began to read Duns Scotus, the 13th century Franciscan philosopher who had perhaps the greatest single impact on his mature thought, and developed and clarified Hopkins's sense of individuation, and that this individuation still was held in oneness. Over all this world the Holy Ghost 'broods with warm

breast and with ah! bright wings'. Duns Scotus held a somewhat
heretical belief, a belief now much more widely held, that the incarnation would have happened even without Adam's fall; this
gives a glory to the whole material world, allowing Hopkins a
sort of Pagan faith as in 'Pied Beauty', 'God's Grandeur',
'Starlight Night', 'Hurrahing in Harvest', as well as and most of
all in 'The Windhover'. How sad, then, that in 1889, a loathing of
his life and a barren submission to God's will, has taken over.

In May 1889 he falls ill with a fever that is soon diagnosed as
a type of typhoid. 'And while the official diagnosis is typhoid, it
is quite possible that the illness has been made worse by another
complaint, which will not even be named until 1932: Crohn's, a
disease marked by constant fatigue' (Marinari 424) and by stomach
cramps, indigestion, diarrhea and exhaustion. Around noon on
Saturday, June 8, just short of his 45th birthday, he died; whispering, over and over, 'I am so happy, I am so happy'.

Across my foundering deck shone
A beacon, an eternal beam. Flesh fade, and mortal trash
Fall to the residuary worm; world's wildfire, leave but ash:
In a flash, at a trumpet crash,
I am all at once what Christ is, since he was what I am, and
This Jack, joke, poor potsherd, patch, matchwood, immortal
      diamond,
Is immortal diamond.

Edvard Munch

One of the great painters of the northern countries was Edvard Munch, born in Norway in 1863 and died there in 1944. His life was filled with suffering and his paintings tend to be somewhat bleak, with subjects like fear, illness, death, melancholy, despair. His modernity, his fearlessness in painting what were subjects close to his own spirit, and his determination to explore even the darkest side of our living, always appealed to me. How appropriate, then, that he feature in a study that calls itself 'the works of love'. I have used Munch's life in my own poetry, and used his paintings to order my own thoughts on life, death and love, how my life turned from its attempt at monastic living, to a love and marriage where the beloved died, and turned again to joy and wholeness when I had the incredible good fortune to find love again. And all of this found itself making up the stanzas of a long poem which was called 'The Instruments of Art', and as I believe that great art is a work of love, then that title was most appropriate in its reference to Munch.

There is a picture somewhere of Munch's own gallery and it shows the paintings, finished and unfinished, placed here and there about the great wide space. And so we all appear to move in such draughty, barn-like spaces, spaces that shape our life. I remember in Achill a great loft behind the house where the hay was stored; swallows in the summer found their way inside and flew busily about the beams, the way images fly around the brain and memory. In this large space of our living there is room for the larger canvasses of our living to be displayed, such utterly memorable moments as a marriage, an accident, a love, a loss, a death, a re-marriage, and there are storing-places too for the weaker efforts of our living, the small events, the gifts given or received, the journeys taken or not taken; all of this as if the mind and soul and memory were a large barn where Munch himself would have stored his larger, completed canvasses, and his works-in-progress: in short, to store his works of love. In his barn, Munch needed to wear his warmest clothing, he would have taken his surreptitious nips of spirits to keep his hopes and energies alive, the spirits hidden away behind the instruments of his art. What a life becomes may be compared, then, to a series of self-portraits, bleak or alight, the measured-out reasons for living. Our dreams, our sketches, of heaven and hell: our works of love, self-portrait with computer, self-portrait, nude, with blanching flesh. Self-portrait as artist with his brush, as poet declaiming the latest poem. Self-portrait as Lazarus as he is visible, mid-summons, emerging from the darkness of death, of self seen as Job as he suffers another jolt at the hands of his God.

Always we stand, in our public moments, with the best outward dignity we can maintain, a white shirt, a black tie, a black hat held before the crotch and, in the photograph, in the portrait, little notice can be offered of the turmoil within, of advancing decay. Each painting signed and achieved, as each poem is, announcing itself as the last, in which all effort has been made. The barn door seeming to slam shut on our works of love.

When Nanna came to die, in the hospice in Harold's Cross, Dublin, there was a pungency of remedies on the air, a pungency discernible as soon as one turned down the long corridor towards the wards. This was the pungency the young Munch was constantly aware of, the house in which he grew up hushed for weeks, awaiting the arrival of death. His young life knew too much focus on the sick-room. When I visited the hospice, I remember how her fingers reached for me, in affection, and I responded, though there was that sense of the skeleton beneath about to obtrude. Saliva had gathered at the corners of her mouth and my soul suffered for her, and with her. When I came back that last time, she had been taken from the ward, the bed was newly made up, her sheets and eiderdown spirited away, and a great vase of flowers stood in its place. The room, I sensed, had been disinfected, it had been purged. What was left, the flowers, stood there like a still life painted by Edvard Munch after the death of his mother, and again after the death of his beloved sister, Johanne Sophie. Leaving in me a sense of dread, of abandonment, leaving in Munch a recurring sensation of sorrow and fear, a greyness that would colour living like a dye, darkening the canvas, darkening the page. It was an early mourning, a deeply shuddering *Dies Irae*, that slow fret-saw

wailing of black-vested priests from each side of the coffined
body. It was Ireland that I had come to know, subservient, relishing its purgatory. It was Oslo, winter, in the morbid pietism
of Edvard's sorrowing father. And for me, in the seminary, it
was books that had been indexed and locked away in glass
cases, lest we be touched by doubts, by negative philosophies
with which we could not cope. Munch had written: 'My father
was temperamentally nervous and obsessively religious – to the
point of psychoneurosis. From him I inherited the seeds of madness. The angels of fear, sorrow, and death stood by my side
since the day I was born.' My morbid parent, then, was Roman
Catholic Ireland and I remember how I had often tried to sleep
in my bedroom upstairs, the Bunnacurry dance-hall, that poor
old barn, loud with the noises of the dancing, bicycles laid slack
against a gable-wall, bicycle-clips stored in pockets, minerals offered, a raffle held: but for me it was rosary and bed-time, and
none of that dancing nonsense ought to be allowed enter my
head. But I imagined them, the shy men, the cautious women,
the hesitant, ill-used words of affection or longing, the groping.
What entered my soul was the dark bloom of a fascination, an
imagined Eden, and a sense that would last with me always, of
withdrawal, suspicion, dread.

Father, indeed, had his own artistic endeavours; he read,
voraciously, in the wilder books of European literature, as Munch's
father told ghastly stories to his son from Edgar Allan Poe. He
liked to work in his garden and had a long earth-rake with
which he drew lines neat as copy-book pages on which he could
write his seeds, the everyday ones first, cabbage, carrots,
parsnips, and then the more unusual ones like mange-tout and
cherry tomatoes. For him this was a form of loving the earth;
and now I wonder, sometimes, if you can love, and be loved, yet
never say the word 'love', nor ever hear the word 'love' spoken
to you. Loving was a hidden art in those days in Ireland, as it
was in Munch's day, in Norway.

I followed father round his gardens and watched where the
uncollected apples underneath the trees moved with legged
things and were coloured a chocolate rust. So I, too, grew up reluctant to mention the things of flesh, or the heart's desires, in
case the naming of such things might draw down on me a

masterful punishment. Munch wrote: 'In my art I attempt to explain life and its meaning to myself.' My entering the seminary, I believe, was an attempt to do with my life what Munch was doing, at an early age, with his painting. Mother cut hydrangeas from father's garden and placed them in a pewter bowl close by the tabernacle door in Bunnacurry church. I saw her once, opening the gilt gate along the altar rails, bearing the pewter bowl, and crying, softly, to herself. And like Edvard, I knew a small revulsion and terror at my own swelling flesh and suffered the pangs of puberty, holding my hands against my crotch in fear.

The early colours of Munch's palette were pale and he could paint the skin of his dying siblings a secret-linen white with a smart stubble of dirt. The first fountain-pen I ever owned, gushed a soft, warm blue ink; the first paint-box Munch owned held pristine tablets of Prussian Blue and Burnt Sienna and I found those colours, too, in my own small tin box of watercolours, the names ringing beautifully to me, Prussian Blue, Burnt Sienna, and I put the tip of the brush with its delightful yellow-coloured bristles, softly against my tongue, tasting the words, tasting, too, the words Mother knew from the harmonium she played up in the organ loft, words like *Diapason*, like *Celeste*. By an early age, Munch was already painting the dark night of grief and loss, dipping the hairs of the brush in watered-down colours, and I think of the story of the squirrel who would empty the ocean onto the land by dipping in his squirrel's tail and shaking the water out onto the beach. I lived with the consequences of my inherited faith, trying, in the seminary, to colour it Prussian Blue, Burnt Sienna, stooping over the desk in the long library, trying to find rhymes for love, for faith, reading heavy tomes of cosmology, brushing out the reasoning of Thomas Aquinas, willing to hold the knowledge of God within our soul. Dawn chorus became *laudetur Jesus Christus*; and the smothered, smothering answer: *in aeternum. Amen.* Loneliness hanging about our frames, like cassocks, while Edvard Munch, moving about the canvas in a big, stained smock, painted his *Standing Nude* in a secret corner of the barn, far from his father's eyes.

When I left the seminary it was a new world, a new day, but it was difficult to shake off the darkness, the black habit. Munch

could paint the sky at sunset a fire-red, opening its mouth to
scream. Now it was all questions of adulthood, exploration of
the belly-flesh of a lover. Yet the pale walls of the barn hung
threatening over such daring, for it felt like the rubbling of
revered buildings, it was the moulding of words into new
shapes. The kiss. In the cramped cab of a truck, the woman
fleshed across my knees. Two separate people, shivering, alive,
not singular. It was almost a death already, prowling at the dark
edge of the wood, fangs bared, saliva-white. Munch found himself deeply disturbed by the sexual revolution going on in Oslo
at that time and made his way to Paris where he thought he
might find inner freedom and strength, yet always he feared insanity, the bridge he crossed over seemed humming and shuddering under his screaming (in oil, in casein, in pastel) but there
was nobody there to hear him and the river simply went streaming by, the sky, too, streaming past, scarlet, oil, casein, pastel.
And all too soon, she died, Barbara died, on a dark night, and I
gazed uselessly onto ashes. Helpless again, as was Munch who
carried all the primitive storms within him, and feared once
more, what woman was: saint, and whore and hapless devotee.
Munch wrote, painting his words a deep violet, a pale yellow, a
fearsome scarlet: 'I live with the dead – my mother, my sister,
my grandfather, my father ... Kill yourself and then it's over.
Why live?' but he knew why, to paint, to create his works of
love, his *Winter in Meath*, his *Fugue*, his *Apotheosis of Desire*.

The final terror at that time was that I would not be able to
write, that it would not succeed. Barbara had embraced her own
skeleton and was gone. And what, now, was the colour of *God is
love*, when I watched them draw the artificial grass over the hole
while the rain came down steadily and the gravediggers waited
impatiently under the trees. For too long, disturbing presences
were shadowing the page, darkening the landscapes, the bleak
ego-walls, like old galvanise round what was festering, and that
artificial mass collapsing down on her, releasing a small, essential
spirit, a secular bone-structure, and all my reaching was out of
need, and no longer out of will.

And there was the picture: the woman on the jetty, at the vis-
ceral edge of ocean, where was all the agitated ooze of low tide
across the slobs, and she was watching out to sea. There, I too,

took to watching out on the world again and the woman, dressed in blue, broke from the group on the jetty and came purposefully towards me. I would watch her come as I gazed through the stained glass of the door, and I loved her. And now where was the God, for mine had become the religion of poetry, the poetry of religion, the worthy Academicians unwilling to realise we don't live off neglect. I had two children. I had no, or very little, income. My writing was not to the liking of the Academy. Munch, they said, carried his own Tahiti within him, but found little access to it, and little recognition of the darkness through which he moved, and out of which he created his works of love. It was a painting out of the necessity of his own heart, out of the need to know why and how people breathe, and live, they love, and die.

Munch continued to paint a series of self-portraits, just as Van Gogh had done, in an attempt to understand his own deepest inner being. Is there a way to understand the chaos of the human heart? our slaughters, our carelessness, our unimaginable wars? He suffered greatly under the Nazi persecutions and they attempted to destroy his works of love, his paintings. He hid a great many of them when the Nazis took over Norway and then tried to claim Munch as a sympathiser. In later life he abandoned the Christian beliefs that had shaped his early years, but he remained enthralled by spirituality and religion, forming his own kind of Pantheistic beliefs. He wrote: 'From my rotting body, flowers shall grow and I am in them and that is eternity.'

Without a God can we win some grace? Will our canvases, our poems, their patterns and forms, their rhymes and rhythms, supply a modicum of worth? Or does the Christian faith abandon us in later years? There was that old priest I knew who dragged himself up the altar steps, beginning the old rites; the thurible clashed against its chain; we rose, dutifully, though they have let us down again, holding their forts against new hordes. I had hoped the canvas would be filled with radiant colours, but the word God became a word of scorn, easiest to ignore. We came out again, our heartache unassuaged. The high corral of the Academy, too, is loud with gossipers, the ego-traffickers, nothing to be expected there. Self-portrait, with grief and darkening sky. There is a late photograph of Edvard Munch sitting in a room large as a barn; it is the winter studio; a room, enclosed; you will sit, stilled, on a wooden chair, tweed heavy about your frame, eyes focused inwards, where there is no past, no future; you sit alone, your papers in an ordered disarray; images stilled, like nests emptied; the phone beside you will not ring; nor will the light come on; everything depends on where your eyes focus; when the darkness comes, drawing its black drape across the window, there will remain the stillness of paint, words on the page, the laid down instruments of your art.

Down in the Swamps and Marshes
Patrick Kavanagh (1904-1967)

Perhaps, in the context of Kavanagh, it is time to clarify what is generally meant by the use of the word 'mystical'. It is a word too easily used, and too vague, to cover some moods, feelings, experiences, either aesthetic or religious. If the allusion to a particular experience is imprecise or uncertain, the word 'mystical' is too often, too lazily, flung out. The true meaning of the word, then, is to express the experiential perception of the Presence and Being of God; it is union with God, not merely in conforming to God's will, but an actual and ontological contact between the soul and God. Strictly speaking, then, none of the poets in this book may be termed 'mystics', and their work is not 'mystical' in the way that St John of the Cross, St Teresa of Avila, St Francis of Assisi and others were mystics. If the poetry offered by poets like Traherne, Herbert, Vaughan, springs from a deep awareness of their own dependency on God, their own love of the Creator and his creation, the work is still not strictly 'mystical'. The lazy use of the word to cover some of the poetry of Patrick Kavanagh is quite unacceptable, as is the use of the word Kavanagh himself often employed. This is in no sense intended to demean or lower the value of the poetry, quite the contrary, it is to suggest a more realistic approach to the work.

An 'aspect of mysticism is the embrace of nature, that is, God's creation as a source of rapture which, in its own way, is foremost in Kavanagh's writing' (Stack 34). This use of the word is also somewhat misleading, the 'embrace of nature' being simply a reaction to the awareness of the beauties and inherent value of creation, such as the Romantic poets knew. The dangers of that word are clear; and the fact of nature as a source of rapture does not entail the fact that it's 'God's creation'. Kavanagh himself uses the word in the 'Owl' section of 'Four Birds':

Night-winged
As a ghost
Or a gangster,
Mystical as a black priest
Reading the Devil's Mass.

The inaccuracy of the use of the word here is quite horrific. However, as Father Stack also observed, 'For the Christian, the particularity *par excellence* occurs in the mystery of the incarnation through which God enters the world of the finite, becoming flesh in the person of Christ at the village of Bethlehem, some two thousand years ago' (Stack 15). The centrality of Christ to Kavanagh's life and work is important to note, but must be clearly understood.

Patrick Kavanagh's father, James, was a bastard son who greatly loved his mother and cared for her, and similarities with the life of John Clare may begin with this awareness. James was a cobbler and did well, buying land, some nine acres. He had ten children; Patrick Joseph, born in 1904 was the fourth. Kavanagh suffered primary schooling in Kednaminsha, particularly under one Miss Julia Cassidy: 'He never forgave her the physical abuse which made his school life a nightmare and turned him against all interest in furthering his education' (Quinn 24). Boys being boys and 'sissies' being the most despised of all amongst his peers, 'That he actually enjoyed poetry was a guilty secret' (Quinn 26). His experiences in primary school were quite normal for the time, including the beatings and the mere learning of things by heart without explanation or discussion. Hearing the poetry of James Clarence Mangan spoken aloud moved him deeply at this time. The Catholic liturgy, the vestments, the flowers and candles and incense, appealed to his aesthetic sense but he had ended his schooling by June of 1918.

It looked as if it was his destiny to be apprenticed as a cobbler, but he never did well at the task, nor indeed, it appears, at any other task. 'Local farmers were willing to take him on for seasonal stints, convinced that they could get a good day's labour out of him. Few did' (Quinn 32). But he learned the trade of farming and, if he did not bother getting down to work the land, he made good use in his poetry of the language, the scenery, the trade. He had very little money. At the age of 18 he contracted typhoid fever and spent 3 months in hospital. Reading and talking were what he preferred to do. In 1925 the family bought more land, at Shancoduff, intending to have Patrick farm it, though it was not until 1938 that it was transferred to his name. He was working hard at his verse, reading when he could, enjoying poems in the school textbooks and from Palgrave's 'Golden Treasury'. The habit of rote-learning served him well and he built up a wide-ranging awareness of the central English poets. At about age 21 he discovered the *Irish Statesman*, edited by AE (George Russell) and met real contemporary literature for the first time. However, the poetry preferred by AE and which Kavanagh worked towards so as to please and be published, was a poetry at odds with the texture and idiom of everyday life and rife with the notion of mysticism in the vaguest possible sense of that word. In 1929 AE accepted three poems of Kavanagh's, including 'Ploughman' and 'Dreamer'. However, 'The downturn of AE's influence in the short term was that it led to an erasure of the local, the sensuous and the realist; in the long term it introduced a fondness for lofty abstractions to which he remained prone for most of his career' (Quinn 57). This was the danger of the flat-footed, lazy notion of what mysticism truly means.

Ploughman

I turn the lea-green down
Gaily now,
And paint the meadow brown
With my plough.

I dream with silvery gull
And brazen crow.
A thing that is beautiful
I may know.

Tranquility walks with me
And no care.
O, the quiet ecstasy
Like a prayer.

I find a star-lovely art
In a dark sod.
Joy that is timeless! O heart
That knows God!

The simple faith that is underlying this early poem is close to sentimentality, and yet rings with the honest truth of a genuine faith. It is a going-with the turning of the earth, a sense of being close to and involved in the very movements of nature that gives a young man a sense of well-being and pleasure. Earth, sky, star and God are linked in one experience as is art – the 'painting' with the plough, and worship, the 'prayer'. It signals a new era in Irish poetry, this man so close to earth, as was John Clare, taking joy in work and contact with the earth, though in Kavanagh the Christian movement is more explicit. There is, however, a tone of unreality in the use of the 'O', and in the final line, a note of willed imposition on the experience, rather than a necessary outcome. Kavanagh, brought up in the strict Catholic framework of the early twentieth century in Ireland, was wet with Christian imagery, tanned with its faith certainties, muscled with its general rules and regulations; as indeed were so many Irish people, who accepted the overall notion of a church and its commandments that would lead one who remained faithful to eternal glory, rather than a people who developed their beliefs out of their living and found the faith through their own inner demanding.

In 'April', for instance, Kavanagh has written:

… in the green meadows
The maiden of Spring is with child
By the Holy Ghost

all of which is lovely if one already accepts all the premises. 'The religious content of his poetry is … extensive and of considerable weight. It represents a large, remarkable and even something of a self-contained segment of Kavanagh's creative work with its own particular substance and strain' (Stack 9), and this is what has been innovative in Irish poetry, this personal response to the Christian message, born out of a will to write, and out of a locale where the Christian imagery was prevalent as rain. It was instinctive in Kavanagh at this early stage, self-taught, ordained in the following of the AE prescription of 'mystical' awareness, a message, a worldview that Kavanagh cultivated so as to succeed in publication.

Kavanagh was taken, in early childhood, with the wonder of the Christmas message and with the Christ who was child, God and man, the wonderful mystery of the incarnation. 'The authentic Christian way is the long plod through our material world, through our lived lives, with all the ordinariness, puzzlement and pain that this entails. In other words, the incarnational way' (Stack 20).

Street Corner Christ

I saw Christ to-day
At a street corner stand,
In the rags of a beggar he stood
He held ballads in his hand.
He was crying out: - 'Two for a penny
Will anyone buy
The finest ballads ever made
From the stuff of joy?'

But the blind and deaf went past
Knowing only there
An uncouth ballad-seller
With tail-matted hair.

And I whom men call fool
His ballads bought,
Found him whom the pieties
Have vainly sought.

For Kavanagh, hope and faith reside in the state of innocence; and yet Kavanagh was no idiot, he was already aware that the given, the accepted image of the Christ was not that of the merely pious, the Christ offered through the static and limited lessons of catechism and sermon. Yet the innocence of childhood he knew in the Christ of the Christmas celebrations, remained the deepest root of his humanity, offering him an immediacy of awareness of a primal truth and beauty, associated with the sanctity possible through creation and through the Christ. There may be an echo of

Vaughan sounding through such a learned innocence, and there
was Wordsworth, with his phrase 'The child is father to the man'.
Kavanagh has 'a knack of presenting material objects as bespeak-
ing God's handiwork and a sense of the transcendent mirrored in
the physical realities of our environment' (Stack 16).

So the early poems are a-glitter with the beauty of creation,
and the special wild beauties of the Monaghan landscape where
he grew up. There was in the poetry an awareness of light and
freshness, so that for him, nativity scenes predominate in the
poetry, spring, the re-birth of innocence, and baptism, all of which
will appear, deepened and more assured through the vicissitudes
and self-centred banalities and foolishness through which he
pushed himself, in later poems like 'Canal Bank Walk'. Innocence
is closely linked, however, to lack of knowledge here and one
wonders if Kavanagh was scared of losing his faith, and his poetry,
if too much knowledge entered in; this, from 'To Knowledge':

> You taught me far too many things,
> Filling my singing void
> With signs and sounds until the kings
> Creative could not bide.

and in 'Sensualist':

> Realise the touch kingdom
> Do not stray
> In the abstract temple of love.

Christmas, innocence, childhood, they flowed together, as in
the poem 'Christmas, 1939' he writes:

> O Divine Baby in the cradle
> All that is poet in me
> Is the dream I dreamed of Your Childhood
> And the dream You dreamed of me.

The poem 'Primrose' makes clear to us and to the poet himself his dependence on the innocence of childhood, the wish
that, perhaps, notions of the crucifixion of life, may not cast their
long shadow, their tree-like ('Dream of the Rood') shadow, their
'tired soldiers' shadows, on such innocence. Suffering and reality,
it is hinted, will not allow such glad moments again.

Primrose

Upon a bank I sat, a child made seer
Of one small primrose flowering in my mind.
Better than wealth it is, I said, to find
One small page of Truth's manuscript made clear.
I looked at Christ transfigured without fear –
The light was very beautiful and kind,
And where the Holy Ghost in flame had signed
I read it through the lenses of a tear.
And then my sight grew dim, I could not see
The primrose that had lighted me to Heaven,
And there was but the shadow of a tree
Ghostly among the stars. The years that pass
Like tired soldiers nevermore have given
Moments to see wonders in the grass.

Kavanagh starts, then, 'in bright certainty' (as Pádraig J. Daly will write); and yet it was a certainty fraught with an awareness of his own failure in academic knowledge. Kavanagh had accepted his inherited faith; in these early poems so many of the statements are beautifully put, and echoed again in a very late poem where they still resonate but without that early ease of acceptance:

The One

Green, blue, yellow and red –
God is down in the swamps and marshes,
Sensational as April and almost incred-
ible the flowering of our catharsis.
A humble scene in a backward place
Where no one important ever looked;
The raving flowers looked up in the face
Of the One and the Endless, the Mind that has baulked
The profoundest of mortals. A primrose, a violet,
A violent wild iris – but mostly anonymous performers,
Yet an important occasion as the Muse at her toilet
Prepared to inform the local farmers
That beautiful, beautiful, beautiful God
Was breathing His love by a cut-away bog.

A poem written many years after Kednaminsha, the awareness of the 'swamps and marshes' is still fresh for Kavanagh, 'a
humble scene in a backward place'. But for years he came to reject
this kind of country innocence and simplistic faith, and challenged, as a form of defence, those whom he regarded as more
educated than he, here ironically telling how 'the Muse at her
toilet' is urging the local farmers to gaze into their own bog.
'Kavanagh insisted that the poet's vocation, like that of the
prophet, is to confront what is shallow and unreflective' (Stack
30), but for too many years Kavanagh confronted too violently,
too personally, quickly rejecting the innocence he knew in himself so as to 'fit in' with the learned crowd in the Dublin pubs;
Father Stack quotes Kavanagh: 'In every poet there is something
of Christ writing the sins of the people in the dust.' Kavanagh
roared them out, those sins of the people, while remaining fully
aware that those same sins were in himself, and (sadly, as I see
it), hiding his true self from himself.

Kavanagh comes across in those early years as something of
a country bumpkin, awkward at dances, awkward with friends
and with female company. But he was athletic, and took part in
the local games, joining the Rovers Gaelic football team where
he played in goal and took frees, with some success and a good
deal of inconsistency. The circumstances of his first visit to
Dublin and to AE are well known. To emphasise the fact that he
was a 'rough peasant genius', Kavanagh dressed badly, and
walked, over three days, the sixty or so miles to Dublin. AE was
kind to him, and remained so, giving him books and introduc-
ing him to the literati of the day. Kavanagh's early poems had
been written to impress AE and, even though the 'religious'
content of these pieces may have been forced, they yet sprang
from his inner conviction and experience. 'Both the paganism
and the piety were affectations; he was an intellectual poseur'
(Quinn 76). I am inclined to argue the point. Perhaps the expression of both 'paganism' and 'piety' were affected, but they could
not have been so and produce such memorable poetry, without
a genuine depth of commitment to both notions. It was the ex-
ternal, manipulative Kavanagh who hid the inner one of which
he was a little embarrassed. He also worked hard to write 'realistic' poetry and in his love poems of the early years, he thought

it fine to take on what he saw as the tragic poet's sense of loss and suffering in his failures in wooing a woman. He imitated many of the romantics in those, very poor, verses, and saw himself for a while as similar to John Clare in giving his love to an unresponsive and even unaware young woman. 'From first to last the affair seems to have been as much a construct as one of his own poems and as little grounded in actuality – he was indulging in a poetic experience of love' (Quinn 80). 'Peasant quality' was very much in demand at the time. *Ploughman and Other Poems*, a slim volume, came from Macmillan in 1936; Kavanagh took to wearing a stetson to Mass but was hesitant between comforts of home and giving himself to poetry.

Christmas, 1939

O Divine Baby in the cradle,
All that is poet in me
Is the dream I dreamed of Your Childhood
And the dream You dreamed of me.

O Divine Baby in the cradle,
All that is truth in me
Is my mind tuned to the cadence
Of a child's philosophy.

O Divine Baby in the cradle,
All that is pride in me
Is my mind bowed in homage
Upon Your Mother's knee.

O Divine Baby in the cradle,
All that is joy in me
Is that I have saved from the ruin
Of my soul Your Infancy.

The 'O', repeated, the proud yet hesitant notion of mentioning 'All that is poet in me', even the awareness that his 'philosophy' is yet that of a child, still mar the poem somewhat though the genuineness of the feeling, of the urge, cannot be questioned. Already he is self-conscious about 'the ruin' of his soul, aware that the road he was taking was away from what was native to him and to his essential spirit. Yet he was to carry that same

Infant Christ with him across all the turmoils he put himself through.

Christmas Eve Remembered

I see them going to the chapel
To confess their sins. Christmas Eve
In a parish in Monaghan.
Poor parish! and yet memory does weave
For me about those folk
A romantic cloak.

No snow, but in their minds
The fields and roads are white;
They may be talking of the turkey markets
Or foreign politics, but to-night
Their plain, hard country words
Are Christ's singing birds.

Bicycles scoot by. Old women
Cling to the grass margin:
Their thoughts are earthy, but their minds move
In dreams of the Blessed Virgin,
For One in Bethlehem
Has kept their dreams safe for them.

'Did you hear from Tom this Chrismas?'
'These are the dark days.'
'Maguire's shop did a great trade,
Turnover double – so Maguire says.'
'I can't delay now, Jem,
Lest I be late in Bethlehem.'

Like this my memory saw,
Like this my childhood heard
These pilgrims of the North …
And memory you have me spared
A light to follow them
Who go to Bethlehem.

Another poem that demonstrates Kavanagh's self-awareness, that he was viewing his Monaghan living and the people there as under a 'romantic cloak'. It is a poem where he is standing back from what he knew and loved; he is watching 'them', the people with whom he should be sharing this experience, from a distance; he is envious, too, that their simple words may be 'Christ's singing birds'. Even the old women he envies, whose dreams are kept safe. All the gladness he can find (this in 1939) is being able to envy them and follow them in memory.

In May 1937 Kavanagh was already heading to London where Helen Waddell got Constable to commission *The Green Fool*, allowing him to spend five months in the city. This work helped him achieve a precise particularity and honesty. The book was published, by Michael Joseph, in 1938, to good reviews. By now he was beginning to make a name for himself among the Dublin literati whom he was also treating with some contempt, though it was among them that he was to seek affirmation and support. In 'The Irony Of It', a poem published in the *Irish Times* in 1938, Kavanagh was still musing on the intimidating situation of being under-educated. 'I have not the fine audacity of men/Who have mastered the pen/Or the purse.' He goes on to say: 'Mine was a beggar's mission'.

> I should have been content to walk behind,
> Watching the mirror-stones
> For the reflection of God's delight:
> A second-hand teller of the story,
> A second-hand glory.
> It was not right
> That my mind should have echoed life's overtones,
> That I should have seen a flower
> Petalled in mighty power.

He was 'profoundly self-centred', according to Antoinette Quinn, his biographer, and this developed throughout his life. It appears to have begun as a defence-mechanism; it eventually brought about the diminution of his talent. In 1939 Oliver St John Gogarty took a libel action against an innocent-enough comment in *The Green Fool* and the book was withdrawn in March of that year. In August he began to live with his brother Peter (off his brother) in Dublin; it is difficult, reading the details of the life, to be sympathetic to such a free-loader, such a selfish, big-headed, rough man. And yet, the poems!

To the Man After the Harrow

Now leave the check-reins slack,
The seed is flying far today –
The seed like stars against the black
Eternity of April clay.

This seed is potent as the seed
Of knowledge in the Hebrew Book,
So drive your horses in the creed
Of God the Father as a stook.

Forget the men on Brady's hill.
Forget what Brady's boy may say,
For destiny will not fulfill
Unless you let the harrow play.

Forget the worm's opinion too
Of hooves and pointed harrow-pins,
For you are driving your horses through
The mist where Genesis begins.

This poem has the movement of true inspiration, its fine shaping and rhymes, its impulsive onward movement. It contains that instinctive faith that Kavanagh was reared in and the poem gives that faith a rich articulation. There is the Hopkins sense of pain and suffering as necessary to the ongoing growth of being, that being begun in Eden garden, in 'The mist where Genesis begins'. Disculping Kavanagh from Pantheism, Father Stack wrote: 'A helpful distinction which banishes the pantheistic suspicion … is the difference between a God reduced to created, finite being and a God in whom all being is included' (Stack 27). In his best work, this is the overarching God, the indwelling Christ of the original Christian faith; Kavanagh was absorbed by the incarnation, by Christ.

Advent

We have tested and tasted too much, lover;
Through a chink too wide there comes in no wonder.
But here in the Advent-darkened room
Where the dry black bread and the sugarless tea
Of penance will charm back the luxury

Of a child's soul, we'll return to Doom
The knowledge we stole but could not use.

And the newness that was in every stale thing
When we looked at it as children: the spirit-shocking
Wonder in a black slanting Ulster hill,
Or the prophetic astonishment in the tedious talking
Of an old fool, will awake for us and bring
You and me to the yard gate to watch the whins
And the bog-holes, cart-tracks, old stables where Time begins.

O after Christmas we'll have no need to go searching
For the difference that sets an old phrase burning –
We'll hear it in the whispered argument of a churning
Or in the streets where the village boys are lurching.
And we'll hear it among simple, decent men, too,
Who barrow dung in gardens under trees,
Wherever life pours ordinary plenty.

Won't we be rich, my love and I, and please
God we shall not ask for reason's payment,
The why of heart-breaking strangeness in dreeping hedges,
Nor analyse God's breath in common statement.
We have thrown into the dust-bin the clay-minted wages
Of pleasure, knowledge and the conscious hour –
And Christ comes with a January flower.

'Through a chink too wide there comes in no wonder'.
Kavanagh offers the worth of the imagination over that of intellect and learning. It is when Kavanagh puts a halt to his own
imagination and pushes the will towards satire and intellectual
musings in an effort, I believe, to top the literati whom he envied
and yet despised, that his own poetry slumped. In 'Advent', that
time that is to prepare for the coming of the Christ, it is once
more the child's view, that clear-eyed, unselfconscious longing
for incarnation, that gives the poem its magical quality. It is
where the ordinary, the simple, the truly known are allowed
take on the wonder that the imagination endows them with, that
Kavanagh finds peace and fulfillment, and great poetry. This is
life and wonder beyond 'reason's payment', a richness alert
with immediacy of experience, but an experience coloured by

the sacred, by the incarnation, by the taking flesh by the Godhead. As Kavanagh suggests, it is the analysis and argument that reason brings that stifle love and hope and wonder. The early poetry 'is supplied with a strong physical presence and is full of the recognitions which existed between the poet and his place' (Government 4). Seamus Heaney recognises in Kavanagh's early work the same lien that exists in Heaney's own work, between place and spirit, between contact with the actuality of one's living and the presence of the human in that actuality. In the case of Kavanagh, the late places become 'sites where the mind projects its own force' (Government 5), and in this case Kavanagh loses touch with the sources of his poetry. Heaney was stirred by 'the unregarded data of the usual life', that poetry can be born from such 'a primitive delight in finding world become word' in his own life. Kavanagh however turns from Monaghan to the self as poetic subject; his removal to Dublin and his quick and overwhelming success, became a resource to maintain an inner sense of worth in spite of the world; he was in flight, over the world, above the world; no longer seeking a destination.

A Christmas Childhood

I
One side of the potato-pits was white with frost –
How wonderful that was, how wonderful!
And when we put our ears to the paling-post
The music that came out was magical.

The light between the ricks of hay and straw
Was a hole in Heaven's gable. An apple tree
With its December-glinting fruit we saw –
O you, Eve, were the world that tempted me

To eat the knowledge that grew in clay
And death the germ within it! Now and then
I can remember something of the gay
Garden that was childhood's. Again

The tracks of cattle to a drinking-place,
A green stone lying sideways in a ditch

Or any common sight the transfigured face
Of a beauty that the world did not touch.

II
My father played the melodeon
Outside at our gate;
There were stars in the morning east
And they danced to his music.

Across the wild bogs his melodeon called
To Lennons and Callans.
As I pulled on my trousers in a hurry
I knew some strange thing had happened.

Outside the cow-house my mother
Made the music of milking;
The light of her stable-lamp was a star
And the frost of Bethlehem made it twinkle.

A water-hen screeched in the bog,
Mass-going feet
Crunched the wafer-ice on the pot-holes,
Somebody wistfully twisted the bellows wheel.

My child poet picked out the letters
On the grey stone,
In silver the wonder of a Christmas townland,
The winking glitter of a frosty dawn.

Cassiopeia was over
Cassidy's hanging hill,
I looked and three whin bushes rode across
The horizon – The Three Wise Kings.

An old man passing said:
'Can't he make it talk' –
The melodeon. I hid in the doorway
And tightened the belt of my box-pleated coat.

I nicked six nicks on the door-post
With my penknife's big blade –
There was a little one for cutting tobacco,
And I was six Christmases of age.

My father played the melodeon,
My mother milked the cows,
And I had a prayer like a white rose pinned
On the Virgin Mary's blouse.

Only the innocence apparent in childhood can allow Kavanagh get away with the first stanza of this poem; and 'Now and then / I can remember something of the gay / Garden that was child-hood's.' Here is where the poet found something of beauty that the harsh world with its skepticism and its learning has not touched. The rest of the poem, the second section, is masterly, a delightful romping in innocence, in the mystery that is accepted as mystery, in the imagination untrammeled by intellect or rea-son. As Michael Schmidt observed, here is 'The immanent God, perceived always in the more earthy places, in the new leaves, in the ploughed soil' (Schmidt 657). But Kavanagh had taken up his post in the city and the city was not in his blood, as the immediacy and locale of Monaghan were in his blood. The city quenched the light of the incarnation within his childlike soul, then drew that childhood into a raw and cynical centre with which he tried to cope for the rest of his life, without success, with scarcely an occasional glimpse of the early light. Schmidt writes: 'God becomes difficult, but there is still a hunger for him in the later poems' (Schmidt 657).

Without education he found getting work in Dublin, or in London, difficult. Quinn says he was 'anxious to conceal his ed-ucational deficiencies' (Quinn 124). John Charles McQuaid, Archbishop of Dublin, who came from Cootehall in Cavan, not far from Kavanagh's home, became a patron. 'During his first years in Dublin, Kavanagh's notoriety as a journalistic trouble-maker was beginning to overtake his reputation as a lyric poet' (Quinn 138). He was forcing himself through a life to which he was not naturally inclined. It is teasing to wonder how he would have developed had he stayed in Monaghan and pursued his poetry without the mixed blessings of the Dublin literary society which admired itself in the pint-glasses and whiskey glow of the pubs. Truly astonishing all the literati, he completed 'The Great Hunger', without doubt his major work and one that al-tered the ground of Irish poetry from then on.

The 'Great Hunger' of which Kavanagh wrote is not the famine in Ireland whose consequences ruled on well into the twentieth century; rather is it the failure of small farmers to marry. It is the poverty of a country living that is kept poor and broken by the dominance of an overweening church and the minions of that church. The poem is not an attack on Christianity, but it does focus on the failures of an institutional church that backs up the ways of living and believing that actually destroyed growth of spirit in country people.

> Clay is the word and clay is the flesh
> Where the potato-gatherers like mechanized scare-crows move
> Along the side-fall of the hill – Maguire and his men.

Kavanagh sets up his people to see if there is 'some light of imagination in these wet clods'. He sees the Christian message manipulated by eldering farmers, whose whole aim is to stifle in the younger men and women the claims of body as well as the claims of the spirit in order to preserve what they see as an age-old tradition, the holding on to land at all costs, the shared value-system by which they haggled and hustled, dug and plotted and harvested, a family-thing, that kept the son from bringing a woman into the house as long as the mother remained alive. It was a terrible dominance by those who did own land, and Kavanagh will hold the poem to 'watch the tragedy to the last curtain'. The poem is rich with the acutely-observed details of the clenched young farmer's living: 'Three heads hanging between wide-apart legs'. Maguire makes futile attempts to hide the truth of what was happening to himself, as he watched the seasons pass, fertile enough in the land he laboured, but infertile in his own personal life:

> Patrick Maguire, he called his dog and he flung a stone in the air
> And hallooed the birds away that were the birds of the years…
> His dream changes again like the cloud-swung wind
> And he is not so sure now if his mother was right
> When she praised the man who made a field his bride.

Patrick Maguire's slow dance of fear and distraught desire around young girls and women is wonderfully portrayed, as are his poor efforts to satisfy himself by masturbation and dreams.

What he comes to know is that 'God's truth is life – even the grotesque shapes of its foulest fire.' The Catholic Church has preached a morality that backs up this manipulation of sons and daughters of landowners, offering a heaven to come, insisting on the worthlessness of present bodily demands. 'The Christ who dignified the human body and spirit by choosing to become incarnate has been replaced by the Irish country version of Catholicism by a false clay god, an agricultural divinity who is simultaneously a graveyard deity' (Quinn 177).

> Maguire was faithful to death:
> He stayed with his mother till she died
> At the age of ninety-one.
> She stayed too long,
> Wife and mother in one.
> When she died
> The knuckle-bones were cutting the skin of her son's backside
> And he was sixty-five.

The mother in the poem bears no resemblance to Kavanagh's own beloved mother but it is true to much of what anyone alive in the forties and fifties Ireland was well aware of. Yet through all of the misery and frustration of the living of such men, they were instinctively aware of the truth of the Christian message as Kavanagh himself caught it in his early poems:

> Yet sometimes when the sun comes through a gap
> These men know God the Father in a tree:
> The Holy Spirit is the rising sap,
> And Christ will be the green leaves that will come
> At Easter from the sealed and guarded tomb.

Kavanagh was instinctively right about Christ, and he saw the incarnation as a blessing on flesh and on sexuality; if he remained self-conscious about his lack of education, he yet remained instinctively true to Christian verities. And above all, to the incarnation, to the belief in Christ as redeemer and in the Godhead who gave meaning to life. Yet what the Catholic Church was preaching at the time was Sin! and sin was equated with sexual longings: 'And he saw Sin/Written in letters larger that John Bunyan dreamt of.' Kavanagh spoke of the Eucharist:

'In a crumb of bread the whole mystery is', yet the bread is nourishment, but the church and the landowners took the savour from the bread and turned it into clay.

'Now go to Mass and pray and confess your sins
And you'll have all the luck,' his mother said.
He listened to the lie that is a woman's screen
Around a conscience when soft thighs are spread.

Maguire suffers the gradations of the seasons, in his fields, in his home, in his body and there was nothing in the living to raise his spirits or to teach him the real truth of the incarnation. He read only the rags of newspapers, 'sometimes an old almanac brought down from the ceiling', he put an odd bet on a race-horse and still 'Patrick Maguire was six months behind life'. Kavanagh's aim in the poem is to debunk the romantic and lyrical notions of 'the peasant' that the learned folk indulge in, 'The peasant ploughman who is half a vegetable',

Who can react to sun and rain and sometimes even
Regret that the Maker of Light had not touched him
        more intensely,
Brought him up from the sub-soil to an existence
Of conscious joy.

If Kavanagh has painted a bleak picture of Patrick Maguire and his kind, he did succeed in fashioning a real character, a real tragedy in the poem. And the picture is bleak indeed, a bleakness later echoed in the early poetry of the Welsh poet R. S. Thomas, a bleakness Kavanagh congratulated himself he had escaped. He came to reject the poem in later years, perhaps because of the unrelieved blackness of the vision of the country farmer, yet it remains a scaldingly rich and imaginative piece of writing that opened up new worlds for poets who came after him. Maguire stands alone at the end of his life of futility and loneliness and watches out on the world:

He stands in the doorway of his house
A ragged sculpture of the wind,
October creaks the rotten mattress,
The bedposts fall. No hope. No lust.

The hungry fiend
Screams the apocalypse of clay
In every corner of this land.

The poem has often been read as an attack on Catholicism but that is far from the truth. 'An obsession in some quarters with Kavanagh's "mysticism" has deflected attention from his quite complicated attitude towards Catholicism: a compound of belief and skepticism, affectionate tolerance and fierce criticism, superstitious fear and anticlericalism and, as in 'The Great Hunger', the imaginative and intellectual power to conceive of an alternative to the popular Irish conception of a prudent and sexually prudish Deity, a God who always said yes' (Quinn 192). He continued as a practising Catholic; went to Mass and the sacraments regularly but when he visited Lough Derg to find a poem out of his experience as a pilgrim, he was quite unsure how to respond. His attitude to Monaghan and 'the peasant' also remained quite ambiguous, as may be seen in a poem he wrote in 1942/43, during the war:

Peace

And sometimes I am sorry when the grass
Is growing over the stones in quiet hollows
And the cocksfoot leans across the rutted cart-pass,
That I am not the voice of country fellows
Who now are standing by some headland talking
Of turnips and potatoes or young corn
Or turf banks stripped for victory.
Here Peace is still hawking
His coloured combs and scarves and beads of horn.

Upon a headland by a whinny hedge
A hare sits looking down a leaf-lapped furrow;
There's an old plough upside-down on a weedy ridge
And someone is shouldering home a saddle-harrow.
Out of that childhood country what fools climb
To fight with tyrants Love and Life and Time?

Such a melting mood did not occur too often and Kavanagh turned to writing more satirical pieces in a mood he termed 'comic'. The 55 pages of his second collection, *A Soul for Sale* were published by Macmillan in 1947 and it was generally acknowledged that 'The Great Hunger', having its first major publication here, was a masterpiece.

The satires and the sideswipes took too much of his energy; in 'Irish Poets Open Your Eyes', written around 1950, there is a glimpse of this antagonism towards learning:

> Could you ever pray at all
> In the Pro-Cathedral
> Till a breath of simpleness
> Freed your Freudian distress?

And the poem 'Innocence' demonstrates his awareness of where he has come from and suggests a nostalgia for that earlier time:

> They laughed at one I loved –
> The triangular hill that hung
> Under the Big Forth. They said
> That I was bounded by the whitethorn hedges
> Of the little farm and did not know the world …

And the poem concludes: 'I cannot die/Unless I walk outside these whitethorn hedges'. The fact that he associated poetry with innocence, with the freedom of the imagination, with an unquestioning faith in God, is seen in the 1951 poem:

Having Confessed

> Having confessed, he feels
> That he should go down on his knees and pray
> For forgiveness for his pride, for having
> Dared to view his soul from the outside.
> Lie at the heart of the emotion, time
> Has its own work to do. We must not anticipate
> Or awaken for a moment. God cannot catch us
> Unless we stay in the unconscious room
> Of our hearts. We must be nothing,
> Nothing that God may make us something.
> We must not touch the immortal material,
> We must not daydream tomorrow's judgement –
> God must be allowed to surprise us.

We have sinned, sinned like Lucifer
By this anticipation. Let us lie down again
Deep in anonymous humility and God
May find us worthy material for His hand.

The line 'God must be allowed to surprise us' rings to the very soul of the best of Kavanagh's work and perhaps helps explain why he could not relish most of the poetry being written by his contemporaries. Intellect and will, he found, were inimical to poetry. But he does not seem to have been fully aware that that had been happening to him, too: 'The rich measured achievement of his early poems is betrayed by the prolixity and unbridled anger of his later satires' (Schmidt 655). Yet he held on to his belief in the power of the imagination over that of reason and learning; in the poem 'To Hell with Commonsense', written about 1958, there are the lines:

And I have a feeling
That through the hole in reason's ceiling
We can fly to knowledge
Without ever going to college.

With his brother Peter financing him, he published *Kavanagh's Weekly*, for some time before it failed, mainly because of a lack of backing to circulate it, but also because of the vituperation with which he filled it. He was now famous in Dublin and throughout the country; many coming to see him, a few daring to try and chat with him, so that 'though he was filling McDaid's coffers, he wasn't making any money in his own right' (Quinn 330). This would have been around 1954 when he was very much in debt. In 1955 he suffered lung cancer, had a lung and a rib removed; he was in Rialto hospital for two months where he relished the care and enjoyed the security. In 1955 his patron, Archbishop McQuaid, banned a soccer match between Ireland and Communist Yugoslavia; 'In private ... Kavanagh was opposed to the ecclesiastical ban on the match; publicly, as when addressing a meeting of the L and H in UCD, he applauded the Archbishop's stance' (Quinn 347).

He was literally killing himself with drink; he insulted and alienated almost everyone he met, he was self-focused, self-aggrandising at the expense of everybody he knew, boorish in the extreme, aware of his own lack of learning and contemptuous of it in others. The difficulty has always been to reconcile the exquisite nature of some of his poems with such unacceptable behaviour. He set himself up as the unwanted outsider who was yet clever enough to beat the literati at their own game. In the 'Paddiad', he also set himself up as the Conscience of the country, dramatising his freedom from what he termed a tame, scholarly and dry approach to life and literature. He was a cynical Irish Catholic, cynical about Roman Catholicism but braced by his upbringing, unable to let go that basic Christian faith. He fought with the armour of cynicism a milieu of educated people. He pretended cynicism about being published so that he could manipulate his own work. He was cynical with the truth so that he could persuade others to take care of him and pay his debts.

Yet in the later poems he sometimes returns to the instinctive religious imagery he used at the beginning of his career. After the cynical and often poorly wrought poems of his satirical period, he returns to a celebratory mode and the poems are once more love poems to street, canal, lane and bog. The imposition of religious imagery, consciously manipulative in the early poems, recurs here but with an emotional truth to them, a necessity to the actual inspiration. Poetry now has become more irrational for him, independent of will or intellect or education, and influenced, perhaps, by his contact with the Beat poets among whom he spent several weeks during a stay in New York. 'Canal Bank Walk', written around 1958, shows Kavanagh aware of being 'redeemed' by his attention to nature once again, creation presenting another 'person' to consort with those able to take pleasure in nature. There is an echo of Francis Thompson in the poem, a longing to be whirled away by the strength of the innocence of a world untainted by the depredations of humanity.

Canal Bank Walk

Leafy-with-love banks and the green waters of the canal
Pouring redemption for me, that I do
The will of God, wallow in the habitual, the banal,
Grow with nature again as before I grew.
The bright stick trapped, the breeze adding a third

Party to the couple kissing on an old seat,
And a bird gathering materials for the nest for the Word,
Eloquently new and abandoned to its delirious beat.
O unworn world enrapture me, encapture me in a web
Of fabulous grass and eternal voices by a beech,
Feed the gaping need of my senses, give me ad lib
To pray unselfconsciously with overflowing speech,
For this soul needs to be honoured with a new dress woven
From green and blue things and arguments that cannot be
    proven.

In 1959 he met Katherine Barry Moloney in London and they became instant friends. For several years she took care of him, ministering to him, loving him and he came to rely greatly on her. In many ways she was a 'redeemer' for him in the years when he most needed someone to see past his gruff and angry exterior and find the child still skulking within. 'As alcoholism prematurely aged him and he was increasingly racked by ill health, he was avid for youth and gaiety, the qualities that he thought all good poetry should possess' (Quinn 437). It was around this time he wrote the poem 'The One', quoted above, that speaks of 'that beautiful, beautiful, beautiful God/Was breathing His love by a cut-away bog'. A real God, through the incarnation of Christ in creation, informs his later poetry:

Miss Universe

I learned, I learned – when one might be inclined
To think, too late, you cannot recover your losses –
I learned something of the nature of God's mind,
Not the abstract Creator but He who caresses
The daily and nightly earth; He who refuses
To take failure for an answer till again and again is worn.
Love is waiting for you, waiting for the violence that she
    chooses
From the tepidity of the common round beyond exhaustion
    or scorn.
What was once is still and there is no need for remorse;
There are no recriminations in Heaven. O the sensual throb
Of the explosive body, the tumultuous thighs!

Adown a summer lane comes Miss Universe,
She whom no lecher's art can rob
Though she is not the virgin who was wise.

He married Katherine in April of 1967 and was dead by November 30 of that same year. It was pneumonia, aggravated by all the other illnesses severe drinking had developed. He left behind him a body of work which is uneven, magnificent when it works, flawed and a little careless too often, but at its best and richest it is a work that touches deeply on the Irish Christian psyche and on the instinctive companionship with nature that is common in the country.

The Meadows of Asphodel

Bog cotton flourishes on the wild acres of bog on Achill Island. The thin stems offer a fine and woolly head of white that blows gallantly in the sea winds. Here and there amongst the cottons you will find the fine yellow heads of bog asphodel. Asphodel, according to the great stories of our mythology, is beloved of the dead and covers the plains of Hades. I came to have a vision of the surface of the bogs of Achill Island as imaging those rich and wind-blown plains of the afterworld, and the beautiful and delicate bog cotton plants stirring like a chorus of souls arrayed for paradise, prepared to utter into praise.

My grandfather lies in Bunnacurry graveyard, closed now, and allowed to run wild with dogrose, montbretia, clumps of soiled-white lilies and long and withering grasses. Robins burst into song from the wild hedgerows round about and the wheatear scolds from her hidden places; the wren gads contentedly about in the dense undergrowth of fuchsia. All this is neglect, I said to Ursula, my wife and she said no, it is repose, the way the dead have abandoned us and become seeds curled up in darkness, whose only task now is to wait the nourishment and ripening; here, she said, it is the living who are blown about by the winds.

The gate leans crookedly and blue binding-twine clamps it against strays. We untied the twine and entered, to pay our respects to my grandfather, to an aunt, and to all the quiet dead who lie beneath the fine wilderness of growth. The asphodel, of course, is sacred to Persephone, queen of the underworld, and daughter of Demeter, earth-mother, goddess of the grain and fructifier of youth and the green earth. Strange, I thought, how the burial-place is also close allied to the productive side of our living and of our earth. Strange, and beautiful. We searched among the gravestones and grasses and eventually found my grandfather's resting-place. If it is, indeed, a place for resting. The stones with their weathering, their burthen of names and aspirations, face, Ursula said, all in the same direction, and I said East, they are waiting for that great disturbance, the final opening of the gate when we will all stir out of repose, and lift, prepared for counting, like the pale down of bog-cotton shivering before the breeze.

Grandfather's grave lies amongst rank disorder; a high stone cross holds the history of the world carved in pastel-coloured lichens; the graveyard path around his grave hides in the weeds and grasses; it is creation's original chaos of delight – where the old man lies, at peace, like God before he shook himself out of lethargy and spoke: In the beginning ... For grandfather had been a carpenter, among other things, and flourished in those decades when a man had to be all in all, capable of multiple tasks, like turf-cutting, hay-making, milking, shoe-mending, electrics, and carpentry. His tool-shed held every instrument needed for the making of chair, cupboard, sideboard and all was ordered to perfection, the tools ranged according to make and size and purpose, the bench kept free of clutter, the floor swept clean of shavings. Order above all; everything in its place, and every human being in his or her place, too. His children, my mother and my uncles and aunt, had to call him Sir. For me he was always big, that great moustache, that certainty of order, that command.

Today I imagine him, like the creator God, that first Carpenter, busy about the asphodel meadow in Bunnacurry. At times, on quiet summer nights, I see the old man take a turn about the yard, tidying away the empty beer and cider cans, the condoms, I see him work a while on polishing his soul against the final word that will draw everything back to stillness. The way he used to hone his workshop tools, because the old man's God was a carpenter God whose every word sent some new craftwork out into the universe to spin, and swell, and reproduce.

Perhaps the dead do not know repose. Perhaps the work of creation goes on and on across the afterworld the way the bog-cotton dies away in the winter and flourishes again over the peat acres every summer. And perhaps, I thought, and thought with happiness, as I tied again that blue binding-twine around the squealing gate, perhaps, before the dawn you can hear grandfather make his way back down, his night's work ended, to rest amongst the asphodel, perhaps you can hear those sounds like woodshavings being swept, like a workshop door being shut.

So many other images rule the mind, the most vivid of these, after the asphodel meadow of Bunnacurry, is the slightly larger meadow outside the village of Bunclody, in County Wexford, where my father and mother lie at rest. They had retired here, and spent their last years in quietness. On the day of his death I was with my father in the hospital in Wexford; when I came into the ward he was seated at the foot of the bed, wrapped in an old red dressing-gown, and he was absent from the world, his mind concentrated on somewhere we could not follow, his thoughts intent on the past, or the present, or the future, or all of that together, and we did not dare interrupt. He came out of that deep reverie and greeted us warmly, with his usual humour and diffidence, but had to make his way, with great effort, back into bed. We sat with him a long time that day, and slowly he abandoned us, slowly moving away into that ultimately dark mystery which is death. My prayer was that the Christ he had been so true to, would be there, wherever or whatever 'there' is, when he had gone from us. When I saw him again, the shock was terrible:

On Another Shore

The worn-out Otherthing
rigid on its slab, the fluids
stagnant;
dressed up and parcelled – the Offence;

someone had set a plastic rose
upon the chest,
and we, attendants,
faces unmasked by grief,

murmured our studied words:
he is not dead, but sleeping,
he is not here,
he has stepped out on another shore

beautiful beyond belief;
and we have crept back out
into weakened sunshine,
knowing our possibilities

diminished.

When we laid him in his grave in Bunclody, I knew that now we, the next generation, were at the head of the queue, at the edge of the cliff, and there was nobody there to guide or shelter us; we were on our own to face the living and dying we would have to do, our burden heavier, our loss almost unacceptable.

On This Shore

They laid him on his back
in the flat-bottomed
ramshackle boat that the dead use
and carried him down to the shore;

quickly he sank
into the current's hold
and did not come up again for air;
when I had kissed his forehead

he was already cold
and had begun to sweat;
soon he will have shed all baggage,
the great gannet of life

will be gliding over him like a dream;
he has cast off at last
from the high white cross
to which he was anchored

and I have turned back,
carrying his burden,
leaving a deeper set of footprints
across the sand.

Mother had died on Christmas Eve some time before. Her mind had gone a little astray in her last months and when I visited her for the last time, she did not know me. The funeral procession wound its way slowly from the hospital along by the river Slaney and there was frost everywhere, the trees holding it as if it were small wool-flecks of tinsel, the puddles at the side of the road thickened into ice. The journey seemed an endless one and what kept coming into my mind was the time she and I had picked our way so carefully over the frozen road on Achill, so many, many years ago. When we laid her down, what struck me most was the silence, a silence in which you almost expected to hear the frost crackling a little, the naked branches of the trees crack, and break off. And deep within me was a frosting of guilt that I had not loved her enough, that I had resented the demands of her strict Catholicism, that I had struggled against the fortress she had built up around herself, to hold her safe, with her own Christ, against a hostile world. In these meadows of asphodel I knew that it would be a duty of remembrance to study and speak the works of love, to work to make some sense of the beauty of this earth, the beauty of the souls departed, the wonder of the Eucharist we share, the incarnation of the God we honour.

Winter Silence

Ice came, regularly as the grey lag,
to lay its weight over the island.
I watched her

pick her way through morning,
step like a high-stilted bird
astonished across its frozen lake;

all afternoon we watched
through reflected images of ourselves
the disconcerting coming down of snow;

sometimes our faces swayed like ghosts
looking in at us from another world;
we wrote our names on glass with our fingertips.

She sat, finally, on the edge of the bed,
her feet dangling;
where are you now? I whispered

searching her face for traces of the dream;
her eyes were glazed, her lips pursed.
Field and hedgerow, after long snowfall,

are like a sheet drawn up
on the newly dead;
we lit tall candles about her cot

and I called again into winter silence –
are you? expecting no reply.
Came the slow slushing of tyres over a bridge,

procession of cars along a road
that turned with the turns of a river, long
black ribbons binding the earth together;

words bounced back at us from a grey sky
where we stood, drawn close together,
black ghosts adrift through a white world. Morning

and the world outside was a white ocean
while here, at the ocean's edge,
her name outlined in froth across our pane.

Rain in Boston

Many years after my mother's death I spent a winter teaching in Boston College. Through the frosting that eventually took over the streets, I remembered her, and my guilt, and I made a promise to myself that I would go back to Bunclody and whisper my plea for forgiveness over her grave. I wrote to her, and the radio in Ireland took the letter, and broadcast it. Perhaps she heard it, wherever, or whatever she has become. These, the words of that letter:

There have been days of rain here in Boston, this late winter. It comes as a surprise to me who prepared long and hard for snow, and frost and ice. I am brought back out of the unfamiliar to days I had thought long faded out of memory and have been smitten again by the vagaries of the mind. Do you remember those long rainy days we would sit inside and watch through half-fogged windows, boredom holding us, tired of the books? Oh yes, you were bustling about, forever busy, a lot of it unnecessary, passing the time, I think, as if time were a threat and not something that would run out for you, as it will for me, sometime, and who knows when? Things here are strange, familiar too. Small hard banks of snow remain and no, there's no sign yet of spring. I remember how excited you used to be as the buds appeared, as if suddenly, on the fuchsia hedge. Here the winter holds, it has longer arms, winds stretching down over Canada with thin and chilling fingertips. I remember that story of the Snow Queen you used to read to me, well over half a century ago. I was stirred by the tale of ice lodged in the eye and heart, throwing a different view of love about the world, where the Snow Queen ruled in her palace of ice, where the northern lights, the aurora borealis, were a kind of chill and lovely firework display.

And then there are the birds, or not. During the snowstorm that came through like a vast, rushing express train some weeks ago, all the birds seemed to have disappeared, as if they had caught that train and moved on south. There was an eerie silence in the garden, and among the trees by Boston College a dreary absence. I heard a chuckling sound one day and saw a congregation of sparrows in under the shelter of a bush where the snow had never reached; they were setting up a rumpus, a debate, no doubt, on weather but all of them were chattering at once and not a word of sense amongst them. I stopped and watched, feeling, well, here are familiar creatures, behaving as they did when you and I stood out one winter and flung them tiny moistened crumbs of bread. You must remember? How we shooed the eager cat away indoors? And when that bully magpie came, scolding and threatening from the garden wall, how you took pity on it, too, aren't they all God's little creatures, you said. Isn't it strange how you may be walking down miles-long Commonwealth Avenue and all that you can think about is the back yard of home, the blue-black apron of your mother speckled with the tiniest of daisies, and the squabbling of house-sparrows, familiar as the old rusty gate you swung on. Then today, along with the rain, there came a kind of clearance, that work of sunshine to get through and you can sense a glow in the world, a light that sings already deep in the heart, like the promise of lilac back into the world.

And there he was, the cardinal bird, perky red crest and aggressive red beak, there in flesh and feather, a brilliant red with a black bib that takes nothing away from his preening glory. I took his coming as a welcome to this stranger from the west of Ireland, a loud halloo as if to say Now just you wait, all this dull, damp city of Boston will clarify itself, and will become a playground filled with sunshine and good cheer. And there, right beyond the cardinal, the catbird, oh yes I had heard of him, grey and secretive, but with that strange and haunting cry like the mewing of a sorry cat, and he called out, that sharp-shriek mewling sound and all I could think of was your phrase, little boys should be seen and not heard. And here I am, talking to you, and you have been gone now a quarter of a century. Something about the heart, and its ongoing will to lift into bright skies of hope and love, something about walking here, in a strange city, growing aware of a love that was offered to me so many years before I grew aware of it, and relished it. Thank you. And God speed.

And then we were slowing down the long hill
into Bunclody; a varied shrubbery, the small town
laying itself out below; a soft-toned town, to retire to.
I ease the car to a halt, opposite the bungalow, memories
like exhaust fumes stirring through the heavy air; there
the plants he nursed, soil he laboured; that window
was her room, her privacy, her prayer-time, ministries;
blank now, reflecting this bleak day, and unresponding.
After her death, the house loud with visitors, I slept
alone in her room and in her bed; the moon sent a dull,
pre-Christmas light through the curtains; I knew, at last,
a weight of sadness, a slow welling of loss; a scent
remained, her talcs and creams, the dressing-table things,
a glass tea-tray for rings and hairpins, and there
in the empty hours after dawn, I saw
her tortoise-shell hand-mirror, dusted,
and a crinkled prayer-card to Saint Anthony, patron
of all lost things. Mother. Who has taken away with her
her bundles of sufferings, inflated anxieties
for her children's souls, and every possibility
of mutual understanding and forgiveness.
On then,
the river again on our left, through the rich and fallow fields
till we drew up, at last, by the graveyard wall
under dripping trees. That certain pause, a small
silence, and then the gathering of coats, umbrellas,
the pot with its three pink hyacinths. The car doors
closed, startling through the almost stillness of the rain,
intrusive ping-song of the automatic lock, and then,
destination, the rising recurrent sorrow of the merely
human before loss, its unacceptability, its disdain.

  *

8th December. 1943.
The world was stretched
feverish under war. There was a fall
of snow, they told me, over the heathlands.
Achill. My island. Call me
John. After the Evangelist. And Francis, after the poor

and love-tossed fool. And call me
Mary, for the day that's in it, and for mother, worn
after the pain and tearing. There were men
wading through an underworld of blood and muck
uncomprehending. I hear the winter storms
crying through the pine grove. Mother. Mary.
Mother and son. Madonna. A winter child.

*

After it all, after all this, the years, the distances,
after the days and absences and angers, what can I do
but stand in stillness by the grave, her name
and his, only a dream breeze touching
the trees and a soft rain falling. Stand,
nothing to say, all said, winter, and grey,
my presence I hope amounting to something,
to sorrow, pleading, the three pink hyacinths.
I step across her grave to lay them by the headstone,
offering a presence more eloquent than mine.
And can you hear them all, the women?
mothers, daughters, sisters … their cries
across time and space, joining with her in ongoing silence
that shatters the world across every century,
crying against war and killing, against crucifixion, torture,
    rape,
the fact of the disappeared, the pulling down of love.

The Galilean Myth
Pádraig J. Daly

Pádraig J. Daly offers the most sustained attempt at serious religious poetry in Ireland. His poetry begins with easy nostalgia for that innocent land we knew in our youth, when Roman Catholic Ireland moved like a Titanic through untroubled waters. Daly's work, however, moves quickly into the Augustinian concept that all our living is praise of God. But Luther, too, was an Augustinian and quickly his spirit enters Daly's work, subjecting his own life, and ours, to examination, an examination in the light of the incarnation. Nicholas Boyle outlines how Catholic theology works always to rediscover its roots in the scriptures. He tells of the Bible as literature, and not as a system of ideas. It is interesting to keep this in mind when reading a poet whose work is wholly based on scripture, too. Boyle writes: 'In some formal sense every poetic text may be a revelation, but the revelations offered by most texts may be so similar as to make that sense not just formal, but trivial. A Catholic approach to literature, sacred and secular, requires a discrimination of revelations' (Boyle 118). The language of such a poetic, as opposed to the language of the Bible, is non-purposive, non-utilitarian, disinterested; there is no sense of imposing the standards or the will or the outlook of the poet, the work is not a set of rules of engagement. In Daly's work, the interior desert imagery and the drudgery of serving before an absent God make their first, startling appearance in Irish poetry. The language becomes sparer, the immediacy and closeness of the experience are conveyed quickly and with the accuracy of anguish. The biblical author does not expose his or her own heart, but offers the words of God in prophecy or in ordinance.

An early Daly poem is alert with the joy of the discovery of Christ in the world about us:

Immanuel, A Name Which Means ... (Mt 1:23)

He is the stray dog
Who brushes himself timidly against you in the street,
The city river that quietly climbs along the river wall,
Caressing in its loneliness the dull stone
And bringing dried-up weed to life;

The clouds when they lie in weariness over the earth.
The sun that touches them with black silver;
He is the rain flowing tenderly over the tar,
The leaves' excitement in the evening wind,
The frost like lichen on warehouse walls.

The world is a great sea
And he, the boat of varnished pine
That slips into the water at noon.

As consequence of the incarnation (*kenosis*: the humbling taking on of flesh by the Godhead) and Christ's presence amongst humanity and amongst the whole of creation, everything is part of God, and God is part of everything. Immanuel therefore means, 'God with us'. Pádraig J. Daly was born in Dungarvan, Co Waterford, in 1943. He entered the Augustinian order and studied in Ireland and in Rome. He has worked as a priest in Dublin and in New Ross, Co Wexford. He has published several collections of poetry, amongst them *Nowhere But in Praise* (Profile Press 1978), *A Celibate Affair* (Aquila 1984), *Out of Silence* (Dedalus 1993), *The Voice of the Hare* (Dedalus 1997) and *The Last Dreamers, New & Selected Poems*, (Dedalus 1999). A further collection, *The Other Sea*, appeared from Dedalus in 2003, and *Clinging to the Myth*, also Dedalus, in 2007. Another collection, *Afterlife*, appeared in 2010. So there has been a steady stream of work from this priest poet, work that has moved on a downward curve in terms of trust and hope, and on an upward curve in terms of language, form and imagery.

From the beginning there has been an eye on locale, an acute awareness of the physical world, captured always with an engaging sympathy. This has already been noted in the poem to, and on, St Augustine in the early chapters of this book. Very early in the work the Augustinian note is struck, a belief that everything in the world exists to praise God, a note that is developed and deepened as the poet (and the priest) matures. Here is an early poem written on the birth of a daughter to a friend:

Magnificat for Catherine

Your mother's body
Softly glowing as alabaster,
You danced in her eyes.

Before ever you saw light
Or learned to scream
So lustily,

When you were totally unwashed,
I watched you
Move beneath her body,

Swimming in primeval fluid,
Sole inhabitant
Of your close and shadowy universe;

And when I reached out my hand
To touch you,
You kicked at me suddenly

Till like those mountain women
In our book,
I heard my words becoming song.

The reference is, of course, to Mary's visit to her cousin Elizabeth, and the leaping of the child in Elizabeth's womb in joy at the forthcoming birth of the Saviour. There is, in the poetry, such a sense of joy at the being of things, without there being any sense of necessary ecology; it is something humanity has become forgetful of, this ease and praise before the glories of our human nature and before the whole of creation. This poetry survives because of its music and the accuracy of its observation, not because of its content which resorts so often simply to statement. The voice is unique; the lines move with a sense of breathing, slowly capturing a mood of awed certainty; the language is quite simply honed to perfection, 'sole inhabitant/Of your close and shadowy universe'. In many ways, here we have an early George Herbert, relishing the world about him, and relishing it in terms of the music of poetry and the lifting of the heart towards God. In the following poem it is the priest who speaks, conscious of God, conscious too of the grace and promise that faith in a loving God can bring. Only when the deeply personal note is allowed in are we aware of any possible darkness in this picture.

Sagart

In many ways you're like an old man. Perhaps
You walk alone more than most people twice your age.
You notice each change of weather, the drift
Of smoke to sky. There is a certain decorum
You follow in your dress, the way you comb your hair.

You have many acquaintances, few friends;
Besides your unreplying God you have no confidant.
Nevertheless you lift your hat to all. Old ladies
Especially will seek you out, sometimes a sinner.
You are guest at many celebrations, a must at birth or death.

Sometimes you wonder whether this is how God intended it.

Here is the 'unreplying' God literature has made us so aware of. It is my belief that great religious poetry appears only when the individual heart and experience of the poet are faced straight on; what smacks of proselytising in any way, tends to alienate the reader and move language and shape into artificial ways. 'Sagart' (meaning 'Priest') is an achieved poem because the music, the words, the slow lines, all move deftly with the sentiment, the experienced matter of the poem. The music of the second line, for instance, with its open vowel sounds, sings effortlessly, but sing it does and in so doing the final line fits perfectly in place. Literature must not have a purpose extraneous to itself and Daly is aware of this stricture. A great deal of 'devotional' writing has a sermonising purpose to it that leaves it simply in the realm of restating theories or ideologies. Daly is so much aware of creation that his sense of awe, his need to praise, overcomes any urge to offer dogma or lesson or advice.

Among the Nettles

When we turn our backs to the sea,
It trembles still and climbs and falters;

On quiet hillsides families of foxes
Sport at evening
Where green pines slice the sun.

Glorious butterflies flit where no one watches,
Dun horses ramble by rivers and shake miraculous manes.

The willow grouse sits on her eggs all day
And holds her breath when danger comes
And stills at her will the beating of her heart.

In lakes far into the marshland
The grebe treads water in his courtship dance.

All day long the world is tumbling,
Stars follow their ordered ways,
Clouds form and reform.

A mind moves endlessly among the nettles
Full of the thrive of leaf and flower,

Hardly breathing or heaving,
Still as the willow grouse.

The simple things are done well, and are not intrusive: the vowel sound of 'quiet' repeated in 'hillsides' and again in 'pines slice', so holding this stanza musically together; the 's' sounds everywhere suggesting the sport, the alliteration of 'families of foxes' suggestive of the togetherness of the animals. All is well, and all manner of thing appear well, and God is in his heaven ... and the poem is in itself a work of love, a celebration, a hymn of praise. Now it is time to focus in on the Christ, the Master, the priest of priests:

Encounter

Monotony of sun
On sand and scrub,
A place of wild beasts
And long shadows;

At last he comes
To green and olivegroves,
Vineyards,
Houses climbing beyond walls
Along a hillside.

Here the tempter waits,
Full of candour,
Offering for easy sale
All the green kingdoms of the world.

And he,
Though gaunt from fasting,
Needing rest,

Some perfect star
Seen a lifetime back
Determining him,

Passes slowly by.

This is the figure of Jesus testing his own calling in the desert, drawing up out of the depths of his belief some original, promising motive for his fasting, his choosing the desert rather than the green paths. We have moved on a great distance from the ease of Augustine's songs of praise, to a sparer view of the natural world, and to a harsher view of the interior spirit. 'A place of wild beasts / And long shadows', has replaced the more fulsome language of, for instance, a poem like 'Tertullian on Prayer': 'The red cow / Coming from her stall / Looks up, moves forward, / Bellowing praise.' Without questioning the validity of language or mood of either the earlier poetry, or of this middle ground, one finds that the poems are already shadowing forth an interior journey that is marked out in exceptionally honest and moving terms. The poet associates himself with the dryness that Christ himself must have known, with the doubts and anxieties that are perhaps not so severe as those aided and abetted in Hopkins by his illness, yet daunting none the less. The poetry is self-searching, the poet knowing himself and his world better as he proceeds; there is no goal being aimed at save that of truth, integrity and honesty. 'Both sacred and secular literature involve the non-instrumental, non-purposive use of words and in differ-

ent ways assert our freedom from the tyranny of functional,
goal-directed thought and language; secular literature by using
words to give pleasure and so enabling us to enjoy what is;
sacred literature by using words to utter obligation, and so to give
us our identity, not as beings who perform a function, but as creatures who know what ought to be' (Boyle 140). The imperative
'thou shalt!' is the border line; secular literature does not have
the authority to command; it cannot strip itself of authorship as
the Bible stories can, in order to assume the authority of God; it
is, however, deeply moving in its own truth and undemanding
reach.

Pádraig J. Daly published a collection, *Out of Silence*, in 1993
and its guiding genius is Thomas Merton. Although this is a benign presence in the work, there is in it, too, a strong suggestion
of sterility that follows on from the desert imagery in earlier
work. In one poem, 'Pentimento', a note of menace is struck for
the first time in Daly's work, and the menace comes not from
human antagonisms but from a perceived indifference of God to
the beings he has created.

> He created emptiness first;
> Then threw the world out like wool
> To dangle amid the planets.

'Dangle' does not suggest much care, nor does 'threw'. He created
animals, too, and humanity, the latter 'bound by clay and death and
foolishness.'

> Sitting back, he laughed;
> While men and women
> Built draughty palaces.

We have moved a very great distance indeed from the hymn
of praise the creation is to lift to its creator. Worse, this God begins to be seen as not really involved in human living: 'We cry
out;/But if he hears,/He moves away from our voices'. Countering
this sense of foreboding are figures like Merton and St Thérèse;
the latter is, of course, the saint of small things, of isolation, of a
dogged loyalty to her beliefs:

And in her room at night,
She shivered at the thought of God growing strange
And a death as final as the death of stars.

What, then, is left? Silence? Further hints of menace and awareness of human suffering recur throughout this collection; there is a terrifying image of people on a cattle train in 1943, the menace real, the slaughter impending: 'Never before was murder so innocently done.' Another poem, 'Apocalyptic', touches on the horror man himself has threatened on his world in the form of a nuclear holocaust. It is the struggle with the *Deus absconditus*, the hidden or absent God, that strikes all Christians at some stage in their journey of faith. With Fr Daly it came to be a dispute with an (at best) indifferent God:

He

He is somewhere in the garden,
Kicking up the leaves with his feet.

Nothing disturbs him.

He does not care any longer
Whether we eat the fruit or no.

The dispute becomes more serious when the poet, as priest, finds this apparent indifference quite unacceptable. In a collection published in 1997, *The Voice of the Hare*, the unrestrained anger at a sense of betrayal by that God over human suffering bursts out for this poet priest; gone is the possibility of simple praise; this will not do any more. Gone is the simple statement of God's glory, and of humanity's sacred destiny; such unquestioning faith will not suffice any longer. But the priest's deeply committed care and humanity respond, not to a great cosmic calamity, nor to any national disaster, but to a small and individual pain, the small and individual things of life having already been focused on all through the poetry. Here is the servant of God and humanity, who has done his utmost in care and hope, and who finds that the apparent cheat in all of this is God himself. In a most stark and powerful poem, 'Complaint', all the previous poetry is turned on its head; a depth of sorrow and bleakness is reached, and the sense of a personal God responding to a personal plea, becomes a cry of rage against the unresponsive 'Sir'. To name somebody is to suggest a certain degree of closeness and friendship; the coldness and distance of this repeated 'sir', in this context, is deeply moving.

Complaint

I will tell you, Sir, about a woman of yours,
Who suddenly had all her trust removed
And turned to the wall and died.

I remember how she would sing of your love,
Rejoice in your tiniest favour;
The scented jonquils,

The flowering currant bush,
The wet clay
Spoke to her unerringly of benevolence.

I remind you, Sir, of how, brought low,
She cowered like a tinker's dog,
Her hope gone, her skin loose around her bones.

Where were you, Sir, when she called out to you?
And where was the love that height nor depth
Nor any mortal thing can overcome?

Does it please you, Sir, that your people's voice
Is the voice of the hare torn between the hounds?

The depth of care, frustration and anger contained in this poem is immense. On its own the poem is one of the finest written in the human questioning of a benign God, of a Providence, of a Creator who cares for what has been created. But given all the fine work that has gone before, the rich texture of the poems, the music of language, the gentle and firm breath-movement of the lines, this poem is even more of a shock and a disturbance. If silence leaves only a sense of sterility, then the rage that is put into the questioning of what had been held for truth, may be a way out. But for the priest, what can this do? If the priest frames his faith in such terrible questions, how can he then speak with comfort to his people.

I watch one I have grown to love,
Beautiful as the wind, languish;
And I flounder in the grief around her ...

Your people mutter bitterly against you;
How can I carry them?
('Sorrow')

There is another poem that sums up a life, a faith, a hope and
a loss of strength; a point has been reached of utter honesty, of a
genuine search that began with optimism and has floundered in
doubt and anger before the sufferings of the world, before the
challenges to that original optimism:

The Last Dreamers

We began in bright certainty:
Your will was a master plan
Lying open before us.

Sunlight blessed us,
Fields of birds sang for us,
Rainfall was your kindness tangible.

But our dream was flawed;
And we hold it now,
Not in ecstasy but in dogged loyalty,

Waving our tattered flags after the war,
Helping the wounded across the desert.

A great many of the images used in the earlier work re-
appear, though changed, changed utterly. Perhaps this is the
lowest point to which this particular poet has sunk, in terms of
his own capacity for joy, hope and faith. But it is a high point in
his work, the most convincing poetry, the most piercing imagery
and language. Here Daly has touched on the same cold flame that
drove the poems of the later R. S. Thomas, this sense of an absent,
worse, an uncaring God. And where can he go from here? The rest
of this collection, *The Voice of the Hare*, is taken up with things a
little distant from the instant pain that these poems touch on,
memories of relatives and friends. It is a kind of cooling down
period, a gathering of energies, a smoothing of crumpled sheets.

Will it lead anywhere? Will it help? 'Secular literature … articulates the world for us, puts it into words, as the material of our prayer – as the place of redemption, as the place that has received redemption, and as the place that our own lives are called to cooperate in redeeming' (Boyle 187). From here forward, the poetry of Pádraig J. Daly is a searching after redemption. The questioning remains, as it must, but the awareness achieved begins to lead towards a new and vitally alive Christian belief.

Real God

Once we were in a grey country
With a grey and dismal God.

Now we are in a bright country
With a bright, flourescent God.

But Real God hides
In unfathomable light.

One may travel a great journey with Pádraig J. Daly, a journey that shifts from the outer world of lovely things to a dark interior world where grey mists prevail. Those mists persist. But so does that doggedness in belief that he set out with. Perhaps this is the way forward, this dogged loyalty? The thought patterns in the poetry become more complex, and the language more concerned, yet the power of his observation and the vigour of the language have brought about a new vision of the impossible glory of a triune God:

Trinity

The sea by itself is water merely:
Its miracle is in its beating against the shore,
Spreading out across flat sands,

Shifting shingle and stone,
Flowing over piers and jetties,
Halting before rock

And falling backward on itself to try again,
Leaping high in the storm,
Quietly attacking the very base of land.

And God and God and God are love merely
Until they find foolish us
To take love's overflow.

Dogged loyalty, foolishness, though a readiness to believe?
Perhaps this is the most genuine contemporary response to belief in a world where all the pieties appear to have foundered. In
'Trinity' the last three lines may be willed lines, but then faith,
after going through all the doubts and dismays a genuinely caring life goes through, comes down to an act of will, a choice, a
decision to opt for what may well be the only hope that gives
meaning to our lives. We are left with loyalty, a dogged loyalty,
but that loyalty, hard-earned, is perhaps the most true approach
to religious faith, a loyalty urged and lived by people like
Simone Weil. But the poetry is achieved, moving with a flow
and certainty to those last lines, building up an image and
sound pattern that earn the music of that last statement. The
long 'e' sound of that first line, is echoed in the third last line by
the repetition of the word God and is re-echoed in the vowel of
'love'; and note those sound patterns that lead to the very final
word, 'overflow': 'flat sands', the 's' music of the fourth line, the
short and halted sixth line with its long and back-flowing seventh, and that forceful line that leads into the final triplet. And
there are the exciting words that hit the mark so well, 'the very
base of land', 'foolish us', 'love's overflow'.

What, then, of ecology, of Christ, of Eucharist, of peace? Is all of
what Christianity has been about to become museum curiosities?
Or does it still contain the seeds, roots and stems of our hope?

Monstrance Museum, Prague

Diamonds, in circles, dance
Around the vacant space of the host.

Row upon row,
Shrines constructed to display the ineffable
Are themselves displayed.

I gasp at the ice beauty of stones,
Platinum sunbursts,
Plump cherubim swimming in gold.

Caught in a frenzy of camera clicks
And surging tourist flesh,
I crave a place to kneel

Before the God of absences,
Of empty tabernacles
And empty hearts.

More than ever, in a world apparently bereft of purpose other than the accumulation of wealth and property, there is an urgency to find Christ again, to know the roots of lasting peace, to preserve the created universe from destruction at the hands of human carelessness. In 2007 the title of Daly's new collection said a great deal: *Clinging to the Myth*.

Toytown

In this toytown world we have created,
Even the few who come before You,
Come unbelievingly.

Among the others,
There is no hostility;
Only mystification

That there are those alive
Who cling still
To the Galilean myth,

Consider a God become flesh,
The word 'God' itself
Describing unnecessary matter.

A handful of terse, telling poems develop this notion; 'Fever' tells how a glimpse of the incarnate God may occasionally be found but when that is pointed and shouted out 'No one has any wish to hear'. The incarnation itself is ignored and, 'to the kings who have come from afar, All we offer is our emptiness'. People in another poem come to church, 'Believing, / Wanting to believe', yet the incarnation, Christ's moving through the fields and streets of Galilee, is the source of all our hope.

Touch

We have never known miracles,
Yet believe that once in Galilee
God touched the world glancingly;

And nothing moved.
Yet all that saves us from despair
Resides there.

Along with this loss of faith, Daly sees a loss of a sense of wonder, echoing in this way Kavanagh's notion that 'through a chink too wide comes in no wonder'. In a poem, 'New Country', Daly says 'We go and come/In rooms, sealed/From the spectacular'. Naturally there is a failure, then, of the great need in humanity to offer praise. In these poems it is not now only the individual writer who is crying out of a loss of hope and a sense of emptiness; the most common pronoun used is 'we', humanity as a whole, in our beleaguered times, suffering its pointlessness. The only answer is to cling hard to the myth, to hold Christ, Eucharist, peace up still as possibilities. Faith is a question of will, then, of a willed hope, of a staying with it to the bitter end.

Resurrection

There will be a day in the end
When there will be no need
To explain anything,

When we will row
Across the short channel
To the island

And find You standing
Where the white shingle
Drops steeply into sea,

Waiting to gather us
Under Your russet coat.

The 'russet coat' is a fine reminder of the Holy Spirit, or Hopkins's 'bright wings', of Christ himself and his wish to gather the people into the safety of his presence. And the rich and subtle use of wonder in his own poetry, leaves this priest poet with a warm image of hope in the end of all:

Lore

There was a tribe in that place,
Whose savants strapped a tiny bird
To the breasts of all their corpses;

Perhaps to startle their hearts to life again,
Perhaps to sing them
Into the fields of death.

Sometimes still we tread on sward,
Where deep under earth
Small birds stir their clay-encumbered wings.

The poetry of Pádraig J. Daly offers a paradigmatic journey for the contemporary Christian. As poet and priest he occupies a special, a difficult and a privileged place. His work moves from the innocence of instinctive praise through the desolation of near despair, back through a sense of real redemption into a hope, through the incarnation, of ultimate salvation. As quoted earlier from Nicholas Boyle's book, *Sacred and Secular Scriptures*, 'Both sacred and secular literature involve the non-instrumental, non-purposive use of words and in different ways assert our freedom from the tyranny of functional, goal-directed thought and language; secular literature by using words to give pleasure and so enabling us to enjoy what is; sacred literature by using words to utter obligation, and so to give us our identity, not as beings who perform a function, but as creatures who know what ought to be' (Boyle 140). Daly's work offers the distinct pleasure of the exquisite use of language and the basic response to that work is one of joy and gratitude; there intrudes no preaching, no urging, merely the beguiling and compelling study of personal identity and the sharing of the results of that study through the form and music of poetry.

And, from the new collection, *Afterlife*, this poem that puts it all together succinctly and memorably:

Knowing

We know how stars divide,
How atoms race and run,
How the first explosion
Sent planets hurtling,
How there is a maw in the spheres,
Lurking to swallow everything;

And miss the small perfection
Of bird alighting,
Dilettante butterfly,
The oak over the river
Sheltering the sensitive fish;

And sometimes
If we fold ourselves
Into that quiet and wait,
The Other comes,
Touching us with madness
And certitude.

The courage for love: an emergent universe
Wendell Berry (1934-)

We are living in a time when harmony between humanity and creation must be restored. 'The difficulty comes when the industrial mode of our economy disrupts the natural processes, when human technologies become destructive of earth technologies' (Dream 71). This has become abundantly clear over the last decades; there has been an utter dichotomy between human behaviour in its effort at 'progress' and the well-being of the planet on which this progress was to have occurred. We were moving, we believed, towards Wonderland, but forgetting the 'land' part of that word and destroying the ground upon which we walked. It has become evident that we are so intimately bound with the universe that we must take care how we treat every other being in that universe. 'While we emerge into being from within the earth process and enable the universe to come to itself in a special mode of psychic intimacy, it is evident that we have also a special power over the universe in its earthly expression' (Dream 198). But we have betrayed that trust; we have misused that power.

In his epistle to the Colossians (1:15-20), St Paul speaks of Christ: 'He is the image of the invisible God, the firstborn over all creation. For by him all things were created: things in heaven and on earth, visible and invisible, whether thrones or powers or rulers or authorities; all things were created by him and for him. He is before all things, and in him all things hold together. And he is the head of the body, the church; he is the beginning and the firstborn from among the dead, so that in everything he might have the supremacy. For God was pleased to have all his fullness dwell in him, and through him to reconcile to himself all things, whether things on earth or things in heaven, by making peace through his blood, shed on the cross.' If our cosmos is, indeed, a cosmogenesis, then Christ is the Omega point as well as the Alpha, and for too long we have missed Paul's linking of human salvation with 'things on earth or things in heaven'.

Paul was stressing Christ's divinity, and also countering a world-denying asceticism which has had perhaps too much focus in the churches for far too long: 'The first part of this hymn expresses a cosmic christology as that which encompasses the whole creation: Jesus Christ is the one through whom and for whom the whole creation was made. The second half of the hymn points to cosmic redemption: all things will be reconciled with Christ' (Deane-Drummond 101). Of course there is the uneasy question of such parts of creation that are destructive, what of those poor creatures the scorpions? what about mosquitoes? and those creatures that cause illness and death?

It is time that the churches focus on all of these questions and shift the emphasis from the teaching that all of creation was made merely to be subject to humanity's whims. Even in *Gaudium et Spes*, 1965, a milestone in 20th century Catholic vision, it is written: 'For man, created in God's image, received a mandate to subject to himself all that it contains, and govern the world with justice and holiness.' Justice and holiness are not enough; this is still anthropocentricism, and it is the view that has allowed our earth come to the sorry pass it now finds itself in. Not until 1990 and John Paul II did environmental awareness gain some purchase: 'Christians, in particular, realise that their responsibility within creation and their duty towards nature and the Creator are an essential part of their faith', sentiments undermined in 1991 by *Centesimus Annus:* 'The text views the universe as a collection of objects to be transformed, rather than as a communion of subjects' (McDonagh 107). *The Catechism of the Catholic Church*, which appeared in 1994, has very little concern for the potential extinction of natural things, nor for the welfare of the poor, nor awareness of women's concerns.

Referring to the 2009 social encyclical of Benedict XVI, *Caritas in Veritate*, Donal Dorr remarks: 'I think it is a pity that Benedict, who is so committed on environmental issues, did not locate everything he has to say about business activity in this time of economic crisis within the broader context of the ecological crisis of our time. Indeed, I feel that the encyclical does not sufficiently emphasise the urgency of adopting a model of human development which respects the environment and repairs the damage already done to it' (*The Furrow*). And Seán McDonagh

writes: 'The church should challenge our earth-consuming culture and unmask the contemporary idols which are seducing
many people and fostering untold pain, exploitation and destruction' (McDonagh 124). But individuals, too, must examine
their own value-systems and see whether it is economics that
drives them on, or love.

In this context I would refer to a fine poet, Wendell Berry.
Berry was born in 1934 in Kentucky. His family has farmed the
same land for several generations and Wendell bought a farm in
that area, Lanes Landing, which he continues to work. He came
to know Thomas Merton and is a fellow of Kathleen Raine's
Temenos Academy. Berry's life and writings work towards
maintaining, or restoring, sustainable agricultural practices, a
meaningful connection to local communities, and to celebrating
the miracle that is life. He rails against violence of any kind, to
humans or to any part of creation, inspired by his reverence for
God as creator, and the possibilities of true Christian development. He is a Protestant, and was baptised in the Baptist Church.
He has published a great deal, in poetry, fiction and essays, and
has won many awards, including the T. S. Eliot Prize, and the
Cleanth Brooks Medal for Lifetime Achievement.

Berry's work offers a challenge to the secular notion that the
sciences are sufficient to solve our environmental problems. He
holds that, as producers and consumers cease to care about the
source of their food, the motives for taking care of the land itself
diminish. He insists that 'land cannot be properly cared for by
people who do not know it.' Governments are controlled by
special interests unconcerned with the sustainability of land,
seeking instant profits. He seeks to recover ethical standards
and ecological questions are often underpinned with his religious sense of the sacredness of creation. He touches on
Christian Bible myths and sacred traditions. There is no question,
in his work, of a pantheistic outlook; his sense of the original
Genesis covenant, and of the world as the work of a loving
Creator, simply rule out that charge. A clarification is still needed
here: we speak of 'Panentheism': that God is in everything and
that everything has its being in God: to be distinguished clearly
from 'Pantheism' which simply holds that everything is God.

Leonardo Boff, a theologian working in Brazil, links liberation theology with ecology, suggesting kinship with humans and other things in a cosmic harmony. This cosmic approach is part of Berry's thinking but the great advantage of Berry's work is that it is embodied in the poetry and therefore lifted from mere statement and teaching. Boff echoes Teilhard de Chardin: 'God is in the world and beyond it, continually creating it, permeating it, and drawing it toward ever more complex, participatory, and communing forms' (Cry 148), and indeed he says: 'Teilhard de Chardin saw in the omega point the great attractor, calling the universe to its supreme culmination in the theosphere' (Cry 144). All this is relevant to the actual day-to-day view we take of ecology and our own part in it, in our own local area and experience. 'From its very beginning, evolutionary cosmogenesis has produced ever richer complexities, from the first two particles interacting one with another to the complexity of life, and especially human life, in its biological, sociological, and historic aspects, to the complexity of civilisations, dreams, ideas, religions, and human faces' (Cry 150). Ecology, particularly in the eye of Christian thinking, permeates all aspects of our living. Wendell's namesake, Thomas Berry, writes: 'Concern for the well-being of the planet is the one concern that, it is hoped, will bring the nations of the world into an international community. Since the earth functions as an absolute unity, any dysfunctioning of the planet imperils every nation on the planet' (Dream 218).

Wendell Berry takes the Amish people as excellent workers of the land in terms both of economy and ecology. From his love of farming and the land, Berry outlines the enormous damage done to local communities by large and distant corporations taking over smaller local enterprises, as the purpose of these take-overs is to make ever bigger and bigger profits, faster and faster than ever. If they think they have to, large conglomerates will cut and run after they have sucked the people and places dry. '… In the last half century we have added to our desecrations of nature a deliberate destruction of our local communities' (Crank 11). To fight these corporations is to discover that there is no individual who will take responsibility. The 'buck never stops'. The wonderfully real and wonderfully vague 'shareholders' are always the ones to blame, their need to make money on their shares, the need of the corporations to keep them always on

board. Because of exploitation: 'From now on we should disbe-
lieve that any corporation ever comes to any rural place to do it
good, to "create jobs", or to bring to the local people the benefits
of the so-called free market' (Crank 33). Berry describes how huge
corporations, even in the dragging away of felled trees that they
have 'harvested', carelessly leave the land in a dreadful condition, new growth destroyed, gullies left that may never 'heal'.

Every Sabbath, then, Wendell Berry takes a solitary walk out
into the woods and onto the hillside where he lives in Kentucky;
'… the Sabbath is primarily about re-connection with God and
with all creatures in order to allow the flourishing and plenitude that is spoken about in the Genesis account' (Deane-
Drummond 182). Berry's collection, *A Timbered Choir*, published
in 1998, contains the poems written on those occasions between
1979 and 1997; the book is dedicated to Kathleen Raine and to
Donald Hall. Many of these poems pay some homage to traditional forms and to rhyme but they develop Berry's individual
voice and ethics in a particularly rich way, threading his passage over and back between creation and faith, the ever-present
reality of objects and the wisdom of Christian thought, from sorrow to prophecy.

The special tone of the poems comes from Berry's love of
working on his own farm among the natural rhythms of the seasons, planting, harvesting, and caring for the soil and the community. For Berry, one of the aims of farming is to nurture the ground
by careful husbandry, instead of exploiting it for immediate or
short-term gain. So the language of the poems is immediate and
concerned, it is quietly conversational and meditative, as becomes the occasion for the poems, and is alert with the love of
creation itself and with homage to the Creator. The forms of
these poems, too, mirror the sense of shaping and husbandry
that the poems encapsulate, thereby offering a poetic that holds
its strong roots in traditional poetic forms.

The Holy Spirit is related to the universe in her role as per-
fector and completer of creation. The Spirit, associated in the
Old Testament particularly with Wisdom, moves towards per-
fecting and redeeming creation. The material world is permeated
by Spirit: the Spirit's activity is incarnational in the community
of believers, and is liberating. To go against the natural develop-

ment of creation is, therefore, sin. This is not to identify Spirit with the process of evolution but it is to identify the Holy Spirit with care for creation, and with those who develop creation in accordance with the inherent movements of evolution. This, of course, will also cast up questions on the nature and place of suffering, evil and death in God's covenant with the world and with humanity.

For the purposes of this study, those poems of Berry's that directly focus on the themes of 'nature' or creation, on incarnation, Eucharist and peace, are offered here. The accuracy of physical detail to determine place is pronounced in most of these poems, an awareness acutely adding to the sense of the importance of creation to Berry's views. The sense of an order to the march of the seasons, the growth of trees and crops, the migrations of birds and animals, echoes this sense that there is a plan to the growth of the universe. The regular use of Christian imagery and reference simply extends Berry's wealth of observation, thought and emphasis to a cosmic consciousness that is religiously whole and important to the matter of his living; humanity is body and spirit, and 'spirit' forms part of creation as a whole.

What this through-other spirit may be is relevant to Berry's ecological thinking; the thrust of 'Resurrection', for instance, often refers to the rebirthing of spring through the land; and goes further than this, moving into his guardianship of the need and value of accepting 'mystery', that which lies beyond human understanding. Indeed, the whole notion of setting aside a particular time for meditation, in the midst of a loved place and space, limns the strength of the title of the gathering of poems as 'Sabbaths', that ending of a work-period, that moment of rest and re-gathering, re-focusing, and then the cycle of work beginning over again. There is the suggestion, too, of relief, however momentary, from the destructive activities of contemporary economic gravities, emphasised and clarified by Berry in his book of essays, *Another Turn of the Crank*. The pause in human, violent despoliation, allows the poet, and his readers, to hear the songs of the birds, indeed to hear the hum of creation in its generation and movement, to hear 'the harmony of the sphere', to hear 'the whole earth singing'.

Hence the title: *A Timbered Choir*. The poems forge strong links between Berry's ecological concerns and his religious intuitions; to call these concerns, then, 'mystical' or 'polytheistic' is to miss what Berry is all about and too readily apply terms that have lost their strict and real meaning. If Berry speaks of creation and its delight, if he worries over human destruction of the land, if indeed he finds the care of creation and the beauties that creation offers to be 'holy', then what humankind ought to be deeply engaged in may be called 'works of love', as the week of God's creating movement proved to be, as the Sabbath is a time to recollect these works of love and meditate on the human response to them. One of the aims of these meditations is to bring together the sense of family and community, past and future generations, the whole ecology of creation, even the dark and suffering portions of that creation, and bless it all under the human acknowledgment of mystery. Boff again: 'Ecological discourse is structured around the web of relationships, interdependencies, and inclusions that sustain and constitute our universe' (Cry 154).

In an essay in *Another Turn of the Crank*, Berry speaks about his dream of a 'forest commons': 'It means a property belonging to the community, which the community members are free to use because they will use it with culturally prescribed care and restraint' (Crank 48). This has echoes of the sadness of poets like John Clare who saw the commons clawed back by the enclosures. There is also an optimism, scarcely credible, that restraint and prescribed care will be used; one can see how greed and the desire for quick profit can quickly undermine such communities. Berry continues: 'The idea of commons applies perhaps to most tribal cultures. It applied to English culture before the long and bitter history of enclosure' (Crank 48). The word 'commons' quickly shifts to 'commonwealth', by which Berry means that land to be used be divided into 'small parcels among a lot of small owners', who will live and work towards the good of the local community. This will depend on the good will and co-operation of both individual and society.

Later, Berry writes: 'Once we have understood that we cannot exempt from our care anything at all that we have the power to damage – which now means everything in the world – then we face yet another startling realisation: we have reclaimed and revalidated the ground of our moral and religious tradition. We now can see that what we have traditionally called "sins" are wrong not because they are forbidden but because they divide us from our neighbours, from the world, and ultimately from God. They deny care and are dangerous to creatures' (Crank 75). This he expands into that duty of care which 'rests upon genuine religion'. Humanity needs to allow creatures their own mystery and presence, to acknowledge that creatures are not ours to exploit as we wish, that they are part of an order and a harmony, just as we ought to be, though it is humanity alone that disrupts and may destroy this harmony.

There follows another definition of love that can be derived from the following: 'We have tried on a large scale the experiment of preferring ourselves to the exclusion of all other creatures, with results that are manifestly disastrous' (Crank 78). The works of love ... 'we must see that we cannot be made kind toward our fellow creatures except by the same qualities that make us kind toward our fellow humans' (Crank 78) and the spiritual sensibility underlying all of this leads to an expression of belief: 'I take literally the statement in the gospel of John that God loves the world. I believe that the world was created and approved by love, that it subsists, coheres, and endures by love, and that, insofar as it is redeemable, it can be redeemed only by love. I believe that divine love, incarnate and indwelling in the world, summons the world always toward wholeness, which ultimately is reconciliation and atonement with God' (Crank 89).

So, to the poems from *A Timbered Choir*.

I go among trees ...

I go among trees and sit still.
All my stirring becomes quiet
around me like circles on water.
My tasks lie in their places
where I left them, asleep like cattle.

Then what is afraid of me comes
and lives a while in my sight.
What it fears in me leaves me,

and the fear of me leaves it.
It sings, and I hear its song.

Then what I am afraid of comes.
I live for a while in its sight.
What I fear in it leaves it,
and the fear of it leaves me.
It sings, and I hear its song.

After days of labour,
mute in my consternations,
I hear my song at last,
and I sing it. As we sing
the day turns, the trees move.

Moments of silence and tranquillity allow the burdens of everyday living to recede, and the mind to focus on more essential things. This was the real purpose of the 'original' Sabbath, when God rested, gazed on his creation and saw that it was very good. In such moments there comes, eventually, through the action of the human becoming one in stillness and presence with the rest of creation, that sense of being a part of the praise that all of creation offers to its maker, the song of the earth. Fear between human and animal kingdoms fades away and that fine, rare sense of the unity of all creatures on earth can be rediscovered.

In another poem he speaks of resurrection 'in the way each maple leaf/Commemorates its kind' and accepts that such connection 'outreaches understanding'.

To sit and look …

To sit and look at light-filled leaves
May let us see, or seem to see,
Far backward as through clearer eyes
To what unsighted hope believes:
The blessed conviviality
That sang Creation's seventh sunrise,

Time when the Maker's radiant sight
Made radiant every thing He saw,
And every thing He saw was filled

With perfect joy and life and light.
His perfect pleasure was sole law;
No pleasure had become self-willed.

For all His creatures were His pleasures
And their whole pleasure was to be
What He made them; they sought no gain
Or growth beyond their proper measures,
Nor longed for change or novelty.
The only new thing could be pain.

This is a following on and a clarification of the first piece, a
'memory' of what that first Sabbath would have been like, life
perfect and at peace. The final line suggests all that will be yet to
come in the forward march of creation. It is, here, only a statement of a possibility, nothing more. The use of regular form and
rhyme underpins the sense of order and tradition that is mooted
in the piece.

What stood will stand

What stood will stand, though all be fallen,
The good return that time has stolen.
Though creatures groan in misery,
Their flesh prefigures liberty
To end travail and bring to birth
Their new perfection in new earth.
At word of that enlivening
Let the trees of the woods all sing
And every field rejoice, let praise
Rise up out of the ground like grass.
What stood, whole in every piecemeal
Thing that stood, will stand though all
Fall – field and woods and all in them
Rejoin the primal Sabbath's hymn.

Creation works its way, through 'misery', through death, towards 'perfection in new earth'. And because of this belief, all of
creation, not only humankind, rejoices, and joins in that first
hymn that was the first Sabbath when God saw 'everything that
he had made and it was very good'. The poem parallels the
thinking of Gerard Manley Hopkins and many contemporary

Christian ecologists. Another passage speaks of a crudely stripped wood, how it will take 'Thousands of years to make it what it was,/Beginning now, in our few troubled days'. And here is an echo of Hopkins's 'long live the weeds and the wilderness':

Enclosing the field ...

Enclosing the field within bounds
sets it apart from the boundless
of which it was, and is, a part,
and places it within care.
The bounds of the field bind
the mind to it. A bride
adorned, the field now wears
the green veil of a season's
abounding. Open the gate!
Open it wide, that time
and hunger may come in.

And what of the presence of created things alongside the destructive activities of humankind? Berry, on the special American day, tells how an area of forest that had been destroyed by mining, has come back to fruitfulness because of 'neglect', that 'American benevolence', allowing heaven's sun back in and urging human beings to see the trunks and limbs of trees, the light leaves and the wings of birds, not as anything other than independent 'fellow presences', but blessed and existing side by side with humans.

Hail to the forest ...
(Sunday, July 4)

Hail to the forest born again
that by neglect, the American benevolence,
has returned to semi-virginity, graceful
in the putrid air, the corrosive rain,
the ash-fall of Heaven-invading fire –
our time's genius to mine the light
of the world's ancient buried days
to make it poisonous in the air.

Light and greed together make a smudge
that stifles and blinds. But here
the light of Heaven's sun descends,
stained and mingled with its forms,
heavy trunk and limb, light leaf and wing,
that we must pray for clarity to see,
not raw sources, symbols, worded powers,
but fellow presences, independent, called
out of nothing by no word of ours,
blessed, here with us.

As another poem says, we are, with creation, 'One household, high and low,' and if we can see our way to allowing this
to be the case then 'all the earth shall sing'.

Who makes a clearing …

Who makes a clearing makes a work of art,
The true world's Sabbath trees in festival
Around it. And the stepping stream, a part
Of Sabbath also, flows past, by its fall
Made musical, making the hillslope by
Its fall, and still at rest in falling, sons
Rising. The field is made by hand and eye,
By daily work, by hope outreaching wrong,
And yet the Sabbath, parted, still must stay
In the dark mazings of the soil no hand
May light, the great Life, broken, make its way
Along the stemmy footholds of the ant.
Bewildered in our timely dwelling place,
Where we arrive by work, we stay by grace.

The harmony that creation contains within itself is delicately
portrayed by Berry in these poems, a harmony that ought to be
part of the whole human effort in conjunction with creation. But
we humans have greatly damaged the earth, we have raked
through the agreement to take care of non-human creation; it is
the task of humanity in the twenty-first century to rebuild that
covenant between human and earth, between earth and human
and God. A great deal has been said and written on the ecological
problems of our time, writers like Thomas Berry, Seán MacDonagh,

Celia Deane-Drummond, Leonardo Boff ... and detailed accounts of the depredations we have caused may be easily found. To counter this destruction it is the lot of every human being to offer works of love, to God, to humanity, to the whole of creation. It is not simply a wish, it is a necessity. A new Spring is required. A new birth. The works of love.

Slowly, slowly, they return

Slowly, slowly, they return
To the small woodland let alone:
Great trees, outspreading and upright,
Apostles of the living light.

Patient as stars, they build in air
Tier after tier a timbered choir,
Stout beams upholding weightless grace
Of song, a blessing on this place.

They stand in waiting all around,
Uprisings of their native ground,
Downcomings of the distant light;
They are the advent they await.

Receiving sun and giving shade,
Their life's a benefaction made,
And is a benediction said
Over the living and the dead.

In fall their brightened leaves, released,
Fly down the wind, and we are pleased
To walk on radiance, amazed.
O light come down to earth, be praised!

And this is where our leaning on the Christ is essential, our participating in Eucharist, our urgent need to register in our own lives the incarnation of Christ. Echoes in this last poem of Kavanagh, of Hopkins, of Herbert, of the great line of poets who have been aware, instinctively, of these wholly pressing issues.

Remembering that it happened ...

Remembering that it happened once,
We cannot turn away the thought,
As we go out, cold, to our barns
Toward the long night's end, that we
Ourselves are living in the world
It happened in when it first happened,
That we ourselves, opening a stall
(A latch thrown open countless times
Before), might find them breathing there,
Foreknown: the Child bedded in straw,
The mother kneeling over Him,
The husband standing in belief
He scarcely can believe, in light
That lights them from no source we see,
An April morning's light, the air
Around them joyful as a choir.
We stand with one hand on the door,
Looking into another world
That is this world, the pale daylight
Coming just as before, our chores
To do, the cattle all awake,
Our own white frozen breath hanging
In front of us; and we are here
As we have never been before,
Sighted as not before, our place
Holy, although we knew it not.

Why are we not Amazed?
Eucharist I

St Francis said: 'Kissing your feet and with all the love I'm capable of, I beg you to render, as far as you can, all reverence and total adoration to the Most Holy Body and Blood of our Lord Jesus Christ, in whom all things in heaven and on earth are made peaceful and are reconciled to God the Almighty' (Bodo 12). This is the centre and focus, the throb and the power, the joy and love and demand of the Christian faith. Elizabeth Jennings says of this: 'Why are we not Amazed?'

Elizabeth Jennings was born in Lincolnshire in 1926, and spent most of her life in Oxford. She worked for a time as a librarian, in advertising and in publishing before she became a full-time writer. She won a Somerset Maugham Award for her first book and over her career as poet and essayist, she won very many awards. The poetry is probably unique in its unostentatious forms and language, though its technical working and its gentle restraint give it a strength and memorability that is refreshing. She was a devout Catholic and much of her poetry touches on her faith. She died in 2001. In a collection entitled *In the Meantime*, published in 1996, she has a series of poems touching on the Mass and Eucharist.

At Mass (I)

Why are we not amazed? How can we kneel
And stare or else, perhaps,
Find our minds wandering? We ought to feel
Awestruck. A bell is rung and the bread wraps

Christ thinly in it. This is for our sake
lest we should feel afraid.
The wine's for drinking and the priest will break
The bread as on that night when Jesus laid

His life down for us. Did they understand,
His chosen, what it meant
To bring God into bread? A human hand
Takes gently what is kind and heaven-sent.

The drama is tomorrow. History has
A place for crucified
God-made-man to teach us to learn peace.
It was for this that Christ bore pain and died.

All he had promised came about. He knew
Peter would deny
His lord and master. So do we also.
The Mass is gentle, prayer is but a sigh.

And yet, and yet … at times most of us hope
That all the world will see
The magnitude, yes, the enormous scope
Of what the Mass means so that all may be

Sorry and say so, mourn and maybe cry,
For all creation here
Has waited for God-man to testify
That he can conquer every kind of fear.

But we are wrong. All that our saviour did
Depended on free-will.
Time ceases when the gold ciborium's lid
Is lifted and Christ comes to us as still

As he was at his birth. Now death and birth
Are changed that we may live,
Yes, live abundantly and by our Faith
Accept what all the Godhead longed to give.

The celebration of First Communion has tended to become more of a circus or fashion parade than a truly understood drawing of a person into the greatest mystery of Christian Faith. The fact that Eucharist has been emphasised perhaps a little too much at the expense of the sacrifice of the Mass where it is best received, has caused communion and the table of the altar to be set apart somewhat from the celebration of the sacrifice of the Mass. Pope John Paul II wrote in the encyclical, *Ecclesia de*

Eucharistia, 2003: 'Stripped of its sacrificial meaning, it is celebrated as if it were simply a fraternal banquet. Furthermore, the
necessity of the ministerial priesthood, grounded in apostolic
succession, is at times obscured and the sacramental nature of
the Eucharist is reduced to its mere effectiveness as a form of
proclamation.' The Mass is Christ's loving sacrifice of himself
offered to his Father in total obedience. The offering of the bread
and wine, his Body and Blood, by Christ to the disciples on the
evening of the institution of the Eucharist, was an earnest of the
coming suffering, the death and resurrection of Jesus. And so,
by partaking of communion during the Mass, we, too, are partaking of the sacrifice of love consummated on the cross. 'Do
this in memory of me.' This echoes the Passover sacrifice of the
Lamb, the memorial of the Exodus, of the liberation of the people from slavery. The event of the Mass, then, is that Christians
offer Christ, the loving Victim, to the Father once again, but we
also offer ourselves and our lives into the unity of Christ with
God, and of God with the whole of creation, so that finally God
may be all in all. It is, of course, a moment for the most joyous
celebration when someone comes to the table for the first time;
but along with the celebration comes a covenant, that now the
participant is part of God's great plan for the universe, and must
act accordingly in the world outside the church. The participant
becomes part of the church, part of the body of Christ, and
brings Christ with him or her out into creation, to sanctify the
whole of God's creation, work, love, earth, neighbour, enemy ...

The form of the meal is the separation of the body and blood,
and is therefore linked to Christ's sacrifice. Jennings sees that
the repetition of this sacrifice at the Mass occurs gently, but
when we partake of the sacrifice and the communion, then
everything is renewed, it is as if Christ were born again, as if the
incarnation, the crucifixion and the resurrection all recur in our
presence and we participate in it. After Christ had left them, the
early Christians would congregate in a believer's home to eat together, to speak of the good news, to celebrate Eucharist. So it
began as a quiet and homely event, without crowds, without distinction of classes, until the numbers became too great to gather
in a home, under the watchful, serving presence of the woman of
the house, and they had to gather in a larger building. In this

way, Eucharist and community meal began to be separated in people's minds. At the Last Supper, Jesus passed around the cup, or chalice, that he was using, and everyone drank from that one cup: 'A hallmark of the eucharistic discourses in Paul is his emphasis on unity and oneness in the breaking of the bread and the sharing of the cup' (Foley 29). So Christianity came into being around the home table. The supper is also a time of blessing, from God, and of one another, and of renewal and memorial of covenant. In our celebration, this memorial is not simply about the past, and the events of Christ's life, it is about the ongoing intervention of God in our human and cosmic history. Jesus prayed for unity that evening, too: and he presents it as the New Covenant, echoing the Passover sacrifice, echoing Moses, and Noah, and Abraham. 'Eucharistic practice in the primitive community was both a celebration and a call to unity' (Foley 52).

At Mass (II)

It is so simple and so quiet that we
Gather round and make small bows and look
At all the others present. Gradually
The celebration works on us.
A book tells us how to be

A part of all the wonder happening
And soon enough we realise the awe
We ought to feel. Here God is opening
His secrets. Human law

Is broken and a great event occurs,
Hidden, yes, but only that we may
Not be afraid. The wine a server pours
Becomes Christ's blood, the same as on the day
He died upon the cross.

This great occasion started long ago
In an Upper Room. Here Christ's own blood
Is present once again. The priest will show
The Little Round to be our daily food,
We pause in what we do,

Every day. Our marvelling to prayer
Nothing matters but this Holy Meal,
The angels bow and time can disappear
As we gaze and simply want to kneel
To show our faith. We're near

Eternity and every bad thing done
By us we're sorry for. Our hearts are made
Bethlehems for God the Father's son
Who is God and wants us unafraid
And only see what's true.

Every moment of enchantment we've
Ever known joy here is present and
Our best love is shown when we receive
God so simply. We can understand
Less than we believe.

For here all intuitions gather to
Show our hopes are valid and made clear.
Passion falters. Love alone will do
As God shows his creation need not fear
Great wishes won't come true.

The rite proceeds. The world comes spinning back
And we return to find all usual things
Are shining with right purpose.
                            What seemed luck
Is given while our hurt creation sings
And there is no more lack.

All usual things are shining with right purpose, and our hurt creation sings. This is what is often forgotten: to partake of the Body of Christ and the Blood of Christ is to will to become the Body and Blood of Christ for humanity's sake, and for creation's. It is also too easy to forget how all of this began as we receive strange bread into our hands and, if we can find a church where it is done, receive a sip of wine from a beautiful chalice. Early Eucharist vessels were those of the home, home-made baskets, pottery plates, glass plates, boxes that became the pyx; some used water, not wine, for ascetic purposes until it became compulsory to use wine; there were home drinking cups and chalices. The early church, too, saw Eucharist as evidence of the new covenant. In the early years the Eucharist was first seen as 'Sacrifice of the Mass'; the notion existed, too, that the bread and wine were changed by miracle; but for all Christians, the Mass and Eucharist were always a memorial of Christ's passion, death and resurrection. And the unity of all Christians is part of the wonder of this celebration: we all partake of the same Eucharist, it is, therefore, a sacrament of unity, and so, of peace. 'Augustine teaches that the church as the Body of Christ participates in the eucharistic Body of Christ, so that they are both identical and different. For Augustine, like Paul, this identity comes about not by mere physical participation in the Eucharist but by authentic Christian living' (Foley 124/5). The partaking in the sacrifice of Christ, the sharing, with so many others, in the Body and Blood of Christ, brings with it the inevitable consecration of the world in which we live, the sanctification of that world, and the bringing about of lasting peace; it entails carrying out, in our lives, the works of love. Pope Benedict spoke to the Roman Curia in December 2005: 'And it is precisely this personal encounter with the Lord that then strengthens the social mission contained in the Eucharist, which seeks to break down not only the walls that separate the Lord and ourselves, but also and especially the walls that separate us from one another.'

Consecration (I)

It all happens so slowly. A few words
Are spoken. Such tiny words
Full of more than this world can ever contain
In its random occasions, its pell-mell actions which we
Have brought about. It is to change what we see
And hear all about us that this Round of bread
Is changed, becomes Christ's life on earth when he
Chose to move among us all, to free
Our trammelled spirits. He loves liberty
So he became for a time what all of us are
All the time. His words go on echoing where
Any will listen. One simple breath of prayer
Will break our chains, abandon our daily fear.
For this he arrived and stays on our desperate star.

Jennings so accurately describes human living here as 'random occasions'. Eucharist will help alter such random occasions into the blessed and redeeming consequences of Christ's incarnation, freeing 'our trammelled spirits'. And that final line wonderfully sums up the incarnation, the love of God for us, our need for him, and all our hopes. It was about the end of the fourth century before the sin of Adam was seen as belonging to everyone: St Augustine reasoned that because of Original Sin, the unbaptised infant could not enter the kingdom of heaven. This brought about such a strain of unworthiness in human beings that the practice of burying such children out of sanctified ground became common and heartbreaking; it also made people believe they were unworthy to partake in Eucharist and for a long time the ordinary laity went to communion very rarely. Those were dark times, indeed. A further sense of distancing from the overwhelming love of God came about when altars began to be moved back from the centre of the church, into the sanctuary so that the faithful could not gather round them. Then the association of sacred relics with the altars became popular and the altars began to look more like sarcophagi than tables. Christ's presence on 'our desperate star' grew more and more distant from ordinary living.

Consecration (II)

'This is ...' The priest lifts up
The Round of Bread and we
Wait for the risen cup.
So that no ecstasy

Should too excite us, God
Hides in this frail Host
And then we drink his Blood,
Wine to us. Our dust

Through all the ages has
Brought us to this event.
In any simple Mass,
Christ is so quietly lent

To all. We fold our hands
And try to pray. Who can
Find words? Mass starts and ends
With hiding God-made-man.

There have been many changes in the way Eucharist has been understood. By the early 16th century, the papacy was in decline, plagues battered Europe and civil unrest challenged rulers, there were new ideas being discussed in universities and there was widespread corruption in the church. Luther received support; but he suffered from a great fear that no contrition would work, the lot of humanity being so vile. In 1517 he posted his 95 theses on the church door in Wittenberg. There were many differences in understanding of the 'real presence' for many years, leading to many and varied forms of belief. By 1530s many countries had broken ties with Rome, including England. The Council of Trent, 1545-63, failed to reconcile with the reformers, but it did bring about a kind of retrenchment, even divisions amongst Catholics. At the same time, developments in science and philosophy were occurring, with Copernicus and Galileo, and with Newton and his laws of gravity. This was the 'Age of Enlightenment'. Some forms of Protestantism diminished the role of the Eucharist, placing more emphasis on the pulpit than on the altar. Church architecture began to draw the laity closer by eliminating rood screens, choirs etc, and this tended to make of the high altar a kind of stage, and the congregation an audience. Once again, in her poem Elizabeth Jennings has caught the sense of God's distance from us, because of our own incapacity for love, and complete understanding. God hides from us because we are unable, in our earthly state, to cope with the great wonder of his love.

We stand amazed!

'From the birth of Christianity there have been questions about what Eucharist is, what it does, what ritual elements should be included, who is invited and who should lead' (Foley 281). Such issues as the number of the sacraments, the duties of ordination, confession, liturgy and, of course, the 'real presence', helped the splintering of Christianity in Luther's age. Luther himself attacked the word and idea of 'transubstantiation:

'He clearly believed that Christ's real flesh and blood were present in real bread and wine – both "substances" together' (Foley 282). This is 'consubstantiation', a notion that was accepted for some time. Zwingli held that nothing physical could affect the soul, that faith was fully attuned to the spiritual, not to created or visible things; that engaging in a sacrament was an announcement of one's commitment to God, not moments for receiving grace; so that Christ's presence was spiritual or metaphorical; in this case the change would not be in the elements of bread and wine, but in people themselves. Calvin held that it united us to Christ's body in heaven. In the Council of Trent, 1551, the Roman Catholic fathers pronounced Christ 'truly, really and substantially contained' under the appearances. Whatever way it is defined, the basic truth is that Christ is present in the Eucharist and our participation in the sacrament brings Christ more closely into his creation.

Holy Communion

There were some miracles intended to
Save us from too much awe and wonderment.
How simple are the things a priest must do
To close Christ in a simple element.
The Round of Bread is so

Tiny, thin and white. It almost makes
Us feel we must protect the Godhead when
The Host looks like what any woman bakes
For her small family. The wisest man
Says nothing when he takes

The little wafer. What can any word
Explain of this kind, gentle element?
Silence is the way God is adored.
Vaster than galaxies, this sacrament
Holds Bethlehem's young Lord.

When Pope John Paul II gave limited permission once again for the use of the Tridentine Mass, it appeared as if a step backward was being taken into a form of nineteenth century baroque, and the moving to a certain distance, once more, of the Eucharist from the faithful. This would be a disaster from every point of

view. 'It is only hoped that the vision of active participation embedded in Vatican II, the voices for inclusion that echo around
the globe, and the promise of charity that resides at the heart of
Christian Eucharist will combine in rich and powerful ways to
serve Christian worship in a new millennium' (Foley 304). We
are speaking of 'the Bread of Life'. Can we partake of this Bread
while so many millions are spent every moment on the development of arms of mass destruction? while so many millions are
starving in the world? 'Each Eucharist, in which we receive the
Bread of Life, should challenge our society to ask why it is that
so much of our resources is dedicated to weapons of death when
there is so much hunger' (Care 172).

The 'last supper' was consciously set up, climactic, full of
deliberate significance. A Passover meal, where the movement
towards liberation and that towards expulsion combine, where
all of this happens before the flight into Egypt: 'The meal inter-
prets the flight which is to follow, and gives Israel a special understanding of itself as a victim people' (Alison 65). The Passover
still keeps this sense alive and this bringing them out of Egypt
establishes a new covenant. Add to this the New Covenant given
to us at the supper, and then the sacrifice of Christ, followed by
the resurrection, the final act that gave clarification to all that
had happened in the life of Christ: 'The reason why he can be
universally present to all men – not just to Christians but to the
whole world – is that his body is risen and in glory' (McCabe
118). 'He was making a new covenant, sealed and testified by
the shedding of his blood' (O'Collins 74). To whom does he address the words, 'Do this in remembrance of me ...'? It is perhaps instructive to read George Herbert's poem, 'Love': 'A short
answer to those tempted to imagine Jesus limiting the saving
impact of the new covenant comes from the meals he shared
with all manner of people, not least with the disreputable. That
table fellowship conveyed forgiveness to sinners and celebrated
in advance the happiness of the heavenly banquet to come, a
banquet to which all were invited' (O'Collins 75).

We partake of Christ's Body and Blood; we share it with one
another; we go back into the everyday world, into creation, a
creation that humanity is gradually destroying; 'The Eucharist
is a celebration of the death and resurrection of Christ, but

through it we also lift up all of creation, and through the cosmic Christ, we remember the victims of ecocide' (Deane-Drummond 181). James P. Mackey develops the relationship of kingdom and meals. There are many meal images throughout the New Testament; Mackey writes of the value and meaning of this table-fellowship. It is beautifully evident in the story of Emmaus. And in Revelation 3:20-22: 'Here I am! I stand at the door and knock. If anyone hears my voice and opens the door, I will come in and eat with him, and he with me. To him who overcomes, I will give the right to sit with me on my throne, just as I overcame and sat down with my Father on his throne.' He points out how the early Christians continued the 'breaking of bread' together, a habit that only gradually grew into the eucharistic meal; before that it was a 'natural sacrament', a giving and sharing for the benefit of all.

Hans Urs von Balthasar speaks of Eucharist as the moment of fulfilment of the institutions of the Old Testment, combined with ideas of sacrifice and meal: 'Moses took the blood and dashed it on the people, and said, "See the blood of the covenant that the Lord has made with you in accordance with all these words"' (Exodus 24:8). Chapter 24 of The Book of Exodus is a major moment when all the people, after offering oxen as sacrifice, promise to keep the ordinances of the Lord; after which moment the people 'ate and drank'. 'What is really important is that Christ, at the end of the ages, once for all, by his own blood, has passed both through the heavens to the Father and into those sharing the meal, as the sacrificial victim poured out as a libation' (Mysterium 98). In the Eucharist 'Christ actively incorporates the participants into his mystical body' (Mysterium 100). 'Why are we not amazed?'

Thou hast bound bones and veins in me ...
Eucharist II

I associate the Feast of Corpus Christi with the month of May on Achill Island. The roads and uplands were brilliant then with the opulence of the rhododendron, great masses of purple flowers contrasting wonderfully with the liquid gold of the furze bushes, also in bloom. And here and there the glorious chestnut tree, alert and worshipful like a thousand-branched candelabrum. The church at Achill Sound was festive with bunting and we, young and old alike, were treated to a festival day; school was out, it was a public holiday, processions were taking place and the great monstrance was carried around the church and sometimes down the village road while hymns were sung raucous across erratically-working loudspeakers. There was a sense of generosity, of wholeness, of togetherness as if the world itself, its root, branch and foliage, were wholly given over to the celebration of this wonderful gift of bread, the Eucharist.

The documents of Vatican II describe the Eucharist as 'the source and summit of the Christian life' and when the faithful participate in it 'they offer the divine victim to God and themselves along with it'. All of which is wonderful, uplifting, and has been quite meaningless to me until recent times. When I was young, of course I accepted with delight such festive days, but they meant nothing to me in terms of sacrament or Eucharist. Our First Communion Day was such another feast; we were dressed in new suits, new shirts, new ties, we were treated as little gods and got ourselves thoroughly sick afterwards on sweets and chocolate and lemonade. But what we were about ... well, that was never clear. We were told we were eating the Body of Christ, really present. And drinking his Blood. But we never got near the wine in the chalice. And what I remember most was the fear of taking communion in a state of sin, 'not discerning the Body of the Lord'. This was grave; it was mortal; it was terror. Where now the generosity and opulence? where the delight and festival? It became a chore, a thing you had to do each Sunday or else, if you failed to leave your pew, you were presumed to have committed a mortal sin and could not go! 'Love bade me welcome, but my soul drew back, guilty of dust and sin.'

Now I partake of Eucharist with a wholly different attitude, the attitude of an unworthy one trying to accept the abundance and opulence of a loving and never-vindictive God. After all, Jesus fed thousands of people on the side of a mountain, at the shore of a lake, so generously that from the loaves and fishes distributed to the people, the fragments gathered up afterwards would have fed many, many more. When the fishermen came to shore that glorious morning after the resurrection, they found Jesus with a banquet prepared for them on the edge of the lake. The disciples fleeing to Emmaus recognised Jesus 'in the breaking of bread', and it is clear that the Christ often and often feasted with his followers, the poor and the starving, the sinners and the outcast, as well as with his own chosen disciples. All of this, and so much more in the story of Jesus's life and death, leads me to believe in Jesus's overt emphasis on love; love, love, love … and nowhere in the events that constitute the institution of the Eucharist do I find anything about 'eating unworthily', or having to confess beforehand. It is up to us, human hesitants, to acknowledge God's abundant giving, his love, and to accept it.

This I began to feel after reading once again the great poem by George Herbert, that poem called 'Love'. The dramatic movement of this poem makes clear the wholeheartedness of the invitation to dine with the Lord and the slow, reluctant response of the human heart to the generosity. There is a wonderful development as the guilt-ridden sinner gradually comes to accept the urging generosity in spite of the awareness of human frailty and sinfulness. It is simply the generosity that is so difficult for us to accept: can our God be as good as all that? Have we spent ages trying to hide this generosity from ourselves, rather emphasising our own unworthiness than accepting the giving? And isn't it much easier to criticise that same God for every natural disaster that occurs on this earth? As if such halting progress the earth makes in its evolution negates God's love. As I go through the canon of poetry written in English, I have found it well-nigh impossible to find poems on the Eucharist, even amongst the Catholic countries, especially in our own. I wonder why this central focus of our faith has so rarely moved a poet sufficiently to write a poem on it? Strange, unless it is the fear of unworthiness, or the slowness to allow a faith in the whole-heartedness of that love, that hesitates the hand. Or perhaps it is the fact that poets tend more to the earthy and pagan movement of our living rather than to the regulated and doctrinaire tenets of a faith: perhaps the poet moves in the reaches of pagan marshlands rather than through the aisles of organised church?

If that is the case then it would be ideal to reconcile both movements. And here, I feel, is where I may well part company with strict orthodoxy, yet, I hope, I do so with reason and with love urging me in this direction. Starting with the idea of sinful-ness: in Matthew's gospel, it is put like this: Jesus takes the bread, blesses it, breaks it and says, 'Take, eat; this is my body'. Then He takes the cup, blesses it, gives it to them and says 'Drink from it, all of you; for this is my blood of the covenant, which is poured out for many for the forgiveness of sins.' Apart from the association of bread with His flesh and wine with His blood, it appears to me that partaking of this Sacrament in itself is 'for the forgiveness of sins'. Thus, the generosity increases. The forgiveness of sins, brought about by the overwhelming fact of Jesus giving His blood for humanity, is available to us in the Eucharist itself. In the gospel of John, where the synoptics have bread and wine, John has the washing of feet as the central event. Now, if a sacrament, as we were taught, is the 'outward sign instituted by Christ to give grace', then this, too, is an act of forgiveness, of cleansing and of unbounded loving. The Eucharist, in its fullest form, is the linking of Christ's body to the bread and His blood to the wine, and all of it links to a cleansing and a forgiveness that is riotous in generosity.

For Gerard Manley Hopkins the Incarnation enriched the whole of creation, not just humankind. Let me push further. In his great poem 'The Wreck of the Deutschland' Hopkins wrote:

> Thou mastering me
> God! give of breath and bread;
> World's strand, sway of the sea;
> Lord of living and dead;
> Thou hast bound bones and veins in me, fastened me flesh ...

It's a stanza that excels in bringing close a sense of God's physical, incarnate, presence, so close that 'I feel thy finger and find thee'. And further on in the same poem:

> I kiss my hand
> To the stars, lovely-asunder
> Starlight, wafting him out of it; and
> Glow, glory in thunder;
> Kiss my hand to the dappled-with-damson west:
> Since, tho' he is under the world's splendour and wonder,
> His mystery must be instressed, stressed;
> For I greet him the days I meet him, and bless
> when I understand.

Once the incarnation has occurred, once God has become flesh, then the whole of creation partakes of incarnation; the bones and veins, the flesh and blood of Christ are bound into the very being of the earth. Simone Weil came close to this, I feel. In an autobiographical letter she wrote: 'Christianity should contain all vocations without exception since it is catholic. In consequence the church should also. But in my eyes Christianity is catholic by right but not in fact. So many things are outside it, so many things that I love and do not want to give up, so many things that God loves, otherwise they would not be in existence … Christianity being catholic by right but not in fact, I regard it as legitimate on my part to be a member of the church by right but not in fact, not only for a time, but for my whole life if need be.' Her insistence that the knowledge and love of Christ pervade the whole universe kept her aloof from Catholicism and suspicious of the Eucharist. But it is my belief that the Eucharist is the way that Christianity – the full following of Christ – actually pervades the universe, as its bones and veins.

'Now there are varieties of gifts, but the same Spirit; and there are varieties of services, but the same Lord; and there are varieties of activities, but it is the same God who activates all of them in everyone … For just as the body is one and has many members, and all the members of the body, though many, are one body, so it is with Christ. For in the one Spirit we were all baptised into one body – Jews or Greeks, slaves or free – and we were all made to drink of one Spirit' (Paul: 1 Cor 12:4-13). Weil held that the whole of creation is subject to the forward-urging power of God's love, which she terms 'necessity', the engine as it were driving the whole creation onward, through its seasons, its births, its deaths, its growth; she also sees this as 'obedience', the whole of the natural world being true to its created nature, and the radiance of this obedience, when humanity grows aware of it, we see as beauty. Weil goes further and equates this beauty with the incarnation. Humankind's closest relationship with this necessity is through suffering: 'To change the relationship between ourselves and the world in the same way as, through apprenticeship, the workman changes the relationship between himself and the tool. Getting hurt: this is the trade entering the body. May all suffering make the universe enter into the body.' The beauty of this creation, the necessary suffering undergone in its and our development, all of this gets its truth and sanctity through the incarnation and the Eucharist, through the faith that the bones of Jesus, the veins of Jesus, have sanctified the whole of creation.

Taking this further, believing that we take within us the Body and Blood of Jesus, and bring that out into the world in which we live and move, do we then become so like Jesus in the eyes of the Father, that we are on the way to becoming truly Sons of God?

Kane's Lane

The substance of the being of Jesus
sifts through the substance of mine; I
am God, and son of God, and man. Times I feel

my very bones become so light I may
lift unnoticed above Woods's Wood and soar
in an ecstasy of being over Acres' Lake; times again

I am so dugged, so dragged, my flesh
falls granite while a fluid near congealed
settles on my heart. The Christ – frozen in flight

on the high-flung frame of his cross
leaves me raddled in the grossest of mercies
and I walk the length of Kane's Lane, on that ridge

of grass and cress and plantain
battening down the centre, I sex my tongue
on the flesh juices of blackberries, cinch my jaws on the chalk

bitterness of sloes, certain and unsettled,
lost and found in my body, sifted through a strait
and serpentine love-lane stretched between dawn and night.

If we are all expecting, together with the whole of creation, our transformation into an eternal entity with God, then it is the Eucharist that spreads this expectation, in a gesture of cleansing and of forgiveness for our being 'guilty of dust and sin', and partaking of this sacrament takes the love of Christ and sprinkles it throughout the whole of creation. 'For the creation waits with eager longing for the revealing of the children of God; for the creation was subjected to futility, not of its own will but by the will of the one who subjected it, in hope that the creation itself will be set free from its bondage to decay and will obtain the freedom of the glory of the children of God' (Rom. 8.19-21) The world is made up, then, as we are, of the Jesus body, the Jesus veins. The whole of creation becomes sanctified by the body and blood of the Son of God and thus redeemed and worthy to stand tall in the sight of God.

What it all comes down to is the immensity of the love of God, his creative power allied to his redemptive Incarnation and suffering, the spreading of the bones and veins of Jesus Incarnate, dead and resurrected, throughout the whole of creation and we, beyond all reasonable hope, are blessed with the possibility of consuming this Incarnate Love into our own being and knowing, by this sharing in love, a healing and forgiveness beyond all common sense. (No wonder a poet as sensitive as George Herbert would hesitate before the greatness of this invitation: are we not all amazed?) All of this I tried to put into a poem written on the island of Gotland, Sweden, after a difficult flight from Stockholm. At midnight on the island a church bell rang out just as a summer storm was dying away. And for a moment my encounter with a poor suffering child and her father brought me back to my days serving Mass on Achill Island, the morning the priest dropped a Host and I, against all my training, picked it up and swallowed it. It was a moment of awareness of how the

whole world is one with Christ through the Eucharist, how this
is a cleansing and forgiving Sacrament, and thus how it heals all
the ills of humankind and of the universe! Oh dear, what a huge
concept to try and convey in a short poem! But here goes. . .

Acolyte

The wildness of this night – the summer trees
ripped and letting fall their still green leaves,
and the sea battering the coast
in its huge compulsion – seems as nothing

to the midnight chime from the black tower,
reiterating that all this tumult
is but the bones of Jesus in their incarnation.
I have flown today onto the island,

our small plane tossed like jetsam on the clouds.
I watched the girl, her mutilated brain,
the father urging, how her body rocked
in unmanageable distress, her fingers

bruising a half-forgotten doll; hers, too,
the Jesus body, the Jesus bones. Once
in early morning, the congregation
was an old woman coughing against echoes

and a fly frantic against the high window;
the words the priest used were spoken out as if
they were frangible crystal: hoc – est – enim –
The Host was a sunrise out of liver-spotted hands

and I tinkled the bell with a tiny gladness;
the woman's tongue was ripped, her chin,
where I held the paten, had a growth of hairs;
her breath was fetid and the Host balanced

a moment, and fell. Acolyte I gathered
up the Deity, the perfect white of the bread
tinged where her tongue had tipped it – the
necessary God, the beautiful, the patience.

I swallowed it, taking within me
Godhead and congregation, the long obedience
of the earth's bones, and the hopeless urge
to lay my hands in solace on the world.

And, on the Eucharist, on ecology, on the overwhelming
love of Jesus, a final word:

The Final Prayer

I stand before him and he says
'Body of Christ' and I chew on flesh, he says
'Blood of Christ' and I taste a bitter, small inebriation;
I take the substance deep into my substance and can say
I, too, am Jesus; and I pray
(thanks to the Jesus body, the Jesus bones)
that the deaf will hear the breezes
siffling through the eucalyptus trees
and the breaking of waves along Atlantic's shingle shores,
that the blind, after darkness and the shadows that darkness
        throws,
will see the moonlight play like fireflies
along the undersides of leaves,
that those of us botched in brain and limb will be
gazelles across an intimate terrain and that the tears
of the too-old woman, inward-dwelling, wheelchair-locked
who lost her lover-man to death some twenty years ago
will step out giddily again
into blue erotic light.

Set The Weapon Down

Stanley Hauerwas writes in an essay titled *The Appeal to Abolish War*: 'Those of us committed to Christian non-violence clearly want to work for a world in which war does not exist. But we also believe … that we are pacifist not because pacifism is a strategy for ending war, but because that is the way we must live if we are to be faithful followers of Jesus' (Between 136). The dream of the total abolition of war is a necessary consequence of being a follower of Christ, of being Christ-ian, and it is also a consequence of an anxiety over the ecological crises of our time. The truest Christian response to the incarnation and to the overwhelming love offered by God to humanity and to the whole of creation is – Eucharist. It stands to reason, then, that the most powerful response to the appeal for the total abolition of war is to partake of the most integral practice of Christian belief. The development of poetry in this context is also edifying, from the 'glory days' of Tennyson's 'Charge of the Light Brigade', through Julia Ward Howe's 'Battle Hymn of the Republic', through the poet-soldiers of Ireland's Easter 1916 uprising, to the war-poems from the First and Second World Wars and our own embattled era.

Wendell Berry

> *Now you know the worst*
>> *To my granddaughters who visited the Holocaust Museum*
>> *on the day of the burial of Yitzhak Rabin*

> Now you know the worst
> we humans have to know
> about ourselves, and I am sorry,

> for I know that you will be afraid.
> To those of our bodies given
> without pity to be burned, I know

there is no answer
but loving one another,
even our enemies, and this is hard.

But remember:
when a man of war becomes a man of peace,
he gives a light, divine

though it is also human.
When a man of peace is killed
by a man of war, he gives a light.

You do not have to walk in darkness.
If you will have the courage for love,
you may walk in light. It will be

the light of those who have suffered
for peace. It will be
your light.

Seamus Heaney says, in *Stepping Stones*, p 456: 'It is possible for the poet to be better than himself in the poem he writes. That is one of the functions of the doing of any art and one of the benefits of putting yourself into the contemplative, receptive and transporting presence of art. It makes you a bit better than yourself for the moment; it doesn't mean that you won't relapse or fail yourself.' This is to suggest that the good poems written by those who have suffered in the wars of our age, will have something most pertinent to add to the story. Back to the Christian alternative to war, which is – not peace – but Eucharist, of which the consequence must be peace. St Paul, speaking of Eucharist (1 Cor 10:16, 17): 'The cup of blessings that we bless, is it not a sharing in the blood of Christ? The bread that we break, is it not a sharing in the body of Christ? Because there is one bread, we who are many are one body, for we all partake of the one bread'. And Teilhard de Chardin wrote: 'The Christian must not falter in his duty to resist evil' (Milieu 58). As we are also speaking of 'the works of love', those masterpieces done by El Greco worked to absorb all the history of human violence into his paintings of Christ, the cross, andresurrection.

  Gerard O'Collins summarises the situation thus: 'Over 100 million men and women were killed in the twentieth century, and the twenty-first century continues the massacre. Violent deaths have always played an enormous role in human affairs. Modern times have, if anything, increased the ways men and women have been prone to seek out and destroy each other – even to the point of straight genocide and the use of nuclear weapons. Auschwitz and Hiroshima have set Jesus' own violent death in a ghastly new context of interpretation. After the Second World War, killing fields have kept turning up – in Bosnia, Cambodia, Darfur, Rwanda, and elsewhere. Even so, no later atrocities raise the question posed for believers by the Holocaust: what does the systematic attempt to eradicate his Jewish brothers and sisters mean for contemporary faith in Jesus Christ and the theology that flows from it?' (O'Collins 227-8).

St Augustine's speaking of the ever-present finger of God in the activities of human beings brought him to hold that it is God who guides all wars, their duration, their validity, their justness. So he suggests that a Barbarian invasion may be sent as a chastisement for human sinfulness, a preparation for eternal life with God. This, too, is the view of Islamic fundamentalists. There is ongoing war in the individual between flesh and spirit, between hope and guilt. Sin, he also holds, is part of the natural makeup of human beings, a propensity inherited from the sin of Adam. Reconciliation with this theory and the absolute need for the freedom of human willing, always caused him some difficulty. We are free to choose evil. There is pressure put upon us by our environs, by the culture and historic movements of the times we live in.

Upon all this, Augustine developed his theory of 'The Just War'. If our world is a 'City of God' then it will need to be defended against its enemies. In the Old Testament, the most cruel and distressing tales of Israel's destruction of the territories and peoples it took to itself as the promised land, gave Augustine part of his belief in God's use of war as a purifying and chastening instrument against a sinful humankind. Soldiers, then, become the means of God's chastising power and in this capacity serve God truly. War is divinely ordained. If war and its sufferings and cruelties really do exist in this world, then it is part of a divine purpose and must prove of value to mankind. Though Augustine is aware of the imperfect willing and reasoning of humankind, yet he does not anywhere hold that such impurities may be the cause of war; all is divinely ordained, nowhere but in praise is humankind's living carried forward. He moves to a consideration of plunder and invasion, such as the Roman Empire had carried out in extending its borders and justifies this because those against whom their wars were waged were wicked peoples. It is stern necessity, then, that justifies such plunders. He writes, in 'The City of God', The peace of the body, we conclude, is a tempering of the component parts in duly ordered proportion; the peace of the irrational soul is a duly ordered repose of the appetites; the peace of the rational soul is the duly ordered agreement of cognition and action. The peace of body and soul is the duly ordered life and health of a living creature; peace between God and man is an ordered obedience, in faith, in subjection to an everlasting law; peace between men is an agreement of mind with mind; the peace of a home is the ordered and perfectly harmonious fellowship in the enjoyment of God, and a mutual fellowship with God; the peace of the whole universe is the tranquillity of order – and order is the arrangement of things equal and unequal in a pattern which assigns to each its proper position.

The guiding principle is order and deviation from order is dangerous and it is God's way of reordering creation to be governor. If war is a deviation from the order of peace, war, too, is a mechanism by which that order may be restored. Augustine saw war as part of our human living, a necessary consequence of The Fall. If it is a 'just war' then God is with the just. Who, then, is to decide on the just side of a war? We speak of a necessary and hereditary evil that is war, and that its justice depends on God's justice and the need to formulate the enemy with precision. It is interesting to note how, in the Greek and Roman era and in other theatres of war, the individual challenge had become a method of deciding the prosecution of a war. *Ecclesiastes* 9:18 says 'Wisdom is better than weapons of war, but one bungler destroys much good'.

In this context it is interesting, and serious fun, to read a recent poem by Thomas Kinsella:

The Last Round: an allegory

I

We were howling down off our benches
at the two figures leaning on each other's bodies,
remote and bare under the lights.

*

All their skills perfected for this meeting,
so that one might defeat the other.

II

It is a long while since they were first heard of;
since the scouts were sent out to confirm the rumours,
and the first serious offers were made.

They were confined immediately, each separate,
far apart; trained by specialists
and strengthened in bodily endurance.

Then their names were made public for the first time,
and the first contests arranged
– unimportant in themselves, but essential
for the experience, and as a first step.

One was sent out to meet a local champion
on his own ground; and floored him,
featuring with startled comment in the local paper.

After a like shock, the other came home
to great acclaim, and the sponsoring of local events.

III

The bell beat,
and echoed up into the dark spaces around us.
It was over.

The two bodies leaned on each other,
intimate under the lights.
Theif rists hung loose in their leather,
their organs damp in their bags.

They were separated.
The arm of one was lifted up.
He was led back into the corner
and sat staring up at the dark,

where the business of the evening
was being completed between the main parties.

We know that 'Human society is a violent place, which creates victims, and the revelation of God is to be found in the
midst of that violence, on the side of the victims' (Alison 43). We
know, too, that 'Estimates of those killed in wars and atrocities
during the twentieth century totalled about 200 million lives'
(Foley 299). There is little doubt that if St. Augustine were witness to the wars and merciless invasions of our age, his 'just
war' theory would not be satisfactory to him. Wars begun were
supposed, according to Augustine, to obey certain rules of conduct to avoid unnecessary cruelties and atrocities. In 1939,
Freud published his essay 'Civilization and its Discontents' and
wrote: 'Men have gained control over the forces of nature to
such an extent that with their help they would have no difficulty
in exterminating one another to the last man. They know this,
and hence comes a large part of their current unrest, their un-
happiness and their mood of anxiety. And now it is expected
that the other of the two "Heavenly Powers", eternal Eros, will
make an effort to assert himself in the struggle with his equally
immortal adversary [Thanatos]. But who can foresee with what
success and with what result?'

David wished to build the great temple but God would not
allow it because David had shed too much blood. And in 1
Chronicles 22: 7-8: 'David said to Solomon, My son, I had intended to build a house to the name of the Lord my God. But the
word of the Lord came to me, saying, "You have shed much
blood and have waged great wars; you shall not build a house to
my name, because you have shed so much blood on the earth
before me".'

The war on Iraq opened up urgent thinking on many fronts.
Initial and pre-action thoughts regurgitated the old questions:
just cause, right intention, legitimate authority, due proportion,
last resort, successful outcome? Most thinking throughout the

world answered all of these in the negative. Yet the war went ahead and, we know now, it was already mooted two years before in the White House; George Bush needed a war. Worldwide cries of protest, marches, prayers: all went unheeded and a general sense of hopelessness settled on the world, like a great dark cloud over the earth. For years the world had grown aware of the impossibility of immunity for the innocent, the non-combatants (both of these now frighteningly negative in the more recent Israeli invasions of both The Lebanon and Gaza). It appeared as if the old 'just war theory' had simply been jettisoned. The phrase that elbowed its way into that place was 'smart weaponry'. There grew up a belief that the 'civilized world' had given over moral and humanitarian values for the sake of political and economic expediency.

Weapons of mass destruction are available, so the innocent will inevitably suffer. There are things like cluster bombs. Such weaponry, with biological and chemical and nuclear weapons, preclude any possible moral justification for war. The Christian viewpoint must remain – can we find how to bring about the total abolition of war? War is the extreme of violence against humans, property or environment. Ecology is intimately involved. 'To learn how to live graciously together would make us worthy of this unique, beautiful, blue planet that evolved in its present splendour over some billions of years, a planet that we should give over to our children with the assurance that this great community of the living will lavish upon them the care that it has bestowed so abundantly upon themselves' (Dream 12). The core affirmation of all protesters against war is the immorality of it and of any kind of violence. It must also be remembered that the need for self-defense may always exist, but here we are speaking of wars of aggression of all sorts. In the question of a Gandhi and non-violent action, versus Patrick Pearse and the bloody self-sacrifice that is intended to be an imitation of Christ's self-imolation: to admit violence at any level must be seen as inconsistent with Christian belief. Christ overcame human violence by his love: Christians return this love; and we are back once more to the concept of Eucharist. It must be admitted, too, that only in the eschaton, in the completion of God's plan, at the Omega point, only then will perfect and lasting peace be a reality.

Wherever, in the meantime, violence or coercion is required, then it is a failure in human terms. Psalm 46: 9-10: 'He makes wars cease to the end of the earth; he breaks the bow, and shatters the spear; he burns the shield with fire.' 'Be still and know that I am God! I am exalted among the nations, I am exalted in the earth'.

Fred Marchant

Fred Marchant has published several collections of his poetry, most recently 'The Looking House', from Graywolf. He is a professor of English and director of creative writing at Suffolk University in Boston. He is also teaching affiliate of the William Joiner Center for the Study of War and Social Consequences at the University of Massachusetts, Boston. From 1968 to 1970 he was a lieutenant in the Marine Corps, served in Vietnam and was one of the first officers ever to be discharged honourably as a conscientious objector.

Tipping Point

Late blue light, the East
    China Sea, a half-mile out …
        masked, snorkelled, finned,

rising for air, longing for it,
    and in love with the green
        knife-edged hillsides, the thick

aromatic forests, and not ready
    for the line of B-52s coming in
        low on the horizon, three airplanes

at a time, bomb-empty after
    the all-day run to Vietnam.
        Long, shuddering wings, and predatory,

dorsal tail-fins, underbelly
    in white camouflage, the rest
        jungle-green, saural, as if a gecko had

grown wings, a tail-fin, and
    nightmare proportions. Chest deep,
        on the reef-edge, I think of the war smell

which makes it back here:
    damp red clay, cordite, and fear-salts
        woven into the fabric of everything not

metal: tarps, webbed belts,
    and especially jungle 'utes',
        the utilities, the fatigue blouses

and trousers which were not
    supposed to rip, but breathe,
        and breathe they do – not so much

of death – but rather the long
    living with it, sleeping in it,
        not ever washing your body free of it.

A corporal asked me if he still stank.
    I told him no, and he said,
        'With all due respect, Lieutenant,

I don't believe you'. A sea snake,
    habu, slips among the corals,
        and I hover while it slowly passes.

My blue surf mat wraps its rope
    around me, tugs inland
        at my hips while I drift over ranges

of thick, branching elkhorn,
    over lilac-pale anemones,
        over the crown-of-thorns starfish,

and urchins spinier than naval
    mines, over mottled slugs,
        half-buried clams, iridescent angelfish.

The commanding general said,
    'Every man has a tipping point,
        a place where his principles give way.'

I told him I did not belong
    to any nation on earth, but
        a chill shift of wind, its hint of squall

beyond the mountain tells me
    no matter what I said or how,
        it will be a long swim back,
            complicities in tow.

It has also been wholly clear that recent wars of aggression have left whole countries devastated in their natural landscapes, their ecosystems, their agriculture. War becomes war against all of creation: 'Aggressions against nature and the will to dominate exist because visions, archetypes, and emotions that lead to exclusion and violence are at work within the human psyche' (Cry 6). When creation is ill, humans are ill. The whole world holds tremblingly to the making of war unnecessary, in abolishing it for ever. Are we truly *homo sapiens* while we allow even the possibility of war?

Michael Longley
from *The Weather in Japan*

   All of These People

Who was it who suggested that the opposite of war
Is not so much peace as civilisation? He knew
Our assassinated Catholic greengrocer who died
At Christmas in the arms of our Methodist minister,
And our ice-cream man whose continuing requiem
Is the twenty-one flavours children have by heart.
Our cobbler mends shoes for everybody; our butcher
Blends into his best sausages leeks, garlic, honey;
Our cornershop sells everything from bread to kindling.
Who can bring peace to people who are not civilised?
All of these people, alive or dead, are civilised.

Israel's incursion into Gaza, beginning immediately after Christmas in 2008 and carried on, in spite of worldwide opposition and protest at the disproportionate response of Israel to Gaza's provocative launching of missiles across its borders, cannot be termed a war, the inequalities being such. The incursion, the murdering, the unrestrained onslaught by Israeli forces, from land, air and sea, the destruction of civilian property and civilian life, including so many children, women and non-combatants, the onslaught against the United Nations attempt to broker some kind of ceasefire – all of that sorry campaign makes this episode in the ongoing shameful history of mankind a sort of watershed, if the will exists to see it as such. The whole notion of a 'just war' was simply not considered. The aim was as total a destruction of Gaza as was possible. Justice and truth were completely sacrificed.

In the question of just cause, of course there was just cause for a limited movement to force the flinging of missiles from Gaza into Israel to stop. This was and is universally accepted. But just cause for the indiscriminate slaughter that failed miserably to concentrate on the missile bases, that was not there. Right intention? It did seem inevitable that Hamas provocation through such missile launching should garner some response. But the intention – and this is clear given the progress and scale of the incursion – was much more than this; the intention was the destruction of Gaza to an extent that even the innocent civilian population would suffer so much they would turn away from Hamas. Due proportion between the end sought and the means used in the furtherance of that end? Absolutely not. Disgrace and worldwide condemnation attended Israel's crimes. And last resort? A certain incursion was inevitable, but the pursuance of the wider agenda took away any pretence that this was an effort of last resort. Was there ever any hope of a reasonable outcome? The thinking behind the incursion merely drove so many otherwise unwilling citizens of Gaza to support their Hamas rulers. The minds of many in the free world turned wholly against Israel. Their official attempts to justify the murders of children, the destruction of hospitals and even United Nations food depots ... all proved a blinded hatred and ungoverned rage that would destroy the hope of any reasonable outcome. And finally, non-combatant immunity? Sadly, Israel's actions simply showed that one of the first and most vital rules of 'just war' theory was simply and coldheartedly abandoned. This is perhaps the clearest proof possible that humankind reached a level of cruelty and indifference both to human values and to creation itself that is breathtaking and depressing in the extreme.

Bruce Weigl
Born in Lorain, Ohio, and has published many collections of
poetry. He has taught at the University of Arkansas and Old
Dominion University, and in the Writing Program at Pennsyl-
vania State University. From 1967 to 1968, he served with the
First Air Cavalry in Vietnam. Bruce also takes part in the
William Joiner Centre programme every year. Here is the title
poem from one of his collections of poetry:

Song of Napalm
for my wife

After the storm, after the rain stopped pounding,
we stood in the doorway watching horses
walk off lazily across the pasture's hill.
We stared through the black screen,
our vision altered by the distance
so I thought I saw a mist
kicked up around their hooves when they faded
like cut-out horses
away from us.
The grass was never more blue in that light, more
scarlet; beyond the pasture
trees scraped their voices into the wind, branches
crisscrossed the sky like barbed wire
but you said they were only branches.

Okay. The storm stopped pounding.
I am trying to say this straight: for once
I was sane enough to pause and breathe
outside my wild plans and after the hard rain
I turned my back on the old curses. I believed
they swung finally away from me. . .

But still the branches are wire
and thunder is the pounding mortar,
still I close my eyes and see the girl
running from her village, napalm
stuck to her dress like jelly,
her hands reaching for the no one
who waits in waves of heat before her.

So I can keep on living,
so I can stay here beside you,
I try to imagine she runs down the road and wings
beat inside her until she rises
above the stinking jungle and her pain
eases, and your pain, and mine.

But the lie swings back again.
The like works only as long as it takes to speak
and the girl runs only as far
as the napalm allows
until her burning tendons and crackling
muscles draw her up
into that final position
burning bodies so perfectly assume. Nothing
can change that, she is burned behind my eyes
and not your good love and not the rain-swept air
and not the jungle-green
pasture unfolding before us can deny it.

Kevin Bowen
Kevin Bowen served in the Vietnam war during 1968-69. He has
published several collections of poetry and is Director of the
William Joiner Centre for the Study of War and its Social
Consequences at the University of Massachusetts-Boston. This
poem comes from his poetry collection, *Playing Basketball with
the Vietcong:*

Incoming

Don't let them kid you –
The mind no fool like the movies,
doesn't wait for flash or screech,
but moves of its own accord,
even hears the slight
bump the mortars make
as they kiss the tubes good-bye.
Then the furious rain,
a fist driving home a message:
'Boy, you don't belong here.'

On good nights they walk them in.
You wait for them to fall,
stomach pinned so tight to ground
you might feel a woman's foot
pace a kitchen floor in Brownsville;
the hushed fall of a man lost
in a corn field in Michigan;
a young girl's finger trace
a lover's name on a beach along Cape Cod.
But then the air is sucked
straight up off the jungle
floor and the entire weight
of Jupiter and her moons
presses down on the back of a knee.
In a moment, it's over.
But it takes a lifetime to recover,
let out the last breath
you took as you dove.
This is why you'll see them sometimes,
in malls, men and women off in corners:
the ways they stare through the windows in silence.

Doug Anderson

Doug Anderson lives and teaches in Hartford, Connecticut. His first collection of poems, *The Moon Reflected Fire*, won the Kate Tufts Discovery Prize. His memoir, *Keep Your Head Down: Vietnam, The Sixties, and a Journey of Self-Discovery*, appeared in 2009. He worked as a medic in Vietnam in 1967. His memoir is one of the clearest and most moving accounts of the horrors a combatant undergoes and the difficulties of overcoming the hangovers of such a war.

    'Snakebrain tells you where the nails are, driven through a plank, smeared with shit and hidden in a shallow pit covered with leaves, tells you before you put your foot down, sniffs the funk of its maker skittering away through the thick tangle just as you arrive. Snake tells you about the length of pipe with the cartridge in it, primer sitting on a nail, waiting for you to put your foot down, the bullet straight up into your groin. Snake tells you where the punji pits are, sharpened bamboo stakes at the bottom. Tells about the Malaysian whip, sprung back on green bamboo with sharpened spikes on the whip end, trip wire stretched across the trail and covered with leaves. Tells you where the wire's strung high up to snag the radio antenna. Tells you about the five-hundred-pound bomb hung in a tree.'

'I'm back in the EM club. It's midnight. I'm the only one there. It's closing time. There are two holes in the tin roof. The blood has been mopped up, leaving a pink film on the plywood floor. I'm drinking as much as I can. I'd drink more if they'd let me. I haven't thought of the morphine syrettes. I'll manage to get out of Vietnam without shooting anything into my veins, but I've got oblivion on my mind. I don't like this war anymore. Come to think of it, I never did. The guys who like it don't even like it once they're too numb to swagger.'

He must make desperate efforts to survive and to remain sane after he returns home. 'On the way back to Northampton on Route 9, I re-enter Hell. I don't have any idea what happiness is. No, I don't have any idea what the absence of pain is.'

'When American vets meet with their former enemies, the sadness pools between them and collects in the shadows around them. Politics go away. There is only one body of grief. Americans lost about fifty-nine thousand killed, more than three hundred thousand wounded, and it is estimated that another sixty thousand died of their wounds, or of the psychological damage they medicated with alcohol and street drugs. The Vietnamese lost three million killed, two-thirds of whom were civilians. Four hundred thousand are still missing in the north alone. They have no veterans administration and the families are supposed to take care of the maimed and maddened.'

'The prerequisite to healing is to tell the truth. No way around it. Place realities into words and put them outside the body a little more each time. The poems I wrote then seemed to come from just-opened veins.'

The poems and prose offered above are also presented as some of the 'works of love' that are placed on the scales of human value, against the weight of war, violence and aggression. The dream remains, of a total abolition of war. The adding to the works of love – and this includes the living out of the Christian

dream to its fullest possible in ordinary lives – will continue to
be one of the best ways that will, some day, bring humanity to
its senses, to an accord with the original covenant of creation,
and to the ultimate fulfilment of human and universal destiny.
In response to this dream, and in response to George Herbert's
great poem 'Love', I wrote this poem:

The Poem of the Goldfinch

Write, came the persistent whisperings, a poem
on the mendacities of war. So I found shade
under the humming eucalyptus, and sat,
patienting. Thistle-seeds blew about on a soft breeze,
a brown-gold butterfly was shivering on a fallen
ripe-flesh plum. Write your dream, said Love, of the total
abolition of war. Vivaldi, I wrote, the four
seasons. Silence, a while, save for the goldfinch
swittering in the higher branches, *sweet*, they sounded,
sweet-wit, wit-wit, wit-sweet. I breathed
scarcely, listening. Love bade me write but my hand
held over the paper; tell them you, I said,
they will not hear me. A goldfinch swooped,
sifting for seeds; I revelled in its colouring, such
scarlets and yellows, such tawny, a patterning
the creator himself must have envisioned, doodling
that gold-flash and Hopkins-feathered loveliness. Please
write, Love said, though less insistently. Spirit, I answered,
that moved out once on chaos ... No, said Love,
and I said Michelangelo, Van Gogh, No, write
for them the poem of the goldfinch and the whole
earth singing, so I set myself down to the task.

The Return from Emmaus
The Completed Introduction

In his book *Grace and Necessity*, Rowan Williams, Archbishop of Canterbury writes how, according to Maritain, art reveals an openness to unseen structures. Maritain wrote: 'Things are not only what they are' – the relationship of mind to the world. 'Mere realism is of no use.' And Williams: 'To make present the underlying structures and relations apprehended may involve a degree of imaginative violence to surface harmonies' (Williams 26). The music of poetry finds a register, then, beyond what is perceived. Williams goes on: '... the artist is always concerned with things as they are in relation to something more and other than the artist' (Williams 149). I am making a further plea for the use of poetry in an understanding of the deepest urgencies of our creation. The world 'is radically grounded in God, in God's "wisdom", to use the traditional language, and just as radically different from God' (Williams 159) and thus 'The artist discovers his own unfinishedness in the work' (Williams 162).

A reliance on man's natural or instinctive urge towards good is insufficient. Over the centuries even the best-intentioned people have caused such destruction to humanity that this proposition is proven without a shadow of a doubt. The forces of grace, the forces of damnation, these sources of good and evil remain forever a mystery to the human heart. The underpinning of the word of God alone, the Spoken Word – who is Jesus – and the assistance of the sacraments, these are necessary to direct the human towards good. Can natural instincts build civilisation? Witness then a civilisation that lived off slavery, a civilisation that condoned the burning of witches, the slaughter of infidels in the name of a holy Crusade, the extermination of non-German peoples, the obscenities of the Twin Towers, of Guantanamo Bay, of Iraq, of Israel's war against women and children in Gaza. And all of this has been done under human boasting of civilisation. Czeslaw Milosz wrote, in a 'Letter to Jerzy Andrzejewski':

'Without religious and metaphysical underpinning, the word man is too ambiguous a term, is it not? From the moment it is deprived of traits such as an immortal soul and redemption through Christ, does it not disintegrate into a vast number of possibilities, of which some are better, others worse, some deserving of protection and cultivation, and others of absolute extinction?' In our economic victories such spiritual defeat!

We have begun to be aware that the sciences are not sufficient to solve our environmental problems. There exist, and will go on existing, the real experiences of suffering, finitude, and sin. Our problems include the growth of population, the overuse of resources, pollution, climate change, an increase in the rise of the sea level, the availability of fresh water, food distribution, world health, economic disasters, environmental disasters, biodiversity loss. Perhaps poetry will help us turn back to viewing the world as the miracle it is, and therefore we may move towards responsible behaviour. Creation has value in itself, independent of its use as human resource. What we seek is stability, harmony, interdependent relationships, respect, admiration for the land, love and the works of love. What we suffer is huge company profits leading to all-powerful corporations, robotic in their dealings. A politics impotent before globalisation; poverty, funding insufficient to develop ecological answers; military conflicts … and many other problems. Do we hide our heads? do we run away? do we flee, as the two disciples did on the road to Emmaus after the brutal murder of Jesus and all their hopes? Hopkins wrote 'There lives the dearest freshness deep down things …' And John Clare wrote, in 'The Eternity of Nature':

> Leaves from eternity are simple things
> To the world's gaze – whereto a spirit clings
> Sublime and lasting – trampled underfoot
> The daisy lives and strikes its little root
> Into the lap of time – centurys may come
> And pass away into the silent tomb
> And still the child hid in the womb of time
> Shall smile and pluck them when this simple rhyme
> Shall be forgotten like a churchyard-stone …

And the small bumble bee shall hum as long
As nightingales, for time protects the song
And nature is their soul to whom all clings
Of fair or beautiful in lasting things
The little robin in the quiet glen
Hidden from fame and all the strifes of men
Sings unto time a pastoral and gives
A music that lives on and ever lives
Both spring and autumn, years rich bloom and fade
Longer than songs that poets ever made

Luke, chapter 24, tells of the two disciples on their way to Emmaus, fleeing Jerusalem; they were joined by Jesus, whom they did not recognise in his resurrected form. He spoke with them, clarifying scripture and 'their hearts burned within them'. They only knew him when 'he was at the table with them, he took bread, blessed and broke it, and gave it to them'. They not only knew now who he was, but the fact of his resurrection threw a light back on all he had taught and done and been during his life amongst them. So much so that they went straight back to Jerusalem to be witnesses to Jesus. As we are to be, taking our courage in our hands and bearing witness, too, to a Christian way of living in the world. The incarnation threw a light back, even over the Old Testament, right through to the original covenant. The Psalms form a collection of poems in which the created world is seen as wonderful, as proclaiming the glory of God; creation is not a dead and useful thing, but living and sacred. Psalm 19:

The heavens are telling the glory of God;
the firmament proclaims his handiwork.
Day to day pours forth speech;
night to night declares knowledge.
There is no speech or language
where their voice is not heard.
Their voice goes out into all the earth,
their words to the ends of the world.
In the heavens he has pitched a tent for the sun,
which is like a bridegroom coming forth from his pavilion,
like a champion rejoicing to run his course.

It rises at one end of the heavens
and makes its circuit to the other;
nothing is hidden from its heat …
May the words of my mouth and the meditation of my heart
be pleasing in your sight,
O Lord my Rock and my Redeemer.

Psalm 29 tells how God has not simply created and abandoned, but is perpetually involved in the workings of his creation.
It is because of this the poet believes that humankind depends
on this creative Presence for strength and for peace. Psalm 65
speaks of the earth's bounty: the urgency here being that if
humankind is aware of God's goodness and care, then we should
also be aware how good that same God can be towards us:

who formed the mountains by your power,
having armed yourself with strength,
who stilled the roaring of the seas,
the roaring of their waves,
and the turmoil of the nations.
Those living far away fear your wonders;
where morning dawns and evening fades
you call forth songs of joy.
You care for the land and water it;
you enrich it abundantly.
The streams of God are filled with water
to provide the people with grain,
for so you have ordained it.
You drench its furrows
and level its ridges;
you soften it with showers
and bless its crops.
You crown the year with your bounty,
and your carts overflow with abundance.
The grasslands of the desert overflow;
the hills are clothed with gladness.
The meadows are covered with flocks
and the valleys are mantled with grain;
they shout for joy and sing.

After all the incredible misery Job has suffered, after all his own muttering about injustice, about the comforters' even more miserable 'comforting', God comes up with the answer and it is that he alone controls and looks over all of creation. In chapter 38 God speaks, 4-13: 'Where were you when I laid the earth's foundation? Tell me, if you understand. Who marked off its dimensions? Surely you know! Who stretched a measuring line across it? On what were its footings set, or who laid its cornerstone while the morning stars sang together and all the angels shouted for joy? Who shut up the sea behind doors when it burst forth from the womb, when I made the clouds its garment and wrapped it in thick darkness, when I fixed limits for it and set its doors and bars in place, when I said, "This far you may come and no farther; here is where your proud waves halt"? Have you ever given orders to the morning, or shown the dawn its place, that it might take the earth by the edges and shake the wicked out of it?'

Examples could be multiplied, but to move forward to the incarnation: 'In Christ, God wedded himself in an irreversible way to the totality of the emergent creation' (Care 118). And on into St Paul: 'Paul had no idea of an emergent universe, but his insight into the cosmic dimension of Christ captures accurately the reality of things' (Care 119). We must never forget, ignore or dismiss the extent and level of suffering and cruelty in nature, however. An emergent evolution appears to proceed through destruction and rebuilding, with an inevitable pain involved; suffering then may appear to be a by-product of progress. There is another evil and cruelty that human actions cause in and to the natural world, slaughter: climate change, habitat destruction … All of this has been taken up in the incarnation, the cross, the resurrection. We now strive towards a fullness not yet achieved but the incarnation has shown how to work towards it. While we struggle to achieve the possible, the whole of creation struggles with us. Romans 8 again: 'For the creation waits with eager longing for the revealing of the children of God; for the creation was subjected to futility, not of its own will but by the will of the one who subjected it, in hope that the creation itself will be set free from its bondage to decay and will obtain the freedom of the glory of the children of God. We know that the whole creation has been groaning in labour pains until now; and not only the creation, but we ourselves, who have the first fruits of the Spirit, groan inwardly while we wait for the adoption, the redemption of our bodies.'

'The universe, earth, life and consciousness are all violent processes' (Dream 216). 'While we reflect on the turmoil of the universe in its emergent process, we must also understand the splendour that finds expression amid this sequence of catast-rophic events, a splendour that set the context for the emerging human age' (Dream 217). We have tried to suppress the creative violence of the natural world, positing human wisdom as more perfect than the creator's. And we have turned from this to con-quer one another.

We are not born Christian; nor does baptism, nor confirm-ation, nor Eucharist, make us full Christians. We spend a lifetime struggling to become more like Christ; at the end of a life, then it may be judged how successful we have been at becoming Christian. Now, a new life stretches ahead: no previously traced path exists from where we are now, save for Emmaus? Conversion involves a break with what has been; then a new path, 1 step for-ward, 2 back, or 2 forward and 1 back. 'He has told you, O mor-tal, what is good; and what does the Lord require of you but to do justice, and to love kindness, and to walk humbly with your God?' (Micah 6:8).

Who, then, is this Christ? Have I been with you so long, and yet you do not know me? 'In his life his word provided hope, and his actions of feeding, healing, forgiving and freeing people from demons and caring for the weak fleshed out that hope. It was out of a hope-filled context that resurrection could burst forth. This resurrection could become real for millions of people today' (McDonagh 122). To be with the disciples turning home from Emmaus would be to grow utterly aware of the centrality of the event of the resurrection. Jesus had given such a new and ravishing testament of God's overwhelming love, he had demonstrated that love in his own living, then he had died in vicious circumstances and the disciples had lost, they thought, the ground of their being. Now they had a new-found ability to understand why Jesus had been murdered, and that this was the same person they had encountered again at Emmaus. James

Alison shows how the marks of his death show the resurrected Jesus as the same man. 'It is as crucified Lord that Jesus is risen' (Alison 21). 'The resurrection of the crucified and risen one had given the complete background to the self-giving victim, showing everything as depending on the self-giving and revealing of God. It is this movement, and this alone, that made possible the emergence of the discovery that God is love' (Alison 50). Discipleship, then, becoming a Christian, means giving witness to the life, death and resurrection of Christ.

Yet it is important to try and get to know, as well as possible, this person whose being we wish to bear witness to, lest he remain only a shade in our lives. The Lord, risen, is still human: 'the crucified and risen Jesus was not only crucified as a human, but rose as a crucified human' (Alison 24). If this were not so, it would make a mockery of the ascension when our human flesh, too, was raised to glory with Jesus; the post-resurrection accounts in the gospels and in Acts take trouble to show how this was the same human Jesus they found again, at Emmaus, on the shores of the lake, in the upper room, the same human being they knew on the roads of Galilee. They had anticipated a warlike Messiah, to liberate them from the rule of Rome: 'Jewish messianic expectations hardly show a hint of envisaging a suffering and martyred Messiah, who would be the persecuted and vindicated "servant" of God. A crucified (and resurrected) Christ was even more alien to Jewish messianic expectations. It was precisely over that point that the Christian proclamation of a crucified Messiah proved so new, strange, and scandalously offensive' (O'Collins 28).

Jesus, during his years among the disciples, brought to bear new insights and a new understanding of the sacred texts of Judaism, but this understanding did not come to them until after his resurrection; this last stumbling-block to hope, this terror that is death, no longer was the end; the disciples became witnesses to the resurrection. 'The efficacy of his sacrifice, his mediation of the new covenant, the perfect consistency between his human life and cultic activity, his divine identity, and his direct appointment by God made Jesus' priesthood quite superior to the Levitical priesthood' (O'Collins 30). John's gospel emphasised the fact that Christ was the Word, the expression of the Father's love; the Word became flesh, and lives still amongst us.

Jesus is the mirror-image of God, the Word always existed, from the beginning, so that all of creation bore a christological face. Jesus said to Philip: 'Have I been with you so long, and yet you do not know me?' Jesus was proclaiming a new kingdom, God's. He never spoke of God as king, but of the divine kingdom already present, or still to come. 'The parables were challenging addresses and essential events in that ministry for the kingdom – stories that called their hearers to repentance, enacted the divine forgiveness, and mediated religious transformation' (O'Collins 55). Miracles, too, were signs of the kingdom. As prophet, he saw himself beyond the normal: 'I was sent', or 'I came'; knew he was greater that Jonah or Solomon ... He showed a powerful personal authority, claiming such authority over Sabbath observance, over the Temple and the law. He forgave sins in his own name and saw himself as the divine judge at the coming of the kingdom. More than that, he presented himself as one of us, on his way to the Father; 'Jesus Christ, who is God and man, is our way to the Father but he is also our way to recognition of others as brothers and sisters' (Gutierrez 112). We are to be made one in Christ, we are Christ's body, we are not to war amongst ourselves. We are to be made one in Christ, and so is the whole of creation: 'The earth and its blessings were the guarantee of Yahweh's continued favour, his eternal covenant. It behoved Israel to respect that earth, and this was enshrined in her law codes' (Freyne 29).

Deuteronomy says: 'But remember the Lord your God, for it is he who gives you the ability to produce wealth, and so confirms his covenant, which he swore to your forefathers, as it is today.' Jesus inherited the view of nature as God's creation. His was an itinerant ministry, returning to desert places for prayer and quiet as needed. 'The supplanting of a mode of production based on Yahweh's seasonal blessings to Israel, for one driven by greed, opulence and exploitation, inevitably fractured the tenuous connection between land, people and religious concerns' (Freyne 46). We cannot separate the incarnation from our obligations to preserve and respect our planet.

The utter self-giving of Christ, in life and death, in Eucharist, does away with division and factions amongst human beings, and between humans and creation. There is no exclusion; life is for building unity. 'Maranatha' means come Oh Lord! and was the prayer of the first Christians; Lord, being the earliest title. The names for Jesus are male, but referring to him as Wisdom is a feminine image. He himself had spoken of his actions as a mother hen gathering her chicks under her wing. The exclusion of women from true ministry in any Christian context goes directly against the urgency of Christ's showing. Jesus had to be fully human and fully divine to bring salvation; a human had to redeem humanity, to fashion us afresh he had to be divine. God became human so we can become divine. Christ, being fully human and fully divine, shows humanity the possibilities of being human.

Hans Urs van Balthasar speaks of 'The natural solidarity of Jesus with all human beings' (Mysterium 90). 'Christ's excess of love made him the more inclined to suffer. The stronger love is, the more painful are the wounds of co-suffering' (104). It is a question of love, pure and simple, love without question, without qualification, without limit. And we are back once more to echoes of George Herbert's poem. Mary, the mother of Jesus, declared her own poem, emphasising the approach of love as opposed to the Old Covenant's approach of obedience, outlining the option for the poor:

Magnificat

My soul extols the greatness of the Lord
and my spirit exults in God who saves me,

for he has heeded and loved
the lowliness of his servant.

And see, from this day out
every generation shall know me blest,

for the mightiest One has worked
wonderful things for me

and holy is his name.
Down all the generations

his mercy swells to those who love him.
And in this way the strength of God
has been made manifest:

the arrogant in the hardness of their heart
have been strewn about,

the powerful have been pulled from their thrones,
our God has lifted up on high

those who had been degraded;
he has fed the hungry full with the best of gifts

and those who are rich have been banished
empty from his sight.

Remembering the greatness of his mercy
he has come to the aid of the oppressed,

for this has been his promise from the distant past
and will be kept down all the centuries to come.

Christ, the hero. On the cross, in the uttermost humility of a slave, the glory shows in the affirmation of the extremity of God's loving. This self-limitation of the Godhead in the incarnation is *the* work of love. The cross itself is the supreme Work of Love; 'God's power shows itself in his weakness; in his folly he demonstrates his superiority *vis-à-vis* the wisdom of men' (Mysterium 55). St Paul insists that the resurrection cannot be separated from the cross. The moment between Good Friday and resurrection morning is that still point where the turning-point in the history of creation is prepared. If we have lost the plot of our human story growing side by side with the growth of creation: 'We must now understand that our own well-being can be achieved only through the well-being of the entire natural world about us' (Dream xv). In a society focused on progress, prosperity, unlimited growth of material goods, possessions, there is an urge towards exploitation, science, technology, industrialism, robotics. We witness the will to power, conquest and profit. We see ourselves as the masters of creation, subjugating nature to our selfish needs. This is the direct opposite to what Jesus came to show us. And Jesus is the Word, the name and nature of the Source and Sustenance of all creation. 'The sea and air and sky and sunlight and all the living forms of earth establish a single planetary system. The human at the species level needs to fulfil its functional role within this life community, for in the end the human community will flourish or decline as the earth and the community of living species flourishes or declines' (Dream 43).

How, then, are we to live after our own awareness of Emmaus? Thomas Berry writes: 'There is an awe and reverence due to the stars in the heavens, the sun, and all heavenly bodies; to the seas and the continents; to all living forms of trees and flowers; to the myriad expressions of life in the sea; to the animals of the forests and the birds of the air.' This is the beginning of a comprehensive vision that will place human and created things in the relationships envisaged in the covenant: that will rediscover the music of the spheres. Berry goes on: 'The human community is passing from its stage of childhood into its adult stage of life. We must assume adult responsibilities' (Dream 46-7). And in the book of Ecclesiastes (7:29): 'See, this alone I found, that God made human beings straightforward, but they have devised many schemes': we need to return to being straightforward. 'After centuries of confronting nature and being isolated from the planetary community, human beings are finding their way back to their shared home, the great, good and bountiful earth. They wish to initiate a new covenant of respect and kinship with it' (Cry 107) and the beginning of this covenant, Leonardo Boff maintains, must be the option for the poor and the oppressed. Thomas Berry summed it up: 'The twentieth century has eliminated the terror of the unknown darknesses of nature by devastating nature herself' (Dream 50).

In the first part of the introduction to this book I quoted from Leonardo Boff: 'Beginning a new covenant with the earth absolutely requires a reclamation of the dimension of the sacred' (Cry 115). Boff goes on: 'If in recent centuries we have been victims of a model of civilisation that has systematically assaulted the earth and led us to close our ears to the music in things and turn our backs on the majesty of the starry sky, it is because the experience of the sacredness of the universe has been lost.' Creation is tremendous and fascinating, it makes us tremble with awe and it draws us to itself. It is not enough to know all of this; it is necessary to experience the awe, the emotion, the love: hence the focus on Christ, on Eucharist, and on poetry. It is the aim to develop what Boff calls 'an ethic of unlimited compassion and shared responsibility' (Cry 135).

The Works of Love: The works of love are to be found scattered throughout the world, such as the Masaccio murals in Florence, the Piero de la Francesca in Arrezzo ... Eliot's 'Four Quartets', Kinsella's 'Hen Woman', Vivaldi's 'The Four Seasons', Caccini's Ave Maria, Elgar's 'Dream of Gerontius' ... The world is love's task, and love must undergo, until the eschaton, the Omega point, the long rehearsal of immature gods. The works of love are in danger.

We need a new spirituality. Jesus has been buried again beneath greed, war, the misuse of language by politicians. Following Christ is something that penetrates the course of history: 'the concrete forms of the following of Jesus are connected with the great historical movements of an age' (Gutierrez 27). We need to respect people more than economics: honesty and integrity in a politics that promotes governance for the people, not for the government: not a renewal necessarily within a church that, as James Mackey shows, is still grounded in the image of itself founded on the model of imperial Rome: 'The phenomenon of a Christian church gradually aping the ethos of the Roman Empire became lapidary with the conversion of Roman dynasts to the Christian faith, beginning with Constantine, perhaps ... So that to this day it is the Roman Catholic Church that still pretends to the ancient secular forms and ethos of the imperial power of ancient Rome, still extant in the continuing dynasty of a self-propagating clerical caste' (Mackey 39-40). This, coupled with the sexual scandals of the last decades, has alienated a great number of people. It is Christ back upon all souls, to be a sacrament of salvation and witness to the living of the risen Christ and thence to God's overwhelming love. Our 'new' spirituality will be a 'a walking in freedom according to the Spirit of love and life' (Gutierrez 35). The point of departure is an encounter with the Lord. We believe in order to understand, not the other way round. We need a firm and distinctive way of being Christian. A renewed commitment to Jesus, to ecology, to the Incarnation, to Eucharist. To the works of Love.

The Last Invocation

At the last, tenderly,
From the walls of the powerful fortress'd house,
From the clasp of the knitted locks, from the keep of the
  well-closed doors,
Let me be wafted.

Let me glide noiselessly forth;
With the key of softness unlock the locks – with a whisper,
Set ope the doors O soul.

Tenderly – be not impatient,
(Strong is your hold O mortal flesh,
Strong is your hold O love)
      Walt Whitman

Books Quoted

Alison ~ Alison, James: *Knowing Jesus,* London SPCK, New edition 1998

Anderson ~ Anderson, Doug: *The Moon Reflected Fire,* Maine, Alice James Books 1994

Anderson ~ Anderson, Doug: *Keep Your Head Down,* a memoir, New York, W. W. Norton & Company, 2009

Armstrong ~ Armstrong, Karen: *A History of God,* Ballantine Books Edition 1994

Barker ~ Barker, Margaret: *An Extraordinary Gathering of Angels,* London, MQ Publications, 2004

Berry ~ Berry, Wendell: *A Timbered Choir,* Washington DC, Counterpoint, 1998

Between ~ *Between Poetry and Politics,* ed Linda Hogan & Barbara FitzGerald, Dublin, The Columba Press 2003

Bodo ~Bodo, Murray OFM: *The Simple Way,* Ohio St Anthony Messenger Press 2009

Bowen ~ Bowen, Kevin: *Playing Basketball with the Viet Cong,* USA, Curbstone Press 1994

Boyle ~ Boyle, Nicholas: *Sacred and Secular Scriptures,* London, Darton, Longman and Todd Ltd, 2004

Care ~ McDonagh, Seán: *To Care for the Earth,* UK, Cassell Ltd, 1986

City ~ Saint Augustine: *City of God,* tr.= Marcus Dods, New York, Modern library 2000.

Confessions ~ Saint Augustine: *Confessions,* tr R. S. Pine-Coffin, USA, Penguin Classics 1969

Clare ~ Clare, John: *Selected Poems,* ed Geoffrey Summerfield; London, Penguin Books 2000.

Coogan ~ Coogan, Tim Pat: *Ireland in the Twentieth Century,* London, Hutchinson 2003

Copleston ~ Copleston, Frederick SJ: *A History of Philosophy, 2 – Mediaeval Philosophy,* USA, Image Books, 1962

Crank ~ Berry, Wendell: *Another Turn of the Crank,* Washington DC. Counterpoint, 1995

Cry ~ Boff, Leonardo: *Cry of the Earth, Cry of the Poor,* tr Phillip Berryman, New York, Orbis Books, 1997

Daly ~ Daly, Pádraig J., *The Last Dreamers: New & Selected Poems,* Dublin, Dedalus 1999.

Daly ~ Daly, Pádraig J., *The Other Sea,* Dublin, Dedalus 2003

Daly ~ Daly, Pádraig J., *Clinging to the Myth,* Dublin, Dedalus 2007

Deane-Drummond ~ Deane-Drummond, Celia, *Eco-Theology*, London, Darton, Longman & Todd 2008

De Paor ~ De Paor, Liam: *Saint Patrick's World*, Dublin, Four Courts Press 1993

Devlin ~ Devlin, Christopher, ed: *The Sermons and Devotional Writings of Gerard Manley Hopkins*, London, OUP, 2nd edition 1967

Dream ~ Berry, Thomas: *The Dream of the Earth*, Sierra Club Books, San Francisco 1988

Donoghue, Denis: *England, their England*, Berkeley, Univ of California Press, 1989

Duffy ~ *Beauty, Truth & Love*, ed Eugene Duffy & Patrick Hannon: Dublin, The Columba Press 2009

Eckhart ~ *Meister Eckhart: Selected Writings*, tr by Oliver Davies, UK, Penguin Books 1994

Farming ~ Berry, Wendell: *Farming: A Hand Book, poems*: New York, Harcourt Brace, 1971

Foley ~ Foley, Edward: *From Age to Age: How Chirstians have celebrated the Eucharist*, Collegeville MN, Liturgical Press, 2nd ed 2008

Freyne ~ Freyne, Seán: *Jesus, A Jewish Galilean*, London, T&T Clark, 2004

Gascoigne ~ Gascoigne, Bamber: *A Brief History of Christianity*, London, Constable & Robinson, 2nd edition 2003

Government ~ Heaney, Seamus: *The Government of the Tongue*, London, Faber & Faber 1988

Gutierrez ~ Gutierrez, Gustavo: *We Drink from Our Own Wells*, London, SCM Press 1985

Heaney ~ Heaney, Seamus: *The Redress of Poetry*, London, Faber 1995

Hill ~ Hill, Geoffrey: *Collected Poems*, London, André Deutsch, 1986

History ~ Morgan, Kenneth O. ed, *The Oxford History of Britain*, Oxford 2001

House ~ House, Humphrey, ed: *The Journals and Papers of Gerard Manley Hopkins*, completed by Graham Storey, Oxford, OUP, 1959

Inge ~ Inge, Denise: *Wanting like a God*, London, SCM Press 2009

Jennings ~ Jennings, Elizabeth: *Every Changing Shape*, UK Manchester, Carcanet 1996

— *In the Meantime*, Manchester, UK Manchester, Carcanet 1996

Julian ~Wolters, Clifton, ed & trans, *Julian of Norwich, Revelations of Divine Love*, New York, Penguin 1966

Kitchen ~ Kitchen, Paddy: *Gerard Manley Hopkins: A Life*, UK Carcanet, 1989

Lalić ~ Lalić, Ivan V.: *The Works of Love*, tr Francis R. Jones, London, Anvil Press, 1981

Levi ~ Levi, Peter: *The Penguin Book of Christian Verse*, London, Penguin, 1984

Mackey ~ Mackey, James P: *Jesus of Nazareth*, Dublin, The Columba Press, 2008

Malone ~ Malone, Mary T.: *Women & Christianity*, Vol 2, (3 vols) Dublin, The Columba Press, 2001

Marchant ~ Marchant, Fred: *Tipping Point*, Washington DC, The Word Works, 1993

McCabe ~ McCabe, Herbert OP: *God Matters*, London & New York, Mowbray 1987

McDonagh ~ McDonagh, Seán: *Passion for the Earth*, London, Geoffrey Chapman, 1994

McKenna ~ McKenna, Megan: *Harm Not the Earth*, Dublin, Veritas 2007

Milieu ~ De Chardin, Teilhard: *The Divine Milieu*, New York, Harper Collins 2001

Mysterium ~ von Balthasar, Hans Urs: *Mysterium Paschale*, Edinburgh, T & T Clark, 1990

O'Collins ~ O'Collins, Gerard: *Christology*, Oxford University Press, 2nd edition 2009

Paul ~ Harrington, Daniel J. SJ: *Meeting St Paul Today*, Chicago, Loyola Press 2008

Pick ~ Pick, John: *Gerard Manley Hopkins: Priest and Poet*, London, OUP, 1966

Plunkett ~Plunkett, Joseph Mary: *Poems*, Dublin, The Talbot Press, 1917

Psalms ~ Stuhlmueller, Carroll CP: *The Spirituality of the Psalms*, MN, The Liturgical Press 2002

Quinn ~ Quinn, Antoinette: *Patrick Kavanagh: A Biography*, Dublin Gill & Mcmillan 2001

Roberts ~ Roberts, Andrew Michael: *Geoffrey Hill*, Writers & Their Work Series, UK Northcote House 2004

Sabbaths ~Berry, Wendell: *Sabbaths*, San Francisco, North Point Press 1987

Schmidt ~ Schmidt, Michael: *Lives of the Poets*, London, Weidenfeld & Nicholson 1998

Scott ~ Scott, David: *Sacred Tongues*, London, SPCK 2001

Shorter ~ *The Theology of the Shorter Pauline Letters*, ed Karl Donfried and I. Howard Marshall, UK, Cambridge University Press, 1999

Stack ~ Stack, Tom: *No Earthly Estate*, Dublin, The Columba Press, 2002

Summerfield ~ Clare, John: *Selected Poems*, ed Geoffrey Summerfield, Penguin Classics, London, 2000

Weigl ~Weigl, Bruce: *Song of Napalm*, New York, Atlantic Monthly Press 1988

Weil ~Weil, Simone: *Gravity and Grace*.

Whitman ~ Whitman, Walt: *The Essential Whitman*, selected by Galway Kinnell, New York, Echo Press 1987

Williams ~ Williams, Rowan: *Grace and Necessity: Reflections on Art and Love;* London, Continuum 2005

Doctrine and Life, September 2009
The Furrow, September 2009